T0226228

Lecture Notes in Computer Science   10793

Commenced Publication in 1973
Founding and Former Series Editors:
Gerhard Goos, Juris Hartmanis, and Jan van Leeuwen

More information about this series at http://www.springer.com/series/7407

Mladen Berekovic · Rainer Buchty
Heiko Hamann · Dirk Koch
Thilo Pionteck (Eds.)

Architecture of Computing Systems – ARCS 2018

31st International Conference
Braunschweig, Germany, April 9–12, 2018
Proceedings

 Springer

Editors
Mladen Berekovic
Chair for Chip Design
  for Embedded Computing
Technische Universität Braunschweig
Braunschweig
Germany

Rainer Buchty
Chair for Chip Design
  for Embedded Computing
Technische Universität Braunschweig
Braunschweig
Germany

Heiko Hamann
Institute of Computer Engineering
Universität zu Lübeck
Lübeck
Germany

Dirk Koch
School of Computer Science
The University of Manchester
Manchester
UK

Thilo Pionteck
Institute for Information Technology
  and Communications
Otto-von-Guericke Universität Magdeburg
Magdeburg
Germany

ISSN 0302-9743   ISSN 1611-3349 (electronic)
Lecture Notes in Computer Science
ISBN 978-3-319-77609-5   ISBN 978-3-319-77610-1   (eBook)
https://doi.org/10.1007/978-3-319-77610-1

Library of Congress Control Number: 2018935900

LNCS Sublibrary: SL1 – Theoretical Computer Science and General Issues

Printed on acid-free paper

This Springer imprint is published by the registered company Springer International Publishing AG
part of Springer Nature
The registered company address is: Gewerbestrasse 11, 6330 Cham, Switzerland

Preface

The 31st International Conference on Computer Architecture (ARCS 2018) was hosted at the Technische Universität Braunschweig, Braunschweig, Germany, April 9–12, 2018. It was organized by the special interest group on "Architecture of Computing Systems" of the GI (Gesellschaft für Informatik e. V.) and ITG (Informationstechnische Gesellschaft im VDE).

With a tradition of 31 annual editions, ARCS has always been a conference attracting leading-edge research outcomes in computer architecture and operating systems, including a wide spectrum of topics ranging from embedded and real-time systems all the way to large-scale and parallel systems. ARCS provides a holistic view of computer architecture as it covers both hardware design aspects as well as a wide range of software techniques required to exploit and build new hardware systems efficiently. ARCS is also a platform covering new emerging and cross-cutting topics, such as autonomous and ubiquitous systems, reconfigurable computing and acceleration, neural networks, and AI as well as outlooks on future topics like post-Moore architectures and organic computing. The focus of ARCS 2018 was on architectures for robotics, autonomous vehicles, and automation systems. With this, ARCS is reflecting the large interest in intelligent systems that are currently emerging and that have disruptive character across the entire research and industry landscape.

ARCS 2018 attracted 53 submissions from authors in 17 countries. With 14 authors, India had more authors submitting papers than the UK (13), China (12), Japan (9), and France (9). Each paper was reviewed by a diverse and dedicated Program Committee providing a total of 199 reviews. The Program Committee selected 23 submissions to be presented at ARCS and published in the proceedings, which corresponds to a 43% paper acceptance rate. The accepted papers were presented in eight sessions: Embedded Systems (3 papers), Multicore Systems (2 papers), Analysis and Optimization (2 papers), On-Chip and Off-Chip Networks (4 papers), Memory Models and Systems (4 papers), Energy Efficient Systems (3 papers), Partial Reconfiguration (3 papers) as well as a session on Large Scale Computing (2 papers). The word "cloud" in the beginning of the preface was compiled from all the paper titles of the ARCS 2018 proceedings.

ARCS has a long tradition of hosting associated workshops. The following five workshops were held in conjunction with the main conference this year:

- VERFE: 14th Workshop on Dependability and Fault Tolerance
- PASA: 13th Workshop on Parallel Systems and Algorithms
- FORMUS³IC: Third FORMUS³IC Workshop
- SAOS: 6th International Workshop on Self-Optimization in Autonomic and Organic Computing Systems
- CompSpace: Second Workshop on Computer Architectures in Space

We thank the many individuals who contributed to the success of ARCS 2018, in particular the members of the Program Committee and all the additional external reviewers for their time and effort in carefully reviewing and judging the submissions. We further thank all authors for submitting their work to ARCS and presenting accepted papers. The workshops were organized and coordinated by Carsten Trinitis, the proceedings were compiled by Thilo Pionteck, and Gerald Krell, the website was maintained by Markus Hoffmann. Thanks to all these individuals and all the many other people who helped in the organization of ARCS 2018.

April 2018

Mladen Berekovic
Dirk Koch
Rainer Buchty
Heiko Hamann

Organization

General Chair

Mladen Berekovic — Technische Universität Braunschweig, Germany

Program Co-chairs

Rainer Buchty — Technische Universität Braunschweig, Germany
Heiko Hamann — Universität zu Lübeck, Germany
Dirk Koch — University of Manchester, UK

Workshop and Tutorial Chair

Carsten Trinitis — Technical University of Munich, Germany

Publicity Chair

Rainer Buchty — Technische Universität Braunschweig, Germany

Publication Chair

Thilo Pionteck — Otto von Guericke University Magdeburg, Germany

Local Organization

Anna Jankowski — Technische Universität Braunschweig, Germany

Web Chair

Markus Hoffmann — Karlsruhe Institute of Technology, Germany

Program Committee

Hamid Amiri — University of Tunis El Manar, Tunisia
Michael Beigl — Karlsruhe Institute of Technology, Germany
Mladen Berekovic — Technische Universität Braunschweig, Germany
Jürgen Brehm — Leibniz Universität Hannover, Germany
Uwe Brinkschulte — Goethe-Universität Frankfurt am Main, Germany
Rainer Buchty — Technische Universität Braunschweig, Germany
João M. P. Cardoso — Universidade do Porto, Portugal
Laura Carrington — San Diego Supercomputer Center/University of California, USA

Sascha Uhrig   Airbus, Germany
Theo Ungerer   University of Augsburg, Germany
Hans Vandierendonck   Queen's University Belfast, UK
Stephane Vialle   CentraleSupelec and UMI GT-CNRS 2958, France
Lucian Vintan   Lucian Blaga University of Sibiu, Romania
Klaus Waldschmidt   Goethe-Universität Frankfurt am Main, Germany
Dominik Wist   BIOTRONIC Berlin, Germany
Stephan Wong   Delft University of Technology, The Netherlands
Sungjoo Yoo   Seoul National University, South Korea

Additional Reviewers

Afzal, Ayesha   Niazmand, Behrad
Becker, Thomas   Ozen, Elbruz
Borghorst, Hendrik   Payandeh Azad, Siavoosh
Brand, Marcel   Perner, Cora
Bromberger, Michael   Procaccini, Marco
Buschhoff, Markus   Pusz, Oskar
Courtaud, Cédric   Reif, Stefan
Dellagostin Souza, Jeckson   Rheindt, Sven
Eitschberger, Patrick   Schirmeier, Horst
Freitag, Johannes   Schmaus, Florian
Frickenstein, Alexander   Schwarz, Alexander
Friesel, Daniel   Shuka, Romeo
Gante, João   Singh, Jasdeep
Ghasempouri, Tara   Sommer, Lukas
Gottschling, Philip   Spiekermann, Daniel
Hoffmann, Markus   Srivatsa, Akshay
Hofmann, Jaco   Stegmeier, Alexander
Hoozemans, Joost   Terraneo, Federico
Joseph, Moritz   Tsiokanis, Ioannis
Jung, Lukas   Wirsch, Ramon
Khalid, Faiq   Witterauf, Michael
Korinth, Jens   Wägemann, Peter
Lorenzon, Arthur   Yang, Dai
Martins, Paulo   Zoni, Davide
Mische, Jörg

Biologically-Inspired Massively-Parallel Computation (Keynote Talk)

Steve Furber

Abstract. The SpiNNaker project has delivered a massively-parallel computer incorporating half a million ARM processor cores (with the ultimate goal of expanding to a million cores) aimed at supporting large-scale models of spiking neural systems that run in biological real time. The project has been 20 years in conception and 10 years in construction, and the machine has been on line for a year and a half as one of two major neuromorphic platforms supported by the EU Flagship Human Brain Project.

The key problem to address in supporting biological neural networks is the very high connectivity of those networks: each neuron typically receives connections from, and connects to, around 10,000 (and sometimes as many as 250,000) other neurons. Biological neurons communicate primarily by issuing action potentials or "spikes", and in SpiNNaker each spike is sent as a small packet through a packet-switched fabric. The high connectivity is achieved by using a multicast communication protocol. Each SpiNNaker chip incorporates 18 ARM968 processor cores and a packet router, where information about packet destinations is held in tables in the router. This exploits the fact that the topology of the biological network is static or, in the case of synaptogenesis or neurogenesis, at most slowly changing.

The equations describing the neurons and the synapses (including learning rules) are implemented on software running on the ARM processor cores, so the problem of mapping a particular network application onto the machine has two parts, both of which are run on a host server or PC: the network topology is mapped onto the machine and the routing tables set up, and separately the neuron and synaptic functionality is compiled into executables to run on the ARM cores. Execution is supported by a small event-driven real-time kernel running on each core.

This talk will cover the relationship between neuromorphic systems and the parallel development of Deep Networks and Convolutional Neural Networks in machine learning, the architecture of the SpiNNaker machine and its packet-routing mechanisms, and examples of applications that run on the machine, with some discussion of the role that neuromorphics may play in future computer architectures.

Steve Furber CBE FRS FREng is ICL Professor of Computer Engineering in the School of Computer Science at the University of Manchester, UK. After completing a BA in mathematics and a PhD in aerodynamics at the University of Cambridge, UK, he spent the 1980s at Acorn Computers, where he was a principal designer of the BBC

Microcomputer and the ARM 32-bit RISC microprocessor. Over 100 billion variants of the ARM processor have since been manufactured, powering much of the world's mobile and embedded computing. He moved to the ICL Chair at Manchester in 1990 where he leads research into asynchronous and low-power systems and, more recently, neural systems engineering, where the SpiNNaker project is delivering a computer incorporating a million ARM processors optimised for brain modelling applications.

Contents

Memory Models and Systems

Energy Efficient Systems

Partial Reconfiguration

Large Scale Computing

Embedded Systems

Trade-Off Between Performance, Fault Tolerance and Energy Consumption in Duplication-Based Taskgraph Scheduling

Patrick Eitschberger[1][(✉)], Simon Holmbacka[2], and Jörg Keller[1]

[1] Faculty of Mathematics and Computer Science, FernUniversität in Hagen,
Hagen, Germany
{patrick.eitschberger,jorg.keller}@fernuni-hagen.de
[2] Faculty of Science and Engineering, Abo Akademi University, Turku, Finland
sholmbac@abo.fi

Abstract. Fault tolerance in parallel systems can be achieved by duplicating task executions onto several processing units, so in case one processing unit (PU) fails, the task can continue executing on another unit. Duplicating task execution affects the performance of the system in fault-free and fault cases, and its energy consumption. Currently, there are no tools for properly handling the three-variable optimization problem: Performance ↔ Fault Tolerance ↔ Energy Consumption, and no facilities for integrating it into an actual system. We present a fault-tolerant runtime system (called RUPS) for user defined schedules, in which the user can give their preferences about the trade-off between performance, energy and fault tolerance. We present an approach for determining the best trade-off for modern multicore architectures and we test RUPS on a real system to verify the accuracy of our approach itself.

Keywords: Scheduling · Fault tolerance · Energy efficiency
Trade-off · Power modeling · Optimization · Runtime system

1 Introduction

Fault tolerance is important for parallel systems like manycores and grids, where a permanent failure of a processing unit (PU), resulting from either a hardware or software fault, might occur during the execution of a scheduled parallel program.

The schedules of parallel programs can be created statically, prior to execution with the help of a task graph that represents the tasks and dependencies between them. To maximize performance in static schedules, it is critical to minimize the length of a schedule, the so-called makespan. However, integrating fault tolerance techniques typically results in performance overhead. This leads to increasing makespans. One kind of fault tolerance is the task duplication where for each task a copy – a so-called duplicate – is created on another PU. In case of a failure, the duplicate is used to continue the schedule execution. The performance of the system in the fault case will then benefit from the

© Springer International Publishing AG, part of Springer Nature 2018
M. Berekovic et al. (Eds.): ARCS 2018, LNCS 10793, pp. 3–17, 2018.
https://doi.org/10.1007/978-3-319-77610-1_1

duplicates, since the progress of the schedule can seamlessly be continued by the tasks' duplicates. Another issue emerging especially in recent years is the problem of minimizing the energy consumption. Duplicating tasks requires additional resources because the task is actually executing simultaneously on various PUs. In the fault-free case this is regarded as energy wasting. The energy consumption is also affected by scaling down the clock frequency of a PU. By executing at different clock frequencies, the makespan is affected by the altered performance, and the energy consumption is affected by the altered power dissipation. This leads to a three-variable trade-off decision to be made between Performance PE, Energy Consumption E, and Fault tolerance FT.

There are several approaches in the literature for two-dimensional optimizations in the area of performance, energy and fault tolerance for various parallel platforms and with different fault tolerance techniques, e.g. in [3,10,12,13,15–17,20]. Although the optimization for all two-dimensional combinations is well researched, the three-dimensional optimization is rarely addressed. There exist a few exceptions that focus on real-time systems where tasks have to be executed in predefined time frames or within a certain deadline. Therefore, PE in corresponding approaches is the major objective. For example Cai et al. [6] present a greedy heuristic to reduce the energy consumption in fault-tolerant distributed embedded systems with time-constraints. Another approach is presented by Alam and Kumar [1]. They assume that only one specific transient fault could occur during the execution of a task. Tosun et al. [19] present a framework that maps a given real-time embedded application under different optimization criteria onto a heterogeneous chip multiprocessor architecture. In all of these approaches, the focus typically lies on transient faults, where checkpointing or backup mechanisms are used to circumvent a fault. In our approach, we focus on permanent faults and present scheduling strategies that combine all three criteria without a real-time constraint. Hence, in this work a broader range is considered, which is not yet addressed in previous work.

We propose a solution for the three-variable optimization problem for cases where the user can inform the scheduler about his preferences. We firstly extend an energy efficient and fault tolerant scheduler by integrating new scheduling strategies that can be set according to the user's preferences. Secondly, to demonstrate the influence of the user preferences we present a runtime system RUPS for scheduling parallel applications with adjustable degrees of fault tolerance on grids, computing clusters or manycore systems. The runtime system utilizes a pre-optimized static schedule with the desired characteristics and trade-off between PE, E and FT. To obtain the energy consumption for a selected schedule, we create a realistic power model based on experiments for an actual real-world processor. Several example models for different platforms are created, and we show that their accuracy is sufficient to predict the requirements for the trade-off between PE, E and FT. Thirdly, with the power model and the given schedule, we can construct the trade-off map to be used during system planning, and we show how the PE, E and FT parameters can affect the planning decisions of parallel fault-tolerant applications. Our results indicate that the power model is accurate and that the experiments match the predictions. Finally the trade-off map shows in detail the relations between PE, E and FT.

The remainder of this paper is structured as follows. In Sect. 2 the trade-off problem is discussed. Sections 3, 4 and 5 present the extended scheduler, the runtime system and the power model. In Sect. 6 the results are presented and analyzed. In Sect. 7, we conclude and give an outlook on future work.

2   The Trade-Off Problem

A combination of all three objectives is possible in general, but there does not exit an overall optimal solution. In this context the degree of FT is rated by the overhead in performance (and energy) that results from the fault tolerance techniques in both the fault-free and fault case. Therefore, a compromise between the optimization criteria must be made. While one criterion is improved, either one or both of the others are worsened.

When we focus on PE of a schedule, it is dependent on the mapping of the tasks. The more an application can be parallelized the better is the performance. Additionally, modern processors support several frequencies at which a processor can run. Thus, tasks should be accelerated as much as possible, i.e. use the highest supported frequency of a PU. In contrast, a more parallelized application results in fewer gaps between tasks and thus in fewer possibilities to include duplicates without shifting successor tasks. This results in a high performance overhead in case of a failure, e.g. a low FT. Additionally, running on a high frequency typically leads to a high E. When we focus on FT, duplicates should be executed completely in the fault-free case and available but unused PUs should also be considered for mapping duplicates to minimize performance loss in case of a fault. In this case, duplicates may lead to shifts of original tasks and thus to a low PE in the fault-free case. In terms of E, both executing duplicates completely and using available PUs not necessary for the original tasks result in a high E. Is the focus put on E, low frequencies and short duplicates are preferable. But low frequencies lead to low PE and short duplicates to a high performance overhead (FT) in case of a failure.

In addition, the main focus of a user varies in different situations. For example, in a time critical environment, PE is the most important criterion next to FT. Thus, in this situation PE and also FT is usually favored over minimizing E. Another situation is, that a failure occurs extremely rarely and thus E is becoming more important. Other examples exist in mobile devices where E is the most important criterion next to PE. The main focus is therefore put on E and PE while FT is neglected. However, the alignment of the optimization is very situational and ultimately depends highly on the user preferences.

3   Fault Tolerant and Energy Efficient Scheduling

We start by reviewing the ideas of [10] and briefly introduce our previous work. Then we present two new strategies to improve either FT or E of the schedules.

3.1   Previous Approach

Fechner et al. [10] provides a fault-tolerant duplication-based scheduling approach that guarantees no overhead in a fault-free case. Starting from an already existing schedule (and taskgraph), each original task is copied and its duplicate (D) is placed on another PU than the original task so that in case of a failure the schedule execution can be continued. We assume homogeneous PUs and a fail-stop model, where a failure of a PU might result from a faulty hardware, software or network. We only consider one failure per schedule execution.

If an original task has finished it sends a commit message to its corresponding D so that it can be aborted. Schedules often comprise several gaps between tasks resulting from dependencies. Ds can be placed either in those gaps or directly between two succeeding tasks. To avoid an overhead in a fault-free case, in all situations where a D would lead to a shift of all its successor tasks only a placeholder, a so called dummy duplicate (DD) is placed. DDs are only extended to fully Ds in case of a failure. To reduce the communication overhead, Ds are placed with a short delay, so called slack. Thus, either the results of an original task are sent to its successor tasks or the results of the corresponding D, but not both. Figure 1(a) illustrates an example taskgraph. For a better understanding the communication times and the slack are disregarded. Figure 1(b) and (c) show the resulting schedules of two strategies, the first uses only DDs the second uses Ds and DDs.

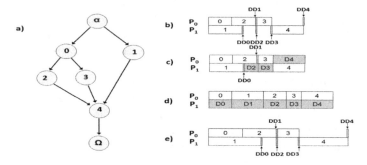

Fig. 1. (a) simplified taskgraph, (b) strategy 1: use only DDs, (c) strategy 2: use Ds and DDs, (d) strategy 3: use half of PUs for original tasks, the others for Ds, (e) strategy 4: select a lower frequency for original tasks

In our previous work [8], we show the importance of considering communication times for the placement of Ds and DDs. We present in [9] an extension to improve E of schedules by calculating a buffer for each task. It indicates how much a task could be slowed down by scaling down the frequency of the corresponding PU without prolonging the makespan. Frequencies are then set to the lowest possibles to fill the buffers. We assume a general power model like explained in [2] and use continues normalized frequencies for our predictions.

3.2   Extensions

We extend the scheduler for supporting also a concrete power model (that we describe in Sect. 5) with discrete frequencies and we include two new simple strategies. In our first strategy, we use a simple list scheduler to create schedules with respect to the dependencies from the corresponding taskgraph. Instead of using as many PUs as possible, only half of the available PUs are used for the placement of original tasks and the remaining PUs are used to include Ds (see Fig. 1(d)). With this strategy we try to focus on FT.

In our second strategy, the user can set a frequency level with which the original tasks should run before including Ds and DDs (see Fig. 1(e)). Thus, we leave the mapping of all original tasks as it is and change only the runtime of the tasks by using the selected frequency level. Then, the start times of tasks are corrected according to the dependencies given by the taskgraph.

4   Runtime System

RUPS (Runtime system for User Preferences-defined Schedules) is a scheduling tool for parallel platforms with features allowing the user to input various preferences e.g. PE, E or FT in the schedule. Schedules are then created with the RUPS tool – optimized for the user defined preference in question. RUPS consists of four main parts illustrated in Fig. 2(a). The processor details are extracted in Part 1 and passed to the scheduler (Part 3), which in turn optimizes the schedule based on the processor parameters and user preferences (Part 2). Finally, the schedule is passed to the runtime system (Part 4), and scheduled on the processor. In this section, we describe the details of these four parts.

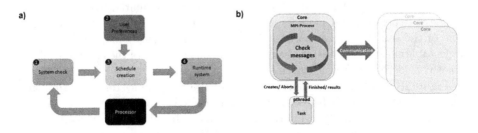

Fig. 2. Overview of (a) RUPS and (b) the runtime system

4.1   System Check Tool

At the first use of RUPS, it has to be initialized once with the system check tool to adjust the power model for the processor used. This tool measures the power consumption of the processor for all supported frequencies and for a different number of cores under full load. We measure the power consumption for 10 seconds (s) with a sampling rate of 10 milliseconds (ms). All cases are repeated five times to compensate high power values that could occur due to unexpected background processes. Between each case, all cores are set to the lowest frequency in idle mode for 5 s to reduce the rise in temperature of the processor and thus the influence on the power consumption. Then the averaged results of the measure points for each case are used as values for the power model.

4.2   Scheduler and User Preferences

The scheduler consists of two main parts. One part for the schedule creation and one part for the simulation of generated schedules to predict the energy consumption in different situations. It supports several strategies for the placement of Ds/DDs and the user can set different options for the behavior during the scheduling process like setting the time for a slack, considering unused cores for the placement of Ds/DDs, simulating failures or only creating the fault-tolerant schedules. The simulator can then be used to simulate for each task in the schedule one failure. It can also handle task slow downs that result from a high load level of a PU. For more details we refer to [8,9].

4.3   Runtime System

The runtime system is based on ULFM-MPI [5], a fault tolerant extension of Open-MPI. For each core a MPI-process is created, that reads the schedule and taskgraph information from files and generates a task queue (sorted by the starting times of tasks). Then, a while loop is executed as long as there is a task in the queue. The loop is used for a polling mechanism that reacts and handles the communication (via messages), starts a task if possible and also aborts a task if necessary. The task execution is separated from the communication process by a (posix) thread. Data transfers between tasks are simulated by only sending the message header, that includes next to others the information about the start time of the sending operation and the transfer time. This simplification has a neglectable effect on the results, as the energy consumption of the communication is not considered in the measurements and models.

Figure 2(b) illustrates a short overview of the runtime system. We simulate a failure by exiting a MPI-process just before the corresponding task is started. The other processes are then informed about the failure by an error handler. We integrate a testing mode where one additional MPI-process is started to measure the energy consumption with the help of Intel RAPL. The measurement process measures the energy with a sample rate of 10 ms.

5   Power Model

To predict the energy consumption for a schedule, an appropriate power model for the processor is necessary. Basically, a model is a simplified representation of the reality. The complexity of a model increases significantly with its accuracy. As the power consumption of a processor depends on several factors, like the temperature, instruction mix, usage rate and technology of the processor, there exist numerous approaches in the literature to model the power consumption of a processor with varying complexities and accuracies, like in [4,7,11] or [18].

In general the power consumption can be subdivided into a static part, that is frequency-independent and a dynamic part, that depends both on the frequency and on the supply voltage.

$$P_{processor} = P_{static} + P_{dynamic} \qquad (1)$$

The static power consumption consists of the idle power P_{idle} and a device specific constant s, that is only needed when the processor is under load.

$$P_{processor} = \begin{cases} P_{idle} + s + P_{dynamic} & \text{if under load} \\ P_{idle} & \text{else} \end{cases} \qquad (2)$$

The dynamic power consumption is typically modeled as a cubic frequency function [2], as the frequency and voltage are loosely linearly correlated[1]. Additionally the supply voltage and thus the dynamic power consumption depends on the load level of a core. As we only consider fully loaded cores or cores that are in idle mode (at the lowest frequency) the influence of a load level can be given by a parameter $w \in \{0,1\}$. If we assume a homogeneous multi-core processor with n cores, a simple power model for the dynamic part can be given by the following equation, where a, b and β are device specific constants, i is the core index and $f_{curr,i}$ is the current frequency of core i:

$$P_{dynamic} = \sum_{i=0}^{n-1} w_i \cdot \beta \left(f_{cur,i}^{3} + a \cdot f_{cur,i}^{2} + b \cdot f_{cur,i} \right) \qquad (3)$$

Only if a core runs at a higher frequency under full load, the dynamic part of the power consumption for the processor is considered.

5.1 Model Validation

To prove the accuracy of the power model, we used three different computer systems with Intel processors as test platforms:

1. Intel i7 3630qm Ivy-Bridge based laptop
2. Intel i5 4570 Haswell based desktop machine
3. Intel i5 E1620 server machine

To construct the power model, we extracted the power values by physical experiments using the Intel RAPL tool. As described in Sect. 4.1, we measured the power consumption for each frequency combination for 10 s with a sampling rate of 10 ms and repeated all measurements five times. We test the power

---

[1] For a given voltage there is a maximum frequency and for a desired frequency there is a minimum voltage required.

model for six different workload scenarios: ALU-, FPU-, SSE-, BP- and RAM-intensive workloads and for a combination of these tests as mixed workload. The measured power values were used to construct the power model for each platform and scenario. The architecture specific tuning parameters (s, β, a and b) in Eqs. 2 and 3 were then determined using a least squares analysis.

Table 1 shows exemplary the individual parameters for each platform for a mixed workload after fitting the physical measurements to Eqs. 2 and 3 and optimizing the tuning parameters. The results of the least squares analysis for the other tests only differ slightly from the mixed workload scenario. The different parameters for the power model can be determined and saved in advance and used for several classes of applications with a specific workload type dominating. Then the power consumption can be measured during the execution of the first application and compared to the different power models to find the best suitable for the whole class.

Table 1. Values of the architecture specific tuning parameters for a mixed workload

	P_{idle}	s	β	a	b
i7 3630	3.781 W	1.29 W	0.340 W/Hz^3	-3.42 Hz	5.88 Hz^2
i5 4570	5.976 W	0.42 W	0.091 W/Hz^3	1.02 Hz	12.08 Hz^2
i5 E1620	8.728 W	3.83 W	0.344 W/Hz^3	-2.87 Hz	6.13 Hz^2

Table 2 shows the difference between the data and model as the maximum and average deviation. The maximum deviation was lowest using the desktop CPU (i5 4570). The reason for having a less exact fit using the server (i5 E1620) and laptop CPU (i7 3630) is because of the significantly higher power output using the turbo boost on these CPUs, which is more difficult to fit to the curve than the more smooth power curve of the i5 4570 CPU. However, with a low average error value we consider this model feasible for our experiments. In Fig. 3 we present exemplary the resulting power curve for the server test platform for the real data and for the model.

Table 2. Difference between the data and model as error values squared from Fig. 3

	i7 3630	i5 4570	i5 E1620
Avg. deviation	1.09%	0.84%	1.13%
Max deviation	15.56%	7.28%	17.07%

5.2   Real-World Evaluation

For our real-world evaluation we used the server system as a common platform for clusters and grids. We tested 922 schedules in total that are related to 40 taskgraphs with random properties and between 19 and 24 tasks (see Sect. 6).

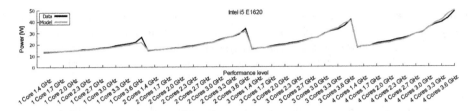

Fig. 3. Power consumption and power model for the server platform

For each taskgraph we first let the already existing schedule run without any changes and thus without any failures. Then, the fault-tolerant schedules that result from the first strategy – using only DDs – (see Sect. 3) were calculated and executed by the runtime system. And we let run all fault-tolerant schedules with a simulated failure at each task by exiting the corresponding MPI-Process directly before the task execution started.

We validate the accuracy of the prediction by comparing the predicted energy values that result from the scheduler with the real measurements of the runtime system. In Fig. 4 we present the predicted and real energy consumption for all schedules. With a maximum deviation of 7.14% and 1.64% on average, our prediction fits the reality quite well.

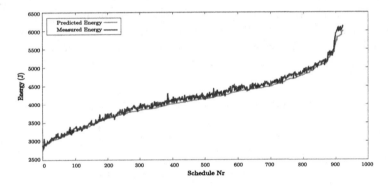

Fig. 4. Predicted and measured energy consumption (for a mixed workload)

6 Experimental Results

For our experiments we used a benchmark suite of synthetic taskgraphs [14] with 36000 performance optimal schedules, that can be subdivided by the number of PUs (2, 4, 8, 16 and 32), the number of tasks (7–12, 13–18 and 19–24), the edge density and length and the node and edge weights. The schedules were generated with a PDS-algorithm (Pruned Depth-first Search). To find optimal solutions in an acceptable time, the search space is reduced by pruning selected paths in the search tree. As the scheduling problem is NP-hard, there have been some taskgraphs where no optimal schedule could be found even after weeks of computation. Those taskgraphs are excluded from this study. As seen in Sect. 5.2, our system model closely reflects the real system in terms of energy consumption. We used this fact to simulate nearly 34500 of the given schedules using the RUPS system. We evaluate the trade-off between PE, FT and E with four scenarios in which we use the four strategies from Sect. 3. These scenarios reflect system setups with one of the three parameters as inherently dominating. This choice will give a wide range of experiments with the extreme corner cases covered, and everything between them. The following scenarios were used for our simulation, where we do not consider the turbo frequency to avoid throttling effects:

(A) Strategy 1: Use only DDs and start with the highest supported frequency (3.5 GHz). In this scenario we focus on PE.
(B) Strategy 2: Use Ds and DDs and start with the highest supported frequency (3.5 GHz). This scenario mainly targets on PE, but also on FT.
(C) Strategy 3: Create the schedules with a simple List Scheduler that uses half of the PUs for original tasks, the other for the Ds and start with the highest supported frequency (3.5 GHz). Here the focus is on FT.
(D) Strategy 4: Select a lower frequency for original tasks and start with frequency level 7 (2.3 GHz). With this scenario we try to focus on E.

To visualize the trade-off between PE, FT and E the results of the four strategies are relatively related to the following estimated upper and lower boundaries for each criterion (see Table 3) where m is the makespan in cycles, m_{seq} is the makespan, when all tasks are running in sequence and m_{ft} is the makespan in case of a failure. $p_{max} \in PU$ is the maximum number of PUs used and $f_{highest/lowest}$ is the highest or lowest frequency respectively.

Table 3. Upper and lower boundaries for PE, FT and E

	Best case	Worst case
PE	$\dfrac{m_{seq}}{p_{max} \cdot f_{highest}}$	$\dfrac{m_{seq}}{1 \cdot f_{lowest}}$
FT	$\dfrac{m_{ft}-m}{m} \cdot 100 = 0\%$	$\dfrac{2 \cdot m - m}{m} \cdot 100 = 100\%$
E	$\dfrac{m_{seq}}{p_{max} \cdot 2.3 \ GHz}$	$\dfrac{m_{seq}}{1 \cdot f_{lowest}}$

Focusing on performance PE, the best solution is to parallelize an application as much as possible. Furthermore, the highest available frequency $f_{highest}$ should be selected, if the system in use supports different frequencies. A lower bound for the performance can be achieved by running all tasks in sequence on one PU with the lowest possible frequency f_{lowest}.

While a schedule is either fault-tolerant or not, the fault tolerance FT is rated by the performance overhead in case of a failure. Therefore, when focusing on the fault tolerance the best solution is to copy the whole schedule and execute it simultaneously (completely independent) to the original one on other PUs.

Then, both the performance, i.e. the makespan m_{ft} in case of a failure and in a fault-free case m are equal. Accordingly, the performance overhead results to zero percent. However, the worst solution is when the schedule is not fault-tolerant and a failure occurs directly before the end of the schedule execution. Then, the whole schedule has to be repeated on $p-1$ PUs and the makespan $m_{ft} = 2 \cdot m$ in case of a failure is at least doubled in comparison to the fault-free case m. Thus, the performance overhead in case of a failure results in 100%.

While the estimation of upper and lower bounds for PE and FT are independent of a certain system, E depends highly on the system in use. Therefore, we calculated the best and worst energy consumption of the i5 E1620 processor with the measured power values from the system check tool for a perfectly divisible workload. In this case, the most efficient frequency is at 2.3 GHz. The boundaries for E in Table 3 have to be multiplied with the corresponding power values from the system to get the energy consumption in Joule.

In Fig. 5 the results of all scenarios are presented. For a better illustration we only show the results for systems with 4 PUs (in total 6500 schedules with different properties). But the results for the other number of PUs (2, 8, 16 and 32 PUs) are similar with respect to the overall trends. They differ only slightly by small shifts. The left column of the figure presents for all scenarios (A, B, C and D) the trade-off between E and PE, the middle column between E and FT and the right column between PE and FT.

Starting with scenario A, we can see that a better performance also leads to a better energy consumption. With a performance of nearly 100% the energy consumption goes down to around 5% (related to the best and worst cases from the boundaries). This behavior seems to be related to the high idle power of the system compared to the dynamic power. The higher the idle power is, the better it is to run on a high frequency, e.g. at the highest like here. If we now focus on the trade-off between E and FT we can see, that the lower the energy consumption in the fault free case is, and thus the higher the performance of the schedule, the higher is also the performance overhead in case of a failure. This behavior results from the decreasing number and size of gaps within a schedule, when improving the performance. Because then each DD leads directly to a shift of its successor tasks. The trade-off between PE and FT shows directly the same behavior. The higher the performance the higher is also the performance overhead. In scenario B we used Ds and DDs for the fault tolerance. We see that the left part $(E \leftrightarrow PE)$ of the figure is more spread. This indicates, that especially for a lower performance more gaps can be filled with Ds. This leads to an increased energy. The middle part of the figure $(E \leftrightarrow FT)$ shows the resulting improvement of the performance overhead in case of a failure. And also on the right part $(PE \leftrightarrow FT)$ we see the slightly shift of all results to the left. In scenario C we try to use a simple strategy to get a good FT result. Looking on the left side, we see that the performance is much lower and the energy consumption is much higher than for scenario A and B. As the performance does not change in case of a failure, the middle and right part of the figure are empty. Scenario D shows the results for schedules that run with a lower frequency (frequency level 7, 2.3 GHz). Here we

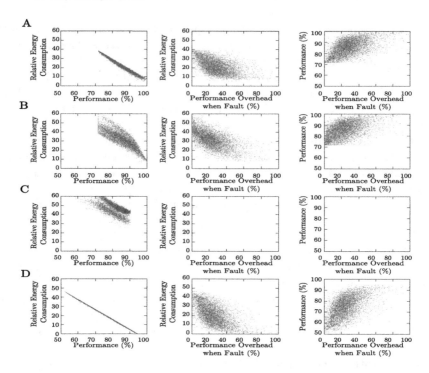

Fig. 5. Results when scheduling according to scenarios A, B, C, D showing: relative energy consumption (lower is better), performance (higher is better), performance overhead when fault (lower is better)

can see that running on a lower frequency results in a better energy consumption, but only if the performance increases. Then we can reach nearly the best energy consumption. The other both trade-offs are the same like for scenario A. They are just a little bit stretched.

We could show, that there does not exist any overall solution for that three-variable problem without giving up at least one of the three parameters. Thus, the decision on which parameter the main focus lies must be made by the user.

Exemplary user preferences and favored strategies are summarized in Table 4. As seen in Table 4, various user preferences are represented by the proposed

Table 4. User preferences and favored strategies.

User preferences		Favored strategies
Fault-free case	Fault case	
PE (E)	–	S1
PE (FT)	PE	S2
FT	PE	S3
E	E	S4

strategies. Next to major objectives, also minor criteria can be considered, resulting in a variety of possible solutions with reasonable results. The worsening of criteria that are not focused is moderate. Thus, the investment for improving favored objectives is low. In addition, the strategies can be hidden from users that do not have any background knowledge about scheduling, so that they only have to give their preferences by selecting a combination of objectives. Then, the corresponding strategies can be chosen automatically by the scheduler.

Please note that the user preference might not only depend on the user, but also on the taskgraph, schedule and deadline at hand. If e.g. the deadline is close to the makespan of the corresponding schedule (i.e. all cores must execute tasks at one of the highest frequencies), then energy savings in the fault-free case are hardly possible, and the user will be better of to focus on other preferences. If the deadline is farther away from the makespan, then energy efficiency can be considered. If the deadline is hard, then the preference will be on keeping the deadline even in each possible fault-case, and energy will only be a secondary preference.

7 Conclusions

We presented a method to quantitatively handle the trade-off between PE, E and FT when scheduling taskgraphs onto parallel machines with DVFS. We also presented a scheduling and execution tool called RUPS that implements these schedules on real machines. Fault tolerance is achieved by adding task duplicates in parallel with the original tasks; affecting both the energy consumption and the time-to-recovery in case a fault occurs in the system. This tool is intended to bridge the gap between Performance, Energy efficiency and Fault tolerance (PE, E, FT), which are the parameters the scheduling decisions are based on. We demonstrate the trade-off between PE, E and FT with four corner case studies, which can heavily impact the decisions needed during system planning. The experiments on real machines also provide evidence on the accuracy of the underlying performance and energy model used in the scheduler. As future work, we plan to extend the scheduler for tolerating more than one failure per schedule and for integrating reconnected PUs after a failure. We also plan to investigate in more strategies that focus on the corner cases E and FT and to integrate real transfer datas next to the message headers into the runtime system.

References

1. Alam, B., Kumar, A.: Fault tolerance issues in real time systems with energy minimization. Int. J. Inf. Comput. Technol. **3**(10), 1001–1008 (2013)
2. Albers, S.: Energy-efficient algorithms. Commun. ACM **53**(5), 86–96 (2010)
3. Aupy, G., Benoit, A., Renaud-Goud, P., Robert, Y.: Energy-aware algorithms for task graph scheduling, replica placement and checkpoint strategies. In: Khan, S., Zomaya, A. (eds.) Handbook on Data Centers, pp. 37–80. Springer, New York (2015). https://doi.org/10.1007/978-1-4939-2092-1_2

4. Basmadjian, R., de Meer, H.: Evaluating and modeling power consumption of multi-core processors. In: Proceedings of the 3rd International Conference on Future Systems: Where Energy, Computing and Communication Meet (e-Energy 2012), pp. 1–10 (2012)
5. Bland, W.: User level failure mitigation in MPI. In: Caragiannis, I., Alexander, M., Badia, R.M., Cannataro, M., Costan, A., Danelutto, M., Desprez, F., Krammer, B., Sahuquillo, J., Scott, S.L., Weidendorfer, J. (eds.) Euro-Par 2012. LNCS, vol. 7640, pp. 499–504. Springer, Heidelberg (2013). https://doi.org/10.1007/978-3-642-36949-0_57
6. Cai, Y., Reddy, S.M., Al-Hashimi, B.M.: Reducing the energy consumption in fault-tolerant distributed embedded systems with time-constraint. In: 8th International Symposium on Quality Electronic Design (ISQED 2007), pp. 368–373 (2007)
7. Cichowski, P., Keller, J., Kessler, C.: Modelling power consumption of the Intel SCC. In: Proceedings of the 6th Many-Core Applications Research Community Symposium (MARC 2012), pp. 46–51 (2012)
8. Eitschberger, P., Keller, J.: Efficient and fault-tolerant static scheduling for grids. In: Proceedings of the 14th IEEE International Workshop on Parallel and Distributed Scientific and Engineering Computing (PDSEC 2013), pp. 1439–1448 (2013)
9. Eitschberger, P., Keller, J.: Energy-efficient and fault-tolerant taskgraph scheduling for manycores and grids. In: an Mey, D., et al. (eds.) Euro-Par 2013. LNCS, vol. 8374, pp. 769–778. Springer, Heidelberg (2014). https://doi.org/10.1007/978-3-642-54420-0_75
10. Fechner, B., Hönig, U., Keller, J., Schiffmann, W.: Fault-tolerant static scheduling for grids. In: Proceedings of the 13th IEEE Workshop on Dependable Parallel, Distributed and Network-Centric Systems (DPDNS 2008), pp. 1–6 (2008)
11. Goel, B., McKee, S.A.: A methodology for modeling dynamic and static power consumption for multicore processors. In: Proceedings of the 30th IEEE International Parallel and Distributed Processing Symposium (IPDPS 2016), pp. 273–282 (2016)
12. Hashimoto, K., Tsuchiya, T., Kikuno, T.: Effective scheduling of duplicated tasks for fault tolerance in multiprocessor systems. IEICE Trans. Inf. Syst. **85**, 525–534 (2002)
13. Hongxia, W., Xin, Q.: Dynamic replication of fault-tolerant scheduling algorithm. Open Cybern. Syst. J. **9**, 2670–2676 (2015)
14. Hönig, U., Schiffmann, W.: A comprehensive test bench for the evaluation of scheduling heuristics. In: Proceedings 16th IASTED International Conference on Parallel and Distributed Computing and Systems (PDCS 2004), pp. 437–442 (2004)
15. Kianzad, V., Bhattacharyya, S., Ou, G.: CASPER: an integrated energy-driven approach for task graph scheduling on distributed embedded systems. In: Proceedings of the 16th IEEE International Conference on Application-Specific Systems, Architectures and Processors (ASAP 2005) (2005)
16. Pruhs, K., van Stee, R., Uthaisombut, P.: Speed scaling of tasks with precedence constraints. Theory Comput. Syst. **43**(1), 67–80 (2008)
17. Singh, J., Auluck, N.: DVFS and duplication based scheduling for optimizing power and performance in heterogeneous multiprocessors. In: Proceedings of the High Performance Computing Symposium (HPC 2014), pp. 22:1–22:8 (2014)
18. Takouna, I., Dawoud, W., Meinel, C.: Accurate mutlicore processor power models for power-aware resource management. In: Proceedings of the 9th IEEE International Conference on Dependable, Autonomic and Secure Computing (DASC 2011), pp. 419–426 (2011)

19. Tosun, S., Mansouri, N., Kandemir, M., Ozturk, O.: An ILP formulation for task scheduling on heterogeneous chip multiprocessors. In: Levi, A., Savaş, E., Yenigün, H., Balcısoy, S., Saygın, Y. (eds.) ISCIS 2006. LNCS, vol. 4263, pp. 267–276. Springer, Heidelberg (2006). https://doi.org/10.1007/11902140_30
20. Zhao, L., Ren, Y., Xiang, Y., Sakurai, K.: Fault-tolerant scheduling with dynamic number of replicas in heterogeneous systems. In: 12th IEEE International Conference on High Performance Computing and Communications (HPCC), pp. 434–441 (2010)

Lipsi: Probably the Smallest Processor in the World

Martin Schoeberl[✉]

Department of Applied Mathematics and Computer Science,
Technical University of Denmark, Lyngby, Denmark
masca@dtu.dk

Abstract. While research on high-performance processors is important, it is also interesting to explore processor architectures at the other end of the spectrum: tiny processor cores for auxiliary functions. While it is common to implement small circuits for such functions, such as a serial port, in dedicated hardware, usually as a state machine or a combination of communicating state machines, these functionalities may also be implemented by a small processor. In this paper, we present Lipsi, a very tiny processor to make it possible to implement classic finite state machine logic in software at a minimal cost.

1 Introduction

This paper presents Lipsi, a tiny microcontroller optimized for utility functions in an FPGA. Lipsi can be used to implement a peripheral device or a state machine as part of a larger system-on-chip. The design goal of Lipsi is a very small hardware design built around a single block RAM for instructions and data.

Using a single block RAM for instructions and data means that this memory is time shared between instruction fetch and data read. Therefore, Lipsi is a sequential and not a pipelined architecture. Most instructions execute in two clock cycles.

Lipsi is such a simple processor that it is possible to completely describe its datapath, instruction set and instruction encoding in a paper. Besides being a useful processor for auxiliary functions, we also envision Lipsi being used in teaching basic computer architecture. For example, it can be used to learn programming at the machine level. Or it should be possible for students to develop a simulator for Lipsi in a single lab session.

Lipsi is part of a family of processors, which all have been designed during an inspiring vacation on Greek islands, which gave the processors their names. The name for each processor was chosen from that island where the first sketches were drawn. The three sisters are: Patmos, Leros, and Lipsi. Patmos is a dual issue, 32-bit RISC pipeline optimized for real-time systems [1] and used in the multicore T-CREST platform [2]. Leros is a 16-bit processor for small embedded systems [3] and can execute a small Java virtual machine [4]. Lipsi is the smallest sister and an 8-bit accumulator architecture using a single on-chip block RAM, which is the topic of this paper.

© Springer International Publishing AG, part of Springer Nature 2018
M. Berekovic et al. (Eds.): ARCS 2018, LNCS 10793, pp. 18–30, 2018.
https://doi.org/10.1007/978-3-319-77610-1_2

This paper is organized in 5 sections: The following section presents related work. Section 3 describes the design of Lipsi. Section 4 evaluates and discusses the design. Section 5 concludes.

2   Related Work

Altera provides a softcore, the Nios II [5], for Altera FPGAs. The Nios RISC architecture implements a 32-bit instruction set like the MIPS instruction set architecture. Although Nios II represents a different design point from Lipsi, it is interesting to note that Nios II can be customized to meet the application requirements. Three different models are available [5]: the *Fast* core is optimized for high performance; the *Standard* core is intended to balance performance and size; and the *Economy* core is optimized for smallest size. The smallest core can be implemented in less than 700 logic elements (LEs). It is a sequential implementation and each instruction takes at least 6 clock cycles. Lipsi is a smaller (8-bit), accumulator-based architecture, and most instructions execute in two clock cycles.

PicoBlaze is an 8-bit microcontroller for Xilinx FPGAs [6]. The processor is highly optimized for low resource usage. This optimization results in restrictions such as a maximum program size of 1024 instructions and 64 bytes data memory. The benefit of this puristic design is a processor that can be implemented with one on-chip memory and 96 logic slices in a Spartan-3 FPGA. PicoBlaze provides 16 8-bit registers and executes one instruction in two clock cycles. The interface to I/O devices is minimalistic in the positive sense: it is simple and very efficient to connect simple I/O devices to the processor.

The Lipsi approach is, like the concept of PicoBlaze, to provide a small processor for utility functions. Lipsi is optimized to balance the resource usage between on-chip memory and logic cells. Therefore, the LE count of Lipsi is slightly lower than the one of PicoBlaze. PicoBlaze is coded at a very low level of abstraction by using Xilinx primitive components such as LUT4 or MUXCY. Therefore, the design is optimized for Xilinx FPGAs and practically not portable. Lipsi is written in vendor agnostic Chisel and compiles unmodified for Altera and Xilinx devices.

The SpartanMC is a small microcontroller optimized for FPGA technology [7]. One interesting feature is that the instruction width *and* the data width are 18 bits. The argument is that current FPGAs contain on-chip memory blocks that are 18-bit wide (originally intended to contain parity protection). The processor is a 16 register RISC architecture with two operand instructions and is implemented in a three-stage pipeline. To avoid data forwarding within the register file, the instruction fetch and the write-back stage are split into two phases, like the original MIPS pipeline [8]. This decision slightly complicates the design as two phase-shifted clocks are needed. We assume that this phase splitting also limits the maximum clock frequency. As on-chip memories for register files are large, this resource is utilized by a sliding register window to speedup function calls. SpartanMC performs comparable to the 32-bit RISC processors LEON-II [9] and MicroBlaze [10] on the Dhrystone benchmark.

Compared to the SpartanMC, Lipsi is further optimized for FPGAs using fewer resources and avoiding unusual clocking of pipeline stages. Lipsi simplifies the access to registers in on-chip memory by implementing an accumulator architecture instead of a register architecture. Although an accumulator architecture is in theory less efficient, the resulting maximum achievable clock frequency offsets the higher instruction count.

The *Supersmall* processor [11] is optimized for low resource consumption (half of the NIOS economy version). Resources are reduced by serializing ALU operations to single bit operations. The LE consumption is comparable to Lipsi, but the on-chip memory consumption is not reported.

The Ultrasmall MIPS project [12] is based on the Supersmall architecture. The main difference is the change of the ALU serialization to perform two bit operations each cycle instead of single bits. Therefore, a 32-bit operation needs 16 clock cycles to complete. It is reported that Ultrasmall consumes 137 slices in a Xilinx Spartan-3E, which is 84% of the resource consumption of Supersmall. Due to the serialization of the ALU operations, the average clocks per instructions is in the range of 22 for Ultrasmall. According to the authors, "Ultrasmall is the smallest 32-bit ISA soft processor in the world". We appreciate this effort of building the smallest 32-bit processor and are in line with that argument to build the smallest (8-bit) processor of the world.

The Ø processor by Wolfgang Puffitsch[1] is an accumulator machine aiming at low resource usage. The bit width of the accumulator (and register width) is freely configurable. Furthermore, hardware is only generated for instructions that are used in the program. An instance of an 8-bit Ø processor executing a blinking function consumes 176 LEs and 32 memory bits. The Ø processor is designed with a similar mind set to Lipsi.

A very early processor targeting FPGAs is the DOP processor [13]. DOP is a 16-bit stack oriented processor with additional registers, such as address registers and a work register. As this work register is directly connected to the ALU, DOP is similar to Lipsi an accumulator oriented architecture. No resource consumption is given for the DOP design.

Leros is, like Lipsi, an accumulator machine [3]. The machine word in Leros is 16-bit and Leros uses two on-chip memories: one for instructions and one for data. Therefore, Leros is organized as a two-stage pipeline and can execute one instruction every clock cycle. The Leros 16-bit architecture is powerful enough to run a small Java virtual machine [4].

3   The Lipsi Design

Lipsi is an 8-bit processor organized as an accumulator machine and has been designed and optimized around FPGA specific block RAMs. The focus of the design is to use just a single block RAM.

Different FPGA families contain differently organized and differently sized on-chip memories, which are also called block RAMs. The current minimum

---

[1] https://github.com/jeuneS2/oe.

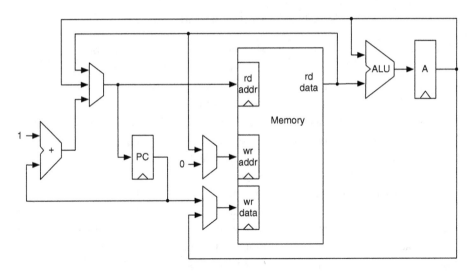

Fig. 1. The datapath of Lipsi.

block RAM[2] is 4096 bits (or 512 bytes) large and has an independent read and write port. Lipsi is an 8-bit processor in its purest form. Therefore, we can use 256 bytes from that memory as instructions and 256 bytes for register and data. We use the lower half of the memory for the program, as the address register powers up at zero to fetch the first instruction.

Using a single block RAM for instructions and data means that this memory is time shared between instruction fetch and data read. Therefore, Lipsi is a sequential and not a pipelined architecture.

Most instructions execute in two clock cycles: one for instruction fetch and one for data access and ALU operation. As on-chip memories in FPGAs usually have independent read and write ports, a store instruction can execute in a single cycle.

Most instructions are single byte. Only immediate and branch instructions contain a second byte for the immediate value or the branch target.

3.1   The Datapath

Figure 1 shows the datapath of Lipsi. The processor consists of a program counter (PC), an on-chip memory, an arithmetic-logic unit (ALU), and an accumulator register (A). Besides those basic components, one adder and three multiplexers are needed. The decode logic, which basically drives the multiplexers and the ALU function is not shown in the figure.

The memory is divided into three areas: (1) program area, (2) a register file, and (3) data memory. A single on-chip memory in most FPGAs is 512 bytes.

---

[2] This number is for relative old FPGAs, such as Xilinx Spartan-3 and Altera Cyclone II. Actual FPGAs from Xilinx have 16 Kbit and Altera have 8 Kbit memory blocks.

Table 1. Lipsi instruction set with encoding

Encoding	Instruction	Meaning	Operation
`Offf rrrr`	f rx	ALU register	A = A f m[r]
`1000 rrrr`	st rx	Store A into register	m[r] = A
`1001 rrrr`	brl rx	Branch and link	m[r] = PC, PC = A
`1010 rrrr`	ldind (rx)	Load indirect	A = m[m[r]]
`1011 rrrr`	stind (rx)	Store indirect	m[m[r]] = A
`1100 -fff nnnn nnnn`	fi n	ALU immediate	A = A f n
`1101 --00 aaaa aaaa`	br	Branch	PC = a
`1101 --10 aaaa aaaa`	brz	Branch if A is zero	PC = a
`1101 --11 aaaa aaaa`	brnz	Branch if A is not zero	PC = a
`1110 --ff`	sh	ALU shift	A = shift(A)
`1111 aaaa`	io	Input and output	IO = A, A = IO
`1111 1111`	exit	Exit for the tester	PC = PC

This memory is split into two 8-bit addressable areas: one for instructions and one for data. The data area itself is split into 16 bytes treated specially as a register file, while the rest is for general data storage.

We can perform a back of an envelope estimation of the resource usage, the number of logic elements (LE). For each LE we assume a 4-bit lookup table for combinational logic and one register. As the design will be dominated by the logic used, we estimate the resource consumption based on combinational logic. The ALU supports addition and subtraction. With careful coding, it should be possible to implement both functions together in 8 LEs. Four logic functions (and, or, xor, and load) can be implemented in a single LE per bit. The shift operations should consume one LE per bit. The selection between adder/subtractor, the logic function, and the shift needs a 3:1 multiplexer with two LEs per bit. Therefore, the ALU should consume about 32 LEs. The adder will consume 8 LEs, the two 2:1 multiplexers each 8 LEs and the 3:1 multiplexer 16 LEs. This sums up to 64 LEs. Branch condition on zero or nonzero of A consumes 3 LEs Instruction decoding is performed on 4 bits, which fit into one LE. Therefore, 4 LEs are needed for the multiplexer driving and another LE for the PC register enable. The multiplexer and add/sub selector in the ALU decode from 3 function bits and need another 3 LEs. Therefore, Lipsi should consume around 84 LEs.

3.2   The Instruction Set

The instruction set of Lipsi includes ALU instructions with register and immediate operands, accumulator store, register indirect load and store, unconditional and conditional branch, branch and link for function call, and shift operations. Instruction length is one or two bytes.

Table 1 shows all instructions of Lipsi and their encoding. A represents the accumulator, f an ALU function, PC the program counter, m[] the memory,

Table 2. ALU operation and encoding

Encoding	Name	Operation
000	add	$A = A + op$
001	sub	$A = A - op$
010	adc	$A = A + op + c$
011	sbb	$A = A - op - c$
100	and	$A = A \wedge op$
101	or	$A = A \vee op$
110	xor	$A = A \oplus op$
111	ld	$A = op$

r a register number in the range of 0 to 15, n an immediate constant, a an 8-bit address, and IO an input/output device. As Lipsi is an accumulator machine, all operations (except unconditional branch) involve the accumulator register A. Furthermore, we use the notion of additional registers, which are the first 16 bytes in the data memory. Lipsi implements ALU operations with those registers and with immediate values. The accumulator A can be stored in any one of the registers. Memory load and store operations are implemented as register indirect. Those operations need three memory accesses: fetch the instruction, read the register content for the address, and finally load from memory into A or a store A in the memory. Register indirect load executes therefore in 3 clock cycles and an indirect store in 2 clock cycles.

Table 2 lists all ALU operations, including addition, subtraction, and logic operations. For an 8-bit architecture it is also useful to support addition with carry and subtraction with borrow for arithmetic on larger numbers. With careful coding these additional operations are almost for free (by adding one lower bit to the adder, setting one input to 1 and using the carry flag as second input). Furthermore, current FPGAs have an dedicated Xor gate in front of the LUT, so that an adder can also be used as subtractor (when using the additional input bit as well.).

Furthermore, three logic operations and a bypass operation for a load instruction are available. Again, we could be very minimalistic to support only a single inverting logic function, such as nand. However, implementation of these base operations is very cheap in an FPGA.

3.3   Implementation and Assembly in Hardware

For the implementation of Lipsi we use the relatively new hardware construction language Chisel [14]. In Chisel, the hardware is described in two classes: one for the processor and one for the memory. Describing the memory component in its own class allows future optimization to use an initialized memory (described in VHDL), which is currently not possible with Chisel.

```scala
val tokens = line.trim.split(" ")
val Pattern = "(.*:)".r
val instr = tokens(0) match {
  case "#" => // comment
  case Pattern(l) => if (!pass2) symbols += (l.substring(0, l.length - 1) -> pc)
  case "add" => 0x00 + regNumber(tokens(1))
  case "sub" => 0x10 + regNumber(tokens(1))
  // and similar pattern
  case "addi" => (0xc0, toInt(tokens(1)))
  case "subi" => (0xc1, toInt(tokens(1)))
  // and similar pattern
  case "st" => 0x80 + regNumber(tokens(1))
  case "ldind" => 0xa0 + regIndirect(tokens(1))
  case "stind" => 0xb0 + regIndirect(tokens(1))
  case "br" => (0xd0, if (pass2) symbols(tokens(1)) else 0)
  case "brz" => (0xd2, if (pass2) symbols(tokens(1)) else 0)
  case "brnz" => (0xd3, if (pass2) symbols(tokens(1)) else 0)
  case "io" => 0xf0 + toInt(tokens(1))
  case "exit" => (0xff)
  case "" => // empty line
  case t: String => throw new Exception("Assembler error: unknown instruction")
  case _ => throw new Exception("Assembler error")
}
```

Fig. 2. The central statement of the Lipsi assembler in Scala

The hardware abstraction level of Chisel is not so different from VHDL or Verilog. Hardware is described at the register transfer level. However, the power of Chisel lies in that Chisel is a language embedded in Scala [15], a modern general-purpose programming language. Scala itself runs on top of the JVM and can use libraries written in Java. Therefore, all these libraries and a modern object oriented and functional language are available at hardware construction time.

One of the first tools a processor developer needs is an assembler. A common approach is to write an assembler in some general-purpose language, e.g., Java, and spit out a VHDL table for the code that shall go into the ROM. This approach is also used for generating any hardware table which is needed, such as for function lookup or binary to binary-coded-decimal translation. As we can read in data with Scala and then generate a hardware table from Scala, the assembler can now instead generate a binary file that we read in at hardware construction time.

We have, however, gone a step further and have written the assembler itself in Scala, invoking it at hardware generation time, reading in the assembler code, and directly generating the hardware table to the ROM. With the power of the Scala `match` statement the assembler itself is just a handful of lines of code. Figure 2 shows this statement, which is the core of the assembler. The full assembler is less than 100 lines of code and was written in a few hours.

3.4   Simulation and Testing

Chisel supports testing of hardware with a so-called tester. Within the tester one sets input signals with **poke**, advances the simulation by one clock cycle with **step**, and reads signals with **peek**. This is similar to a testbench in VHDL, except that the tester is written in Scala with the full power of a general purpose language available.

Furthermore, the tester also generates waveforms that can be inspected with ModelSim or gtkwave. We used this form of testing for the initial design.

As a next step, we wrote some test programs in assembly code with the convention that the test shall result in a zero in the accumulator at the end of the program. Furthermore, we defined an IO instruction to mark the end of the program. The testing against the zero in the accumulator has been integrated into the tester. With a handful of assembler programs we have, with minimal effort, achieved a first regression test.

As a further step, we have implemented a software simulator for Lipsi in Scala. The software simulator reuses the assembler that was written in the context of the hardware generation. Having a software simulator of Chisel opens up for testing of the hardware with co-simulation. As the hardware and the software simulator for Lipsi are all written in the same language (Scala with the Chisel library) it is possible to execute both together. Therefore, we also implemented a tester that executes the Lipsi hardware and the software simulation in lock step and compares the content of the program counter and the accumulator at every clock cycle. As all data will pass through the accumulator any error in the implementation (hardware of software simulator) will manifest itself at some stage as a difference in the accumulator.

The assembly of code and co-simulation of hardware and a software simulator in the very same language shows the power of Chisel as a hardware construction language. This usage of Chisel/Scala is probably just scratching the surface of new approaches to hardware design and testing.

With two implementations of Lipsi available, we can also explore random testing. As a next step, we plan to generate random byte patterns, which result in random instructions, and to compare the execution of the hardware and software simulator.

3.5   Developing a Processor

Although it is unusual to write about the history of the development in a scientific paper, we will provide here a brief history of the project. Actually, the development of Lipsi follows a pattern that we have observed several times. Therefore, the description of this development pattern for a moderately small digital design project, such as a processor, may be a contribution on its own.

Initially the processor was designed on paper in a notebook. Not really starting from scratch, as the author of this paper has designed several processors before. The Leros processor had been designed just a few days before, on paper as well. The pattern is that one often builds on previous designs. However, one should not restrict always oneself to reuse older designs, as this might restrict the design to not try entirely different approaches for a new system. And the author is convinced that a sketch of the datapath and some timing diagrams of execution traces on a piece of paper is important before coding any hardware.

From the detailed datapath design on paper, almost identical to Fig. 1, and an initial instruction set encoding we started with coding of the hardware in Chisel. First we setup the infrastructure, describe a small part of the datapath in hardware, and started with simple testers (the name of test benches in Chisel).

From there we bootstrapped the implementation of the first instructions, the immediate instructions. We provide test code in very small programs as hexadecimal values in a static array that is then translated into a hardware table (ROM). First tests are manual checks with a Chisel tester (*printf debugging*) and manual inspection of waveforms. In parallel we also setup a Quartus FPGA project to observe the hardware cost development as we add features to the processor.

As manual assembly becomes too tedious, we developed an assembler. First just for the instructions that have already been assembled by hand for the test of the assembler by comparing with the manually generated instructions.

From that point in time on, the instructions in Lipsi and the assembler were developed in tandem. With more instructions being implemented, some automation of the testing is desirable. Especially some regression testing to make sure that newly added functionality does not break older functionality.

To perform some form of automated testing we need two functions: stopping of the test and an indication of success or failure. To stop the simulation (tester), we *invented* an `exit` instruction (which is just an IO instruction to a special address). For an indication of test success, we defined as success that the accumulator has to contain zero at the end of the test. All tests are written to have a dependent data flow from all operations into the accumulator. The tester checks at the end for zero and exits itself with an exit value different from zero when a test fails. This will also exit the `make` based automation of the testing code so we can observe the failure.

For further testing of Lipsi we wrote a software simulator of Lipsi, also in Scala. That software simulator is designed to be cycle accurate, modeling the timing of the Lipsi hardware. With that additional implementation we can perform co-simulation of the hardware description and the software simulator.

Now those tests are triggered manually with a `make` target. This project is too small for automated regression test. However, for larger projects, such as the Patmos project, we use nightly regression tests that follow a similar pattern.

Maybe this design flow with a relatively early automation of testing sounds like a lot of work and distracts from the fun of hardware design. The opposite is true. From the creation of the first file to contain Chisel code until the automation of the tests and implementation of around 2/3 of the functionality of Lipsi, just 8 h have been spent on coding and testing. This very short development time was *because* of early automation with an assembler and smart testing not *despite* of it.

The message of this subsection is to start early with very low effort automation and testing. Invest into the infrastructure of your project just what is needed at the moment.

4 Evaluation and Discussion

For the evaluation, we have synthesized Lipsi for a Cyclon IV FPGA, as this is the FPGA on the popular DE2-115 FPGA board. We used Quartus Prime Lite Edition 16.1 with the default settings and did not introduce any constraints related to the maximum clock frequency. Cyclone IV is the last generation of Cyclone FPGAs where a logic element (LE) contains a 4-bit lookup table (LUT).[3] Therefore, we can compare the resource numbers with designs on older FPGAs (e.g., Xilinx Spartan 3).

4.1 Resource Consumption

Table 3 shows the resource consumption in LEs and on-chip memory blocks, the maximum clock frequency, and the FPGA used for obtaining the results for different small processors. We synthesized Lipsi with a test program that slowly counts and puts the result on the LEDs. This configuration also contains one input port and one output port. Indeed, we can see that Lipsi is the smallest processor in this table. However, it is closely followed by Leros, which is a 16-bit, pipelined processor. With respect to the maximum clock frequency, Lipsi is in the same range as the other processors. We can see that the two pipeline stages of Leros result in a higher clock frequency than Lipsi where the critical path is in a memory read and an ALU operation.

The main reason why Lipsi is not even smaller is that with the current version of Chisel we cannot express an initialized block RAM. Therefore, the program is described in a table, which is then synthesized to logic. This logic for the instruction memory consumes 66 out of the 162 LEs. With the current workaround (using an on-chip memory and a logic table) we also need an additional

Table 3. Comparison of Lipsi with Leros, PicoBlaze, Ultrasmall, and SpartanMC

Processor	Logic (LE)	Memory (blocks)	Fmax (MHz)	FPGA
Lipsi	162	1	136	Cyclone IV
Leros	189	1	160	Cyclone IV
PicoBlaze	177	1	117	Spartan 3
Ultrasmall	235	3	65	Spartan 3E
SpartanMC	1271	3	50	Sparten 3

---

[3] Newer generations is FPGAs use a 6-bit LUT, which can be split into two smaller LUTs.

multiplexer at the output of the memory component. Therefore, the processor core is smaller than 100 LEs.

As future work, we plan to describe the block RAM, including the initialization data, in VHDL or Verilog and instantiating it as a black box in Chisel. However, this solution is not very elegant as we mix languages and need to use different implementations of the memory for testing and synthesis. Another approach would be to extend Chisel to generate Verilog for initialized memory.

4.2   The Smallest Processor?

Is Lipsi now the smallest possible processor? No – if we really want a minimal implementation that can compute, we could drop several instructions. E.g., subtraction can be performed with xor and addition.

However, our target was a very small but useful processor. When we compare Lipsi with other processors, we think we have achieved that goal. With around 100 LEs and one block RAM we can fit many Lipsi cores into a low-cost FPGA.

4.3   A Lipsi Manycore Processor

We have explored how many Lipsi cores we can fit into the low-cost EP4CE115 FPGA from the DE2-115 board. Each processor contains one input and one output port. All processors are connected into a pipeline, which is the minimum useful connection of those processors. The first processors's input port is connected to the keys on the FPGA board and the last processor's output port is connected to the LEDs. Each processor reads the input, adds one to it, and puts the result to the output port.

The EP4CE115 contains 432 memory blocks. Therefore, we have configured 432 Lipsi processors in this computing pipeline. The resource consumption in the FPGA 67,130 is LEs out of 114,480 LEs, which is a resource consumption of 59%. This shows that this kind of design is memory bound and we can add more functionality to the processor for a balanced use of the available resources.

This experiment is just meant as a proof of concept to build a manycore processor in a low-cost FPGA. Future work will be to use the remaining resources to add a simple network-in-chip to the 432 processor cores. This will enable more flexible communication paths and enable exploring network-on-chip designs within a high count of processing cores.

4.4   Lipsi in Teaching

The instruction set of Lipsi is so simple that it can be explained completely in this paper. However, it is complete enough to write useful programs. Therefore, we envision that Lipsi can serve as an example processor for a first semester introduction course in computer systems. Besides writing small assembler programs and running them on a simulator for Lipsi, writing a full simulator for Lipsi can serve as an exercise for a two-hour lab.

4.5 Source Access

We strongly believe in open-source designs for research, as far as legal possible. Especially when the research is funded by public funds, the full results (data and source code, not only a paper) shall be available to the public. Open-source enables independent researches to reproduce the published results. Furthermore, it also simplifies to build future research on top of the published research.

Lipsi's source is available at GitHub: https://github.com/schoeberl/lipsi. The README.md describes which tools are need to be installed and how to build Lipsi.

5 Conclusion

This paper presents Lipsi, a very tiny processor core. We believe that Lipsi is one of the smallest processors available. The intention of a small processor is to serve for auxiliary functions like an intelligent peripheral device, such as a serial port with buffering. Lipsi and the supporting assembler are all written in the same language, Chisel, which itself is based on Scala. This gives the power that the whole compilation flow from assembling the program till testing and hardware generation is driven by one description. Besides being a processor for peripheral devices, Lipsi can also serve as a small, but non-trivial example for the relatively new hardware construction language Chisel. Furthermore, as the processor structure is so simple that it can be drawn on half a page, it can also be used in an introductory course on computer architecture.

References

1. Schoeberl, M., Schleuniger, P., Puffitsch, W., Brandner, F., Probst, C.W., Karlsson, S., Thorn, T.: Towards a time-predictable dual-issue microprocessor: the Patmos approach. In: First Workshop on Bringing Theory to Practice: Predictability and Performance in Embedded Systems (PPES 2011), Grenoble, France, pp. 11–20, March 2011
2. Schoeberl, M., Abbaspour, S., Akesson, B., Audsley, N., Capasso, R., Garside, J., Goossens, K., Goossens, S., Hansen, S., Heckmann, R., Hepp, S., Huber, B., Jordan, A., Kasapaki, E., Knoop, J., Li, Y., Prokesch, D., Puffitsch, W., Puschner, P., Rocha, A., Silva, C., Sparsø, J., Tocchi, A.: T-CREST: time-predictable multi-core architecture for embedded systems. J. Syst. Architect. **61**(9), 449–471 (2015)
3. Schoeberl, M.: Leros: a tiny microcontroller for FPGAs. In: Proceedings of the 21st International Conference on Field Programmable Logic and Applications (FPL 2011), Chania, Crete, Greece, pp. 10–14. IEEE Computer Society, September 2011
4. Caska, J., Schoeberl, M.: Java dust: how small can embedded Java be? In: Proceedings of the 9th International Workshop on Java Technologies for Real-Time and Embedded Systems (JTRES 2011), pp. 125–129. ACM, New York, September 2011
5. Altera Corporation: Nios II Processor Reference Handbook, May 2011. http://www.altera.com/literature/lit-nio2.jsp, Version NII5V1-11.0
6. Xilinx: PicoBlaze 8-bit embedded microcontroller user guide (2010)

7. Hempel, G., Hochberger, C.: A resource optimized processor core for FPGA based SoCs. In: Kubatova, H. (ed.) Proceedings of the 10th Euromicro Conference on Digital System Design (DSD 2007), pp. 51–58. IEEE (2007)
8. Hennessy, J.L.: VLSI processor architecture. IEEE Trans. Comput. **C-33**(12), 1221–1246 (1984)
9. Gaisler, J.: A portable and fault-tolerant microprocessor based on the SPARC v8 architecture. In: Proceedings of the 2002 International Conference on Dependable Systems and Networks (DSN 2002), p. 409. IEEE Computer Society, Washington, DC (2002)
10. Xilinx Inc.: MicroBlaze processor reference guide (2008). Version 9.0
11. Robinson, J., Vafaee, S., Scobbie, J., Ritche, M., Rose, J.: The supersmall soft processor. In: 2010 VI Southern Programmable Logic Conference (SPL), pp. 3–8, March 2010
12. Nakatsuka, H., Tanaka, Y., Chu, T.V., Takamaeda-Yamazaki, S., Kise, K.: Ultrasmall: the smallest MIPS soft processor. In: 2014 24th International Conference on Field Programmable Logic and Applications (FPL), pp. 1–4, September 2014
13. Danecek, J., Drapal, F., Pluhacek, A., Salcic, Z., Servit, M.: DOP—a simple processor for custom computing machines. J. Microcomput. Appl. **17**(3), 239–253 (1994)
14. Bachrach, J., Vo, H., Richards, B., Lee, Y., Waterman, A., Avizienis, R., Wawrzynek, J., Asanovic, K.: Chisel: constructing hardware in a scala embedded language. In: Groeneveld, P., Sciuto, D., Hassoun, S. (eds.) The 49th Annual Design Automation Conference (DAC 2012), pp. 1216–1225. ACM, San Francisco (2012)
15. Venners, B., Spoon, L., Odersky, M.: Programming in Scala, 3rd edn. Artima Inc., Mountain View (2016)

Superlinear Scalability in Parallel Computing and Multi-robot Systems: Shared Resources, Collaboration, and Network Topology

Heiko Hamann$^{(\boxtimes)}$ ⓘ

Department of Computer Engineering, University of Lübeck, Lübeck, Germany
hamann@iti.uni-luebeck.de

Abstract. The uniting idea of both parallel computing and multi-robot systems is that having multiple processors or robots working on a task decreases the processing time. Typically we desire a linear speedup, that is, doubling the number of processing units halves the execution time. Sometimes superlinear scalability is observed in parallel computing systems and more frequently in multi-robot and swarm systems. Superlinearity means each individual processing unit gets more efficient by increasing the system size—a desired and rather counterintuitive phenomenon.

In an interdisciplinary approach, we compare abstract models of system performance from three different fields of research: parallel computing, multi-robot systems, and network science. We find agreement in the modeled universal properties of scalability and summarize our findings by formulating more generic interpretations of the observed phenomena. Our result is that scalability across fields can be interpreted as a tradeoff in three dimensions between too competitive and too cooperative processing schemes, too little information sharing and too much information sharing, while finding a balance between neither underusing nor depleting shared resources. We successfully verify our claims by two simple simulations of a multi-robot and a network system.

Keywords: Parallel computing · Multi-robot systems
Distributed robotics · Swarm robotics · Scalability · Speedup

1 Introduction

Superlinear scalability is a desirable phenomenon in both parallel computing and multi-robot systems. It is counterintuitive because one seemingly receives a profit without paying for it. Also our experience of working together in human groups dominantly gives a different impression, as indicated, for example, by the Ringelmann effect. According to Ingham et al. [1] the Ringelmann effect implies a nonlinear decrease of individual performance with increasing group size.

© Springer International Publishing AG, part of Springer Nature 2018
M. Berekovic et al. (Eds.): ARCS 2018, LNCS 10793, pp. 31–42, 2018.
https://doi.org/10.1007/978-3-319-77610-1_3

We call the improvement in speed of the task execution achieved by adding more processing units 'speedup': $S = T_1/T_p$, for latency T_1 of the smaller system (typically one processing unit) and latency T_p of the bigger system ($p > 1$ processing units); efficiency is $E = T_1/(pT_p)$. Scalability describes how far we can go in keep adding processing units p without getting $E < 1$.

As superlinear speedups seem special, they were frequently discussed and studied [2,3]. There even exists a proof showing the impossibility of superlinear speedups but it assumes fixed problem size [4]. Superlinear speedups are rather infrequently observed in parallel computing (e.g., cache-size effects [5]) compared to rather frequent observations in multi-robot and swarm systems (e.g., inherently collaborative tasks [6]). When observed, superlinearity is often a discrete effect, such as a workpackage happening to fit into the processors cache [5] or a robot group being able to form a bucket brigade [7,8]. Superlinear scalability has much potential that should be enough motivation to investigate it across different domains and to understand how one can provoke it.

1.1   Superlinear Performance in Multi-robot Systems

Superlinear performance increases are observed in multi-robot systems due to physical effects in tasks, such as pulling, passing gaps, and passing steps [9]. Analyzing the literature on multi-robot systems and, in particular, swarm robotics, one finds that plots of system performance over system size (number of robots) have similar features independent of the investigate task (see Fig. 1 as example).

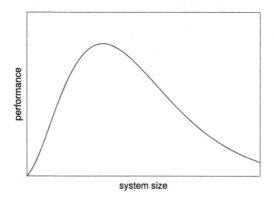

Fig. 1. Generic diagram of system performance over system size for multi-robot systems, without units, function $P(N) = N^b \exp(cN)$ (Eq. 1) depending on parameters $b > 1$ (profits from cooperation, N^b), $c < 0$ (overhead due to interference, $\exp(-N)$), and system size N [10,11].

It was noticed that there is an optimal robot density, that is, how many robots should share the same area [12]. Initially the performance curve increases with increased number of robots but then first levels off and then decreases [13].

The most obvious shared resource in robotics is space. Adding robots to the system while keeping the provided area constant, the additional robots may generate more possibilities to cooperate but they may also physically interfere [14,15]. So we identify a first tradeoff between options for collaborations and an increased overhead due to physical interference. Østergaard et al. [16] discuss the existence of a general multi-robot performance diagram with a focus on its peak performance:

> We know that by varying the implementation of a given task, we can move the point of "maximum performance" and we can change the shapes of the curve on either side of it, but we cannot change the general shape of the graph.

Examples of such performance diagrams are found across the literature, for example, in multi-robot foraging [14,17–20], collective decision making [21], the emergent taxis scenario [11,22,23], and aggregation behaviors [24,25].

In previous works [10,11], the author has proposed the following simple model of performance $P(N)$ in multi-robot and swarm systems:

$$P(N) = C(N)(I(N) - d) = a_1 N^b a_2 \exp(cN), \tag{1}$$

for a cooperation function $C(N) = a_1 N^b$, an interference function $I(N) = a_2 \exp(cN) + d$, parameter $c < 0$, and scaling constants $a_1, a_2 > 0$, d for translation up/down. For $b > 1$ we have potentially superlinear scalability but interference is counteracting exponentially with $\exp(-N)$. This rather rough and abstract model was successfully fitted to a number of multi-robot scenarios [10,11].

Out of the multi-robot domain, other systems are worth mentioning. Although they are much harder to measure, similar diagrams are also found for natural swarms, such as the hypothesis for per capita output in social wasps by Jeanne et al. [26]. The well-known 'fundamental diagram' of traffic flow is also similar but symmetric [27].

1.2   Universal Scalability Law

There is a model for parallel processing performance in distributed systems by Gunther [28]. He calls it the Universal Scalability Law (USL). For a relative capacity $R(N)$ (i.e., X_N/X_1, for throughput X_N achieved using N processors and throughput X_1 for one processor) he defines

$$R(N) = \frac{N}{1 + \alpha((N - 1) + \beta N(N - 1))}, \tag{2}$$

for a coefficient α that gives the degree of contention (inference) in the system and coefficient β that gives the lack of coherency in the distributed data. Contention occurs because resources are shared. Whenever the capacity of a shared resource is used completely and another process requests to use that

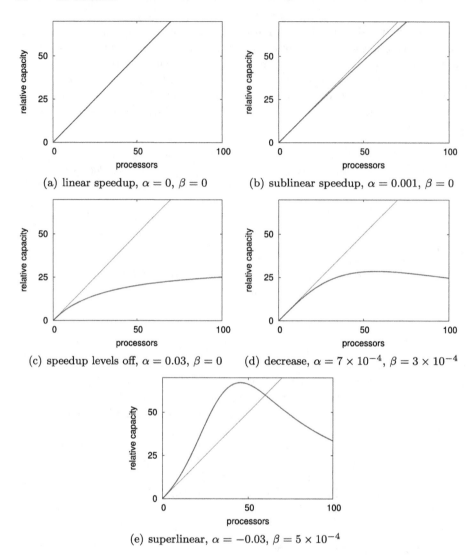

Fig. 2. Universal Scalability Law following Gunther [28], four standard situations and superlinear speedup [5] depending on parameters α (degree of contention) and β (lack of coherency).

resource, then the process has to wait. Contention increases with increasing system size, while keeping resources at the same capacity. Lack of coherency occurs because processes, to a certain extent, operate locally. For example, they have local changes in their caches that are not immediately communicated to all other processes. Maintaining coherency is costly and the costs increase with increasing system size.

Gunther identifies four qualitatively different situations:

a. If contention and lack of coherency are negligible, then we get "equal bang for the buck" and have a linear speedup ($\alpha = 0$, $\beta = 0$, Fig. 2a).
b. If there is a cost for sharing resources in the form of contention, then we have a sublinear speedup ($\alpha > 0$, $\beta = 0$, Fig. 2b).
c. If there is an increased negative influence due to contention, then the speedup clearly levels off ($\alpha \gg 0$, $\beta = 0$, Fig. 2c).
d. If in addition there is also an increased influence of incoherence then there exists a peak speedup and for bigger system sizes the speedup decreases ($\alpha \gg 0$, $\beta > 0$, Fig. 2d).

In the original work of Gunther [28], superlinear performance increases are basically not allowed. In a more recent work [5], superlinear speedups are discussed and negative contention coefficients $\alpha < 0$ are allowed now (see Fig. 2e). While contention $\alpha > 0$ refers to capacity consumption due to sublinear scalability, $\alpha < 0$ refers to a capacity boost due to superlinear scalability. In parallel computing, superlinear speedups can occur due to some interplay between problem size per computing unit and available memory. For example, if the problem can be divided into pieces that fit completely into a CPU's cache, then one can observe a considerable speedup. In swarm robotics, superlinear performance increases occur due to qualitatively different collaboration modes that are accessible with increasing swarm size as in the bucket brigade example [7,8] or when assembled swarm robots cross a hole in a team.

In the context of swarm robotics we can interpret contention as interference between robots due to shared resources, such as an entrance to a base station or generally space. Following this interpretation, the collision avoidance behavior between robots can be understood as a waiting loop because the shared resource *space* is currently not available. That is intuitive and similar to an airplane flying a holding pattern because the resource *runway* is currently in use and should certainly not be shared. Incoherence, in turn, can be interpreted as inconsistencies or overhead due to limited communication of information or due to imperfect synchrony.

While Gunther assumes that there cannot be a system-wide deadlock situation due to contention (speedup monotonically increases with increasing α), that could occur in a swarm robotics system. For example, the swarm density could be too high, such that all robots permanently try to avoid collisions resulting in zero performance.

2   Unified Interpretation Across Fields of Research

Both the simple multi-robot performance model (Eq. 1) and the Universal Scalability Law (Eq. 2) are phenomenological macroscopic models, that is, they are not derived from elementary microscopic features that could be tracked back to concrete procedures and behaviors of robots and processing units. Hence, also their interpretation and specifically the interpretation of individual mathematical terms are abstract considerations that make the chosen function more plausible and understandable but they are also subject to speculation. For example, Gunther's assumption that coefficient α corresponds to contention is a widely applicable concept. However, his assumption that coefficient β corresponds to the lack of coherency is much more specific. Similarly, in the simple multi-robot model the assumed exponential increase of interference is a rather strong assumption. We follow that both models allow or even invite reinterpretations and have potential to be generalized. In the following, we make a number of assumptions of how this can be done, which are then verified in Sect. 3.

We argue that interacting entities in parallel computing, multi-robot systems, and networks are facing tradeoffs in three categories: (R) utilization of shared resources, (I) information flow, and (C) degree of collaboration. A typical system has to deal with several instances from one or more of these categories (e.g., two shared resources and one type of collaboration). They are usually mutually dependent, which is the cause of their complexity. For example, maximizing the utilization of a resource $r_1 \in R$ may be necessary to maximize a type of collaboration $c \in C$, but before r_1 is fully utilized another resource $r_2 \in R$ is already depleted causing overhead.

In Fig. 3 we give a schematic overview of our interpretation. We separate the interval of system size $N \in \{1, 2, \dots\}$ into three regions. First, the region of underused resource, too little collaboration, and too little information flow (left-hand side in Fig. 3). Second, the region of optimally balanced tradeoffs corresponding to optimal achievable performance (middle part in Fig. 3). Third, the region of depleted resources, too much collaboration, and too intensive information exchange (right-hand side in Fig. 3).

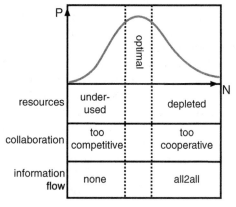

Fig. 3. Schema of how to interpret scalability challenges across fields

While it is intuitive to understand that depleting resources is disadvantageous and creates overhead (e.g., long queues, interference), it is maybe less intuitive to understand why there can be too much of collaboration or too much information flow. For the degree of collaboration, we distinguish between a competitive approach without or with little collaboration and a cooperative approach with a high degree of cooperation. In parallel computing, we can relate that to the distinction between competition parallelization (a parallel race to solve the same problem with different methods) and partitioning parallelization (standard approach to parallelization). Without collaboration all processing units work on their own and create a competitive environment. With a maximal degree of collaboration all processing units cooperate and may, hence, work on too similar potential solutions to the problem. Similarly, for the information flow we can avoid any exchange of information or share information all-to-all. Without sharing any information we may fall back to a purely competitive approach but in a multi-robot setting this could still be a useful parallelization, for example, of a cleaning task. With all-to-all communication we may loose diversity in the solution approaches and end up with a homogeneous approach where each processing unit basically processes the same workpackages.

3   Results

To verify and further investigate these interpretations, we study two example scenarios. In the stick pulling scenario, we investigate the tradeoff between properly exploiting shared resources while not depleting them. In the parallel optimization scenario, we investigate the tradeoff between intensifying collaboration but not loosing too much diversity.

3.1   Stick Pulling: Shared Resources and Collaboration

We investigate the tradeoff between not depleting resources while creating sufficiently many opportunities for collaboration in the well-known stick pulling task [6]. A group of robots equipped with grippers is supposed to collect sticks. The sticks are found standing upright in holes. The sticks are too long as if a single robot could remove them from the hole in one grip. Instead robots have to cooperate. A first robot does the first grip and removes the stick half-way. A second robot then grips the stick and removes it completely from the hole. The task is interesting as for an efficient solution a proper balance of the robot number relative to the number of sticks and the provided area is required as well as an optimized waiting time (for how long should the robot wait for support after the first grip).

To make our point here, we restrict ourselves to a simplified, non-embodied model. We only model that $N \in \{2, 3, \ldots, 20\}$ robots are randomly distributed among $M = 20$ stick sites, wait there for a defined waiting time $w_{\text{atStick}} = 7$ [discrete time steps], and the commute time T between sites is also modeled. We scale the commute time T with the system size N in two variants. First, we scale it linearly

$$T_l(N) = N + \xi, \tag{3}$$

for a random number $\xi \in \{0, 1, 2\}$. Second, we scale it quadratically

$$T_q(N) = cN^2 + \xi, \tag{4}$$

with an arbitrary constant $c = 0.12$ to scale T_q to intervals comparable to T_l and again a random number $\xi \in \{0, 1, 2\}$. The underlying idea is that with increased system size there is more traffic, robots physically interfere, and have delays due to collision avoidance behaviors. The following simulations are separated in two sets where we either use T_l or T_q to calculate how long a robot has to travel from any stick site to any other stick site.

Each robot can be in one of $M+1 = 21$ states. In state s_0 a robot is currently commuting. In state s_i with $i > 0$ a robot is currently positioned at stick site i and waits for help. In addition, each robot has a current waiting time w that represents for how long a robot has been waiting already. Once at least two robots meet at a stick site at the same time step, we say they instantaneously remove the stick, they immediately start to commute to another, randomly selected site, and the stick is put back ready to be removed again. System performance is measured in the total number of removed sticks over the full duration of an experiment (1000 time steps). Each experiment setting was repeated 5000 times.

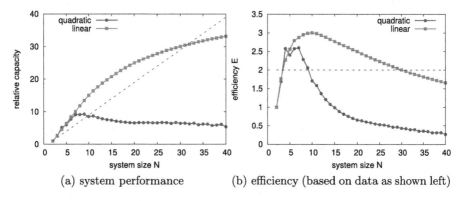

(a) system performance   (b) efficiency (based on data as shown left)

Fig. 4. Stick pulling experiment, relative capacity and efficiency $E = T_2/(NT_N)$ over system size N, averaged over 5000 repetitions (Color figure online)

The results are shown in Fig. 4. First, Fig. 4(a) gives the relative capacity, that is, the total number of pulled sticks normalized by the performance for system size $N = 2$, over system size N for linearly scaled commute time T_l (green) and quadratically scaled commute time T_q (blue; standard deviation for linear commute time: $N = 2$, 2.16; $N = 10$, 7.5; $N = 15$, 8.1; $N = 20$, 8.6; $N = 30$, 9.1; $N = 40$, 9.5; standard deviation for quadratic commute time: $N = 2$, 2.6; $N = 10$, 6.8; $N = 15$, 6.4; $N = 20$, 6.2; $N = 30$, 5.4; $N = 40$, 4.4). For the linear commute times, the system performance improves with increasing system size for all tested system sizes. For the quadratic commute times, the system performance decreases starting with $N = 8$. As expected, the quadratic scaling increases the commute times much faster (despite discount factor $c = 0.12$). The dashed line gives the linear scaling. The relative capacity is superlinear for $N < 10$ (quadratic commute times) and for $N < 32$ (linear). Figure 4(b) gives the efficiency normalized with the mean execution time observed for system size $N = 2$. Both efficiencies decrease for too big system sizes. The efficiencies shown in Fig. 4(b) correspond to case **d.** in Gunther's USL ($\alpha \gg 0$, $\beta > 0$).

3.2   Parallel Optimization: Network Topologies and Information Flow

Here, we follow a network model described by Lazer and Friedman [29] but extend it to random geometric graphs instead of predefined network topologies and small-world networks. Random geometric graphs are more closely related to typical setups in multi-robot systems. Initially we place robots in a 2-d plane (i.e., a point process), which is here the unit square. Hence, each robot has a position x. We say, all robots have a given sensor range r. A considered robot has an edge to another robot if that robot is within range r, that is, for robot positions x_1 and x_2 we test the Euclidean distance $|x_1 - x_2| < r$.

The task is to solve an optimization problem in parallel. The problem is generated using Kauffman's so-called NK model [30]. That is a standard technique to generate test problems with rugged fitness landscapes, for example, in evolutionary computation [31]. For details about the optimization problem see Lazer and Friedman [29]. Each robot (or processing unit) could, in principle, try to solve the problem on its own. That is actually also what a robot needs to do if it happens to have no neighbors in the geometric graph. The idea is, however, that the robots cooperate and share information about the optimization problem. Neighboring robots can compare their current best solutions, the robot with the worse solution can replace it with the other robot's better solution, and continue to optimize the problem starting from there.

The network model iterates over the following procedure. Each of the $N = 100$ robots checks whether a neighbor has currently a better solution. If yes, it replaces its own current solution with the best solution of its neighbors. If not, the robot does a local search, that is, a brute force approach to improve its current solution by checking small changes of it. This is iterated for 20 time steps. We test different sensor ranges $r \in [0.001, 1]$ and each experiment setting is repeated 1000 times.

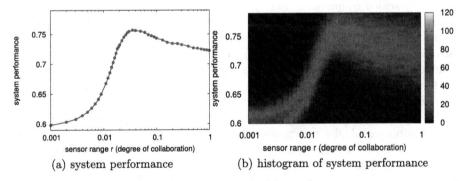

(a) system performance   (b) histogram of system performance

Fig. 5. Parallel optimization experiment, system performance, note logarithmic scale on the horizontal axis (left: mean, right: histogram) over sensor range r, averaged over 1000 repetitions

In Fig. 5 we give the results. In these plots we use a logarithmic scale for the horizontal axis, which does not change the shape qualitatively (e.g., in comparison to Fig. 1). Figure 5(a) gives the mean performance (i.e., best solution in the multi-robot system) averaged over 1000 repetitions of the experiment setting. Figure 5(b) gives a histogram of the same data set and indicates that there is rather little variance. The sensor range r determines how many neighbors a robot has in average. The number of neighbors determines how often a robot adapts solutions from other robots instead of doing a local search to optimize the problem. Having more neighbors helps to gather better solutions but if each robot has many neighbors the overall system reduces its potential for exploring the problem's search space.

4   Discussion and Conclusion

The stick pulling experiment clearly indicates the tradeoff between creating chances to collaborate and ensuring that resources are not depleted. Each stick site can be seen as a resource that needs to be populated, because if they are underused the system performance suffers. However, the resource 'space' between the sites is limited. Hence, we find an optimum system size that balances the use of stick sites and space.

The parallel optimization experiment indicates the tradeoff between collaborating while not loosing too much diversity. If there is no collaboration, each robot independently tries to optimize the problem. If each robot is connected to every other robot, then the search is not parallelized anymore but all robots investigate the same problem instances in parallel. There is clearly an optimum between sharing some information (a medium information flow through the system) and sharing too much information.

Gunther's interpretation of his Universal Scaling Law speaks of contention (i.e., overhead in sharing resources) and lack of coherence (e.g., as in cache hierarchies). While contention can be easily identified in the multi-robot setup (e.g., for linearly scaled commuting times in the stick pulling scenario, see Fig. 4(b)), a correspondence to 'lack of coherency' is difficult to be identified. Instead we see two contradicting uses of shared resources in the stick pulling scenario. One resource is supposed to be populated to increase profit (stick sites) but the other resource is already depleted and creates overheads (space). In the parallel optimization scenario, there is also no lack of coherence but instead a too intensive communication that then crucially reduces exploration in the system.

Superlinearity seems more frequent in multi-robot systems and swarm systems probably mainly due to physical effects. In tasks, such as collectively pulling a heavy object and passing a gap or a steep hill, one or a few robots basically achieve zero performance (they cannot pull the object at all due to friction, they can just not pass the gap or the hill) but once a certain threshold N_c of system size $N > N_c$ is reached the performance increases rapidly. Superlinearity as seen in the stick pulling scenario, however, is more subtle and less easily connected directly to such a single cause. Obviously it is the interplay of not underusing one resource while not depleting another.

As mentioned above, the generic swarm performance curve (Fig. 1) is observed frequently. Hence, we follow that the above described phenomena observed in the two investigated scenarios must also be frequent. It is encouraging to see that similar phenomena emerge in such different domains as multi-robot system, networks, and parallel computing. This is a clear indicator that universal models across all fields must exist.

References

1. Ingham, A.G., Levinger, G., Graves, J., Peckham, V.: The Ringelmann effect: studies of group size and group performance. J. Exp. Soc. Psychol. **10**(4), 371–384 (1974)
2. Gustafson, J.L.: Fixed time, tiered memory, and superlinear speedup. In: Proceedings of the Fifth Distributed Memory Computing Conference (DMCC5), pp. 1255–1260 (1990)
3. Helmbold, D.P., McDowell, C.E.: Modelling speedup (n) greater than n. IEEE Trans. Parallel Distrib. Syst. **1**(2), 250–256 (1990)
4. Faber, V., Lubeck, O.M., White Jr., A.B.: Superlinear speedup of an efficient sequential algorithm is not possible. Parallel Comput. **3**(3), 259–260 (1986)
5. Gunther, N.J., Puglia, P., Tomasette, K.: Hadoop super-linear scalability: the perpetual motion of parallel performance. ACM Queue **13**(5), 46–55 (2015)
6. Ijspeert, A.J., Martinoli, A., Billard, A., Gambardella, L.M.: Collaboration through the exploitation of local interactions in autonomous collective robotics: the stick pulling experiment. Auton. Robots **11**, 149–171 (2001)
7. Lein, A., Vaughan, R.T.: Adaptive multi-robot bucket brigade foraging. Artif. Life **11**, 337 (2008)
8. Pini, G., Brutschy, A., Birattari, M., Dorigo, M.: Interference reduction through task partitioning in a robotic swarm. In: Sixth International Conference on Informatics in Control, Automation and Robotics-ICINCO, pp. 52–59 (2009)
9. Mondada, F., Bonani, M., Guignard, A., Magnenat, S., Studer, C., Floreano, D.: Superlinear physical performances in a SWARM-BOT. In: Capcarrère, M.S., Freitas, A.A., Bentley, P.J., Johnson, C.G., Timmis, J. (eds.) ECAL 2005. LNCS (LNAI), vol. 3630, pp. 282–291. Springer, Heidelberg (2005). https://doi.org/10.1007/11553090_29
10. Hamann, H.: Towards swarm calculus: universal properties of swarm performance and collective decisions. In: Dorigo, M., Birattari, M., Blum, C., Christensen, A.L., Engelbrecht, A.P., Groß, R., Stützle, T. (eds.) ANTS 2012. LNCS, vol. 7461, pp. 168–179. Springer, Heidelberg (2012). https://doi.org/10.1007/978-3-642-32650-9_15
11. Hamann, H.: Towards swarm calculus: urn models of collective decisions and universal properties of swarm performance. Swarm Intell. **7**(2–3), 145–172 (2013)
12. Schneider-Fontán, M., Mataric, M.J.: A study of territoriality: The role of critical mass in adaptive task division. In: Maes, P., Wilson, S.W., Mataric, M.J., (eds.) From animals to animats IV, pp. 553–561. MIT Press (1996)
13. Arkin, R.C., Balch, T., Nitz, E.: Communication of behavioral state in multi-agent retrieval tasks. In: Book, W., Luh, J. (eds.) IEEE Conference on Robotics and Automation, vol. 3, pp. 588–594. IEEE Press, Los Alamitos (1993)
14. Lerman, K., Galstyan, A.: Mathematical model of foraging in a group of robots: effect of interference. Auton. Robots **13**, 127–141 (2002)

15. Goldberg, D., Matarić, M.J.: Interference as a tool for designing and evaluating multi-robot controllers. In: Kuipers, B.J., Webber, B., (eds.) Proceedings of the Fourteenth National Conference on Artificial Intelligence (AAAI 1997), pp. 637–642. MIT Press, Cambridge (1997)
16. Østergaard, E.H., Sukhatme, G.S., Matarić, M.J.: Emergent bucket brigading: a simple mechanisms for improving performance in multi-robot constrained-space foraging tasks. In: André, E., Sen, S., Frasson, C., Müller, J.P., (eds.) Proceedings of the Fifth International Conference on Autonomous Agents (AGENTS 2001), pp. 29–35. ACM, New York (2001)
17. Beckers, R., Holland, O.E., Deneubourg, J.L.: From local actions to global tasks: stigmergy and collective robotics. Artificial Life IV, pp. 189–197 (1994)
18. Lerman, K., Martinoli, A., Galstyan, A.: A review of probabilistic macroscopic models for swarm robotic systems. In: Şahin, E., Spears, W.M. (eds.) SR 2004. LNCS, vol. 3342, pp. 143–152. Springer, Heidelberg (2005). https://doi.org/10.1007/978-3-540-30552-1_12
19. Khaluf, Y., Birattari, M., Rammig, F.: Probabilistic analysis of long-term swarm performance under spatial interferences. In: Dediu, A.-H., Martín-Vide, C., Truthe, B., Vega-Rodríguez, M.A. (eds.) TPNC 2013. LNCS, vol. 8273, pp. 121–132. Springer, Heidelberg (2013). https://doi.org/10.1007/978-3-642-45008-2_10
20. Brutschy, A., Pini, G., Pinciroli, C., Birattari, M., Dorigo, M.: Self-organized task allocation to sequentially interdependent tasks in swarm robotics. Auton. Agents Multi Agent Syst. **28**(1), 101–125 (2014)
21. Hamann, H., Schmickl, T., Wörn, H., Crailsheim, K.: Analysis of emergent symmetry breaking in collective decision making. Neural Comput. Appl. **21**(2), 207–218 (2012)
22. Nembrini, J., Winfield, A.F.T., Melhuish, C.: Minimalist coherent swarming of wireless networked autonomous mobile robots. In: Hallam, B., Floreano, D., Hallam, J., Hayes, G., Meyer, J.A., (eds.) Proceedings of the Seventh International Conference on Simulation of Adaptive Behavior on From Animals to Animats, pp. 373–382. MIT Press, Cambridge (2002)
23. Bjerknes, J.D., Winfield, A., Melhuish, C.: An analysis of emergent taxis in a wireless connected swarm of mobile robots. In: Shi, Y., Dorigo, M. (eds.) IEEE Swarm Intelligence Symposium, pp. 45–52. IEEE Press, Los Alamitos (2007)
24. Meister, T., Thenius, R., Kengyel, D., Schmickl, T.: Cooperation of two different swarms controlled by BEECLUST algorithm. In: Mathematical Models for the Living Systems and Life Sciences (ECAL), pp. 1124–1125 (2013)
25. Hamann, H.: Modeling and investigation of robot swarms. Master's thesis, University of Stuttgart, Germany (2006)
26. Jeanne, R.L., Nordheim, E.V.: Productivity in a social wasp: per capita output increases with swarm size. Behav. Ecol. **7**(1), 43–48 (1996)
27. Lighthill, M.J., Whitham, G.B.: On kinematic waves II. A theory of traffic flow on long crowded roads. Proc. Royal Soc. London **A229**(1178), 317–345 (1955)
28. Gunther, N.J.: A simple capacity model of massively parallel transaction systems. In: CMG National Conference, pp. 1035–1044 (1993)
29. Lazer, D., Friedman, A.: The network structure of exploration and exploitation. Adm. Sci. Q. **52**, 667–694 (2007)
30. Kauffman, S.A., Levin, S.: Towards a general theory of adaptive walks on rugged landscapes. J. Theor. Biol. **128**(1), 11–45 (1987)
31. Eiben, Á.E., Smith, J.E.: Introduction to Evolutionary Computing. Natural Computing Series. Springer, Heidelberg (2003). https://doi.org/10.1007/978-3-662-44874-8

Multicore Systems

Closed Loop Controller for Multicore Real-Time Systems

Johannes Freitag[(✉)] and Sascha Uhrig

Airbus, Munich, Germany
johannes.freitag@airbus.com

Abstract. In critical and hard real-time applications multicore processors are still not used very often. One of the reasons is the lack of timing predictability or the high Worst Case Execution Time (WCET) overestimation caused by the use of shared resources. Nevertheless, multicore processors can significantly increase system integration density also in critical and hard real-time applications.

We present a Closed Performance Control Loop that enables a standalone WCET estimation of a hard real-time application and execution on a multicore system concurrently to other applications. The advantage of our proposal is that it is transparent and non-intrusive to the critical application. Moreover, it is implemented as an external safety net and no additional software functionality on the multicore is required. The previously presented Fingerprinting approach to measure an application's performance is used as sensor element, extended by a Pulse Width Modulated core thwarting technique and two different control algorithms are combined to a Closed Control Loop.

Keywords: Embedded multicore systems · Critical systems
Safety net · Real-time systems

1 Introduction

Future avionic applications will require higher computation performance while at the same time a reduction in space, weight and power is needed. These needs are shown for example in the concept of the Airbus *Vahana*, *Pop-up*, or *CityAirbus* [1] aircrafts which will be ultra lightweight electrical helicopter-style vehicles providing novel autonomous urban transportation. In comparison to current aircrafts the avionic systems must be much smaller and lightweight while at the same time provide sufficient performance to compute not only the flight control data similar to current aircrafts but additionally compute the complex algorithms for autonomous flying, navigation, and collision avoidance. One solution for these demands is the consolidation of flight applications, currently running on multiple single core computers, on a small number of multicore processors. Furthermore, legacy applications shall be reused without major modifications.

© Springer International Publishing AG, part of Springer Nature 2018
M. Berekovic et al. (Eds.): ARCS 2018, LNCS 10793, pp. 45–56, 2018.
https://doi.org/10.1007/978-3-319-77610-1_4

Even though first ideas of the regulations on how to apply multicore systems to avionics are presented in the CAST-32 position paper and its follow-up CAST-32a [2], both authored from the Certification Authorities Software Team (CAST), concrete design details are still open. One of the major challenges in this context is the interference between applications since theoretically one application can compromise another one, at least in the timing domain. Accordingly, an essential requirement for certification is a clear and reliable isolation of safety-critical applications that needs to be demonstrated to the certification authorities.

The *Fingerprinting* technology presented in [3] allows non-intrusive tracking of an application's progress. Moreover, it allows continuous online quantification of an application's slowdown caused by interferences on shared resources compared to the stand-alone execution of the same application. Starting from this ability, we developed a closed loop controlling mechanism that keeps the current slowdown of an application inside given acceptable boundaries compared to stand-alone performance. This is done by thwarting the execution of other cores if necessary, in order to reduce interferences. Consequently, an estimated Worst Case Execution Time (WCET) of the stand-alone execution can hold for the multicore execution with the same acceptable bounds. The fingerprinting technology is targeting applications that are executed in a periodical way which is a typical feature of applications used in aircrafts.

The contributions of this paper are

- adjustable performance reduction techniques based on a Pulse Width Modulated (PWM) signal,
- a complete closed control loop system controlling an application's performance.

The remainder of this paper is organized as follows. Section 2 provides an overview of mature techniques and related work. The closed loop control techniques including a background on the Fingerprinting is described in Sect. 3 while the evaluation is presented in Sect. 4. The paper concludes with Sect. 5 including an outlook on future work.

2   Related Work

The use of multicore systems in avionic applications is still not wide spread. One reason is the difficulty to obtain suitable Worst Case Execution Time (WCET) estimates since application performance can theoretically drop significantly if multiple cores (i.e. applications) are sharing bus and memory [4]. Furthermore, it is not possible to identify all interference channels on COTS multicore processors [5]. Therefore, a WCET analysis on possible worst case scenarios leads to a high WCET overestimation (WCET to average execution time ratio) for current COTS MPSoCs. Hence, the performance gain of the multicore is neglected.

There exist several approaches to limit or even control the interferences between high and low critical tasks on multicore systems to relax the worst case scenario and, hence, improve WCET analysis results. Most of them focus on task or even thread granularity and are integrated into the scheduling of the system. The main idea of these approaches is counting e.g. bus accesses and limiting them by suspending the corresponding thread. Examples of such approaches are presented in [6–9]. An overview of these and other approaches is given in [10]. Even though these approaches are interesting for newly developed applications, they are not suitable for combing multiple legacy single core avionic applications on a multicore processor because the legacy applications or the underlying operating system would either have to be modified completely, which leads to a high effort in certification, or restrict the applications in a way that the performance gain of the multicore is neglected.

A previous approach for characterizing an application's execution is presented in [11]. It is used in high performance systems to predict an application's future behaviour and needs for adjusting architectural parameters for performance optimizations. It is not related to embedded real-time systems but successfully uses a similar, but intrusive, technology for tracking an application's performance.

The use of feedback controllers in the utilization of real-time systems is not novel. For example, a closed loop controller is used in [12] for dynamic resource allocation and power optimization of multicore processors. An example for closed loop control in a real-time scheduler is presented in [13,14] while a controller for thermal control of a multicore processor is introduced in [15]. However, all of these methods require intrusive measurements and no non-intrusive approach for controlling the interferences between cores by an external device has been presented in the past.

3   Closed Performance Control Loop

In the following the basic idea of the *Fingerprinting* approach is briefly described. This *Fingerprinting* is used as the sensor element of the closed control loop. Subsection 3.2 describes the *actuator* to influence the performance of the other cores and, hence, the interferences. The complete closed control loop is presented in Subsect. 3.3. Figure 1 shows the setup of multicore processor and safety net system with the integrated closed control loop. Note that our proposed closed performance control loop does not require any additional software functionality running on the multicore.

3.1   Basic Fingerprinting

During the execution of an application, a flow of instructions is executed. This flow is not homogeneous in terms of type of instructions, source of the instructions, and execution time of instructions. Accordingly, measuring for example the number of executed floating point instructions per time unit will lead to a characteristic curve of an application or a part of the application. If the application is executed several times with the same input parameters the measured curves are very similar (if sample rates greater than $1\,\mu s$ are applied). For tracking the progress of a known application, its measured curve can be compared to the recorded reference curve.

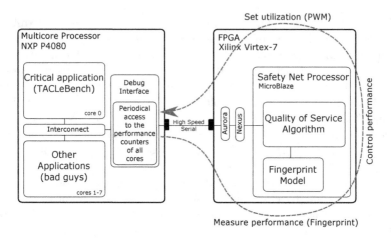

Fig. 1. Hardware setup with closed performance control loop implemented in the safety net system

In case an application executed on a multicore processor suffers from interferences with other applications on the shared memory hierarchy, its progress is slowed down. Slowing down the application will result in a stretched (in time) but shrunk (in the value range) curve. When comparing such a mutated measured curve with the original reference curve, the actual slowdown can not only be identified but also be quantified at any time during execution.

Many current MPSoC (e.g. based on ARM, PowerPC) include performance counters implemented in hardware which can be configured to increment every time a given event is raised. While the amount of events which can be configured is usually more than 100, the amount of counters that can be incremented simultaneously is small (around 4 to 6) [16]. An example of such curves is shown in Fig. 2.

The Fingerprint model is obtained by the execution of the main application several (thousand) times without other applications running in parallel. The performance counter values of the selected events are recorded with the frequency defined by the safety net system (100 μs period in the prototype FPGA case). Afterwards, the recorded characteristics are clustered in order to reduce the amount of curves that are combined into a model. With a *bisecting k-means* algorithm slight variations of the curves are filtered out. As the *bisecting k-means* algorithm does not need a predefined number of clusters, the resulting amount of clusters is depending on the similarity of the curves which is defined by the distance function[1]

$$d(\mathbf{x}, \mathbf{y}) = \sum_{i=1}^{n} [|x_i - y_i| > limit] \qquad (1)$$

---

[1] Please note the Iverson brackets: $[P] = \begin{cases} 1 & \text{if } P \text{ is true;} \\ 0 & \text{otherwise.} \end{cases}$

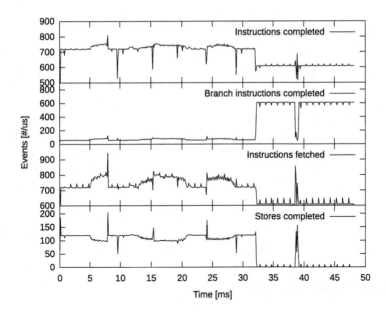

Fig. 2. Measured curves of four event counters when executing an avionic application

with **x** Runtime measurement vector, **y** Centroid vector and n length of the pattern. Finally, the medians of the resulting cluster centroids are combined into a tree model, the *Fingerprint*. The tree data structure is used because it can be accessed in a simple way to allow a fast access when the application is tracked. The root of the tree is the beginning of a new period of the application.

During the actual execution, the Fingerprint safety net system compares the performance counter values with the stored Fingerprint model and the actual execution path along the tree is tracked. In contrast to the generation of the Fingerprint model which can be created offline on a powerful compute node, timing is crucial for the tracking phase.

In case the slowdown of a critical application executed on one core exceeds a given limit (acceptable delay based on the single core WCET), other cores running less critical software are thwarted to reduce concurrency and, hence, increase performance of the critical application.

In summary, the fingerprint safety net approach [3] tracks the application's progress on the basis of characterized behavior of hardware event counters integrated inside the core of a multicore. Periodically reading and resetting such counters results in a curve that is characteristic for an executed application, more specifically, for the progress of that application. When comparing a recorded reference curve with the performance counter values measured online, the current progress with respect to the reference execution can be measured.

3.2   Pulse Width Modulated Interferences

The P4080 multicore system used in this paper provides means to halt and resume cores individually. Both actions can be triggered by messages on the back channel of the trace interface, i.e. by writing to control registers. This means that the *Safety Net* processor (see Fig. 1) is able to control the activity of the cores individually and externally. This way the cores that interfere with the memory accesses of the core under observation with the fingerprinting technique can be halted to not further increase the slowdown of the main application.

To provide a not only digital (on/off) way of setting the performance of the cores, we implemented a (software-based) Pulse Width Modulated (PWM) enabling/disabling of the individual cores, according to the signals from the closed loop controller. By halting and resuming a core, the application on this core can still make progress in contrast to suspending the application completely.

We have chosen a PWM period of 1 ms which is equal to 10 times the $100\,\mu s$ period used for tracking the application's progress. Hence, we can reduce the performance of cores competing with our main core in steps of 10% from 0 to 100% utilization. For example, a utilization of 60% means that the corresponding core is halted for 0.4 ms and runs for 0.6 ms per millisecond.

3.3 Closed Loop Controller

Two algorithms are used as control element, a simple threshold-based algorithm and a proportional controller. Both techniques affect all concurrent cores synchronously. The threshold-based algorithm disables the concurrent cores when the slowdown of the main application exceeds a given threshold and enables the cores again when the slowdown falls below the same threshold again. The second technique uses a proportional controller and the PWM-based activity control as described in the previous section.

4   Evaluation

We evaluated the effectiveness of the PWM-based activity setting on the main core's performance followed by the evaluation of the full closed control loop system. The selected performance counter values for the evaluation are *Instructions completed*, *Branch instructions completed*, *Stores completed* and *Bus interface unit accesses*. This selection results in very diverse curves which lead to a more robust model. Some paths may look similar in one curve but can be distinguished when taking different curves into account. Furthermore, the *Bus interface unit accesses* curve is an important measurement as it shows the operations that lead to cache misses. Therefore, this curve shows the possible interference hot spots.

4.1 PWM Effectiveness

The main application benchmarks in two different scenarios is used for the evaluation of the effectiveness of the PWM-based activity setting, i.e. the interference control. On the main core, the *TACLeBench benchmark* is executed in every case. The two benchmarks for the competing application cores are

- Read benchmark: This artificial benchmark generates high read traffic on the shared interconnect and the memory by performing read accesses to memory and does not profit from local data caches,
- TACLeBench [17]: A benchmark suite which is application oriented and generates realistic traffic on the shared interconnect and memory and profits from local data caches. Example algorithms used are *JPEG image transcoding routines, GSM provisional standard decoder, H.264 block decoding functions, Huffman encoding/decoding* and *Rijndael AES encoding/decoding*.

The two benchmarks are executed in the two scenarios with and without local caches enabled (L1 instruction and data caches). These scenarios show that the technique also works for very high interference configurations. Furthermore, disabling the caches is relevant for creating the single core WCET as mentioned in Subsect. 3.1. In both scenarios, no external memory is accessed and the internal L3 platform cache is configured as shared SRAM to reduce memory access delay and focus on interferences in the interconnect. The activity of the competing cores has been set by the PWM signal in parallel for all cores from 0% to 100% in steps of 10%. The execution time of the main application is measured. Figure 3 shows the results of the scenario without local caches. It can be observed that for the *Read* benchmark thwarting the competing cores by 10% still reduces execution time of the main application by nearly 30%. The decrease stays very intensive until the competing cores reach an activity rate of 60%. Below 60% the execution time of the main application decreases nearly linearly. The TACLe benchmark performs nearly 15% better in case competition is reduced from 100% to 90%. Below this value, the execution time decreases more or less linear until the competition is zero.

We ran the same set of benchmarks with active L1 data and L1 instruction caches for all cores. Here, the overall slowdown is not as dramatical as without caches. Even when running the *Read* benchmark as opponent the main core performs significantly better with a factor of 1.5 on execution time compared to nearly 4.5 as maximum slowdown without caches. This effect is not based on data accesses since the benchmark is constructed to generate the maximum cache miss rate on the data path but the L1 instruction cache is also enabled (disabled in previous scenario) now, which relaxes the pressure on the interconnect and memory significantly. The TACLeBench shows a maximum increase in execution time of only 10%, compared to a factor of 2.15 in the previous scenario. If the performance of the competing TACLeBench cores is reduced, the main core improves nearly linearly while execution time with *Read* opponents is reduced intensively for duty cycles over 80%. Below 80% the performance improvement is also linear.

Our evaluation of the PWM-based thwarting of competing cores show a suitable performance improvement of a memory intensive main application if the reduction is only 10–20%, depending on the use of instruction caches (data caches have no effect on this benchmark) (Fig. 4). In case of an application that is using shared resources to a realistic extend, PWM-based thwarting leads to nearly a linear improvement. The choice of the *Read* and *TACLeBench* shows that the

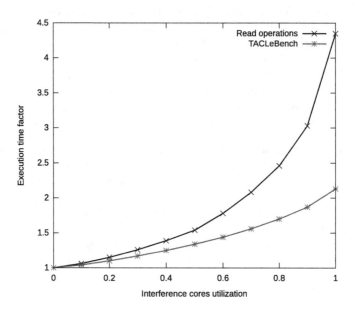

Fig. 3. Execution time of the TACLe benchmark without any local caches and different activity of competing cores

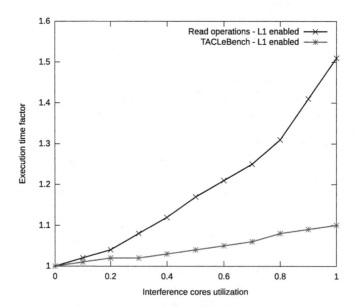

Fig. 4. Execution time of the TACLe benchmark with enabled local instruction and data L1 caches and different activity of competing cores

slowdown with realistic applications running in parallel on other cores are small and may also be within the acceptable delay (e.g. 10%) when the L1 caches are enabled. However, in case one of these applications turns into a *bad guy* (e.g. by a fault) similar to the *Read* benchmark, PWM-based thwarting can protect the correct timing of the main application.

4.2   Closed Loop Controller

We evaluated the closed control loop using TACLeBench as main application and *Read* as *bad guys* running on seven cores in parallel. We set a maximum slowdown of 4% as target performance of the main application compared to stand-alone execution.

Figure 5 shows the performance of the TACLeBench over time (upper part) and the development of the slowdown over time (lower part) without any interference control and with simple threshold-based control. The upper part presents the number of executed instruction per μs. It can be seen that the uncontrolled execution takes about 10% longer for execution at the end. The diagram in the lower part represents the slowdown of the main application as tracked by the *Fingerprinting*. Since tracking of progress is based on discrete steps, the performance reductions are manifested in sharp steps. The following phases of smooth performance increases are caused by relative distribution of a slowdown over a longer time, i.e. a one-time delay at the start of the application of 5% is reduced over the total execution time to a much lower slowdown. The dotted line represents the threshold (4%) i.e. the maximum target slowdown of the main application.

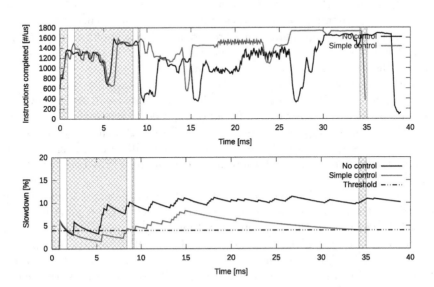

Fig. 5. TACLe performance over time without control and with applied simple threshold controller

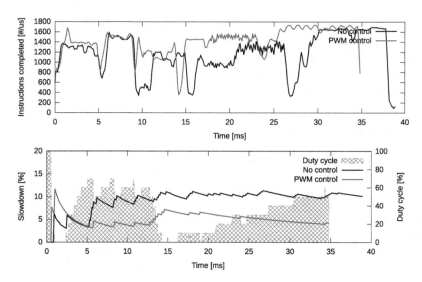

Fig. 6. TACLe performance over time without control and with applied PWM controller

As can be seen in the figure, TACLeBench experienced a slowdown of about 10% over the complete execution time if no control mechanism is applied. With our simple control, the target of 4% maximum slowdown is reached at the end. The grey shaded boxes identify the times when the other seven cores are active. No grey shading means that the other cores are disabled by the control mechanism. At first glance, the competing cores are most of the time disabled meaning that applications running on these cores will not get much execution time. But, note that the competing applications are seven *bad guy* applications flooding the shared resources with maximum traffic. However, even in this simple control case, the other cores each get 23.4% processing time.

In Fig. 6 we show the behaviour of the PWM controller. The duty cycles of the competing cores are set according to the actual slowdown. A slowdown of less than 2% allows full performance for all cores, a slowdown above 7% leads to completely disabled competing cores. Between 7% and 2%, the duty cycles are adjusted in 10% steps from 0% to 100% (one step per half percent of slowdown). The grey shaded areas represent the duty cycles of the PWM core activation signal.

As can be observed that the 4% target slowdown of the main application is also reached at completion. Moreover, the active phases of the competing cores are much longer in time but less intensive. Since we are using a PWM signal, this means that the cores are active for many but smaller periods. The period of a PWM signal is 1 ms (10 times the sampling period of the *Fingerprinting*). With this PWM control, the seven *bad guys* get 34% of the cores' performance while the main application still meets the performance requirements.

5   Conclusion

In this paper a closed control loop for interferences on a multicore processor is presented. It enables a stand-alone WCET estimation of a hard real-time application and execution on a multicore system concurrently to other applications by defining an acceptable slowdown. The presented approach is transparent and none-intrusive to the critical application as it is implemented as an external safety net using the debug/tracing interface for extraction of performance counter values. Furthermore, no additional software functionality on the multicore is required. The fingerprinting approach is used to measure an application's progress. In the closed control loop it is used as sensor element while a simple core on/off switch or, alternatively, a pulse width modulated core thwarting technique represents the actuator.

Our evaluations show that both control techniques perform well and can guarantee the given maximum slowdown factor. We used a *Read* benchmark application flooding the shared resources with maximum traffic and the TACLeBench benchmark suite as competing applications. With the simple control mechanism, a digital enable/disable of competing cores, the competing cores can still get 23.4% performance. When applying a PWM-based controller, the same competing applications will get 34.0% performance.

In the future we will add another performance setting actuator that modifies the frequency of competing cores such that they can stay active all the time but with reduced clock frequency. Moreover, evaluations with other realistic traffic applications and different cache settings can be interesting. Moreover, we plan providing a formal analysis and, hence, a prove of our approach.

References

1. Airbus: future of urban mobility. http://www.airbus.com/newsroom/news/en/2016/12/My-Kind-Of-Flyover.html
2. Certification Authorities Software Team (CAST): position paper CAST-32A: multi-core processors, November 2016
3. Freitag, J., Uhrig, S.: Dynamic interference quantification for multicore processors. In: Proceedings of the 36th IEEE/AIAA Digital Avionics Systems Conference (DASC), pp. 1–6, September 2017
4. Nowotsch, J., Paulitsch, M.: Leveraging multi-core computing architectures in avionics. In: 2012 Ninth European Dependable Computing Conference, pp. 132–143, May 2012
5. Agirre, I., Abella, J., Azkarate-Askasua, M., Cazorla, F.J.: On the tailoring of CAST-32A certification guidance to real COTS multicore architectures. In: Proceedings of 12th IEEE International Symposium on Industrial Embedded Systems (2017)
6. Kritikakou, A., Rochange, C., Faugère, M., Pagetti, C., Roy, M., Girbal, S., Gracia Pérez, D.: Distributed run-time WCET controller for concurrent critical tasks in mixed-critical systems. In: Proceedings of the 22nd International Conference on Real-Time Networks and Systems, RTNS 2014, New York, NY, USA, pp. 139:139–139:148. ACM (2014)

7. Nowotsch, J., Paulitsch, M., Buhler, D., Theiling, H., Wegener, S., Schmidt, M.: Multi-core interference-sensitive WCET analysis leveraging runtime resource capacity enforcement. In: ECRTS, pp. 109–118. IEEE Computer Society (2014)
8. Bak, S., Yao, G., Pellizzoni, R., Caccamo, M.: Memory-aware scheduling of multicore task sets for real-time systems. In: 2012 IEEE International Conference on Embedded and Real-Time Computing Systems and Applications, pp. 300–309, August 2012
9. Agrawal, A., Fohler, G., Freitag, J., Nowotsch, J., Uhrig, S., Paulitsch, M.: Contention-aware dynamic memory bandwidth isolation with predictability in cots multicores: an avionics case study. In: 29th Euromicro Conference on Real-Time Systems (ECRTS), June 2017 (to appear)
10. Girbal, S., Jean, X., Rhun, J.L., Gracia Pérez, D., Gatti, M.: Deterministic platform software for hard real-time systems using multi-core COTS. In: 2015 IEEE/AIAA 34th Digital Avionics Systems Conference (DASC), pp. 8D4-1–8D4-15, September 2015
11. Duesterwald, E., Dwarkadas, S.: Characterizing and predicting program behavior and its variability. In: International Conference on Parallel Architectures and Compilation Techniques (PACT), pp. 220–231 (2003)
12. Maggio, M., Hoffmann, H., Santambrogio, M.D., Agarwal, A., Leva, A.: Power optimization in embedded systems via feedback control of resource allocation. IEEE Trans. Control Syst. Technol. $21(1)$, 239–246 (2013)
13. Sahoo, D.R., Swaminathan, S., Al-Omari, R., Salapaka, M.V., Manimaran, G., Somani, A.K.: Feedback control for real-time scheduling. In: Proceedings of the 2002 American Control Conference (IEEE Cat. No. CH37301), vol. 2, pp. 1254–1259, May 2002
14. Cucinotta, T., Checconi, F., Abeni, L., Palopoli, L.: Self-tuning schedulers for legacy real-time applications. In: Proceedings of the 5th European Conference on Computer Systems, EuroSys 2010, New York, NY, USA, pp. 55–68. ACM (2010)
15. Fu, Y., Kottenstette, N., Lu, C., Koutsoukos, X.D.: Feedback thermal control of real-time systems on multicore processors. In: Proceedings of the Tenth ACM International Conference on Embedded Software, EMSOFT 2012, New York, NY, USA, pp. 113–122. ACM (2012)
16. NXP Semiconductors: e500mc Core Reference Manual (2013). Rev. 3
17. Falk, H., Altmeyer, S., Hellinckx, P., Lisper, B., Puffitsch, W., Rochange, C., Schoeberl, M., Sørensen, R.B., Wägemann, P., Wegener, S.: TACLeBench: a benchmark collection to support worst-case execution time research. In: Schoeberl, M. (ed.) 16th International Workshop on Worst-Case Execution Time Analysis (WCET 2016). OpenAccess Series in Informatics (OASIcs), Dagstuhl, Germany, vol. 55, pp. 2:1–2:10. Schloss Dagstuhl-Leibniz-Zentrum für Informatik (2016)

Optimization of the GNU OpenMP Synchronization Barrier in MPSoC

Maxime France-Pillois[1,2](✉), Jérôme Martin[1,2], and Frédéric Rousseau[3]

[1] Univ. Grenoble Alpes, 38000 Grenoble, France
{maxime.france-pillois,jerome.martin}@cea.fr
[2] CEA, LETI, MINATEC Campus, 38054 Grenoble, France
[3] TIMA, CNRS Grenoble INP, Institute of Engineering,
Univ. Grenoble Alpes, 38000 Grenoble, France
frederic.rousseau@univ-grenoble-alpes.fr

Abstract. Synchronization mechanisms have been central issues in the race toward the computing units parallelization. Indeed when the number of cores increases, the applications are split into more and more software tasks, leading to the higher use of synchronization primitives to preserve the initial application services. In this context, providing efficient synchronization mechanisms turns to be essential to leverage parallelism offered by Multi-Processor Systems-on-Chip.

By using an instrumented emulation platform allowing us to extract accurate timing information, in a non-intrusive way, we led a fine analysis of the synchronization barriers of the GNU OpenMP library. This study reveals that a time expensive function was uselessly called during the barrier awakening process. We propose here a software optimization of this library that saves up to 80% of the release phase duration for a 16-core MSoCs. Moreover, being localized into the middle-ware OpenMP library, benefiting this optimization requires no specific care from the application programmer's point of view, but a library update and can be used on every kinds of platform.

Keywords: GNU OpenMP library · Emulation platform
Synchronization barrier optimization
Generic middle-ware optimization

1 Introduction

For almost 20 years, high performance computing systems are made of several computing elements (typ. processors) implemented on the same die, called multi-processors system-on-chip (MPSoC). MPSoCs incorporate more and more computing units and presently reach several hundreds of cores. In this case, they are refereed to as manycores. Examples of this kind of chip are the Tile-Gx72 of Tilera that embeds 72 cores [4], or the MPPA of Karlay integrating 256 cores [2].

To benefit from these highly parallel manycore architectures, the software has to be parallelized. Parallelizing an initially sequential software code consists

© Springer International Publishing AG, part of Springer Nature 2018
M. Berekovic et al. (Eds.): ARCS 2018, LNCS 10793, pp. 57–69, 2018.
https://doi.org/10.1007/978-3-319-77610-1_5

in dividing the program into several sub-tasks. These sub-tasks have to exchange data to achieve the required service. To ensure data integrity, the inter-task communication requires synchronization operations such as synchronization barrier.

To ease the parallelization process, some "user-friendly" libraries came-up, like the OpenMP standard, allowing programmers to parallelize programs just by adding specific preprocessor directives. Interpreting these primitives, the compiler can then produce a parallelized program split into several sub-tasks synchronized with each other. Synchronization mechanisms are managed by the library. Users don't have to worry about them.

The first step to optimize fine grain software mechanisms is to get representative runtime behaviors. Indeed to solve slowdowns implies to get accurate measurements of the time spent in the different phases of these mechanisms. Thanks to an ad-hoc designed non-intrusive measurement tool chain, we are able to analyze the GNU implementation of OpenMP standard on a fully coherent shared memory MPSoC platform. This accurate study reveals a sub-optimal library code, starting point to an improvement proposal.

The rest of this paper is organized as followed. Section 2 exposes main categories of solutions proposed to reduce synchronization mechanisms slowdowns. In Sect. 3, we describe the OpenMP library and its synchronization barrier mechanism. Then, Sect. 4 presents the experimentation environment and the methodology set-up to study the synchronization slowdown issues. Section 5 details the GNU OpenMP synchronization barrier study and the cross-platform optimization.

2   Related Work

The aim of our study is to improve synchronization mechanisms on MPSoC and specifically the synchronization barrier. This subject has been largely studied and many solutions, based either on software or hardware optimizations, have been proposed. In this section we first present an overview of existing solutions and then expose research directions that are still worth exploring.

Software-based solutions usually aim at speeding-up barriers by improving barrier algorithms. In [8], Hoefler et al. present the principal algorithms designed to implement synchronization barrier optimizing either the fastness or reducing the potential contention issues resulting from simultaneous accesses to the same resource (memory).

Nevertheless, some studies such as [6,12,14], highlight the fact that overheads resulting from software processing are very expensive. Hence hardware proposals have been formulated. Two trends can be identified:

(1) The addition of communication *media* dedicated to synchronization mechanisms like the "G-barrier" of Abellán et al. [6], which consists in implementing a barrier with fast propagation link (g-line) and dedicated barrier controllers. This proposal exposes very good results, however, the "G-barrier", like other solutions in the same trend [9,11], does not scale very well since the addition of a processor requires extra barrier-dedicated

hardware (link and controllers). Another drawback of the "g-barrier" is that the processors taking part in the barrier have to be known before the beginning of the barrier. Moreover only a thread by processor can take part in the barrier. All these restrictions make this proposal hard to use in real operational systems.

(2) The second trend is the addition of a dedicated buffer to manage synchronizations like the "synchronization buffer" of Monchiero *et al.* [10]. The strength of this proposal is to unload the software from the synchronization management, allowing it to perform other tasks during this time.

Proposed optimizations are numerous. All of them target the synchronization primitive itself, trying to offer a new optimized mechanism. The main flaw of these approaches is the poor studying of the mechanisms within their realistic ecosystem environments before proposing a solution. Hence the majority of these solutions have never been implemented in real operational systems. Our approach differs on this point because we have chosen to carefully study an already wide spread solution, in our case the OpenMP library, and then to improve it. We do not directly target the low-level hardware mechanism nor the high-level software algorithm but the middleware layer between the two. Thanks to our methodology we are able to target real issues and to offer solutions usable seamlessly by programmers.

3   The GNU OpenMP Synchronization Barrier Mechanism

OpenMP is a library designed to help users to develop parallel software by adding an abstraction layer over the classic parallel services (threads management, synchronization mechanisms, ...). In this section, we present the key principles of this library.

3.1   Code Parallelization and Synchronization

The Listing 1.1 exposes an example of a simple "high abstraction level" code.

Listing 1.1. Original high level C code with openMP directives

```
1   #include <omp.h>
2   #define TAB_SIZE 1000

3   int main (void){
4       unsigned int n=0;
5       unsigned int sinTable[TAB_SIZE];
6       omp_set_num_threads(16);

7       #pragma omp parallel for shared (sinTable)
8       for(n=0; n<TAB_SIZE; n++)
9           sinTable[n] = n*2;

10      print_table(sinTable);
11      return 1;}
```

The aim of this program is to compute the elements of an array (line 9) then to display them (line 10). The array computation is parallelized into sixteen threads thanks to the OpenMP directives lines 6 and 7. During the compilation phase OpenMP directives are interpreted by the compiler, and the code is expanded with threads creation and management services. In our example, the *for* loop will be replaced by the creation of sixteen threads. Each thread processing one sixteenth of the array. The OpenMP library inserts also a synchronization barrier after the parallel loop (between lines 9 and 10) in order to wait for the completion of all thread computations before going forward to the display of the array (line 10). The display of the array is processed by only one thread (the main thread) since the parallel section ends with the end of the *for* loop.

At first sight, in this example, we note the heavy impact of synchronization mechanisms on parallelized code since the OpenMP library inserts a synchronization barrier at the end of each parallel section.

Delays introduced by synchronization mechanisms are of two kinds. (1) Application dependent delays which are most of the time due to bad load balancing. In our barrier example, all the tasks have to wait for the slowest to complete its computation, which can lead to inefficient use of computing power and reduced application performance. (2) Synchronization mechanisms intrinsic delays: delays resulting from the establishment of the synchronization itself.

When we speak about synchronization optimization, we aim to reduce the second type of delays since the first one, which is more a global application optimization issue, is out of our scope of action.

3.2   Active Wait and GNU OpenMP Policy

To synchronize threads means that a thread could wait until others become in states allowing the establishment of the synchronization. This waiting phase can be fulfilled in two different ways: (1) active wait, and (2) passive wait.

The active wait consists in doing polling (periodic reads) on a waiting flag until this one reaches an expected value. This kind of waiting is very efficient in term of execution resuming speed since as soon as the flag state changes, the thread can resume its nominal execution flow. However periodic reads may lead to a waste of computing time and power consumption for long waiting periods.

The passive wait involves putting the waiting thread to sleep. When a thread changes the state of the waiting flag from the waiting state to the release state, this thread is also in charge of awakening at least one sleeping thread.

The default GNU OpenMP library waiting policy is the following: active wait is performed by a waiting thread until a predefined amount of time is elapsed. When this amount of time is elapsed, wait policy switches to passive wait and the thread goes to sleep till the barrier completion. Waiting modes can also be forced using explicit directives.

The active wait is used when highly reactive applications are expected, reducing as much as possible the synchronization delays. In this study we decided to focus on these applications, for which reducing the total computation time is the main challenge.

4   Experimentation Environment

This section first presents the architecture of the MPSoC used to perform the initial study. Then we give a description of the evaluation platform set up. And finally we describe our non-intrusive measurement tool chain.

4.1   TSAR Manycore Architecture

The evaluation was carried out on the TSAR full coherent shared memory many-core platform [5]. TSAR is a clustered manycore architecture based on NoC which makes it well representative of modern MPSoCs. As represented in the Fig. 1, each cluster is mainly made of four MIPS32 processors with a private L1 cache, and a L2 cache which is also a shared memory segment. Each L2 memory is designed to cache a section of the global memory and the L2 cache of a cluster can be accessed by cores inside and outside the cluster.

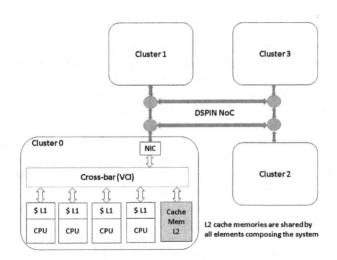

Fig. 1. 4-cluster (16 cores) TSAR MPSoC architecture

4.2   Evaluation Platform

Regarding the hardware side, our evaluation platform is based on a *Veloce2 Quattro* emulator. Emulation platform allows us to fast emulate a full Register Transfer Level (RTL) system, with a cycle accurate precision. Indeed, to lead timing measurement campaigns on operating system primitives (e.g. synchronization mechanisms), we have to get information from software execution (operating system boot + application run) during a very large number of clock cycles. With the "classical" simulation limitations, accurate simulation of these mechanisms is extensively long. For example, the boot of a Linux kernel on top of cycle accurate SystemCass [7] simulation system could take several days for a 16-core TSAR platform. Hence it is hard to imagine a full measurement campaign with a so long kernel boot duration. Commonly, people choose to deteriorate the accuracy of the simulated model to improve the running time. On our side, we use hardware support to speed-up simulation time without losing accuracy.

As for the software aspect, we use a port of Linux kernel 4.6 and the μClibc to boot the TSAR platform in our measurement campaign.

The GCC version used to compile applications for this platform is the 4.8.2. Note that the GNU OpenMP library is part of GCC. Hence the GNU OpenMP library version is directly related to the GCC release version. The GCC version used is quite old, but the synchronization barrier management of the GNU OpenMP library has not changed in more recent GCC releases. Slowdown issues are the same in the release 4.8.2 that in the latest 7.2 GCC release.

To avoid interferences of the scheduling policy on our measurements, we bound each thread to a different core, by setting the suitable OpenMP directive.

4.3   A Non Intrusive Measurement Tool Chain

Obtaining accurate timing information is the central point to analyze slowdowns in software program. To reach this goal, we set up a non-intrusive measurement tool chain. Unlike the traditional software timing instrumentation, our method allows to measure delays without interacting with the software program or distorting its execution flow. Hence software behavior is still the same than in regular operating mode, and actual issues can be identified.

The co-emulation feature of the emulation platform allows communication between the emulator and a workstation. Based on co-emulation, we implemented a spy module in the platform to extract at runtime, by this side channel, useful signals like processors program counters and registers. The extracted signals are dumped into files. The content of these files is then processed by different tools that analyze signal values and provide relevant information of time spent in the studied mechanisms. Leveraging accurate non distorted timing measurements, this tool chain allows to expose synchronization mechanisms slowdowns in real working conditions.

5   Active Wait Optimization for GNU OpenMP Synchronization Barrier

This section describes the study and the optimization proposed for the GNU OpenMP library. We chose to study the GNU implementation of the OpenMP standard because of its large adoption in real operational systems.

5.1   Barrier Mechanism Measurements and Study

The GNU OpenMP library implements a central-counter algorithm for the synchronization barrier. The Fig. 2 shows a time chart of this algorithm. Each thread

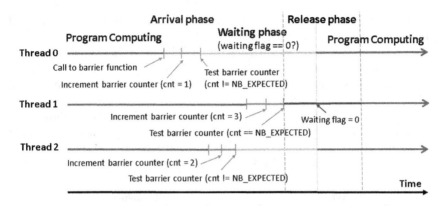

Fig. 2. Synchronization barrier time chart for 3 threads.

is initially in a computing phase corresponding to the nominal program execution. Then each thread calls the barrier function and enters its "arrival phase". It increments the barrier counter. If the barrier counter has not reached the expected value, the thread waits until its release. It is the case of the threads 0 and 2 in the figure. Once the counter reaches the expected number (thread 1), the thread causing this event has to release all waiting threads, refereed to as the "release phase". In theory, the "arrival phase" and the "release phase" can both be sources of slowdowns: (1) resulting from contention issues caused by concurrent access to the shared central counter variable during the "arrival phase", (2) due to the threads release policy for the "release phase".

Actually, as observed by Wei *et al.* [13] threads do not reach the barrier simultaneously resulting from diverse sources: cache misses, I/O management, ... Thus contention risk during the "arrival phase" is very low. Moreover, since the thread will then switch to a waiting phase, most of the arrival phase delays are masked by the waiting phase and do not increase the whole program duration.

"Release Phase" Timing Observations. Regarding the "release phase", the delays measured for our 16-core platform are presented in the Fig. 3a. In order to get relevant reproductive behaviors by limiting operating system artifacts, we loop 400 times over the *for* loop of the Listing 1.1.

This figure shows the release phase delays by thread. The Y-axis represents the number of cycles between the moment the last thread became aware that it is the last one and has to start the release process, and the instant a thread leaves the barrier to resume its nominal execution flow. The X-axis represents the threads in order of release. For example, the first column represents the first thread that resumes its execution whatever its thread ID is. The figure shows box plots in which the red line is the median. The blue box contains 50% of the values. The minimum value is represented by a dot, and the maximum value by an 'X'. We can see on the figure that box plots are well grouped around the median, however the maximum values could be far above the core group of the values.

This is due to contention issues and interrupt management subroutines triggered by the operating system independently from our application, which delay the nominal execution flow of threads. Hence values delayed by these artifacts should not be taken into account in our analysis since these values are not the result of the synchronization mechanism itself. Thus we focus our study on the median value and the box plot for each thread.

We note on this figure that complete process until all threads resume their execution lasts 13194 cycles, and that one thread is especially delayed compared to the others. Hence we decide to analyze more accurately the sources of this large amount of time with our non-intrusive measurement tool chain.

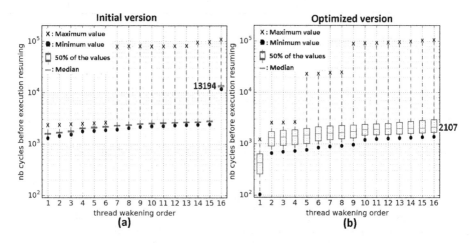

Fig. 3. Delays between barrier completion awareness and thread releases for 16 threads bound on 16 cores for 400 barrier calls without (a) and with optimization (b)

Library Study. Analyzing more precisely the execution flow inside the "release phase" using a time annotated function call stack generated by our tool chain, we remark that GNU OpenMP library calls every time the "threads wake-up function" during the release phase: whatever threads are actually sleeping or not. As a matter of fact, the dual active/passive wait policy implies that some threads can do active wait and others can be sleeping, according to the thread waiting time. In this case, threads performing active wait should be released by switching the state of the waiting flag, whereas sleeping threads should be awaken by calling the wake-up function. However, if the software is well balanced, which is the case most of the time with the OpenMP workload split policy, threads do not sleep but just perform active wait due to short waiting durations. The program shown in Listing 1.1 simulates this case of relatively well balanced threads.

We found that the time spent in the wake-up function is about 12891 cycles whereas no thread has to be awakened, that is to say about 97.7% of the whole release process for 16 threads. This observation leads us to consider a workaround to speed-up the release phase in the case of fully active wait policy.

5.2   Optimization Proposal

GNU OpenMP library wait policy implies that on the same barrier some threads can do active wait whereas others can sleep. When no thread is sleeping, the expensive call to the wake-up function ("futex_wake") is not required. Hence, we propose to keep an information of the waiting mode of the threads participating to the barrier. If no thread is sleeping, we skip the call to the wake-up function. Else, we perform the call if at least one sleeping thread has to be awaken.

The idea is to tag the barrier as "barrier to be awaken" as soon as one thread of the barrier calls the function to go to sleep. To achieve this purpose, we keep a list of "barriers to be awaken". We chose to implement a global list and not a scalar in the barrier structure to ease the implementation by reducing as much as possible the impact on the existing code.

When the last thread of a barrier starts the awakening process, it reads this list. If the identifier (address) of the current barrier is in the list, the thread removes the identifier from it and calls the wake-up function. Else, if the current barrier identifier is not in the list, the call to the wake-up function is skipped.

The list implemented is a single linked list without peculiar requirements. Indeed, since the number of simultaneous barriers in OpenMP programs is reduced, the search process in the list is relatively fast. Based on this assumption and on the use cases of the list (only a thread performing the release process), concurrent access to the list is supposed very sporadic. Hence we decide to simply protect the list by a global lock. After its registration in the list, but before going into sleep mode, a thread checks again the wait flag, thanks to the linux sleeping futex function, in order to prevent potential race between threads.

This optimization is only 50 lines of codes long affecting 2 files of the library.

The use of this optimization requires only a library update to speed-up program execution, while the application code does not change at all.

5.3   Micro-benchmark Results

We evaluated our proposal by running a micro-benchmark executing successively the implicit barrier primitive of the GNU OpenMP library (400x Listing 1.1).

Large Gain on the 16-Core Reference Platform. On our TSAR 16-core reference platform, our optimization brings large time saving. The Fig. 3b shows the delays of the "release phase" by thread with our optimization for 16 threads bound on 16 cores.

We remark that the first thread to resume its execution (first column) is faster than the first thread of the non optimized version (Fig. 3a). Indeed, the first thread is now the one in charge of the release process. Spared from calling the wake-up function, this thread is able to perform the release of all threads (toggle the waiting flag of the active wait) and to return to its nominal execution very quickly.

As represented in the Fig. 3, the optimized barrier is completed for 16 threads in approximatively 2107 cycles (median value) against the previous 13194 cycles.

Hence, our optimization provides a significant gain of 81% of the time required to perform the "release phase" on our 16-core platform.

Since other OpenMP libraries (LLVM, Intel, ...) are not available on our platform, we can not compare them to our optimization. However, once our solution evaluation performed, we watched the LLVM open-source library which seems to implement an analog strategy calling wake function only when it is required.

Platform Size Generalization. Concerned by extending our optimization for various MPSoC sizes, we measure the gain obtained for a TSAR platform made of 8, 16 and 24 cores (Table 1).

In the Table 1, we remark the decrease of the gain with the increase of the number of threads. Indeed, discarding the potential contention issues on the wake-up function, the time spent in this one is constant (when no thread has to be awaken). On the other side time required by threads to resume their execution depends on the number of threads. Thus, when the number of threads is growing the gain reached by our optimization becomes smaller. However, even for 24 threads we get a very good gain of approximatively 43%. Thus these results show that our optimization is attractive for different sizes of MPSoCs with significant time saving.

Table 1. GNU OpenMP library barrier release phase gain

Platform	Threads number	Full release phase delay without optimization	Full release phase delay with optimization	Gain
TSAR	8 on 8 cores	11662 cycles (median)	1481 cycles (median)	87%
	16 on 16 cores	13194 cycles (median)	2522 cycles (median)	81%
	24 on 24 cores	14039 cycles (median)	7975 cycles (median)	43%
Alpha	8 on 8 cores	608 cycles (median)	50 cycles (median)	91%
	16 on 16 cores			
	24 on 24 cores			

Applicability on Other Platforms. In order to validate this optimization with other platforms, we set-up a similar test case on Gem5 simulator [1]. In line with the current MPSoC architecture, the simulated system is made of clusters of 4 *Alpha* cores sharing L2 caches. Each core owns its private L1 cache. However, this system differs from the TSAR system in two major points: (1) Clusters are linked to each other by a crossbar interconnect and not anymore by a NoC. Hence there is no time gap to access different distant L2 caches. (2) The L2 cache policy is a round robin like policy. In TSAR platform each L2 cache is associated to a memory section whereas is this Gem5 platform cache line are spread over L2 caches according to a circular policy. Regarding the software environment, the linux kernel run is the 2.6.27. The micro-benchmark

(Listing 1.1) was compiled with a GCC 4.7.3. The implementation of the barrier mechanism is the same in this GCC version and the version 4.8.2 used with the TSAR platform.

We used the previous methodology on this platform, running 400 loops of the Listing 1.1 and measuring by a side channel the "release phase" duration for platforms made of 8, 16 and 24 cores (Table 1). Considering components as perfect (caches, interconnects, ...), the simulation platform discards memory access delays and contention issues coming up when increasing the number of threads. This is why the measured time are the same for the three platform sizes. Thereby we can notice the large gain provided by our optimization, around 91%. It confirms the attractiveness of our optimization for different kinds of MPSoC.

Moreover, we can theoretically enlarge these experimentations to affirm that our optimization is working for all kinds of platforms. Indeed, our optimization aims at removing unnecessary function calls at the middle-ware level. The alternative strategy proposed is fully independent of platform since this function is still non-useful whatever the platform is. Hence by skipping it, we can guarantee a time saving. However, the amount of time saved depends of the host system.

Table 2. GNU OpenMP library optimization results for 40 runs (20 with optimization, 20 without) of the IS (class S) NAS Benchmark reference application for 16 threads

	Total release time	Total execution time
IS with optimization	93393049 cycles	1069602910 cycles
IS without optimization	162493024 cycles	1228012444 cycles
Gain with optimization	42.5%	12.9%

5.4 Performances Evaluation on the NAS Benchmark IS Application

The second phase of our evaluation consists in measuring the impact of our optimization on a full application. We choose the Integer Sort application of NAS benchmark [3] as reference. We measure the total time spent in the barrier release phases and the total application duration on the 16-core TSAR emulated platform. In order to get results as representative as possible by averaging operating system artifacts, we ran 20 times the IS application class 'S' (Small) with and without optimization. The results are shown in Table 2. We can note that the gain on the total time spent in the release phase for the reference application is 42.5%. This gain is smaller than the one measured on the micro-benchmark due to operating system interferences which parasite the results despite the 20 runs.

We note a gain of 12.9% concerning the total execution time of the benchmark application. This gain can be explained by the time saved in the barrier mechanism itself, but also by the removal of memory accesses (resulting from the optimization) which reduces memory contention issues.

6   Conclusion

Proposing a new approach to deal with synchronization slowdowns, we demonstrate that software middle-ware level is interesting to improve system performances and provide optimization easily set up in various industrial systems.

Based on an accurate study of the GNU OpenMP barrier synchronization we detected, thanks to our custom tool chain, a sub-optimal code section in this wide-spread library. Fine analysis of this mechanism allows us to propose a workaround to the library weakness leading to a large gain, with a reduction of 81% of the "release phase" for 16 threads/cores on our TSAR platform.

Running it on several MPSoCs, and thanks to a theoretical analysis, we disclose the expandability of this optimization on different platforms. Hence, our approach allows us to provide significant gains with no change of the OpenMP programmers habits since no special care is required to benefit from our patch.

We plan in future works to leverage the designed tool chain to improve other mechanisms of the OpenMP library or other middle-ware software libraries.

References

1. gem5. http://gem5.org
2. Kalray. http://www.kalrayinc.com/kalray/products
3. NAS parallel benchmarks. https://www.nas.nasa.gov/publications/npb.html
4. Tilera corporation. http://www.mellanox.com/repository/solutions/tile-scm/docs/UG130-ArchOverview-TILE-Gx.pdf
5. Tsar. https://www-soc.lip6.fr/trac/tsar
6. Abellan, J., Fernandez, J., Acacio, M.: Efficient hardware barrier synchronization in many-core CMPs. IEEE Trans. Parallel Distrib. Syst. **23**(8), 1453–1466 (2012)
7. Buchmann, R., Greiner, A.: A fully static scheduling approach for fast cycle accurate systemC simulation of MPSoCs. In: 2007 International Conference on Microelectronics, pp. 101–104 (2007)
8. Hoefler, T., Mehlan, T., Mietke, F., Rehm, W.: A survey of barrier algorithms for coarse grained supercomputers. Chemnitzer Informatik Berichte **04**(03) (2004). ISSN: 0947-5152. http://www.unixer.de/~htor/publications/
9. Leiserson, C.E., et al.: The network architecture of the connection machine CM-5. In: Proceedings of the Fourth Annual ACM Symposium on Parallel Algorithms and Architectures, SPAA 1992, pp. 272–285. ACM (1992)
10. Monchiero, M., Palermo, G., Silvano, C., Villa, O.: Efficient synchronization for embedded on-chip multiprocessors. IEEE Trans. Very Large Scale Integr. (VLSI) Syst. **14**(10), 1049–1062 (2006)
11. Soga, T., Sasaki, H., Hirao, T., Kondo, M., Inoue, K.: A flexible hardware barrier mechanism for many-core processors. In: Asia and South Pacific Design Automation Conference (ASP-DAC), 2015 20th Asia and South Pacific, pp. 61–68 (2015)

12. Villa, O., Palermo, G., Silvano, C.: Efficiency and scalability of barrier synchronization on NoC based many-core architectures. In: Proceedings of the 2008 International Conference on Compilers, Architectures and Synthesis for Embedded Systems, CASES 2008, pp. 81–90. ACM (2008)
13. Wei, Z., Liu, P., Sun, R., Ying, R.: TAB barrier: hybrid barrier synchronization for NoC-based processors. In: 2015 IEEE International Symposium on Circuits and Systems (ISCAS), pp. 409–412 (2015)
14. Zhengbin, P., Shaogang, W., Dan, W., Pingjing, L.: Hardware acceleration of barrier communication for large scale parallel computer. In: 2013 8th International ICST Conference on Communications and Networking in China (CHINACOM), pp. 610–614 (2013)

Analysis and Optimization

Ampehre: An Open Source Measurement Framework for Heterogeneous Compute Nodes

Achim Lösch$^{(\boxtimes)}$, Alex Wiens , and Marco Platzner

Paderborn University, Paderborn, Germany
{achim.loesch,platzner}@upb.de, awiens@mail.upb.de

Abstract. Profiling applications on a heterogeneous compute node is challenging since the way to retrieve data from the resources and interpret them varies between resource types and manufacturers. This holds especially true for measuring the energy consumption. In this paper we present Ampehre, a novel open source measurement framework that allows developers to gather comparable measurements from heterogeneous compute nodes, e.g., nodes comprising CPU, GPU, and FPGA. We explain the architecture of Ampehre and detail the measurement process on the example of energy measurements on CPU and GPU. To characterize the probing effect, we quantitatively analyze the trade-off between the accuracy of measurements and the CPU load imposed by Ampehre. Based on this analysis, we are able to specify reasonable combinations of sampling periods for the different resource types of a compute node.

Keywords: Heterogeneous computing · Measurement · Energy
Open source

1 Introduction

Application profiling is a major step in software development. Most commonly, developers focus on performance analysis based on hardware performance counters provided by the target resource and on timing information. Using these data, developers gain knowledge about runtime metrics such as number of executed instructions, cache misses, page-faults, or the costs of called functions. Understanding runtime behavior is instrumental for optmizing applications performance. A widely-used open source performance analysis tool is `Perf` which was introduced in Linux 2.6.31 and since then is an inherent part of the Linux infrastructure [1]. Other similar open source tools are `IgProf` [2] and `Likwid` [3]. Vendors have implemented closed source professional profiling tools to support application development for their devices, e.g., the Intel VTune Amplifier [4] or the Nvidia GPU development IDE Nvidia Nsight and command line tool `nvprof` [5]. Since the introduction of the Running Average Power Limit (RAPL) interface for Intel CPUs, developers are able to perform energy measurements on CPUs

© Springer International Publishing AG, part of Springer Nature 2018
M. Berekovic et al. (Eds.): ARCS 2018, LNCS 10793, pp. 73–84, 2018.
https://doi.org/10.1007/978-3-319-77610-1_6

although some source code modifications are required. For example, in [6] the authors add an energy profiling module for Intel CPUs to `IgProf`. Their changes allow for basic power analysis and optimization. Optimizing the energy consumption of applications has become an emerging topic in high performance computing and will continue to grow in importance, given the rising electricity costs.

All the mentioned tools lack an easy-to-use and extensible application programmer interface (API) that allows user applications to read comparable performance and energy data from different resource types. The Performance Application Programming Interface (PAPI) project [7] has been developed to solve these issues. Particularly with the PAPI version 5 release, developers are able to add capabilities for power or temperature analysis by implementing so-called *PAPI components*, extending PAPI to new platforms and other sensor types [8]. These capabilities make dedicated measuring equipment such as digital multimeters redundant. PAPI provides a unified API that hides the underlying device-specific measuring procedures when reading power, energy, and temperature sensors. However, even with PAPI the retrieved data must be interpreted to gain semantically comparable measurement results across the resource boundaries. Such comparable measurements are particularly important for developing and optimizing applications as well as system software for heterogeneous compute nodes.

To overcome these limitations, we have developed the novel framework *Ampehre*, short for *Accurately Measuring Power and Energy for Heterogeneous Resource Environments* [9], with the key features: (i) easy integration into other projects by providing a clear API covering all resource types, (ii) extensible to new resources and sensors through the use of PAPI, and (iii) open source under the terms of the 2-clause BSD license.

In Sect. 2 of this paper, we present an overview of the Ampehre framework architecture. Section 3 illustrates the measuring procedure with Ampehre explained by an example for measuring energy on CPU and GPU. In Sect. 4 we evaluate the trade-off between data accuracy and the additional CPU load imposed by Ampehre. In Sect. 5 we show how to extend Ampehre to new computing resources and sensors. Finally, Sect. 6 concludes the paper.

2   Architecture and Components of Ampehre

Ampehre is designed for heterogeneous high-performance compute nodes running Linux. In this paper, we refer to an implementation on a heterogeneous server using a *Dell PowerEdge T620* with two *Intel Xeon E5-2609 v2* CPUs as host processors, a PCIe-connected *Nvidia Tesla K20c* GPGPU based on the Kepler microarchitecture, and a PCIe-connected *Maxeler Vectis* FPGA board based on Xilinx Virtex 6 (xc6vsx475t). The server runs CentOS 6.8 Linux with kernel v2.6.32. In Sect. 5 we explain the necessary adaptations to Ampehre when deployed on different compute resources. Figure 1 presents the architecture of the Ampehre framework, which comprises three layers in user space: an extended PAPI library, the Ampehre library, and the Ampehre tools. In this section, we describe each of these layers.

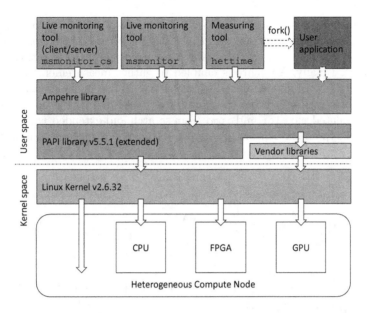

Fig. 1. Ampehre architecture comprising an extended PAPI library, the Ampehre library, and Ampehre tools. Orange blocks denote components we have implemented or extended. (Color figure online)

2.1   Extended PAPI Library

We base the Ampehre framework on *PAPI*, which is short for Performance Application Programming Interface [7]. PAPI is a well-known and widely-used Linux library for gathering performance data on CPU-based systems. The use of PAPI makes Ampehre inherently portable to other systems running a Linux OS distribution. We have extended the *PAPI library* to support not only CPU and system-wide sensors but also to retrieve performance data gathered at the accelerator components.

Figure 2 denotes the main components with their interfaces utilized by Ampehre to obtain measurements from the heterogeneous computing resources and the main board of our server node. Overall, for use with Ampehre PAPI must be compiled with four software components enabled: The PAPI component `rapl` supports CPU measurements, including the cores, last-level cache, memory controller and DRAMs. Modern Intel CPUs provide several so-called Model Specific Registers (MSR) to retrieve data related to energy consumption, temperature, etc. Already with the first Pentium processor family, Intel introduced MSR read and write instructions, `RDMSR` and `WRMSR`, in the instruction set. The PAPI component `ipmi` is necessary to retrieve system-wide measurements such as the system-wide power dissipation measured at the power supply. For this, the component communicates with the *Baseboard Management Controller* (BMC) by means of the Linux OpenIPMI library. IMPI, short for Intelligent Platform Management Interface [10], is a standard to unify server platform management. The *Nvidia GPU* is supported if PAPI is compiled with the `nvml` component. This component includes the Nvidia Management Library (NVML) [11], which is used to obtain the current power dissipation and die temperature. Finally, Ampehre is enabled to gather measurement data on the *Maxeler Vectis* by linking against the MaxelerOS library if the `maxeler` component is enabled in PAPI. From the overall four described PAPI components, we have implemented `maxeler` and `ipmi` from scratch and extended `rapl` and `nvml` in order to support the sensors of interest on our heterogeneous compute node.

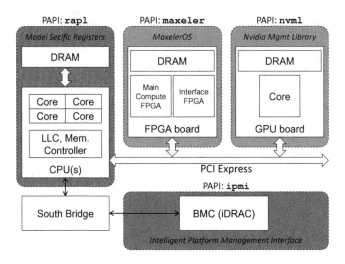

Fig. 2. PAPI components required to retrieve measurements from the heterogeneous computing resources and the main board. We use Linux OS kernel interfaces to sample CPU and BMC sensors (red blocks), while vendor libraries provide functions to retrieve measurements from the FPGA and GPU boards (green blocks). (Color figure online)

2.2 Ampehre Library API

While PAPI simplifies the resource and vendor-specific measuring procedures by a unified interface, the sampled raw data must be properly interpreted in order to provide comparable measurements for all resources. For example, PAPI directly measures the energy consumption on Intel CPUs, but for our Nvidia GPU it can only retrieve the latest power dissipation readings. Therefore, we have developed the *Ampehre library* with the goal to hide all computations and data interpretations from the application developer. Extending PAPI functionality, the Ampehre library unifies the meaning of gained data across resource boundaries and provides the developer with a set of functions having the same semantics for all resource types. The Ampehre library is used by the Ampehre tools and must also be included by any measured user application (see Fig. 1).

The application programmer interface (API) of the Ampehre library is written in C. Table 1 lists the essential functions that must be invoked to perform

Table 1. Ampehre library C interface. The function call sequence ⓪–⑨ presents a correct use of the library. Actual measurements are obtained between `ms_start_measurement()` and `ms_stop_measurement()`

#	Function	Explanation
⓪	`MS = ms_init ();`	Initialize Ampehre and PAPI libraries
①	`MD = ms_alloc_measurement ();`	Allocate data containers storing measured and calculated data
②	`ms_set_timer (MD, Component, Sampling_Period);`	Set component-specific sampling period. Repeat function call for all required PAPI components
③	`ms_init_measurement (MS, MD);`	Register data containers with Ampehre. Initialize timers for periodic sampling
④	`ms_start_measurement (MS);`	Start measuring. Each component is periodically sampled by a dedicated thread. Data are stored in priorly registered MD
⑤	`ms_stop_measurement (MS);`	Stop measuring. Terminate sampling threads
⑥	`ms_join_measurement (MS);`	Wait until all sampling threads have terminated
⑦	`ms_fini_measurement (MS);`	Clean up environment
⑧	`ms_free_measurement (MD);`	Free data containers
⑨	`ms_fini(MS);`	Shut down Ampehre and PAPI libraries

measurements. The sequence of function calls in the table shows the correct use of the library. The library implementation as well as the API isolate the data structures storing the measurement results from the actual measuring system. We refer to these two parts as measurement data MD and measuring system MS, respectively. Step ⓪ initializes the MS, i.e., the underlying Ampehre library, the PAPI library, the Linux OS drivers, and the vendor libraries are opened and configured to retrieve measurements. The MD is allocated subsequently in step ①.

Step ② sets the sampling period for the measurement, where for each underlying PAPI component a separate sampling period can be chosen. Setting sampling periods involves a trade-off since short sampling periods lead to measurements with high accuracy, but can increase the CPU load caused by the measuring framework unacceptably. Long sampling periods lead to smaller increases of CPU load but also to less accurate measurements. We discuss this trade-off in more detail in Sect. 4. The next step ③ links the MD with the MS and initializes one periodic timer per PAPI component. Whenever a timer expires, it triggers the actual measuring procedures in the PAPI respective component followed by internal calculations mainly in the Ampehre library. The measurement framework starts with step ④, that creates a POSIX thread for each component. This way, we can perform the required computations for the components independently. The gained results are stored in the registered MD structures. Properly stopping the measurement framework requires the steps ⑤, ⑥, and ⑦. These steps terminate the measurement threads and performs cleanups. The accumulated measurements remain stored in MD until ⑧ and ⑨ are called to free the data structures and shut down all libraries.

Table 2. Quantities that can be measured or computed with the extended PAPI library and the Ampehre library.

Component	Energy	Power	Temperature	Utilization	Frequency	Alloc. memory
	Accumulated	Current, Minimum, Average, Maximum				
`rapl`	✓	✓	✓	✓	✓	✓
`nvml`	✓	✓	✓	✓	✓	✓
`maxeler`	✓	✓	✓	✓	✗	✗
`ipmi`	✓	✓	✓	✗	✗	✗

Table 2 gives an overview of the quantities that can be reported by the Ampehre framework for each of the four PAPI components. All measurements follow the sequence shown in Table 1 and thus the reported quantities are with respect to a specific measurement period, determined by the function calls ④ and ⑤. The measured energy is by definition a value accumulated over the measurement period. For the other quantities, which are power, temperature, utilization, frequency, and amount of allocated memory, Ampehre reports the current (latest) value and the minimum, maximum, and average over the measurement period.

2.3   Ampehre Tools

Developers can instantiate the Ampehre library in their applications to use our measurement framework, or they can use one of the following *Ampehre tools*:
`hettime` extends the well-known Linux utility *time* by reporting comprehensive measurements for an executed binary. While `time` returns the system resource usage of a binary given as argument, `hettime` additionally reports the energy consumed by the overall system, the average power dissipation and maximum temperature for each component, etc. The results can be stored in JSON files, CSV tables, or simply printed to the shell. `hettime` is highly configurable through 19 different flags in total. For example, the flags -c, -g, -f, and -s set the sampling periods for the CPU (PAPI component `rapl`), GPU (PAPI component `nvml`), FPGA (PAPI component `maxeler`), and the system (PAPI component `ipmi`).
`msmonitor` is a Qt-based live monitoring tool plotting the most recent measurements. `msmonitor` can display the measurement data in form of an array of curves or as heat maps. These features are exemplary illustrated in Fig. 3. The screenshot displays data taken while an arbitrary set of 15 tasks is concurrently executed on CPU, GPU, and FPGA. The array of curves on the left side of Fig. 3 represent the current power dissipation of the three computing resources, while the heat maps on the right side of Fig. 3 show device utilizations.
`msmonitor_cs` is a server-client implementation of `msmonitor` for reducing probing effects on the measured server by transferring the GUI rendering to a client connected via TCP/IP.

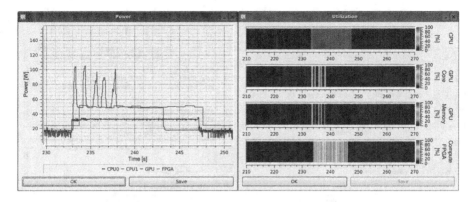

Fig. 3. Power dissipation and utilization plotted by `msmonitor` while an arbitrary set of 15 tasks are executed on CPU, GPU, and FPGA.

3   Example: Measuring Energy on CPU and GPU

We illustrate the interaction of the different layers of our framework, the operating system, and the vendor libraries on the example of measuring energy on the Intel CPU and the Nvidia GPU. Figure 4 gives an overview over the measurement data processing layers.

The energy measurement procedures for CPU and GPU are very different. For the CPU, we read energy counters at two different points in time and the difference denotes the energy consumed during that period of time. Yet, we sample the energy counters periodically to handle register overflows appropriately and to be able to provide the user with power dissipation values. The GPU allows us to only measure the power dissipation and not the consumed energy. Based on the sampling interval T_{nvml}, set in step ② of Table 1, we estimate the energy E_{GPU} consumed over a period of time Δt as shown in Eq. 1. Ampehre hides the essentially different approaches for CPU and GPU to obtain the energy consumption. Developers including Ampehre can thus use energy variables without being required to know about the actual measuring procedures.

$$E_{GPU}(t_0, \Delta t) = \int_{t_0}^{t_0+\Delta t} p(t)\, \mathrm{d}t \approx \sum_{j=1}^{N} p(t_j) \cdot T_{nvml} \text{ with } N = \left\lceil \frac{t_0 + \Delta t}{T_{nvml}} \right\rceil \quad (1)$$

As shown in Fig. 4, the energy and power dissipation readings for CPU and GPU are obtained from the compute elements using an OS driver and a vendor-specific library, respectively. Intel CPUs based on Sandy Bridge or newer microarchitectures implement the Running Average Power Limit (RAPL) interface which is a set of Model-Specific Registers (MSR) to measure CPU energy counters [12]. Xeon CPU energy counters can be derived for three power domains, each one represented by a dedicated MSR: The *Package* power domain refers to the entire die including cores, caches, and the memory controller. The *Power Plane 0* domain is a subset of the Package domain and considers only

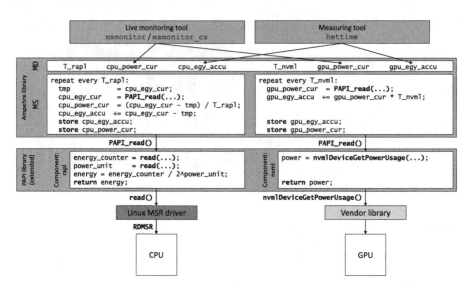

Fig. 4. Interaction of the Ampehre tools, libraries and the Linux OS exemplary illustrated with energy and power measurements obtained from the CPU and GPU. The abbreviations MS (measuring system) and MD (measurement data) are references to the pointers used by the functions in Table 1.

the energy consumption of the cores as well as L1 and L2 caches. The *DRAM* domain represents the energy consumption of the main memory. Linux provides an MSR driver executing the RDMSR instruction to retrieve the values stored in the MSRs. In contrast, for the GPU the function nvmlDeviceGetPowerUsage() of the Nvidia Management Library (NVML) [11] provides the current power dissipation in single device power domain.

The next layer is the PAPI library that fetches the data from the Linux MSR driver and the Nvidia Management Library. Abstracting from the resource-specific interfaces and measuring methods, the main advantage of PAPI is to provide the function PAPI_read() to the next layer in a component-independent way. For the GPU, PAPI_read() returns the latest power dissipation. For the CPU, determining the energy value requires some computations such as adjusting the energy counters by so-called power units that are also retrieved from MSRs.

The Ampehre library continues data processing and provides comparable and equally interpretable measurements to user applications, as shown in Fig. 4. To this end, the Ampehre library employs several threads that periodically sample the PAPI components by invocations of PAPI_read() and similar functions. Data processing in the library's measuring system MS leads to two data fields in the library's measurement data MD with almost equal semantics for CPU and GPU: The data fields cpu_power_cur and gpu_power_cur store the current power dissipation of the resources and are always updated after the corresponding timer has expired. Likewise, the data fields cpu_egy_accu and gpu_egy_accu continuously increase by the energy consumed since the last measurement has been received. Together with the selected sampling periods for the CPU and GPU, T_rapl and T_nvml, the current power dissipation and accumulated energy values are available for further processing by user applications or, as shown in Fig. 4, by the Ampehre live monitoring tools `msmonitor` and `msmonitor_cs` or by the Ampehre measuring tool `hettime`. User applications have full access to MD whether or not MS is active.

4   Balancing Accuracy and Overhead

The selection of sampling periods involves a trade-off between accuracy of the measurements and overhead on the system CPUs for running the measurement system. Shorter sampling periods better approximate continuous signals and thus increase the accuracy, but also result in higher CPU load. To quantify this trade-off, we have conducted a series of measurements on our heterogeneous compute node with the `rapl`, `nvml`, and `maxeler` components enabled in PAPI. Each measurement has lasted for a period of 60 s on an idling system, i.e., except the operating system no tasks have been executed. The sampling periods have been varied between 10 ms and 100 ms with an increment of 10 ms. Each measurement has been repeated 41 times and the results have been averaged.

Figure 5 shows the results and displays the average power dissipation and the utilization, combined for both CPUs, as functions of the sampling period. As a baseline, we have developed a minimal program which is just able to read the CPU energy consumption and utilization without making use of the Ampehre framework, i.e., Ampehre and PAPI libraries. This simple program has been executed under (i) an entirely booted CentOS Linux (black curve) and (ii) a Linux kernel executing BusyBox [13] (gray curve). The blue, red, and green curves in Fig. 5 illustrate the impact of Ampehre when sampling the CPU, GPU, and FPGA, respectively. In addition, the purple curve shows Ampehre's impact if all three components are enabled with identical sampling periods.

As expected, the results show that longer sampling periods lead to less over-heads on the CPUs for both utilization and average power dissipation. For example, when increasing the sampling period (purple curve) from 10 ms to 100 ms the average power dissipation drops from 33.56 W to 16.66 W, and the CPU utilization decreases from 13.29% to just 1.24%. Moreover, it can be seen that higher sampling periods show results close to the baseline implementation executed under CentOS. When comparing Ampehre with the minimal measurement program executed under CentOS for sampling all three components, the average power consumption drops from 17.57 W at a sampling period of 10 ms to 1.83 W at 100 ms. Contrasting the two baselines, it becomes apparent that a fully booted operating system leads to a distinct increase in power dissipation which varies in the range of 4.24 W and 6.97 W between the baselines.

In a real use of Ampehre the heterogeneous components are likely to be sampled at different periods, which makes the estimation of the CPU overheads more involved. We have conducted a second series of measurements where we

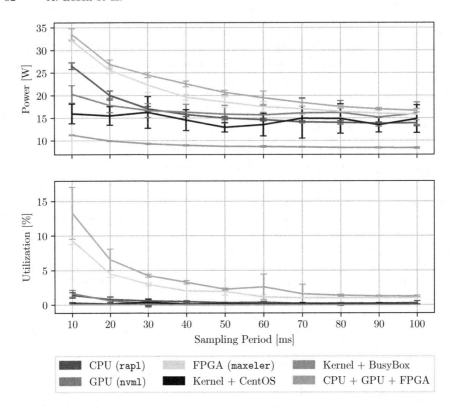

Fig. 5. Average power dissipation and utilization as well as their standard deviations of both CPUs as functions of the sampling period. (Color figure online)

have varied the sampling periods for the three components independently, again ranging from 10 ms to 100 ms with an increment of 10 ms. Overall, 1000 combinations of sampling periods have been evaluated. Then, we have filtered the results with different thresholds on the CPU utilization and recorded the resulting combinations in a multi-dimensional space. Table 3 lists the achieved Pareto frontiers for five different utilization thresholds, with their sampling periods and the average power consumption. Thus, the sampling period combinations in this table represent optimal selections, subject to guaranteed maximum CPU load increases.

5   Availability and Extensibility of Ampehre

Ampehre is open source and freely available [9]. The framework has been developed to support research on heterogeneous computing. For example, in [14] novel scheduling techniques featuring heterogeneous task migration are studied and Ampehre measures the energy consumption of CPU, GPU, and FPGA during the execution of a set of dynamically scheduled tasks. In [15], Ampehre is

Table 3. Valid sampling period combinations for Ampehre taking utilization thresholds between 1.5% and 10% into account. The measurements are performed on our heterogeneous compute node. These data are collected while sampling all sensors available in the `rapl` (C), `nvml` (G), and `maxeler` (F) components. Furthermore, we show the average power dissipation of the CPUs ($\bar{P}$) for the listed sampling period combinations.

≤1.5%				≤5%								≤7%				≤10%			
C	G	F	$\bar{P}$	C	G	F	$\bar{P}$	C	G	F	$\bar{P}$	C	G	F	$\bar{P}$	C	G	F	$\bar{P}$
ms	ms	ms	W	ms	ms	ms	W	ms	ms	ms	W	ms	ms	ms	W	ms	ms	ms	W
50	60	100	18.7	10	10	50	29.5	100	10	30	25.4	10	10	30	30.3	10	10	20	31.8
70	30	100	18.2	10	20	40	28.7	40	100	20	26.3	10	20	20	31.0	20	40	10	33.0
50	70	90	18.1	40	10	40	25.6	60	70	20	26.3	30	10	20	28.4	30	30	10	32.6
80	30	90	18.8	10	30	30	30.8	70	50	20	26.8					80	20	10	32.6
70	40	70	19.6	20	20	30	25.7	80	40	20	25.6								
70	90	60	18.9																

instrumental for developing energy-centric schedulers by quantifying the energy consumption of multi-resource binaries on a heterogeneous compute node with idling resources. Since easy extensibility and portability to other servers are major design objective of the framework, users can extend Ampehre to support additional resources and sensors. Basically, the following three major modifications have to be realized to add a new sensor to Ampehre:

1. **Extend the PAPI library.** First, an existing PAPI component must be extended or a new one must be created, according to the official PAPI documentation [7]. Hereby, developers implement the abstract PAPI API and hide resource-specific details. This step allows for retrieving the new component-specific measurements by invoking `PAPI_read()`.
2. **Configure the Ampehre library.** Depending on the new sensor, the Ampehre library must be configured to properly process the raw data read from the PAPI library. This can be done by simply modifying a configuration file.
3. **Enable measurements.** Add the event name for the new sensor to the event list stored in a file. PAPI-internally, sensors are represented as events. Thus, each sensor must be assigned an event name. Data is read from sensors and processed only if their event names appear in the event list.

6   Conclusion

In this paper we have presented Ampehre, an open source measurement framework for heterogeneous compute nodes. Ampehre is based on the widely-used PAPI library, which greatly facilitates its adaptation to other resources and sensors. Ampehre unifies the measuring procedures and interpretation of gained data across different resource types such as CPU, CPU and FPGA, which makes it easily usable. An important issue in any measurement framework are probing effects. We have quantified the overhead of Ampehre and determined sets of reasonable combination of sampling periods for the different resources types, such that the CPU load imposed by the framework can be limited.

Acknowledgement. This work has been partially supported by the German Research Foundation (DFG) within the Collaborative Research Center 901 "On-The-Fly Computing".

References

1. Linux Kernel: perf: Linux Profiling with Performance Counters (2017). https://perf.wiki.kernel.org/index.php/Main_Page
2. Eulisse, G., Tuura, L.: IgProf, the Ignominous Profiler (2013). http://igprof.org/
3. Roehl, T.: Performance Monitoring and Benchmarking Suite (2017). https://github.com/RRZE-HPC/likwid/
4. Intel Corporation: Intel VTune Amplifier (2017). https://software.intel.com/en-us/intel-vtune-amplifier-xe
5. Nvidia Corporation: Nvidia Nsight (2017). http://www.nvidia.com/object/nsight.html
6. Khan, K.N., Nybäck, F., Ou, Z., Nurminen, J.K., Niemi, T., Eulisse, G., Elmer, P., Abdurachmanov, D.: Energy profiling using IgProf. In: 2015 15th IEEE/ACM International Symposium on Cluster, Cloud and Grid Computing, May 2015
7. Innovative Computing Laboratory, University of Tennessee: Performance Application Programming Interface (PAPI) (2016). http://icl.utk.edu/papi/
8. McCraw, H., Ralph, J., Danalis, A., Dongarra, J.: Power monitoring with PAPI for extreme scale architectures and dataflow-based programming models. In: 2014 IEEE International Conference on Cluster Computing (CLUSTER), September 2014
9. Lösch, A., Knorr, C., El-Ali, A., Wiens, A.: Ampehre: Accurately Measuring Power and Energy for Heterogeneous Resource Environments (2017). http://ampehre.uni-paderborn.de/
10. Intel Corporation: Intelligent Platform Management Interface (IPMI), IPMI Technical Resources (2015). https://www.intel.com/content/www/us/en/servers/ipmi/ipmi-technical-resources.html
11. Nvidia Corporation: Nvidia Management Library (NVML) (2017). https://developer.nvidia.com/nvidia-management-library-nvml/
12. Intel Corporation: Intel 64 and IA-32 Architectures Software Developer Manuals, October 2017. https://software.intel.com/en-us/articles/intel-sdm/
13. Vlasenko, D.: BusyBox: The Swiss Army Knife of Embedded Linux (2017). https://busybox.net/
14. Lösch, A., Beisel, T., Kenter, T., Plessl, C., Platzner, M.: Performance-centric scheduling with task migration for a heterogeneous compute node in the data center. In: 2016 Design, Automation Test in Europe Conference Exhibition (DATE), pp. 912–917, March 2016
15. Lösch, A., Platzner, M.: reMinMin: a novel static energy-centric list scheduling approach based on real measurements. In: 2017 IEEE 28th International Conference on Application-specific Systems, Architectures and Processors (ASAP), pp. 149–154, July 2017

A Hybrid Approach for Runtime Analysis Using a Cycle and Instruction Accurate Model

Sebastian Rachuj[(✉)], Christian Herglotz, Marc Reichenbach,
André Kaup, and Dietmar Fey

Friedrich-Alexander University Erlangen-Nürnberg (FAU), Erlangen, Germany
{sebastian.rachuj,christian.herglotz,marc.reichenbach,
andre.kaup,dietmar.fey}@fau.de

Abstract. Developing a new microchip for an embedded application these days means that the engineer has to take many different design options into account. Evaluating the different processor cores regarding their runtime for a certain algorithm requires simulation tools which make emulation feasible. They come in two flavors: Cycle and instruction accurate simulation. The first one offers a high accuracy regarding the estimated time but is very slow. The second one offers a high simulation speed but only provides a very imprecise estimation of the real runtime. This paper shows a new approach that allows to combine these kinds of simulation to increase the exactness of the estimated time while limiting the additionally required simulation time.

1 Introduction

Hardware platforms are rising in complexity and have an increasing amount of configurable parts. For example, a developer must decide which processors to integrate into the system. There are a lot of different architectures which are available with different characteristics. ARM offers the Cortex-R series for embedded devices which are more predictable but comparably slow and the Cortex-A series for entertainment devices which achieve a much higher performance but sacrifice the simplicity required for statically determining execution time. Additionally, the single models of the series have different characteristics like in-order (e.g. Cortex-A 53) or out-of-order execution (e.g. Cortex-A 57). Apart from ARM there are also other instruction set architectures like MIPS or PowerPC that might be suitable. Before manufacturing the hardware, the platform architect will evaluate its algorithms on a simulation framework providing certain parameters like performance and energy consumption which she can use to decide which core and system layout to deploy.

Simulation can be done on different levels. The most accurate but also the slowest method is to use tools for Application Specific Integrated Circuit (ASIC) validation. For a brief evaluation, it is not necessary to have a completely exact result on the electrical level. Thus, a simulation approach implementing the

© Springer International Publishing AG, part of Springer Nature 2018
M. Berekovic et al. (Eds.): ARCS 2018, LNCS 10793, pp. 85–96, 2018.
https://doi.org/10.1007/978-3-319-77610-1_7

architectures in a high level language like SystemC is sensible since the execution speed of the target software is increased. The second level offers a cycle accurate simulation of the hardware. Cycle accurate means that the pipeline and superscalar architecture is modelled to behave like the real hardware regarding the cycle count per instruction. In comparison to instruction accurate emulation which just executes an instruction each cycle without considering the actual hardware layout, this approach is still very slow. However, the instruction accurate emulation misses the architectural characteristics. For simple deterministic in-order architectures, this method might suffice. But complex out-of-order processor designs are usually much faster as they can execute multiple instructions per cycle which makes the results of an instruction accurate simulation insufficient for the assessment of the processor.

Combining these two kinds of CPU simulation can result in improved accuracy while avoiding an enormous rise in simulation time in comparison to only using the instruction or cycle accurate model. For this paper such a methodology was developed based on the observation that most programs mainly consist of loops. Not each of the loops' iteration must be simulated in great detail. After a few runs of the loop body, the pipeline is filled with only the instruction stream of the loop. Hence, not much deviation between further iterations is expected. This allows to extrapolate the results of few exactly analyzed iterations to the many inaccurately simulated ones. In this work, gem5 [2] is used as it already provides a cycle accurate and an instruction accurate model which can be exchanged as required.

While this method is capable of increasing the accuracy with only a moderate growth of the simulation time, the real benefits depend on the software that is analyzed. As example applications a radar processing algorithm often used in the automotive industry and the High Efficiency Video Codec decoding implementation known from entertainment products are assessed.

In the following section some related works are presented which try to solve the same issue. Afterwards, the methodology is presented in detail. Subsequently, an evaluation using the aforementioned algorithms is shown. For this, a custom metric was created that uses the default gem5 models as a reference. Finally, a conclusion is drawn.

2   Related Work

There are different approaches in current research to increase the simulation speed of virtual prototyping tools without sacrificing the accuracy. Since the amount of processor cores per SoC steadily rises, a sequential simulation cannot keep up with the new hardware. Therefore, simulators were created which also parallelize the emulation of the multi-core platforms. Manifold [14] is an example for a simulation framework that was exactly designed for this purpose of creating a multi-core system. It shows tremendous speedups of up to 12 times the speed of the sequential emulation of a 64-core platform. The next step is to distribute the threads of the simulation tool across multiple host computers which results in distributed simulation introducing new challenges. An overview of the different issues and methods of parallel and distributed discrete event simulation is given in [7]. While these approaches are the future solutions for handling the systems with many cores, they don't optimize a single complex core very well. This issue is addressed in this paper.

The Sniper [3] simulator is a tool increasing the exactness of the instruction accurate simulation (called one-IPC (instruction per cycle) simulation) without introducing the overhead of a cycle accurate simulator. It separates the instruction stream into intervals which are analyzed regarding their architectural behavior and stored in an execution window during the emulation. This allows to model time penalties of real hardware occurring because of data dependencies between instructions or cache misses. In their paper they also suggested to parallelize the execution of the simulation. They achieve an average absolute error of less than 23.8% for the SPLASH-2 benchmark but have a slow-down of 2–3 times in comparison to the one-IPC simulation. The work presented in this paper is intended as an alternative way to achieve similar benefits like Sniper.

Switching the processor models of gem5 like presented in this work was done before by Hsieh et al. [9]. They use this approach to fast-forward to their region of interest. As soon as the inaccurate (they call it "in-order") model reaches the point which has to be investigated, the accurate out-of-order model is switched in. How this region is found and how they keep track of the instruction flow is not explained. Additionally, since this work was not their main topic, no further comparisons of the accuracy achieved for the simulation time required for the full program was made. The mechanics of gem5 to exchange certain processor models was also used to emulate dynamic voltage and frequency scaling. Haririan et al. implemented this feature for gem5 [8]. However, their main focus for evaluation lied on the accuracy of the method. Thus, they did not try to accelerate their work or to compare it regarding its simulation speed.

This section shows that there are already many approaches to improve the efficiency of CPU simulation. But to the knowledge of the authors, no evaluations integrating both dimensions, the simulation time and the accuracy, were made. Hence, the newly proposed methodology is evaluated in a way that includes both metrics. For the future, it is expected that some of the related work presented here might also benefit from the proposed methodology.

3 Proposed Methodology

As mentioned in the introduction, the methodology is intended to exploit the fact that programs mostly consist of loops which are responsible for the biggest proportion of the required runtime. Thereby, saving simulation time in loops will also result in a greatly decreased total simulation time. This is true all the more since accurate simulators take a multiple of the time for each virtually executed instruction the real hardware needs. Software without many loops is expected to be short enough for a fully cycle accurate simulation and is not required to be executed with the aid of the presented approach.

Therefore, an important part is the analysis of the program to find the loops. This requires the creation of a control flow graph (CFG). After the information is acquired, an augmented simulator based on gem5 is run to perform the actual runtime estimation. The flow of the methodology is depicted in Fig. 1 and is elaborated in the following sections. The reference implementation created for this paper is currently only able to analyze and run programs that were compiled for the ARM AArch64 architecture. However, the methodology itself is agnostic to the architecture and can be adapted for instruction set architectures with a fixed instruction size. Variable instruction lengths require further customizations.

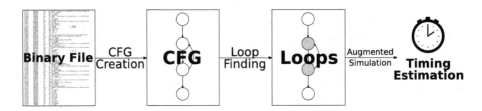

Fig. 1. The flow of the methodology starting with the binary file to the runtime estimation

3.1 Analyzing the Program

Since the key concept of the approach requires to know the addresses of the loops within the binary, the first action is to investigate the instruction stream and to create a CFG consisting of basic blocks. A basic block is defined by Cooper as a maximal length sequence of instructions with only one entry at the beginning and one exit at the end [4]. It allows a more abstract view on the control flow and is used in compilers to analyze the program. There are two possibilities to create a CFG. The first one is to perform a static analysis of the binary file. Reverse engineering tools often provide this functionality and offer a library to use within other software. For the means of this paper, this would suffice. However, the implementation created here uses another method to build a CFG that also delivers information about the actual control flow during the execution. It takes the instruction trace of a fast functional simulation for this purpose. Thereby, the loops and basic blocks can be annotated by the amount of times they were executed. Additionally, dead code is not taken into account. With this knowledge, future enhancements of this methodology might for example use different amounts of accurate iterations for each loop depending on the information gathered from the first run. As of now, a plain CFG extracted from the program under test is enough.

As depicted in Fig. 1, the next step is to find the loops within the CFG. For this, the dominance relationship between the basic blocks inside a function is required. If a node A in a graph dominates another node B, it means that all paths that reach B starting from the function entry block also must contain A. This relationship can be extracted by a simple textbook algorithm that is fast enough in most occasions [5]. A loop consists of basic blocks in between a loop entry block dominating all instructions in the loop body and the backward edge returning to the loop entry. Irreducible loops without an unambiguous head are not taken into account within this work. Since functions called within loops are difficult to handle, a simplification is introduced. A set called "considered blocks" is created that contains all basic blocks of the loop body. Additionally, all called functions are visited and their basic blocks including the basic blocks of other functions called within them are inserted recursively. The set is used to find out if a certain loop is already left or still executed but currently calls another function. While this approach is simple to determine the basic control flow of a program, sophisticated cases containing complex call hierarchies within a loop are not satisfactorily handled. Furthermore, the start and end addresses of all basic blocks are saved to allow the identification of the currently executed block by using the current program counter of the simulated architecture. Additional information that can be annotated to the nodes of the CFG is the amount of executions of a basic block in case an instruction stream was analyzed.

Another simplification that is implemented into the presented system is that only the outer loops are taken into account. This is sensible since all iterations of the inner loops are run during one iteration of an outer loop. However, this is not true for inner loops with different runtimes during each iteration of the outer loop. Thus, future improvements of this methodology might need to also take inner loops into account.

3.2 Running the Simulation

After the analysis step finished gathering the information needed from the program, the simulator can be started. It is written in SystemC and connected to gem5 using the works of Menard et al. [11] to connect TLM (Transaction Level Modeling) compatible modules. This allows more flexibility with custom periphery that might be used in conjunction with other processor simulators. Thus in the future, the whole memory hierarchy and some more complex devices can be exchanged with more accurate or faster models. As a result, not only the microarchitecture but also the connected parts of a platform can be taken into account during loop executions. Most simulation models support connecting to SystemC or even TLM compatible modules.

For the simulation, the O3 model and the Timing Simple (TS) model of gem5 are used. O3 is an implementation of a complex out-of-order pipeline originally based on the Alpha CPUs. It is cycle accurate and as such the reference for the highest possible accuracy and the slowest simulation speed. TS implements an instruction accurate processor model that typifies the most inaccurate but fastest possible simulation.

First attempts showed that it is insignificant whether to use the O3 or the TS model outside of loops. The simulation time and the estimated time are only slightly affected. This confirms our assumption that programs remain most of their time within loops. At the beginning, the implemented simulation starts with an active O3 model to reduce the overhead of switching from TS to O3 when entering a loop.

Keeping track of the currently executed instruction is done by using the tracing functionality of gem5. It logs the committed instructions in the correct order. With the help of the information gathered during the analysis of the program, the basic block of each finished instruction can be found. Whenever the next basic block is reached, the simulation host updates some statistics of the left basic block like the number of its executions and the required estimated time. The latter is tracked for the simulation of each model separately. Additionally, it is checked whether the basic block is the head of an outer loop or, in case a loop was already entered, if the block is still part of the loop. According to the results of these checks, the model is switched accordingly.

The default tracing implementation of gem5 does not log instructions that result in an exception. This behavior is not suitable for the methodology since the knowledge of where the exception occurred is required. Hence, when only relying on the tracing implementation, it is difficult to track which instruction is responsible for the fault. Adding support for tracing these instructions can be achieved by some minor adjustments preventing gem5 from removing the created log data structures in the case of an exception.

For each committed instruction, gem5 writes a line to a C++ stream which can be intercepted by providing an output stream with a custom stream buffer. Parsing the lines allows the extraction of the program counter and the corresponding disassembled instruction. This information is used as described above to find the basic block belonging to the logged line and to keep the statistics up to date.

As soon as a head block of a loop reaches a manually configurable number of executions, the O3 model is replaced by the TS model. This increases the speed of the remaining iterations significantly. When the loop is left, the O3 model takes the simulation over again. In case the loop is executed again (e.g. due to being inside a function called multiple times from sequential code), the models are switched directly at the beginning since enough runtime information was already gathered at the first time.

Changing the model from O3 to TS and backwards is based on functionality of gem5 that was initially intended for checkpointing. To exchange the models, a so-called "drain" can be requested. This leads to gem5 notifying all of its components to come to a consistent state that can safely be serialized, e.g. for writing it into a file as it is done by the checkpointing implementation. Until all components are drained, some further cycles must be emulated since the processor needs to commit all instructions still residing in the pipeline. When the process is finished, the CPU models are exchanged with the help of functions already built into gem5 and the simulation is continued. Enabling a switched out model again works in the same way just with interchanged roles. Due to the latency required by the drain implementation, it is not possible to exchange the simulators exactly at the beginning of a new iteration. Predicting when the draining is completed is also not practicable since the number of cycles depend on the current state of the pipeline. That is why an execution of a basic block is only considered completely accurate, if the O3 model was active from the beginning to the end of the block. Otherwise it is considered inaccurate and not used for the runtime estimation.

After the simulation has come to an end, a correcting calculation of the estimated runtime using the statistics gathered during the run is performed. The following variables for each basic block k are available:

$n_{C,k}$ Amount of times basic block k was reached during the simulation using the O3 (cycle accurate) model.

$n_{I,k}$ Amount of times basic block k was reached during the simulation using the TS (instruction accurate) model.

$t_{C,k}$ Cumulative simulated time of basic block k during the simulation using the O3 (cycle accurate) model.

$t_{I,k}$ Cumulative simulated time of basic block k during the simulation using the TS (instruction accurate) model.

Equation (1) shows the computation used for estimating the global estimated runtime t from these variables. Basic blocks never executed in O3 mode are handled in the else case. Their runtime estimation is equivalent to the instruction accurate simulation. For the other basic blocks the estimated time for one cycle accurate iteration is taken and multiplied by the number of times the block was reached during the run.

$$
t = \sum_k \begin{cases} \frac{t_{C,k}}{n_{C,k}} \cdot (n_{C,k} + n_{I,k}) & \text{if } n_{C,k} > 0 \\ t_{I,k} & \text{else} \end{cases} \tag{1}
$$

By tracking the statistics for each basic block with the help of the tracing functionality and the previously gathered control flow information, a change in the runtime behavior of the following loop iterations is correctly respected by the estimation. However, this is only true if there is no or only a similar fluctuation during the inaccurate execution. This is the main weakness of the methodology. In the future, implementing a mechanics for finding great discrepancies during a loop can allow switching back to the accurate model to solve this issue.

4   Evaluation

To assess the introduced methodology, two real world algorithms were chosen. The first one consists of an algorithm for Frequency Modulated Continuous Wave (FMCW) radars which are often used within vehicles to process the raw data of the radar antennas [15]. With the help of multiple Fast Fourier Transformations (FFTs), it is possible to extract range and velocity information from the delay and the Doppler shift of the signal [16]. A Constant False Alarm Rate (CFAR) algorithm identifies single targets in the output of the FFTs [12]. When using an array of antennas, the direction of the targets can also be determined [1]. The procedure is the same as required for the velocity and range and also includes multiple FFTs and the CFAR approach. For the purpose of evaluating the methodology, an example situation was generated. Its recordings are used for every run of the algorithm.

The second algorithm used for the evaluation of the reference implementation of this methodology is a decoder of the High Efficiency Video Codec (HEVC, also known as H.265) [13]. As a showcase, 30 frames of the akiyo sequence encoded with FFmpeg [6] are decoded. The HEVC decoder [10] is chosen because the complexity of many loops depend on the size of a coded block such that execution times can differ significantly. For example, an inter coded block can have a size of 8×8 to up to 64×64 pixels. Hence, the complexity for predicting the large block is 64 times higher. HEVC is selected as an example to show that the proposed approach can also cope with loops of variable complexity.

4.1   Metric

A quantitative comparison with other approaches that increase the accuracy of instruction accurate models or decrease the simulation runtime of cycle accurate models is not easy. There is no well-known metric that takes the required simulation time as well as the resulting exactness into account. They are most of the time viewed as independent dimensions. For this reason, a new unit is introduced that determines "how much accuracy for each time unit" is achieved. To also allow comparisons of multiple algorithms which are run on a simulated architecture using the presented methodology, the accuracy and simulation time themselves have to be normalized. This enables to compare different approaches, e.g. the ones presented in the related work section, regarding their improvement over the standard approaches with respect to both units. In this paper this approach is used to show how different amounts of accurate iterations for each loop change the quality of the methodology.

To implement the metric, the required simulation time and error of the TS and O3 model are defined as reference points. The O3 model represents the accurate but slow simulator while the TS model is taken as the fast but inaccurate one. We define the exactness of the TS model to one since it is the worst case scenario. In contrast, the O3 model has an exactness of two. The reference implementation of the proposed methodology will have values between these two numbers. Consequently, the accuracy function e_n is defined as shown in Eq. (2). $t_{s,x}$ denotes the estimated time for which the exactness is calculated. $t_{s,O3}$ is the estimated time of the O3 model and $t_{s,TS}$ is the estimated time the TS model provides. The absolute error in comparison to the O3 model can be found in the numerator of the fraction while the absolute error of the TS model is in the denominator. To have the range between one and two, the resulting relative error of the fraction is deducted from two. For the TS model the accuracy, according to the term, is one while for the O3 model it is two.

$$e_n\left(t_{s,x}\right) = 2 - \frac{|t_{s,x} - t_{s,O3}|}{|t_{s,TS} - t_{s,O3}|} \tag{2}$$

In a similar way, the simulation time is normalized and defined. The function t_n is given in Eq. (3). t_x is the required simulation time for which the normalized simulation time is computed. t_{TS} is the simulation time needed by the TS model and t_{O3} is the simulation time the O3 model needs for a full simulation run. In the numerator, the absolute deviation from the TS model is determined and set in relation to the deviation of the O3 model from the TS model. The one is added to have the resulting values within the expected range of one (simulation time of TS model) to two (simulation time of O3 model).

$$t_n\left(t_x\right) = 1 + \frac{\left|t_x - t_{TS}\right|}{\left|t_{O3} - t_{TS}\right|} \qquad (3)$$

The quotient a_n of the two normalized values (shown in (4)) yields a synthetic number that can be used for comparisons of runs with different configurations. For the reference models, it is exactly one. Approaches that achieve a higher number have a better accuracy per simulation time ratio which means that the target was reached. On the other hand, values smaller than one mean that the approach performs worse with regard to the accuracy per time in comparison to the reference models. However, since the accuracy or the time itself might be increased, the methodology might still be beneficial. Different situations of the introduced metric are depicted in Fig. 2. Besides the angle bisecting line that shows where the values are the same as achieved by the reference models, it also shows two examples of lines where the results are better or worse. If a_n yields two, a perfect solution is obtained because the accuracy of the O3 model is reached with a simulation time that is equal to the TS model. This happens within Fig. 2 at the point where the line annotated with "2" has a normalized accuracy of two with a normalized simulation time of one.

$$a_n\left(t_{s,x}, t_x\right) = \frac{e_n\left(t_{s,x}\right)}{t_n\left(t_x\right)} \qquad (4)$$

The presented metric is used to compare the runs of the different algorithms using different configuration options against the TS and O3 model. The results are given in the following section.

4.2   Results

While the estimated time is deterministic for each run using the same configuration options, the required simulation time is variable due to running the simulation on a computer with a preemptive operating system. Therefore, each configuration was measured ten times on the same computer with no additional load and the average simulation time was calculated.

The raw data used for calculating the metric can be seen in Figs. 4 and 5. The latter shows the simulation time required for each iteration while the first one depicts the estimated time. As a reference, the TS and O3 values are also drawn. The plots confirm the previously stated behavior differences. While the estimated runtime of the radar algorithm converges fast and does not change

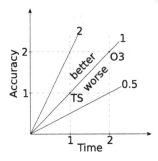

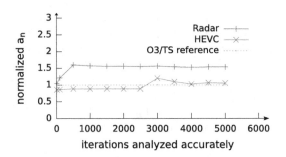

Fig. 2. Plot with the two normalized values used for the axes that shows when a quotient of the values is considered better or worse than the TS and O3 reference

Fig. 3. The value for the metric of both real world algorithms depending on the amount of accurately executed iterations. The reference value is depicted in gray.

much from 500 accurately analyzed iterations upwards, the HEVC algorithm has two points where the estimated runtime decreases tremendously. On the other hand, the simulation time increases in this range while the radar has only small fluctuations which can be traced back to the behavior of the host operating system. It has to be remarked that the estimated time of radar algorithm further increases when using more accurate iterations. However, this means a number of several tens of thousands and is not shown in the figures. The simulation time only rises moderately in this range. For comparison, the total iteration count of the longest loop within our example radar scenario is around 740,000 meaning that only a very small part of the actual runtime was analyzed accurately.

Figure 3 shows the final values of the metric presented in the previous section. The numbers of the different algorithms depending on the number of iterations a loop was executed accurately before switching to the instruction accurate model are depicted. For the radar algorithm the new methodology converges really fast, since it already reaches its maximal accuracy per time with just 500 accurate iterations of the outer-most loops. On the other hand, for the HEVC algorithm, the technique performs worse than the O3 and TS model when only running less than 3000 iterations accurately. However, with 3000 exact iterations, the value rises above the reference. This can be explained by certain loops within the HEVC which have a different runtime characteristic above a certain threshold. When executing iteration 2657 the loop exhibits a greater processing time than all iterations before which results in a dramatic increase in estimated accuracy. Cases like this having a loop displaying a huge difference in runtime between two iterations are only correctly analysable with the methodology when a more detailed examination of the CFG is performed. Due to the rising simulation time when emulating the loop iterations with the greater runtime, the metric results get worse again and approach the reference while still staying slightly above. The loop having the greatest iteration count of the HEVC algorithm spins is executed more than 114,000 times.

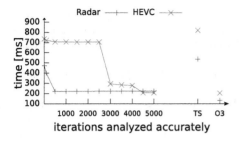
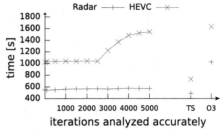

Fig. 4. The estimated times of the algorithms depending on the amount of accurately executed iterations.

Fig. 5. The measured simulation time of the algorithms depending on the amount of accurately executed iterations.

With these results, one can see that the benefits of the methodology is dependent on the algorithm and the configuration of the simulation. The radar processing consists mostly of similar loops that have the same behavior during each iteration. Hence, its value in the introduced metric shows nice results. In contrast, the HEVC has very heterogeneous loop behaviors which make it difficult to get benefits from the methodology without a more detailed control flow analysis. Such an addition could be integrated in the future to achieve a high accuracy with less accurate iterations by a more refined selection of the accurately executed iterations of a loop.

5   Conclusion

In this paper, a new methodology for estimating the runtime of a program with the help of simulation is shown. It tries to reach the accuracy of a cycle accurate simulator while still providing the speed of an instruction accurate emulation. For this, loops are only partially run with the cycle accurate model of the gem5 simulator and the estimated runtime of the remaining loops is extrapolated from the results of the first few. Evaluating a radar algorithm and the HEVC using this new approach shows that simulation based runtime analysis can benefit from the methodology. However, it strongly depends on the behavior of the algorithm. For better results, a more detailed control flow analysis might be required in the future. Though, the first measurements show that the introduced technique is promising.

Acknowledgement. This work is supported by the Bavarian Research Foundation (BFS) as part of their research project "FORMUS³IC".

References

1. Adve, R.: Direction of arrival estimation (2013)
2. Binkert, N., Beckmann, B., Black, G., Reinhardt, S.K., Saidi, A., Basu, A., Hestness, J., Hower, D.R., Krishna, T., Sardashti, S., Sen, R., Sewell, K., Shoaib, M., Vaish, N., Hill, M.D., Wood, D.A.: The gem5 simulator. SIGARCH Comput. Archit. News **39**(2), 1–7 (2011)

3. Carlson, T.E., Heirmant, W., Eeckhout, L.: Sniper: exploring the level of abstraction for scalable and accurate parallel multi-core simulation. In: 2011 International Conference for High Performance Computing, Networking, Storage and Analysis (SC), pp. 1–12, November 2011

4. Cooper, K., Torczon, L.: Engineering a Compiler, 2nd edn. Elsevier, Amsterdam (2012)

5. Cooper, K.D., Harvey, T.J., Kennedy, K.: A simple, fast dominance algorithm. Softw. Pract. Exp. **4**(1–10), 1–8 (2001)

6. FFmpeg (2017). http://ffmpeg.org/. Accessed 10 2017

7. Fujimoto, R.: Parallel and distributed simulation. In: Proceedings of the 2015 Winter Simulation Conference, WSC 2015, pp. 45–59. IEEE Press, Piscataway (2015)

8. Haririan, P., Garcia-Ortiz, A.: Non-intrusive DVFS emulation in gem5 with application to self-aware architectures. In: 2014 9th International Symposium on Reconfigurable and Communication-Centric Systems-on-Chip (ReCoSoC), pp. 1–7, May 2014

9. Hsieh, M., Pedretti, K., Meng, J., Coskun, A., Levenhagen, M., Rodrigues, A.: SST + gem5 = a scalable simulation infrastructure for high performance computing. In: Proceedings of the 5th International ICST Conference on Simulation Tools and Techniques, SIMUTOOLS 2012, pp. 196–201. ICST (Institute for Computer Sciences, Social-Informatics and Telecommunications Engineering), ICST, Brussels (2012)

10. Joint Collaborative Team on Video Coding: HEVC test model reference software (HM). https://hevc.hhi.fraunhofer.de/, https://hevc.hhi.fraunhofer.de/

11. Menard, C., Jung, M., Castrillon, J., Wehn, N.: System simulation with gem5 and systemC: the keystone for full interoperability. In: Proceedings of the IEEE International Conference on Embedded Computer Systems Architectures Modeling and Simulation (SAMOS). IEEE, July 2017

12. Rohling, H.: Radar CFAR thresholding in clutter and multiple target situations. IEEE Trans. Aerosp. Electron. Syst. AES **19**(4), 608–621 (1983)

13. Sullivan, G., Ohm, J., Han, W.J., Wiegand, T.: Overview of the high efficiency video coding (HEVC) standard. IEEE Trans. Circuits Syst. Video Technol. **22**(12), 1649–1668 (2012)

14. Wang, J., Beu, J., Bheda, R., Conte, T., Dong, Z., Kersey, C., Rasquinha, M., Riley, G., Song, W., Xiao, H., Xu, P., Yalamanchili, S.: Manifold: a parallel simulation framework for multicore systems. In: 2014 IEEE International Symposium on Performance Analysis of Systems and Software (ISPASS), pp. 106–115, March 2014

15. Wenger, J.: Automotive radar - status and perspectives. In: IEEE Compound Semiconductor Integrated Circuit Symposium, CSIC 2005, p. 4, October 2005

16. Winkler, V.: Range doppler detection for automotive FMCW radars. In: 2007 European Microwave Conference, pp. 1445–1448, October 2007

On-chip and Off-chip Networks

A CAM-Free Exascalable HPC Router
for Low-Energy Communications

Caroline Concatto[(✉)], Jose A. Pascual, Javier Navaridas, Joshua Lant,
Andrew Attwood, Mikel Lujan, and John Goodacre

School of Computer Science, University of Manchester, Manchester, UK
caroline.concatto@manchester.ac.uk

Abstract. Power consumption is the main hurdle in the race for designing Exascale-capable computing systems which would require deploying
millions of computing elements. While this problem is being addressed by
designing increasingly more power-efficient processing subsystems, little
effort has been put on reducing the power consumption of the interconnection network. This is precisely the objective of this work, in which
we study the benefits, in terms of both area and power, of avoiding
costly and power-hungry CAM-based routing tables deep-rooted in all
current networking technologies. We present our custom-made, FPGA-
based router based on a simple, arithmetic routing engine which is shown
to be much more power- and area-efficient than even a relatively small
2K-entry routing table which requires as much area and one order of
magnitude more power than our router.

1 Introduction

Exascale computing is the next challenge for the supercomputing community
aiming to design systems capable of delivering Exaflops (10^{18} floating point operations per second). To achieve these huge computing capabilities, systems will
require millions of interconnected computing elements to execute massive parallel applications. Traditionally these were High Performance Computing (HPC)
applications where the computation:communication ratio was heavily biased
towards the former. However, the wider availability of increasingly large computing facilities and the new paradigms associated to the ubiquitous digital economy
have favored the emergence of new data-oriented applications arising from the
massive amounts of scientific- or business-oriented data that are being generated. These new application domains (e.g. MapReduce [9], graph-analytics [7] or
new HPC database systems such as MonetDB [21]) impose completely different
needs to the computing systems (and specially to the interconnection and I/O
subsystems). In order to suit the necessities of these new kind of data-intensive
applications, new architectures and platforms are being developed, such as our

J. Goodacre—This work was funded by the European Union's Horizon 2020 research
and innovation programme under grant agreement No. 671553.

novel, custom-made architecture, ExaNeSt [14]. In such systems the Interconnection Network (IN) is crucial to ensure performance, mainly because it needs to support extreme levels of parallelism with applications using tens of thousands of nodes with any latency or bandwidth bottlenecks translating into severe penalties to execution time.

One of the main limitations for the scalability of HPC (and datacentre) facilities is power consumption. The largest current systems based on traditional HPC processors are over one order of magnitude[1] away from Exascale but already require a large, dedicated power station to supply electricity to the system. If we tried to scale computing systems just by putting more components together without changing the architectures or paradigms, we will end up requiring tens of power stations, just to power the system, which is obviously unattainable. Some steps towards reducing power have been taken in the computing subsystems by using ARM processors [4] or accelerators (e.g. GPGPU or FPGAs) that offer high FLOPs/Watt ratios. However, improving the efficiency of other subsystems has been typically ignored. For instance, the network can account for over 10% of the total power during peak utilization and up to 50% when the system is idle [1]. Other authors mention more conservative, but still significant power breakdowns in the range 10–20% [13]. This large share of the power bill of such systems motivates our search for more power-efficient IN designs.

In this regards, we notice that most networking technologies, e.g., Infiniband or 10 Gbps/100 Gbps Ethernet, rely on huge routing tables which are typically implemented as content addressable memories (CAMs). CAMs are an integral part of the design and, indeed, tend to be much bigger than the router logic itself (i.e. buffers, crossbar, flow control mechanisms, etc.). This is because tens of thousands of entries need to be stored to be able to reach all the nodes of the system [22]. In addition, routing tables create other scalability issues. First, as the size of the system increases, the size of the tables (number of entries) needs to grow accordingly. Furthermore, given that routing tables have information distributed across the whole system, they are quite sensitive to routing inconsistencies and, obviously, consistency mechanisms are in themselves another limit to scalability. All the reasons above motivate our design where we get rid of routing tables to achieve substantial savings in terms of area and power footprint. Our FPGA-based router relies on simple arithmetic routing instead. For the purpose of this work we have considered common topologies (fattree [18], dragonfly [16]) but other topologies are possible. Our experiments measure area and power consumption for varying number of ports and CAM entries. Results show that routing tables are not only prohibitive in terms of area, since a relatively small CAM uses more area than a 16-port router, but also that they can consume the whole power allowance of the FPGA.

---

[1] See www.top500.org.

2   Related Work

One of the first steps towards using FPGA for networking was the NetFPGA [25] project which provides software and hardware infrastructure for rapid prototyping of open-source high-speed networking platforms. NetFPGA platform enables to modify parts of it and compare with other implementations. However, there are many differences between NetFPGA and our home-made router. First of all, NetFPGA focuses on IP networks and, thus, relies on routing tables, which as explained we want to avoid. Moreover, IP networking has many overheads that dismiss it as a good infrastructure for HPC networks due to inadequate throughput and latency. Finally, the NetFPGA platform has many features that consume lots of area and power but are not required in the context of ExaNeSt.

While arithmetic routing *per se* is not a new idea, its use in recent years has been restricted to cube-like topologies such as the ones in the BlueGene family of supercomputers [6] or the TOFU interconnect [2]. To our knowledge, flexible architectures relying on arithmetic routing, but capable of being arranged into different topologies just by reconfiguring the firmware (to update the routing logic) such as the one we introduce here have never been proposed before. Arithmetic routing is commonly used in SW to fill the routing tables of the switches of table-based technologies (see, e.g., [23] which generates routes arithmetically and then embed them in the routing tables of an Infiniband IN). There also exist more advanced strategies (also for Infiniband) that take into consideration the congestion of the links by storing this information in the routing tables together with the destination address to perform routing decisions [24]. More recently, the Bull EXascale Interconnect (BXI) [10] has followed a similar approach. They use a 2-stage routing strategy [22]: first an off-line algorithm calculates the paths between each source and destination. These paths are deterministic and populated into the routing tables during system start-up (could be done arithmetically). The second stage is performed on-line, when the system is running, and can change the previously calculated static routes in order to avoid congestion or failures. The 48-port routers, implemented as ASICs, store 64K entries for each port for a total of 3M entries per router. Bull switches use 2 routing tables, a bigger one with the addresses set at start-up and another small table used in case of faults or congestion in which the addresses are used to repair faulty routes.

The only effort on minimizing the impact of routing tables on the networking equipment we are aware of is on strategies to reduce their footprint. For example, using a 2-level CAM routing strategy [3]: the first level stores addresses that require a full match in order to select the output port, the second level stores masks. If the first level does not produce a match, then the selection of the port is performed based on similarity between the mask on level 2 and the destination address. This helps alleviating the impact of routing tables in terms of area and power to some extent, but the other scalability issues of routing tables still hold.

Alternatives to local CAMs do exist, but none of them would keep appropriate performance levels for FPGA-based HPC interconnects. For instance, using an off-chip CAM would severely slow packet processing because of the extra

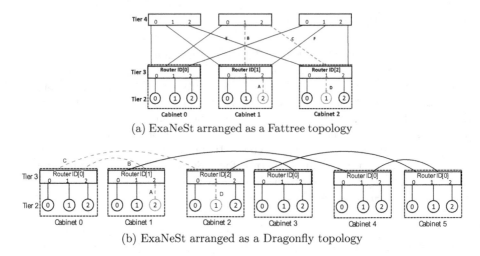

(a) ExaNeSt arranged as a Fattree topology

(b) ExaNeSt arranged as a Dragonfly topology

Fig. 1. ExaNeSt system-level networks with route examples in red (2, 1 to 1, 2). (Color figure online)

delays to go off-chip for routing information. Moreover in a extreme-density design, such as the one we propose in ExaNeSt, adding extra components to the already tightly packed boards is undesirable. Implementing the tables in RAM (as some low-end switches do), would render information fetching even slower due to the lack of parallel access. A proposal that assigns range(s) of addresses to ports [12] and routes to the port which matches the destination was a step towards getting rid of CAMS. However, it is restricted to tree-like topologies and does not scale very well for large networks because range complexity increases with network size.

3   ExaNeSt System Architecture

In this Section we introduce the architecture of ExaNeSt, which will be showcased by means of a small, 2-cabinet, prototype—currently under construction. An ExaNeSt system will require millions of low-power-consumption ARM+FPGA MPSoCs to reach Exascale and includes a unified, low-latency IN and a fully distributed storage subsystem with data spread across the nodes using local Non-Volatile Memory (NVM) storage. Our building block is a quad-FPGA-daughter-board (QFDB) based on Zynq Ultrascale+ MPSoCs[2]. The next level (Tier 1) is the *Blade*, which is composed by up to 16 QFDBs interconnected using a backplane that delivers high-bandwidth connectivity, whilst reducing the costs and power consumption of external cables and transceivers. Six of these Blades are contained in a *Chassis* which also incorporates our FPGA router with a variable number of links that are used to interconnect the blades (Tier 2) as well

---

[2] See https://www.xilinx.com/support/documentation/white_papers/wp482-zu-pwr-perf.pdf.

as to provide uplinks to the system-level interconnect (Tier 3 and above depicted in Fig. 1). As these routers are implemented on FPGAs, the number of uplinks can vary in order to deliver networks with different characteristics. Next, we will focus on describing the architecture of the FPGA-based router used in Tier 3 (and above).

3.1   Router Architecture

The architecture of the router (inside the red square) is depicted in Fig. 2 together with the FIFOs, MACs and PHYs. We built a 3-stage pipelined router using a wormhole switching approach in which the packets (composed of header, payload and footer) are split into multiple flits of size 66 bits (64 bits for data and 2 extra bits to control the beginning and the end of the packets). The router sends and receives flits from and to the FIFO using a handshake flow control mechanism implemented using two signals: `val` and `ack`. When data is ready to be sent in the FIFO the `val` signal is enabled; if there is space to store the data into the router, the `ack` signal will be enabled. When at some point there is no more data available in the FIFO or no more space at the router, the corresponding signal will be disabled. A similar process happens in the output ports. The data sent and received by the FIFO comes from and goes to the 10 Gbps custom-made MAC layer which is connected to the 10 Gbps transceivers (PHY), which serialize/deserialize the data between the routers using an optical fiber. Our router uses *Virtual Output Queues* (VOQs) [8] to reduce Head of Line (HOL) blocking and, in turn, minimize congestion. Although the use of VOQs increases resource utilization, we expect the extra resources to be compensated by the performance gains and the savings of our table-free design.

The three stages of our router are as follows. **Stage-1:**, the router receives the `val` signal (a new packet has arrived to an input port). The header flit will be stored in a register. **Stage-2:** the *arithmetic routing block* decides, based on the destination address of the packet, the output port to forward the packet. Then the desired VOQ is selected and used for the remaining flits of the packet. **Stage-3:** the switch allocator selects one input port (among all the requesting ones) to be forwarded through the crossbar to the required output port. For simplicity we use round robin arbitration, but others are possible.

3.2   Routing Algorithms

Our protocol relies on a geographic addressing scheme in which the location of all the components is embedded in their address. This comes as a side-effect of the highly hierarchical system. The current prototypes would require 22 bits out of the 24 available for encoding end-point ids (2 bits for the chip within a DB, 4 bits for the DB within a mezzanine, 4 bits for the mezzanine within a chassis, 4 bits for the chassis within a cabinet and 8 bits for the cabinet). This would leave 2 free bits within an address that could be used for different purposes, e.g., multipath routing, priority levels or system-level operations. Such a naming convention is enabled by the fact that FPGAs come without a defined address and that

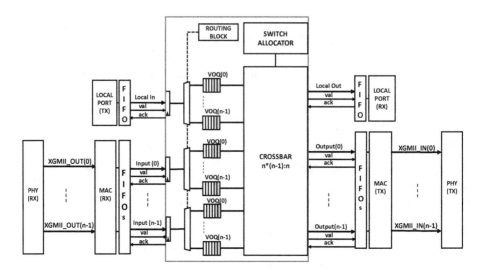

Fig. 2. Block diagram of the 3-stage router plus the FIFOs, the MACs and the transceivers (PHYs). (Color figure online)

initializing it at boot-up time would be trivial and would require barely any overhead, just by leveraging locational information into the different levels, e.g. through system-level controllers or even an EPROM holding this information.

It is our vision that having this hierarchical information within the addressing scheme can be exploited by means of arithmetic routing as many high performance topologies feature very simple routing algorithms that take routing decisions based only on a single coordinate within the hierarchy (e.g. k-ary n-trees and Dragonfly, as provided here or others such as generalised hypercubes [5], Clos [20] or torus [2,6]). Indeed, such arithmetic forms of routing are specially well suited for FPGAs as they would require very simple logic to be implemented and could be changed accordingly to the selected topology as opposed to an ASIC-based implementation, which must be static (or software based).

Algorithm 1 shows the routing algorithm for a fattree. Packets travel up and then down the tree according to the destination address, tier and router ID. This is done in order to avoid deadlocks [19]. First, the algorithm checks if the router is in Tier-4 (the top of the tree), in which case the packet goes down through the port connected to the destination cabinet. If the packet is in Tier-3, the router checks if the destination address is local to its cabinet, in which case it takes the port connected to the corresponding chassis. Otherwise the packet goes through any of the uplink ports (using Round Robin for simplicity), seamlessly performing multipath routing. In the future we expect to investigate improved congestion-aware policies. Figure 1a, shows a route example marked with red dotted lines. We denote addresses as $[Cabinet, Chassis]$. The source, $[1,2]$, sends a packet to the destination $[2,1]$. First $[1,2]$ sends the packet to router 1 in Tier 3 using link A. Then, the packet will be sent through any uplink (B, in the

---

Algorithm 1. Routing strategy for fattree

1: **procedure** ROUTEFATTREE(*header, tier, routerId*)
2:     **if** *tier* = 4 **then**   ▷ top tier
3:         *req* ← *header.cabinet*
4:     **else if** *header.cabinet* = *routerId* **then**
5:         *req* ← *header.chassis*   ▷ go down
6:     **else**
7:         *req* ← *port going up*   ▷ go up
8:     **return** *req*

Algorithm 2. Routing strategy for dragonfly

1: **procedure** ROUTEDRAGONFLY(*header, routerId*)
2:     **if** *header.cabinet* = *routerId* **then**
3:         *req* ← *header.chassis*   ▷ go down
4:     **else if** *group(header.cabinet)* = *group(routerId)* **then**
5:         *req* ← *intraGroupPort(header.cabinet)*   ▷ same group
6:     **else**
7:         *req* ← *interGroupPort(header.cabinet)*   ▷ route to other group
8:     **return** *req*

---

example) to Tier 4, because of line 7 in Algorithm 1. Now the packet is in Tier 4, so Algorithm 1 dictates to follow link C to Cabinet 2 (line 3) and the packet arrives to router 2 in Tier 3. Now the router ID and destination Cabinet are the same, so line 5 in Algorithm 1 selects port 1 (Chassis of destination address is 1) and the packet is forwarded through link D. Finally, the packet arrives to [2, 1], and is routed to the correct QFDB through the lower Tier networks.

Algorithm 2 shows the routing algorithm for dragonfly. Packets travel between groups according to the destination address and router ID. First the algorithm checks if the packet is addressed to the local router, in which case the packet goes down to the corresponding chassis. If not the router checks whether it goes to another cabinet in the group in which case it takes the port connected to the corresponding router. Otherwise the packet needs to move to a different group, either directly through their up-ports or through another router in the group through the intra-group ports. Functions `group()`, `intraGroupPort()` and `interGroupPort()` are arithmetic and use router coordinates and topology parameters only, but are not shown here due to space constraints. Figure 1b shows a route example between nodes [1, 2] and [2, 1]. First [1, 2] sends the packet to router 1 in Tier 3 using link A. Then, the packet will be sent to router 0 through link B, as dictated by line 7. Given inter-group routing is still needed Router 0 will forward to Router 2 following link C, (line 7). Now the router ID and destination Cabinet are the same, so line 3 selects port 1 and the packet is forwarded to the destination chassis through link D.

4   Evaluation

In this Section we firstly present our set-up to measure the area, power and performance (Throughput and latency) required to implement the router and the routing tables. FPGAs have a restricted amount of resources and router design must scale nicely, i.e., do not explode in terms of resources (or power) as the number of ports or the size of the CAMs increase. Therefore we measure the area and power consumption of the approaches to show their scalability. Finally we measure throughput and latency as they are the most important performance metrics for HPC systems.

4.1   Experimental Setup

We implemented the router architecture described in Sect. 3 (and shown in Fig. 2) as a soft core IP in Verilog and synthesise it in a Virtex-709 FPGA. The transceivers (PHY in Figure 2) are hard-core IPs in the FPGA containing a serializer/deserializer (serdes) IP working at 10 Gbps and 156.25 MHz[3]. We use a custom MAC IP which synchronizes the clocks between the transceivers of the sender and the receiver by adding a short preamble and footer in the packets. Finally the router was instantiated with a varying number of ports plus one local port (used as injector/consumer for testing purposes). The FPGA area is measured and considers the amount of Look-up-Tables (LUT), LUTRAM (LUT used as memory), Flip-flops (FF) and Memories (BRAM) consumed by the router and the routing table. To measure the performance, we used two interconnected Virtex FPGAs. In this experiment, the router has 4 external ports plus one local port because our development boards have only 4 SFP ports. Thus the routers were instantiated with 3 downlinks + 1 uplink. The two boards were wire connected using optic fibers and the traffic was generated and received by soft-core MicroBlaze processors attached to the local ports. Traffic was composed of packets with 100 flits length generated at intervals of 11 clock cycles. We provide the local port interface with counters to measure the number of packets received in 1 s and the delay to receive the first packet after the system has started.

4.2   Area

The BRAMs were used to implement the buffers in the MAC layer. The LUT and FFs were used to implement the logic and the LUTRAMs were used to implement the VOQs (with space for 16 flits each) and the memory in the routing table. In case of the routing tables, for the sake of clarity, we just show the resources used to implement them, not the whole router. Given that the footprint of the arithmetic routing block is negligible, implementing the switch with the routing tables will require, at least, the same amount of resources as implementing each of them separately.

---

[3] See seen on 8th January 2018: https://www.xilinx.com/support/documentation/ip_documentation/ten_gig_eth_pcs_pma/v6_0/pg068-ten-gig-eth-pcs-pma.pdf.

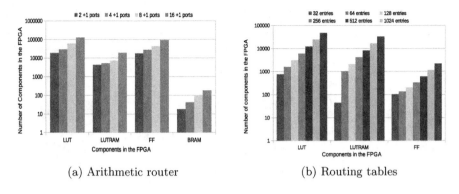

(a) Arithmetic router   (b) Routing tables

Fig. 3. Area used in the FPGA.

Figure 3a shows the area results for our arithmetic router, including the MACs and PHYs, the latter two takes most of the router area. We have measured the area of between 2 and 16 ports (plus the local port, used for evaluation purposes). The maximum area required in the FPGA is around 30% of the LUTs for the 16-port version. More importantly, resource consumption scales roughly linearly with the number of ports which show the scalability of our design. For comparison, Fig. 3b shows the area required to implement routing tables with different number of entries, from 32 up to 2048. Routing tables were implemented following the node-table approach shown in [11] in which one table is shared among all the input ports of the router. The logic of the routing table will match the destination address with the stored node addresses and then, extract from that CAM line the output port to be used. The area required increases roughly linearly with the number of entries requiring almost 20% of the LUTRAMs for 2K entries. Even for a relatively small routing table by today's standards (e.g. 64K entries used by Bull interconnect [10], 48K for Infiniband or 32K for Ethernet [15]) these routing tables take a significant part of the FPGA resources and would seriously limit the scalability and the number of ports we could implement. Moreover tables with 256 entries or more cannot work at our target frequency, as shown in Fig. 3b. This is because the huge MUX/DEMUX trees required to access the tables severely increase the critical path. Comparing the routing table area with the router is not trivial as the routing tables uses more LUTRAM to implement memory and the router uses more FF and LUTs to implement its logic. In terms of LUTs a 4-port router consumes almost the same as a routing table with 1K entries. However for LUTRAMs a 4-port router uses almost the same area as a 256-entry routing table.

4.3   Power Consumption

Figure 4a shows the power consumption estimated by Xilinx tools for routers with 2, 4, 8 and 16 ports (plus the local port) for the different resources used by the router. Notice that the GTH transceivers work at a frequency of

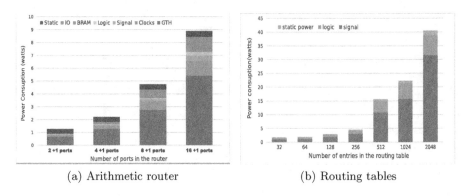

(a) Arithmetic router   (b) Routing tables

Fig. 4. Power consumption in Watts.

156.25 MHz in order to transmit at 10 Gbps. However the router with 16 ports works at a slightly lower frequency, 140 MHz, due to the size of the crossbar that grows exponentially. Other aspect of the implementation in the FPGA that should be noticed is that Virtex-709 only has 4 SFP+ connectors (hence 4 GTH transceivers). For that reason the remaining serial ports for the 8- and 16-port routers were placed in the FMC HPC connector (standard connection for any type of interface) of the FPGA using the same clock source (SFP+ connector). The results clearly show that the GTH transceivers are the resources that consume more power (higher than 50% of the total). The maximum power consumption (for 16 ports) is ~4 W which is relatively low; about 10% of the max FPGA power (40 W) for this implementation. Figure 4b shows the power consumed by the routing tables measured at a frequency of 156.25 MHz. We show both the dynamic (logic plus signal switching) and the static power. As expected the routing tables demand higher power as we increase the number of entries for the same frequency (156.25 MHz). For instance, a routing table with 2048 entries consumes 40 W, which is already the maximum FPGA power rendering the implementation of other elements impossible. In contrast 32 entries consumes less then ~4 W. A 8-ports router plus MACs and PHYs consumes the same power as 256 entries routing table. Moreover a router with a routing table with 2K entries consumes almost 4 times more power than the proposed routers with 16 ports + 1.

4.4   Performance

We close this Section by measuring the throughput and latency of our design. Notice that a VOQ-based router using routing tables would theoretically have the same performance as ours (assuming that accessing the table can be done in one clock cycle and that the frequency remains the same). Our tests showed that the router is able to maintain a throughput higher than 8 Gbps (with 10 Gbps transceivers), which is acceptable for a first prototype. The main culprit for not being able to saturate the links (achieve 10 Gbps) is our custom

MAC implementation which stalls packet-forwarding in order to check whether the transceivers are synchronized. Regarding the latency per hop, our measurements drew between 70 to 80 clock cycles to traverse both routers. This latency is the time required to traverse the source router (3 cycles), MAC (12 cycles), both transceivers TX and RX (25–45 clock cycles each) and the MAC in the destination router (12 cycles). Note that data transmission is much slower than taking routing decisions in our design.

5   Conclusions and Future Work

The interconnection network will play a crucial role in future systems that aim to break the Exascale frontier. One of the main concerns in these systems is the reduction of the power consumption, issue that is being faced by using low-power computing elements or other power-efficient devices delivering high performance/Watt. However in these massive interconnected systems the network can be responsible of consuming a large share of the required power, so traditional approaches are not suitable any more. To deal with this issue we propose a disrupting interconnection architecture that avoids the use of costly and power hungry routing tables. These are deep-rooted in commercial devices for HPC and datacentre networks. Our design leverages an FPGA-based arithmetic router with our geographical addressing scheme.

Our experimental work shows that the amount of resources required to implement the router is small allowing designs with more than 32-ports in this particular FPGA model. Regarding the power consumption the routing tables exceed the maximum power output of the FPGA as early as 2K entries. On the other hand, the router implemented using the arithmetic routing requires less than 5 W, that is, 12.5% of the power delivered by the FPGA. Finally we measured the throughput and latency showing promising figures of 8 Gbps and 70–80 cycles (500 ns) per hop, respectively. Moreover, we found that avoiding the use of routing tables is essential for our design as a small CAM table (2K entries), would not only require ∼20% of the FPGA resources, but would also exhaust the power budget of the FPGA. In the future, we plan to improve the performance of the router optimizing the MAC layer. We will also evaluate the area and power consumption of the arithmetic router using more modern FPGAs like the Virtex UltraScale+ from Xilinx. Finally we want to explore the impact of our VOQs + arithmetic router on the performance of larger networks by using our in-house developed simulator, INSEE [17].

References

1. Abts, D., et al.: Energy proportional datacenter networks. In: International Symposium on Computer Architecture, ISCA 2010, pp. 338–347. ACM, New York (2010)
2. Ajima, Y., et al.: The Tofu interconnect. IEEE Micro **32**(1), 21–31 (2012)

3. Al-Fares, et al.: A scalable, commodity data center network architecture. In: ACM SIGCOMM 2008 Conference on Data Communication, SIGCOMM 2008, pp. 63–74. ACM, New York (2008)
4. Aroca, R.V., Gonçalves, L.M.G.: Towards green data centers: a comparison of ×86 and ARM architectures power efficiency. J. Parallel Distrib. Comput. **72**(12), 1770–1780 (2012)
5. Bhuyan, L.N., Agrawal, D.P.: Generalized hypercube and hyperbus structures for a computer network. IEEE Trans. Comput. **33**(4), 323–333 (1984)
6. Chen, D., et al.: Looking under the hood of the IBM Blue Gene/Q network. In: Conference for High Performance Computing, Networking, Storage and Analysis (SC), pp. 1–12, November 2012
7. Cuzzocrea, et al.: Big graph analytics: the state of the art and future research agenda. In: Proceedings of the 17th International Workshop on Data Warehousing and OLAP, DOLAP 2014, pp. 99–101, ACM, New York (2014)
8. Dally, W., Towles, B.: Principles and Practices of Interconnection Networks. Morgan Kaufmann Publishers Inc., San Francisco (2003)
9. Dean, J., et al.: Mapreduce: simplified data processing on large clusters. Commun. ACM **51**(1), 107–113 (2008)
10. Derradji, S., et al.: The BXI interconnect architecture. In: IEEE Annual Symposium on High-Performance Interconnects, HOTI 2015, pp. 18–25. IEEE Computer Society, Washington (2015)
11. Duato, J., et al.: Interconnection Networks: An Engineering Approach. Morgan Kaufmann Publishers Inc., San Francisco (2002)
12. Gómez, C., et al.: Deterministic versus adaptive routing in fat-trees. In: Workshop on Communication Architecture on Clusters (CAC 2007) (2007)
13. Heller, B., et al.: ElasticTree: saving energy in data center networks
14. Katevenis, M., et al.: The exanest project: interconnects, storage, and packaging for exascale systems. In: 2016 Euromicro Conference on Digital System Design (DSD), pp. 60–67, August 2016
15. Kieu, T.C., et al.: An interconnection network exploiting trade-off between routing table size and path length. In: International Symposium on Computing and Networking (CANDAR), pp. 666–670, November 2016
16. Kim, J., et al.: Technology-driven, highly-scalable dragonfly topology. In: 2008 International Symposium on Computer Architecture, pp. 77–88, June 2008
17. Navaridas, J., Miguel-Alonso, J., Pascual, J.A., Ridruejo, F.J.: Simulating and evaluating interconnection networks with insee. Simul. Model. Pract. Theory **19**(1), 494–515 (2011). http://www.sciencedirect.com/science/article/pii/S1569190X1000184X
18. Petrini, F., Vanneschi, M.: k-ary n-trees: high performance networks for massively parallel architectures. In: International Parallel Processing Symposium, pp. 87–93 (1997)
19. Sancho, J.C., et al.: Effective methodology for deadlock-free minimal routing in infiniband networks. In: Proceedings International Conference on Parallel Processing, pp. 409–418 (2002)
20. Singh, A., et al.: Jupiter rising: a decade of Clos topologies and centralized control in Google's datacenter network. In: ACM Conference on Special Interest Group on Data Communication, SIGCOMM 2015, pp. 183–197. ACM, New York (2015)
21. Vermeij, M., et al.: MonetDB, a novel spatial columnstore DBMS. In: Free and Open Source for Geospatial (FOSS4G) Conference, OSGeo (2008)
22. Vignéras, P., Quintin, J.N.: The BXI routing architecture for exascale supercomputer. J. Supercomput. **72**(12), 4418–4437 (2016)

23. Zahavi, E.: Fat-tree routing and node ordering providing contention free traffic for MPI global collectives. J. Parallel Distrib. Comput. **72**(11), 1423–1432 (2012)
24. Zahid, F., et al.: A weighted fat-tree routing algorithm for efficient load-balancing in infini band enterprise clusters. In: 2015 23rd Euromicro International Conference on Parallel, Distributed, and Network-Based Processing, pp. 35–42, March 2015
25. Zilberman, N., et al.: NetFPGA SUME: toward 100 Gbps as research commodity. IEEE Micro **34**(5), 32–41 (2014)

Lightweight Hardware Synchronization for Avoiding Buffer Overflows in Network-on-Chips

Martin Frieb[✉], Alexander Stegmeier, Jörg Mische, and Theo Ungerer

Institute of Computer Science, University of Augsburg, 86159 Augsburg, Germany
{martin.frieb,alexander.stegmeier,mische,
ungerer}@informatik.uni-augsburg.de

Abstract. Buffer overflows are a serious problem when running message-passing programs on network-on-chip based many-core processors. A simple synchronization mechanism ensures that data is transferred when nodes need it. Thereby, it avoids full buffers and interruption at any other time. However, software synchronization is not able to completely achieve these objectives, because its flits may still interrupt nodes or fill buffers. Therefore, we propose a lightweight hardware synchronization. It requires only small architectural changes as it comprises only very small components and it scales well. For controlling our hardware supported synchronization, we add two new assembler instructions. Furthermore, we show the difference in the software development process and evaluate the impact on the execution time of global communication operations and required receive buffer slots.

1 Introduction

In recent years, more and more many-core processors appeared. Typically, they are connected via a *network-on-chip (NoC)*. In a typical NoC [1,2] all nodes are connected to the network via a *network interface (NI)* containing a send and a receive buffer. As buffers occupy a high amount of hardware logic [18], hardware designers tend to minimize the number of possible buffer entries. Especially the receive buffers need to be of an appropriate size to avoid performance degradation when they are full.

Parallel programs often diverge during their execution, causing some processors executing program parts being far ahead of other processors. In distributed systems, it is often a strategy to send data to some other node without waiting for that node to be at the same part of the program, i.e. needing this data yet [15]. The receiver node just stores this data away in its memory and gets it from there when it actually processes it. This strategy is important because communication is a major bottleneck in distributed systems. However, in NoCs receive buffers are quite small and core-local memory is limited. Therefore, sending data to some node without checking if this node is ready to handle this data might lead to buffer overflows and deadlocks.

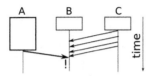

Fig. 1. Node C fills the receive buffer of node B, which is currently waiting for flits from node A. Thus, node B is busy processing received flits before it can answer the request from node A which it was originally waiting for. Boxes represent local computation times and arrows the delivery of flits.

The problem is illustrated in Fig. 1: There are three nodes A, B and C running a parallel application. Each of them does some local computation (boxes), followed by communication (flits represented as arrows). The computation of node A takes a little bit longer than on nodes B and C. Meanwhile, node C finishes its local computation and sends several flits to node B. Node A sends a request to node B, but node B is busy processing flits sent by node C. In the case when the receive buffer of node B is full, the request from node A even cannot be stored there. Thus, A has to wait until C is finished, then it can send its request to B again.

To avoid buffer overflows, we propose to add a synchronization mechanism: each node planing to send data has to wait for a flit from its intended receiver indicating that it is ready to handle incoming flits. A receiver node sends this flit when reaching its receive operation, ensuring that it is fully capable to process incoming flits. When implementing this synchronization in software, there might still arrive a lot of synchronization flits at a node (at most one from each other node). Thus, we suggest to realize it with hardware support. Our hardware implementation stores synchronization information and makes it available for the processing element when it asks for it. Thereby, we focus on minimal hardware and synchronization overhead.

Altogether, the contribution of our paper is a cheap and simple hardware synchronization mechanism which can easily be controlled in software, to increase performance while decreasing receive buffer size and hardware costs. Our approach is independent of router design and network topology.

The remainder of this paper is structured as follows: In the next section, we present related work and backgrounds. Afterwards, first our synchronization concept is explained in Sect. 3, followed by the description of the hardware implementation in Sect. 4 and subsequently it is evaluated in Sect. 5. Finally, the paper is concluded in Sect. 6.

2   Related Work and Background

As described in the introduction, we see the trend that many-core processors employ NoCs and communication takes place via send and receive operations. Some current multi-/many-core processors like the Intel Xeon Phi [4] do not employ send/receive operations or a NoC. Instead, they rely on shared memory and complex coherence protocols. In our opinion, these approaches do not scale well, because shared resources become the bottleneck when adding more cores. Therefore, we see the future of many-cores in employing NoCs, like e.g. in the Intel Single-chip Cloud Computer (SCC) [13]. Thereby, small buffers are benecifial, because otherwise most of the chip area would be occupied with buffers. In the remainder, we only consider architectures working with NoCs and explicit message passing.

Classical synchronization approaches were developed for distributed systems [14,15], where several constraints have to be respected. For example, communication times might be very long, packets or their parts might get lost or a node may drop out surprisingly. In a NoC, all nodes are reliable and communication times are short [1,2]. However, NoCs contribute a lot to the power consumption of many-core chips. The NoC of the Intel 80-core Teraflops research chip consumes 28% of the power per tile [17]. This percentage increases when more cores are put on the chip [3]. A high amount of this contribution stems from buffers. They need a lot of chip area, e.g. 60% of the tile area of the Tilera TILE64 many-core [18]. Nevertheless, compared to buffers in distributed systems, buffers in NoCs seem to be very small.[1] Therefore, flow control has to take place.

Our approach is a variation of *stop-and-wait protocols (s-a-ws)* [8,16]: in the original s-a-w after sending a flit, the sender has to wait for an acknowledgement from the receiver before sending the next flit. This means that each flit has to be acknowledged separately and leads to a high overhead. In contrast, in our approach the sender waits for a synchronization flit before starting to send. Instead of acknowledging each flit several flits can be sent. Then, the next synchronization takes place (see details in Sect. 3).

Another concept is credit-based flow control [7], which works as follows: When a node wants to send data to another node, it asks it for *credit*. Then, the receiver node tells the sender how many receive buffer slots it can use. Therefore, the sender knows how many flits it can send. While sending, the receiver might update the credit, then the sender can send more flits. Credit-based flow control is implemented e.g. in the Æthereal NoC [6]. Thereby, a forward channel is used to send data and a reverse channel to give feedback about buffer utilization. Our approach does not dynamically exchange detailed information about buffer utilization. Instead, it is intended to only find the starting point of the communication.

In Message Passing Interface (MPI), the standard for message-based communication [9], a function MPI_Ssend is defined for synchronous sending/receiving. It requires that the receiving nodes have already called the function before the sending node calls it. Therefore, it implements something similar as our synchronization for synchronous communication. However, this takes place at a higher abstraction level, while our synchronization is realized at low software level or even at hardware level.

---

[1] At distributed systems, there is plenty of buffer space because the main memory and swap space (hard disk) may be employed.

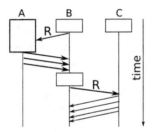

Fig. 2. Communication with **ready** synchronization: each node waits with sending flits until the receiving node is ready (**ready** flits are denoted with *R*).

Ruadulescu et al. [5] describe an approach to optimize the buffer size on NoCs with credit-based flow-control. They employ *time-division multiple access (TDMA)* with an application-specific schedule, i.e. contention-free paths are determined at design time of the *System-on-Chip (SoC)*. Ruadulescu et al. focus on building a SoC with buffers being as small as possible for a specific application. In contrast, our approach works at execution time and is application independent. Instead of determining the optimal buffer size at design time, our focus is on using buffers of a specific size as efficient as possible without having buffer overflows.

3 Synchronization Concept

In NoCs, bandwidth is restricted and a lot of communication takes place between nodes. Therefore, our idea is to avoid buffer overflows with just one synchronization flit – we call it **ready** flit. It does not contain payload and is just used to indicate that the receiver node is ready to receive data.[2] When the receiver node is ready to handle incoming data from the intended sender, it replies with a **ready** flit. This indicates that its receive buffer is free and any incoming flit will immediately be processed by the receiver node.

On the other side, the sender node does not send any flits to the receiver before it receives the **ready** flit. Meanwhile, it has to wait for it or execute some alternative code. When the **ready** flit arrives at the sender, it knows that the receiver is now ready and starts sending. In this way, it is ensured that the receiving node has free buffer slots and is ready to handle the received flits. Should it be necessary to tell the receiver how many flits follow, a header flit containing all relevant data might be sent and processed in software.

The concept of ready synchronization is illustrated in Fig. 2: as in Fig. 1, node B waits for data from nodes A and C. Since it first needs data from node A, it sends a **ready** flit there. Node A starts sending flits after its local computation

---

[2] When implementing **ready** synchronization in software, a particular payload is defined to represent **ready** flits. In the hardware implementation, a payload is not possible because **ready** flits do not reach the processing element of a node.

has finished. After receiving and processing all data from node A, node B sends a **ready** flit to node C, which in turn starts sending. This leads to node C waiting until node B is willing to receive data and avoids any slowdown caused by full buffers. Altogether, problems occuring when nodes do not meet a communication part at the same time are avoided: A node sending flits waits until the receiving node signalizes that it is ready. And a node receiving flits only sends one **ready** flit when it is ready to receive and then waits for flits from the sender (flit transfer starts "on demand"). Should the sender not yet be ready to send data, it just has to store the **ready** flit and can start sending as soon as it has finished its computation.

Our procedure is completely safe when synchronizing each flit (like in s-a-w), but then synchronization overhead is way too high. Instead, we intend that **ready** synchronization takes place only once per packet or program block (which may even imply communication in both directions). This works well as long as a packet does not exceed a certain length and each program block is written in a way that ensures that the receiver can process incoming flits fast enough. When a sender delivers faster than its receiver can process incoming flits and it sends more flits than the receiver node has buffer slots, buffers could still run full. In this case, the maximum number of flits before the next synchronization is limited by the number of receive buffer slots at the receiver node and the difference in time between executing a send and a receive operation.[3] When processing of flits at the receiver is at least as fast as flits are sent from the sender, there is no problem and therefore no restriction on the number of flits to be sent. However, it has to be considered that not all flits might arrive in constant time periods, although they may be sent in such. On their way through the NoC, flits may be hindered (e.g. collisions, deflection routing) on their direct way between sender and receiver. Thus, there might be periods where few flits arrive and others with more flits arriving – which might be more than the receiver node might handle at a time. An ideal number of flits between two synchronizations is up to the software developer and influenced by specific details of the architecture. Therefore, attention has to be paid that **ready** synchronization takes place in appropriate periods to avoid full buffers.

The **ready** synchronization concept is realizable without requiring additional hardware. Thereby, each node maintains a software array with one entry for each other node. These entries indicate if a node is ready to receive data (i.e. if a **ready** flit was received from a particular node). Nodes can send **ready** flits at any time. Thereby, **ready** flits are normal flits with a defined content. Code example 1 illustrates the source code of the sender side: the sender node has to check the array for the state of the receiver node. When it already indicates ready, it can jump over the **while** loop, reset the entry in the array and start sending. Otherwise, the code in the **while** loop is executed: the next flit is taken from the FIFO receive buffer. It has to be checked whether it is a **ready** flit

---

[3] For example, when a **send** operation takes 100 cycles and a **receive** operation takes 105 cycles, it takes 20 sends (2000 cycles) to permanently occupy one more buffer slot.

Code example 1. Code to be executed on sender side with software **ready** synchronization before **send** operation can start

```
// is receiver node ready?
while (ready_nodes[receiver] == 0) {
    // if not, receive next flit ...
    flit f = recv_from_fifo();
    // ... check it and mark corresponding node as ready
    if (f.data == READY) ready_nodes[f.receiver] = 1;
    // if it was the intended receiver, it will be noticed at while
}
// reset ready state of receiver
ready_nodes[receiver] = 0;
// start sending
send(receiver, data);
```

and the corresponding node is marked as ready in this case. Afterwards, the next **while** condition check will show if it was the **ready** flit from the intended receiver node. While receiving data, a node checks each incoming flit if it is a **ready** flit or a data flit. **Ready** flits set the corresponding entry in the array, data flits are processed regularly. Then, the node can go on with the next flit. Code example 1 works without interrupts, it directly checks the receive buffer. On platforms where flit receival is processed via interrupts, code may have to be adapted.

4 Hardware Supported **ready** Synchronization

The software implementation leads to several drawbacks: First, all nodes may receive **ready** flits from other nodes, which might get data at a later point in the program execution. They have to handle these **ready** flits and note that these nodes are ready. The number of these **ready** flits is limited to the number of (other) nodes in the NoC. Therefore, the receive buffer has to be large enough: besides the entries for data flits, there have to be enough entries for **ready** flits (as many as there are other nodes in the NoC). Figure 3 illustrates an example with 8 other nodes: Node D sends a lot of data flits to node E (continuous arrows).

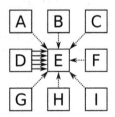

Fig. 3. One node is sending data flits to node E (continuous arrows), all other nodes send **ready** flits (dotted arrows) at the same time. Therefore, buffer space is needed for incoming data as well as for incoming **ready** flits.

Then, all other nodes (A–C, F–I) send their software **ready** flits to node E at the same time (dotted arrows). Therefore, the receive buffer of node E has to be large enough to save the arrived data flits as well as the **ready** flits from all other nodes.

Furthermore, it is possible, though very unlikely, that some data flit has exactly the same payload as a **ready** flit – how can data and **ready** flits be distinguished in a safe way?[4] Finally, program execution is still slowed down by flits that arrive and have to be handled, but are not needed yet. Therefore, **ready** synchronization should be implemented in hardware. Then, **ready** flits can be handled in dedicated hardware logic bypassing the normal receive buffer in the NI. A simple check mechanism for the sender to know whether some node is ready is provided.

4.1   Hardware Implementation

Basically, the hardware implementation works similar to the software implementation. The difference is a dedicated receive logic to process **ready** flits independent from data flits: **ready** flits are processed by our new logic, while data flits are still processed on the processing element. For the differentiation of **ready** and data flits, we introduce an additional 1-bit signal isReady everywhere between sender and receive logic. For data flits, it is 0 and for **ready** flits it is set to 1. Architectural changes besides the additional signal are colored in grey in Fig. 4. A node consists of a processing element with local memory, which is connected to the network router via a NI. The original NI comprises a send and receive buffer. Now we extend the NI by a hardware bit array, which is called Bit Array in the Figure. It stores the source nodes' id of incoming **ready** flits and as such has the same role as the array in the software implementation.

A multiplexer denoted as *MUX* in Fig. 4 is required to distinguish each incoming flit if it is a **ready** or data flit. This is done via the isReady signal. Therefore, data flits are stored in the receive buffer just as normal and when the isReady

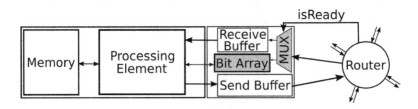

Fig. 4. Hardware structure of a node: processing element with local memory, connected to the NoC router via a NI containing send buffer, receive buffer and hardware bit array. Furthermore, there is a multiplexer to distinguish between **ready** and data flits. Components added by our approach are colored in grey.

---

[4] At some architectures, this might be solved with a header flit. However, not all architectures support this approach, see for example the RC/MC architecture [10].

signal is set the sender's corresponding bit in the hardware bit array is set to 1. Each node has its own bit array where each bit corresponds to one particular node.

When a node wants to send data to some other node, it can check the bit array if the corresponding node is ready. As shown in Fig. 4, the processing element should have direct access to the bit array to check the state. All flits that arrive at the node are either needed by the processing element (data which was requested and is now processed) or they are **ready** synchronization flits. The latter do not reach the processing element, but are processed in the NI and put in the hardware bit array. Therefore, it is avoided that flits which are currently not needed reach the processing element. Furthermore, this is a very scalable solution since each additional node only needs one bit of additional storage per node.

4.2 New Instructions

Received **ready** information is automatically placed in the hardware bit array. However, two new instructions are needed for handling **ready** information: **send ready (srdy)** for sending ready flits and **branch if not ready (bnr)** to check if a specific node is ready. An overview is given in Table 1.

Table 1. Instruction set extension for **ready** synchronization

Mnemonic	Source register	Immediate value	Function
srdy	*Sender node*		Send **ready** flit to *sender node*
bnr	*Receiver node*	*Jump target*	Check if *receiver node* is ready
			When it is not, jump to *jump target*

srdy sends a **ready** flit to the node which is given in the register **sender node**. It does the same like a regular **send** operation with two differences: first, there is no payload. Second, the additional signal **isReady** is set to 1 (for regular data send operations it has to be 0). When the **ready** flit arrives at the target node, it is not put into the receive buffer. Instead, the **isReady** signal allows the detection as **ready** flit. Therefore, the corresponding bit in the hardware bit array is set to 1. This allows the processing element to check if the receiver is ready. srdy might be called some cycles before the **receive** instruction on the same node to reduce waiting times (the time between sending the **ready** flit and receiving the answer from the sender node).

bnr is a branch instruction with the two operands **receiver node** (given in a register) and **jump target** (provided as immediate). It checks if **node** is ready to receive data and jumps to **jump target** if it is not. For this purpose, the corresponding bit is checked in the hardware bit array. Originally, we intended an instruction returning the bit itself in a register, but found a branch instruction to be more efficient: when the receiver node is ready, the following instruction can be directly executed (it is already in the pipeline). Otherwise, the sender node has to wait for the `ready` flit. It can use the waiting time for executing alternative code, spin on the `bnr` instruction or the instruction may be extended to energy saving waiting: the processing element could sleep and be woken up by the NI when the `ready` flit arrives. However, this is beyond the scope of this paper.

Although branch instructions with side effects are uncommon, we designed `bnr` with one small side effect: when the receiver node is ready, the bit in the hardware bit array is reset to 0. This is necessary to ensure that at the next program part which requires synchronization a new `ready` flit is awaited before flits are sent. Alternatives to this behaviour would be a dedicated `reset` instruction or a combination with a normal `send` operation. A dedicated `reset` instruction may be forgotten and lead to time-consuming debugging by the software developer. On the other hand, a combination with a normal `send` operation leads to complex code when several flits are sent in a loop. Then, the first flit would have to be sent outside of the loop via `send and reset` and the rest could be sent via regular `send` in the loop. With the bit being reset at the `bnr` instruction, there is no need for other specialized instructions and code stays simple with only two additional instructions.

Code example 2. Our new instructions `srdy` and `bnr` in a program. The receiver sends the `ready` flit and can afterwards call a blocking receive. On sender side, `bnr` can be utilized for busy waiting or executing alternative code, afterwards sending can start.

```
// Receiver
srdy sender
receive

// Sender
check_ready:
bnr receiver , check_ready //or alternative_code
send receiver , data
```

Code example 2 illustrates how easy hardware `ready` synchronization can be employed in software. The receiver node just sends the `ready` flit to the sender via `srdy`. Afterwards, it receives the requested flits. The sender node spins on its `bnr` instruction (or executes alternative code meanwhile) until it knows that the receiver node is ready. Then, it can directly start sending flits.

4.3   Impact of Ready Synchronization on Hardware Size

`Ready` flit handling requires additional hardware logic: in the focus is the hardware bit array, how it is connected to the processing element and processes incoming `ready` flits. It is the largest part of our hardware synchronization and grows with the number of nodes in the NoC. However, it scales very well as it only grows with 1 bit per additional node (plus management logic). Further logic is needed for the additional isReady signal, which is 1 bit wide and has to be passed through from the senders' send buffer to the receiver. Other signals comprise the flits' source, destination, payload and routing information. Therefore, the overhead should be at a maximum of 1–2% compared to the other information that is sent through the NoC. Finally, the additional send instruction srdy has to be provided. However, it does the same like the regular send besides setting the isReady signal to 1, while the regular send instruction has to set it to 0. This overhead should be negligible.

The additional logic might pay itself by saving buffer slots: Since the processing element is not interrupted by incoming flits anymore, processing times are reduced. The received data flits can immediately be processed. Therefore, fewer buffer slots should be needed. But most promising seems that received ready flits do not enter the receive buffer due to their handling in hardware. Thus, the receive buffer is only needed for data flits and does not have to carry any synchronization flits. Altogether, the load in the receive buffer is drastically reduced and the processing element is not interrupted anymore by flits that are currently not needed. Since ready flits do not carry a payload, even the send buffer might be relieved: dedicated (small) send buffer slots that only save the target node id could be utilized reducing the need for normal send buffer slots.

5 Evaluation

For the evaluation, we use the *reduced complexity many-core (RC/MC)* architecture [10], a 64-bit distributed memory many-core with semi-bufferless routing. It employs a combination of simple RISC-V cores with a lightweight NoC router called PaterNoster [11]. Thereby, the PaterNoster routers realize xy-routing: flits are forwarded bufferless first in x-direction until they reach the target column. There, they are stored in the so-called *corner buffer*. Flits wait in the corner-buffer, until there is a free slot to move them on in y-direction until they reach their target node. Buffers are only needed as send, receive and corner buffers. The NoC is organized as unidirectional torus. A FPGA model as well as a cycle-accurate simulator written in C which was checked against the VHDL model are open source[5]. For our programs, we utilize 4 RISC-V cores with a 5-stage pipeline and the NoC works with TDMA in a One-to-All schedule [12]: in each period each node is allowed to send one flit to any other node. This means that in each period each node can receive at most one flit from each other node. Links between nodes have a width of 69 bits: 64 bits for the payload of each flit, 2 bits for adressing the target node, another 2 bits for adressing the sender node and 1 bit for the ready signal. The platform does not have any speculative components as it is developed to have a predictable behaviour. Therefore, it is sufficient to execute each program once. Repeating the execution leads to exactly the same results.

---

[5] They can be downloaded at www.github.com/unia-sik/rcmc.

5.1   Comparison of Ready Synchronization in Software and Hardware

In the previous sections, we already presented two code examples: On the one hand, Code example 1 illustrates how `ready` synchronization would be realized as software implementation without hardware support. Thereby, the sender executes a `while` loop and an `if` statement, which takes several cycles. On the other hand, Code example 2 shows the minimalistic effort of `ready` synchronization with hardware support: the sender node only needs to execute one assembler instruction. In both implementations, the receiver node has to execute only one instruction: it sends a `ready` flit, in the software implementation with a regular `send` operation and in the hardware implementation with `srdy`. However, at data receival in the software implementation, the receiver always has to distinguish if a received flit is a `ready` or data flit. Altogether, our hardware `ready` implementation saves execution cycles and simplifies code, which is beneficial e.g. for maintainability and code analysis.

5.2   Execution Times

We executed several programs where four nodes work together, e.g. for exchanging data. In the following, we compare software versus hardware implementation of `ready` synchronization. Both are implemented in the way we described in the previous sections. Our programs are (i) four nodes meeting at a barrier and a (ii) broadcast of 1280 values from one node to three other nodes.[6] Furthermore, we have a (iii) All-to-All broadcast, i.e. all nodes broadcast one 64-bit value to all other nodes. Finally, we have a (iv) a global reduce operation, where a global sum is computed from values coming from all nodes.

These programs are small building blocks used in distributed memory programs. The more these building blocks are employed in programs, the bigger is the effect. All numbers are dependent on the hardware as well as the application and its implementation.

Table 2. Overview on benchmarks and their results

Name	Software ready [cycles]	Hardware ready [cycles]	Saving
Barrier	237	116	51%
Broadcast	29 764	18 124	39%
All-to-All broadcast	1 167	1 007	14%
Reduce, global sum	1 208	1 055	13%

Table 2 gives an overview of our results. Compared to the software implementation, the execution time of all programs is reduced in the hardware implementation. The savings reach from 10% to 50%. As Code examples 1 and 2

---

[6] A broadcast operation with one flit would result in numbers similar to the Barrier and All-to-All broadcast. Therefore, we took a larger broadcast to give an idea about what happens when lots of data is transmitted.

already illustrate, less code is executed. It should be noted that no **ready** flits from non-participating nodes interfere these executions. When there would be some, they would interrupt the software **ready** implementation and increase its execution times. However, they would have no impact on the hardware **ready** execution times, because they are handled by specialized hardware.

5.3   Impact on Hardware Costs

Now, we check how many slots in the receive buffer would be needed to avoid overflows. For this, we execute the above programs in the simulator and decrease the receive buffer size until a buffer overflow occurs. The results can be seen in Table 3. Thereby, the numbers at *No Synchronization* represent the buffer space needed in the worst case when there is no synchronization present. It results from the maximum number of flits sent by other nodes to one node. Thereby, it is assumed that all nodes send all their flits at the same time and the receiving node is not yet ready to process them.

Table 3. Overview on required receive buffer slots

Name	No Synchronization [buffer slots]	Software Ready [buffer slots]	Hardware Ready [buffer slots]	Saving
Barrier	2	1	1	0%
Broadcast	1280	251	1	>99%
All-to-All broadcast	3	2	2	0%
Reduce, global sum	2	2	1	50%

Hardware **ready** flits do not occupy receive buffer slots. Therefore, less or in the worst case equal receive buffer slots are required. As before, there are no other nodes sending interfering **ready** flits. Otherwise, more buffer slots would be required in the software implementation. At the barrier and reduce program, only two buffer slots are occupied without synchronization. This is because of the implementation of these programs, where tree-based algorithms are realized. At the broadcast implementation, 1280 64-bit values are to be broadcasted, which are 1280 flits. As can be seen in Table 3, a lot of buffer slots can be saved. The reason is the implementation: it is not one node sending flits to all other nodes. Instead, the broadcast operation is distributed in the network. Thus, there are intermediate nodes having to receive data and forward it to other nodes. In the software **ready** implementation, they need too much time to process flits. New flits arrive faster than the old ones are processed. Therefore, more and more flits retain at the intermediate nodes. In the hardware **ready** implementation, code parts are shorter and processing can take place faster. Therefore, it is avoided that buffers run full.

For estimation of the hardware costs, we made a synthesis of the FPGA model for an Altera Cyclone IV FPGA using Altera Quartus 16.0. Since scaling

Table 4. Overview on required hardware resources

Component	ALMs	Registers	Memory bits
Hardware ready	109	34	0
One 64-bit receive buffer slot	139	65	0

is proportional to the number of nodes, we synthesized 4 nodes and scaled the numbers in Table 4 to one node. Hardware logic is measured in Logic Elements[7] and registers. Table 4 illustrates that implementing hardware ready costs 116 additional LEs at each node and 34 additional registers (the total layout with 4 nodes including hardware ready needs around 53 300 LEs and 21 500 registers). One receive buffer slot requires 139 LEs and 65 registers and there are 32 of them in each node. Therefore, saving only one receive buffer slot already pays the hardware logic needed for ready synchronization.

6   Conclusion

When parallel programs diverge during their execution, nodes may send data to other nodes that are not yet ready to process it. This is no problem in distributed systems, where receive buffers are huge. However, in many-core processors with NoCs receive buffers and core-local memory are limited. Therefore, data should only be sent when receiver nodes are ready to process it. Thus, a systematic synchronization mechanism should be applied. To keep network utilization low, we presented synchronization with one ready flit. It is sent from the node that wants to receive data to the intended sender node. The sender node does not start sending until the ready flit arrives. When it arrives, it knows that the receiver node is ready to handle incoming flits and starts sending. This simple principle can be implemented in software, but is less performant than an implementation in hardware. For an efficient hardware implementation, we added two new instructions srdy and bnr, a 1-bit signal from the send buffer to the receiver node and a hardware bit array (plus management logic) at the receiver. The latter allows to check if a specific node is ready to receive flits. Our evaluation shows that global communication operations execute 10–50% faster and need fewer receive buffer slots. By saving buffer slots, our hardware ready synchronization pays itself as it requires only a small amount of additional logic.

Acknowledgement. The authors thank Ingo Sewing for his efforts implementing our lightweight hardware synchronization in the RC/MC architecture.

---

[7] Altera uses the term *Logic Element* for their elementary logic block, basically a lookup table with 4 inputs and 1 output (4-LUT).

References

1. Agarwal, A., Iskander, C., Shankar, R.: Survey of network on chip (NoC) architectures & contributions. J. Eng. Comput. Archit. **3**(1), 21–27 (2009)
2. Bjerregaard, T., Mahadevan, S.: A survey of research and practices of network-on-chip. ACM Comput. Surv. (CSUR) **38**(1), 1–51 (2006)
3. Borkar, S.: Future of interconnect fabric: a contrarian view. In: Workshop on System Level Interconnect Prediction, SLIP 2010, pp. 1–2 (2010)
4. Chrysos, G.: Intel® Xeon Phi coprocessor (codename knights corner). In: Hot Chips 24 Symposium (HCS), 2012 IEEE, pp. 1–31. IEEE (2012)
5. Coenen, M., Murali, S., Ruadulescu, A., Goossens, K., De Micheli, G.: A buffer-sizing algorithm for networks on chip using TDMA and credit-based end-to-end flow control. In: Proceedings of the 4th International Conference on Hardware/-Software Codesign and System Synthesis, CODES+ ISSS 2006, pp. 130–135. IEEE (2006)
6. Goossens, K., Dielissen, J., Radulescu, A.: Æthereal network on chip: concepts, architectures, and implementations. IEEE Design Test Comput. **22**(5), 414–421 (2005)
7. Kung, H.T., Morris, R.: Credit-based flow control for ATM networks. IEEE Netw. **9**(2), 40–48 (1995)
8. Kurose, J.F., Ross, K.W.: Computer Networking: A Top-Down Approach. Pearson, London (2012)
9. Message Passing Interface Forum: MPI: A Message-Passing Interface Standard, Version 3.1. High Performance Computing Center Stuttgart (HLRS) (2015). http://mpi-forum.org/docs/mpi-3.1/mpi31-report-book.pdf
10. Mische, J., Frieb, M., Stegmeier, A., Ungerer, T.: Reduced complexity many-core: timing predictability due to message-passing. In: Knoop, J., Karl, W., Schulz, M., Inoue, K., Pionteck, T. (eds.) ARCS 2017. LNCS, vol. 10172, pp. 139–151. Springer, Cham (2017). https://doi.org/10.1007/978-3-319-54999-6_11
11. Mische, J., Ungerer, T.: Low power flitwise routing in an unidirectional torus with minimal buffering. In: Proceedings of the Fifth International Workshop on Network on Chip Architectures, NoCArc 2012, pp. 63–68. ACM, New York (2012)
12. Mische, J., Ungerer, T.: Guaranteed service independent of the task placement in NoCs with torus topology. In: Proceedings of the 22nd International Conference on Real-Time Networks and Systems, RTNS 2014, pp. 151–160. ACM, New York (2014)
13. Rattner, J.: An experimental many-core processor from Intel Labs. Presentation (2010). http://download.intel.com/pressroom/pdf/rockcreek/SCC_Announcement_JustinRattner.pdf
14. Raynal, M., Helary, J.M.: Synchronization and Control of Distributed Systems and Programs. Wiley Series in Parallel Computing. Wiley, Chichester (1990). (Trans: Synchronisation et contrôle des systèmes et des programmes réparties, Paris, Eyrolles). http://cds.cern.ch/record/223733
15. Tanenbaum, A.S., Van Steen, M.: Distributed Systems: Principles and Paradigms, 2nd edn. Prentice-Hall, Upper Saddle River (2007)
16. Tanenbaum, A.S., Wetherall, D.J.: Computer Networks. Pearson, London (2010)

17. Vangal, S.R., Howard, J., Ruhl, G., Dighe, S., Wilson, H., Tschanz, J., Finan, D., Singh, A., Jacob, T., Jain, S., Erraguntla, V., Roberts, C., Hoskote, Y., Borkar, N., Borkar, S.: An 80-tile sub-100-W TeraFLOPS processor in 65-nm CMOS. IEEE J. Solid-State Circ. **43**(1), 29–41 (2008)
18. Wentzlaff, D., Griffin, P., Hoffmann, H., Bao, L., Edwards, B., Ramey, C., Mattina, M., Miao, C.C., Brown III, J.F., Agarwal, A.: On-chip interconnection architecture of the tile processor. IEEE Micro **27**(5), 15–31 (2007)

Network Optimization for Safety-Critical Systems Using Software-Defined Networks

Cora Perner$^{(\boxtimes)}$

Airbus Group Innovations, Taufkirchen, Germany
cora-lisa.perner@airbus.com

Abstract. Software-Defined Networking allows to separate traffic handling from network management. This – in combination with potential cost savings – makes it interesting for areas for which it has not been originally designed: safety-critical systems such as aeroplanes or power grids. These require resilience against faults and failures as well as predictable timing and availability. Network optimization provides a mean to incorporate these demands during the design stage of critical systems while taking limitations such as capacities into account.

This paper focuses on obtaining network configurations that satisfy the demands of safety-critical systems. To this end, this paper studies example topologies of both critical and non-critical systems to investigate the effect of resilient routing on network and traffic parameters and solve a minimum cost linear optimization problem that incorporates constraints of safety-critical traffic.

The results thus obtained are then compared with a capacity-constrained and an Earliest-Deadline-First placement heuristic. Hence it can be shown that while heuristics can perform well in some aspects, they violate either capacity or timing constraints, thus making them unsuitable for networks that provide safety-critical services.

1 Introduction

Traditionally, where safety-critical systems such as power grids, aeroplanes or automotive applications require network functionality, a heavy emphasis is placed on hard-wired physical redundancy and methods such as network calculus [1] to ensure that critical traffic can achieve its safety goals. These methods are used to achieve performance goals and to ensure that the critical functionality (e.g. providing control commands to actuators for braking) can be performed safely. Yet only a small percentage of the traffic across the network is actually safety-critical, with a larger quantity related to diagnostics, convenience and management. Notwithstanding, traffic flows with lower requirements obviously influence those with higher demands (e.g. by potentially congestion of the network, starving critical traffic of resources etc.). Consequently, all traffic demands need to be analyzed, not just the most critical ones.

Software-Defined Networking (SDN), on the other hand, allows to separate the handling of traffic from network management. Thus network management

© Springer International Publishing AG, part of Springer Nature 2018
M. Berekovic et al. (Eds.): ARCS 2018, LNCS 10793, pp. 127–138, 2018.
https://doi.org/10.1007/978-3-319-77610-1_10

can be more flexible and effective [2]. Due to these benefits, SDN is receiving some attention in areas for which it was not originally designed: for safety-critical applications. However, safety-critical traffic places some demands that are not inherent properties of SDN. These requirements derive from the underlying certification demand for proof that no single fault may result in a catastrophical failure [3, S.2-F-47]. Additionally, some traffic (e.g. a braking signal) needs to arrive at its destination within a given time. Hence, for each critical demand, the following conditions need to be satisfied:

1. resilience against faults and failures
2. timing/predictability guarantees (some traffic must be delivered to its destination within a given time)
3. availability

Network optimization provides a mean to incorporate these demands of critical systems while taking the limitations of SDN into account. Current network optimization efforts e.g. [4–7] focus mainly on balancing network loads. However, for safety-critical systems a different approach is needed. Here, the demands for network management are based on the functionalities mentioned above rather than performance issues of network management. Notwithstanding, the limitations of network capacity still apply.

This paper focuses on methods to obtain SDN configurations that satisfy the demands given. To this end, an algorithm is obtained that provides optimal routing for a given traffic matrix with a given network topology, provided the network can deal with all demands. The main contribution is to include all traffic demands of safety-critical systems (resilience, timing, availability) in the optimization problem. Here the inclusion of latency is of particular importance, as it accounts the effect that every routing also influences the queuing delay of the other flows sharing that particular link. For safety-critical system, this analysis needs to be performed prior to deployment, hence network changes and thus the effects of the SDN controller are not considered.

The remainder of this work is organized as follows: a brief overview about similar efforts is provided in Sect. 2, while Sect. 3 describes the optimization problem. Details on the networks investigated and the experimental setup are given in Sect. 4. Finally, the results obtained are discussed in Sect. 5.

2   Related Work

In the past years, some research has been conducted in the area of SDN resilience. For example, [6] presents a framework for SDN to abstract resilience functions through so-called *Management patterns* to describe the interactions between different resilience mechanisms. These patterns specify requirements which are satisfied through the assignment to particular components by a combination of a knowledge-base and machine-learning based approaches.

An alternative approach [5] investigates the recovery from failure in SDN by performing run-time optimization using iterative routing of feasible solutions until optimality is achieved. However, their only constraint is the link capacity, they do not take the requirements of the traffic into account. A similar approach is presented in [8]. While not using an iterative approach, it focuses on minimizing operational cost in finding a recovery path while simultaneously trying to minimize the flow operations needed.

Some publications also investigated resilient routing for other network types. The change in complexity between resilient and non-resilient IP routing has been addressed in [9]. The authors compared various heuristic objective functions for their effect on link utilization and average path length. It was found that while heuristics improve certain characteristics, others will be negatively affected, thus special care needs to be taken during network design to select the appropriate strategy.

Optimization for non-resilient networks has also been a prospering research topic. Among them, [7] focuses on minimizing path length of packet forwarding and switch memory usage under the constraints of forwarding table entries. On the other hand, [10] extends the problem by also considering the facility placement i.e. where the traffic sources and demands are placed. While it dynamically changes traffic routing and demands, it does not consider delay-sensitive traffic.

Non-functional safety requirements have been less frequently considered. For example, [11] investigates a delay-constrained routing problem for a M/M/1 arrival rate, while [12] minimize the latency of the flow with the highest delay bound in the network using shortest path and greedy algorithms as well as iterative versions thereof.

Beyond that, some papers have also investigated the safety-critical use of SDN. While [13] reviews general challenges and security issues, [14] provides an overview of how SDN (positively and negatively) can influence the network resilience. Finally, [15] describes a mechanism to provide one-link fault tolerance by using the fast-failover groups feature of OpenFlow.

While these papers address important points, they do not consider the traffic constraints relevant to most critical systems (see Sect. 1). Taking those into account is the key feature of this paper.

3   Problem Formulation

Thus a software-defined network constituting of a number of network switches, with a given topology and links between them is considered. Across this network a number of demands needs to be routed. This network consists of network switches $s \in S$, with the number of forwarding rules r_s and the throughput of the switch c_s. The network links $(i, j) \in L$ have a capacity $c[i, j]$ of the link (i, j) and cost $a[i, j]$ of using this link. This network is used to satisfy the traffic demands $d \in \mathbb{R}^3$ from a source switch src $\in S$ to a destination switch dst $\in S$. Each demand is composed of a bandwidth demand $qnt[d]$, a maximum latency of $d_{\Delta t}$ and the resilience k required, i.e. how many independent paths must be provided. Beyond the requirements originating from the traffic demands, three constraints apply. Firstly, the maximum number of forwarding rules $r_{\max}$ that may be placed at each SDN switch. Secondly, the maximum capacity c_{max} that each switch can handle. Thirdly, the maximum bandwidth bw_{max} of each link.

The traffic demands are satisfied through the according placement of flows by the introduction of the variable $x[r, d, i, j] \in X$ defined as

$$x[r, d, i, j] = \begin{cases} 1 & \text{if } d \in (i, j) \\ 0 & \text{if } d \notin (i, j) \end{cases}. \tag{1}$$

where $r = \{1, \ldots, k\}$ of the resilient path, since this paper does not consider multipath routing. The latency for each demand can be obtained from

$$\sum_{(i,j) \in L} t_q[d] + t_{\mathrm{pp}} + t_t \sum_{s \in S} t_{\mathrm{pr}} = d_{\Delta \mathrm{t}} \tag{2}$$

i.e. the sum of the delay due to propagation t_{pp}, transmission t_t, processing t_{pr} and queueing t_q. This allows to formulate the minimum cost optimization problem:

$$\forall r \in R : \quad \min \sum_{d \in D} \sum_{(i,j) \in L} a[i, j] \cdot x[r, d, i, j] \cdot \mathrm{qnt}[d] \tag{3}$$

subject to the placement of all demands

$$\forall d \in D : \quad \sum_{r \in R} \sum_{(\mathrm{src}[d],j) \in L} x[d, \mathrm{src}[d], j] = k \tag{4}$$

at the source node and all requests at the destination node:

$$\forall d \in D : \quad \sum_{r \in R} \sum_{(i,\mathrm{dst}[d]) \in L} x[d, i, \mathrm{dst}[d]] = k \tag{5}$$

To ensure flow continuation, it needs to be ensured that all required flows are forwarded:

$$\forall r \in R : \forall d \in D : \forall s \in S : \quad \sum_{(j,s) \in L} x[r, d, j, s] + (\text{if } s = \mathrm{src}[d] \text{ then } 1)$$

$$- \sum_{(s,j) \in L} x[r, d, s, j] - (\text{if } s = \mathrm{dst}[d] \text{ then } 1) = 0 \tag{6}$$

Furthermore, the maximum available capacity c_{max} at the node

$$\forall s \in S : \quad \sum_{r \in R} \sum_{d \in D} \sum_{(s,j) \in L} x[r, d, n, j] \cdot \mathrm{qnt}[d] + \sum_{r \in R} \sum_{d \in D} \sum_{(i,s) \in L} x[r, d, i, s] \cdot \mathrm{qnt}[d] \le c_{\mathrm{max}} \tag{7}$$

and the maximum capacity bw_{max} at each link

$$\forall (i, j) \in L : \quad \sum_{r \in R} \sum_{d \in D} x[r, d, i, j] \cdot \mathrm{qnt}[d] \le bw_{\mathrm{max}}[i, j] \tag{8}$$

must not be exceeded. As a full duplex link is assumed in this case, the limit applies to each direction. Since the internal memory for forwarding rules in the SDN switches is limited, the number of flow table entries needs to be constrained likewise:

$$\forall s \in S: \quad \sum_{r \in R, d \in D} \sum_{(s,j) \in L} x[r, d, n, j] \leq r_{\max} \tag{9}$$

Additionally, (10) and (11) ensure that the maximum latency for each demand is not exceeded

$$\forall r \in R, d \in D: \quad \sum_{(i,j) \in L} t_q[d] + t_{\mathrm{pp}} + t_t \sum_{s \in S} t_{\mathrm{pr}} \leq d_{\Delta t} \tag{10}$$

and that no links are shared between resilient flows:

$$\forall d \in D: \forall (i,j) \in L: \quad \sum_{r \in R} x[r, d, i, j] + \sum_{r \in R} x[r, d, j, i] \leq 1 \tag{11}$$

Both requirements follow from the application to safety-critical traffic, where the formulation of (11) assumes that a failure affects both flow directions. In that context, (9) is specific to the utilization of SDN and would need to be adapted accordingly for non-SDN networks.

4   Experimental Setup

To begin with, the networks and traffic parameters under study are described. Two different types of network topologies were used: critical and standard networks. In this context, standard means that they are not commonly associated with critical traffic demands. To this end, the PDH and DI-YUAN networks (see Figs. 1a and b) with the associated traffic demands and link costs were investigated a as well as the AFDX [16] and NOBEL-EU (see Figs. 1c and d) networks as examples for critical networks. For all but the AFDX network, this information has been obtained from the SND-LIB [17] library. In those figures, the circles represent network switches where flows may enter or leave the network, while the arrows represent bidirectional links between switches. Attached to the switches are end-systems (not shown) which generate traffic demands, e.g. a control computer communicating with an actuator.

Due to the additional constraints of our approach, the maximum capacity was selected from each definition. Since maximum latency or resilience was not part of the specification, the resilience was set to $k = 2$, while the maximum latency was set to follow a Gaussian distribution with $\mu = 20\,\mathrm{ms}$ i.e. 10–20% less than the number of demands and $\sigma = 5\,\mathrm{ms}$ for both the DI-YUAN and the PDH network. For the critical networks, k was likewise set to 2, while the latency was set to follow the distribution described in Table 2 which was based on the information for flight data recording in [18, AMC CAT.IDE.A.190]. For reasons detailed in Subsect. 5.2, 200 randomly selected demands were used for those networks. In addition, a fixed value for the link cost of the AFDX network

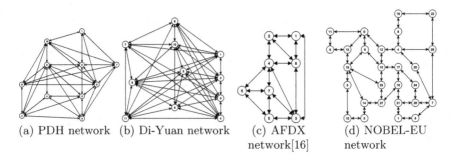

(a) PDH network (b) Di-Yuan network (c) AFDX network[16] (d) NOBEL-EU network

Fig. 1. Network topologies used

Table 1. Network parameters

Network	Nodes	Links	Demands
DI-YUAN	11	42	22
PDH	11	34	24
AFDX	8	15	200
NOBEL	28	41	200

Table 2. Probability distribution for $\Delta t = \Delta t_{\max}[d]$ for critical networks

Δt	125	25	500	1000	2000	4000	8000
$P(\Delta t)$ [%]	2.5	7.5	15	50	15	7.5	2.5

of 10 for every link was assumed. The main properties of the networks under study are provided in Table 1.

The AFDX network used in this study follows the description in [16]. The information useful for the problem considered in this paper is summarized in Tables 3 and 4.

Table 3. Number of VLANs from source src to destination dst [16]

src/dst	1	2	3	4	5	6	7	8
1		71	78					34
2	72			77				34
3	90			212	35		42	52
4		97	134			37	35	48
5			80			72	64	
6				82	61		52	
7			52	47	59	67		
8	51	45	43	52				

Table 4. AFDX Frame lengths [16]

Frame length (bytes)	Number of VLANs
0–150	561
151–300	202
301–600	114
601–900	57
901–1200	12
1201–1500	35
>1500	3

4.1 Assumptions

In order to reduce the problem space, the following assumptions were made with no loss of generality:

- $\text{src}[d] \neq \text{dst}[d]$
- separate output queue for each link

- identical switch capacities
- identical link capacities
- the bandwidth of an SDN switch is 10^7 Bits/s (compare [19])

Generally, the delay for each flow in the network is calculated as in (2). However, as all terms save t_q are constant (and depend on fixed, physical properties of the network), they are assumed to be zero i.e. $t_{pp} = t_t = t_{pr} = 0$. Thus the latency solely depends on the number of flows sharing the link and the sending capacity of the link.

Since the focus of this paper does not lie on the queuing model, a worst case scenario is assumed (i.e. all demands need to be satisfied simultaneously) with no preemption (FIFO). Thus a simplified model for the delay can be constructed as follows:

$$\Delta t = \begin{cases} \sum_{d \in D} \sum_{(i,j) \in L} \frac{x[r,d,i,j] \cdot \text{qnt}[d]}{bw_{\max}[i,j]} & \text{if the path traverses} (i,j) \\ 0 & \text{otherwise} \end{cases} \qquad (12)$$

To avoid including an additional dimension into the problem (and thus being no longer able to use linear programming) an auxiliary variable $y[r, d, i, j]$, with $r \in R, d \in D, (i,j) \in L$ is introduced where

$$\forall r \in R : \forall d \in D : \forall (i,j) \in L : y[r,d,i,j] \leq u \cdot x[r,d,i,j] \qquad (13)$$

with $u = \max(d_{\Delta t})$.

$$\forall r \in R : \forall d \in D : \forall (i,j) \in L : y[r,d,i,j]$$
$$\geq \sum_{r1 \in R} \sum_{d1 \in D} \frac{x[r,d1,i,j] \cdot \text{qnt}[d1]}{bw_{\max}[i,j]} - (u \cdot 1 - x[r,d,i,j]) \qquad (14)$$

and

$$\forall r \in R : \forall d \in D : \forall (i,j) \in L : y[r,d,i,j] \geq 0 \qquad (15)$$

applies. Consequently, the constraint for time delay of a flow can be simplified from (10) to

$$\forall r \in R, d \in D : \sum_{(i,j) \in L} y[r,d,i,j] \leq d_{\Delta t} \qquad (16)$$

4.2   Baseline

For comparison with the optimization algorithm in this paper, the shortest path and Dijkstra algorithm of Python's `networkx` software package as well as two simple heuristics are used. Additionally, the first heuristic (*Heur. Capa.*) uses Dijkstra's algorithm until the link capacity is exceeded, at which point that link can be no longer used, while the second (*Heur. EDF*) implements a simple Earliest Deadline First (EDF) schedule, where the path with the smallest resulting latency is selected for placement first and the placement of successive flows must not violate the requirements of the previous ones. Those were selected as the capacity and latency requirements were observed to be frequently violated by applying the shortest path algorithms.

5   Numerical Results and Discussion

For critical systems, it is likely that the optimization will be performed prior to deployment. Hence, no detailed timing analyses are included in this paper. However, some observations are made in that respect in Subsect. 5.2. What is more, since the results of the shortest path did not noticeably differ from those of the Dijkstra algorithm, only the latter is discussed in the analysis. Additionally, as no significant additional insights could be gained, only one standard and one resilient network is discussed in detail.

Since the latency requirements have been randomly generated (see Sect. 4), ten problem instances were created and solved for each network. The effect of the placement on cost, flow table entries as well as latency and number of hops (for the standard and resilient case) have been investigated further. These results are described in more detail in the following paragraphs.

5.1   Standard Networks

The results for the flow placement with the various algorithms can be obtained from Fig. 2, detailing the various performance characteristics. It can be noted that the results for the Dijkstra algorithm and the capacity- constrained heuristic are identical in this case, since the largest possible capacities from the definitions were obtained, as $k \cdot \text{qnt}$ has to be transported due to the resilience requirement. However, this cannot generally be assumed to be the case.

Figure 2a shows that the cost varies significantly between the methods. While the cost obtained through Dijkstra and the heuristics was identical through all runs (since the different demands have not been considered), the cost for the optimized rule placement varied significantly. What is more, it was only about half of that obtainable through the other methods. The lower cost of the EDF heuristic can be explained through the consideration of the latency, since expensive links are not used by that many flows as the maximum number of flows is mainly limited by the most critical demand placed there.

The distribution of flow placements is depicted in Fig. 2b. Here, the Dijksta and capacity heuristic both have a lower value since they only use the shortest paths which means fewer hops for each flow and thus fewer flow table entries. Additionally, the EDF heuristic has more than the optimization, since the former uses the shortest path until one flow's latency requirement is violated.

The time delay Δt for the resilient case is shown in Figs. 2c and d. Here, the optimization produces higher values than the other methods, since the cost minimization leads to on average, a significantly lower link utilization, which is shown in Fig. 2e and further illustrated by the number of hops for the resilient case in Fig. 2f. In the standard case (not depicted) it was uniformly one (safe for one flow in the optimization) and thus has a negligible impact.

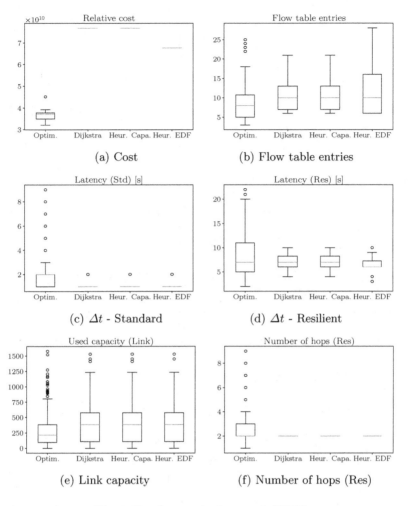

Fig. 2. Results standard network (PDH)

5.2 Critical Networks

Empiric performance analyses showed that calculation time for optimization has a nearly quadratic growth rate for every hundred demands (e.g. if a problem with 100 demands needs about 60 s to run, one with 200 needs about 275 s), while the number of links and nodes do not have a pronounced effect. This is due to the significant number of constraints that need to be created and evaluated, as the placement of every demand influences every other demand in the network and also the reason to use a smaller number of demands of 100 for AFDX.

What is more, while standard networks with around 20 demands can easily and generally quickly be calculated with standard hardware and open-source software, the constraints needed for the full AFDX dataset need more than the

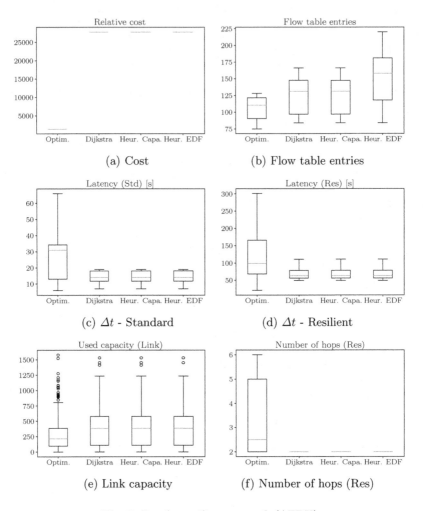

Fig. 3. Results resilient network (AFDX)

internal memory of the GNU Linear Programming Kit and half the dataset already requires about 64 GB of RAM, thus making it only solvable on special hardware and commercial software. The results for the flow placement with the various algorithms can be obtained from Fig. 3. As for the PDH network, the results for the Dijkstra algorithm and the capacity-constrained heuristic are identical in this case, as the largest possible capacities were taken from the definitions, but this will not generally be the case.

The distribution of flow placements is depicted in Fig. 3b. Here, the optimization has the lowest number, while the Dijkstra and heuristics have a much larger value on average. This is due to the much higher amount of hops for the resilient path, which of course results in fewer entries per switch. This is also reflected in the time delay Δt for the standard and the resilient case as shown in Figs. 3c and d. As with the standard networks, since the main goal of cost minimization results on average in a significantly lower link utilization, which is shown in Fig. 3e and further illustrated by the number of hops for the resilient case in Fig. 3f. With one exception in the optimization solution, the number of hops was uniformly one for all algorithms.

6 Conclusion and Future Work

This paper has shown that while heuristics may theoretically result in better performance, they cannot be practically applied since they violate some or all constraints or result in unnecessarily costly design. Using the optimization method discussed, it could be shown that network optimization can take all necessary traffic considerations into account, which is paramount in using SDN for safety critical system. While alternative shortest path algorithms are significantly faster, they are unable to account for all requirements, thus proving unsuitable for safety-critical systems.

For future work, it is planned to investigate the effect of various objective functions as well as parameter variation on overall network performance.

Acknowledgment. This work was partially funded by the German Federal Ministry of Education and Research (BMBF) under Grant Nr. 16KIS0537K (DecADe).

References

1. Le Boudec, J.-Y., Thiran, P. (eds.): Network Calculus: A Theory of Deterministic Queuing Systems for the Internet. LNCS, vol. 2050. Springer, Heidelberg (2001). https://doi.org/10.1007/3-540-45318-0
2. Kreutz, D., Ramos, F.M.V., Verssimo, P.E., Rothenberg, C.E., Azodolmolky, S., Uhlig, S.: Software-defined networking: a comprehensive survey. Proc. IEEE **103**(1), 14–76 (2015)
3. European Aviation Safety Agency: Certification specifications and acceptable means of compliance for large aeroplanes. Technical report CS-25 and AMC, EASA (2015). http://www.easa.europa.eu/official-publication/certification-specifications. Accessed 11 Dec 2017
4. Mao, H., Alizadeh, M., Menache, I., Kandula, S.: Resource management with deep reinforcement learning. In: Proceedings of the 15th ACM Workshop on Hot Topics in Networks, HotNets 2016, pp. 50–56. ACM, New York (2016)
5. Paris, S., Paschos, G.S., Leguay, J.: Dynamic control for failure recovery and flow reconfiguration in SDN. In: 2016 12th International Conference on the Design of Reliable Communication Networks (DRCN), pp. 152–159, March 2016
6. Smith, P., Schaeffer-Filho, A., Hutchison, D., Mauthe, A.: Management patterns: SDN-enabled network resilience management. In: 2014 IEEE Network Operations and Management Symposium (NOMS), pp. 1–9, May 2014
7. Prabhu, S., Dong, M., Meng, T., Godfrey, P.B., Caesar, M.: Let me rephrase that: transparent optimization in SDNs. In: Proceedings of the Symposium on SDN Research, SOSR 2017, pp. 41–47. ACM, New York (2017)

8. Astaneh, S., Heydari, S.S.: Multi-failure restoration with minimal flow operations in software defined networks. In: 2015 11th International Conference on the Design of Reliable Communication Networks (DRCN), pp. 263–266, March 2015

9. Hartmann, M., Hock, D., Menth, M., Schwartz, C.: Objective functions for optimization of resilient and non-resilient IP routing. In: 2009 7th International Workshop on Design of Reliable Communication Networks, pp. 289–296, October 2009

10. Papadimitriou, D., Colle, D., Demeester, P.: Mixed-integer optimization for the combined capacitated facility location-routing problem. In: 2016 12th International Conference on the Design of Reliable Communication Networks (DRCN), pp. 14–22, March 2016

11. Hijazi, H., Bonami, P., Ouorou, A.: Robust delay-constrained routing in telecommunications. Ann. Oper. Res. **206**(1), 163–181 (2013)

12. Cattelan, B., Bondorf, S.: Iterative design space exploration for networks requiring performance guarantees. In: 2017 IEEE/AIAA 36th Digital Avionics Systems Conference (DASC), pp. 1–10, September 2017

13. Sampigethaya, K.: Software-defined networking in aviation: opportunities and challenges. In: Integrated Communication, Navigation, and Surveillance Conference (ICNS), pp. 1–21, April 2015

14. Mas Machuca, C., Secci, S., Vizarreta, P., Kuipers, F., Gouglidis, A., Hutchison, D., Jouet, S., Pezaros, D., Elmokashfi, A., Heegaard, P., Ristov, S., Gusev, M.: Technology-related disasters: a survey towards disaster-resilient software defined networks. In: 2016 8th International Workshop on Resilient Networks Design and Modeling (RNDM), pp. 35–42, September 2016

15. Pfeiffenberger, T., Du, J.L., Arruda, P.B., Anzaloni, A.: Reliable and flexible communications for power systems: fault-tolerant multicast with SDN/OpenFlow. In: 2015 7th International Conference on New Technologies, Mobility and Security (NTMS), pp. 277–283, July 2015

16. Charara, H., Scharbarg, J.L., Ermont, J., Fraboul, C.: Methods for bounding end-to-end delays on an AFDX network. In: 18th Euromicro Conference on Real-Time Systems (ECRTS 2006), pp. 193–202 (2006)

17. Orlowski, S., Wessäly, R., Pióro, M., Tomaszewski, A.: SNDlib 1.0-survivable network design library. Networks **55**(3), 276–286 (2009). http://sndlib.zib.de. Accessed 01 Sept 2018

18. European Aviation Safety Agency: Commission regulation (EU) no 965/2012 on air operations and related EASA decisions (AMC & GM and CS-FTL.1). Technical report regulation (EU) 965/2012, EASA (2016). http://www.easa.europa.eu/document-library/regulations. Accessed 11 Dec 2017

19. Durner, R., Blenk, A., Kellerer, W.: Performance study of dynamic QoS management for OpenFlow-enabled SDN switches. In: 2015 IEEE 23rd International Symposium on Quality of Service (IWQoS). pp. 177–182, June 2015

CaCAO: Complex and Compositional Atomic Operations for NoC-Based Manycore Platforms

Sven Rheindt[(⊠)], Andreas Schenk, Akshay Srivatsa, Thomas Wild,
and Andreas Herkersdorf

Chair for Integrated Systems, Technical University Munich, Munich, Germany
{sven.rheindt,andreas.schenk,srivatsa.akshay,thomas.wild,
herkersdorf}@tum.de

Abstract. Tile-based distributed memory systems have increased the
scalability of manycore platforms. However, inter-tile memory accesses,
especially thread synchronization suffer from high remote access latencies. Our thorough investigations of lock-based and lock-free synchronization primitives show that there is a concurrency dependent cross-
over point between them, i.e. there is no one-fits-all solution. Therefore,
we propose to combine the conceptual advantages (no retries and lock-
free) of both variants by using dedicated hardware support for inter-tile
atomic operations. For frequently used and highly concurrent data structures, we show a speedup factor of 23.9 and 35.4 over the lock-based and
lock-free implementations respectively, which increases with higher concurrency.

Keywords: Atomic operations · Remote synchronization
Compare-and-swap · Distributed shared memory · Network-on-Chip

1 Introduction

In the last decade, the power wall limited the increase of processor frequency.
With the advent of mainstream multicore platforms, this technological problem was tackled by distributing applications over multiple cores that still used
one common memory. Further scalability was introduced by transitioning to distributed shared memory architectures to lower memory access contention and
hotspots [1]. An example is our hybrid tiled architecture depicted in Fig. 1, with
Network-on-Chip (NoC)-based interconnect and several bus-connected cores per
tile, sharing a tile local memory.

Most distributed memory platform make use of the Message-Passing-
Interface (MPI) programming model, but there is still a demand for shared
memory programming due to its ease of use [1,2]. But, multicore architectures
in combination with shared memory programming introduce the challenge of providing atomic memory accesses to local/remote shared data structures. Thread

© Springer International Publishing AG, part of Springer Nature 2018
M. Berekovic et al. (Eds.): ARCS 2018, LNCS 10793, pp. 139–152, 2018.
https://doi.org/10.1007/978-3-319-77610-1_11

synchronization is even more challenging for distributed shared than for purely shared memory systems, since the widely used NoC interconnect does not inherently allow for atomic memory accesses. Additionally, distributed shared memory architectures exhibit non-uniform memory access (NUMA) properties. Application performance therefore highly depends on data-to-task locality and efficient synchronization primitives.

Synchronization can be categorized into three classes of atomic primitives. Lock - based primitives atomically lock the critical section. Classical locks are often implemented using hardware support in the form of test-and-set (TAS) or compare-and-swap (CAS). Software based lock-free mechanisms use general-purpose atomic operations like CAS or linked-load/store-conditional (LL/SC), which are lock-free and provided by the underlying hardware often as ISA extensions. Hardware based primitives use so called special-purpose atomic operations to implement the whole critical section in dedicated hardware without using locks. An example is the class of fetch-and-ops [3–6].

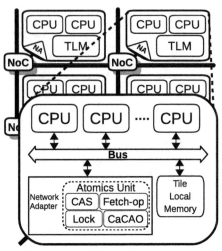

Fig. 1. Hybrid interconnect distributed shared memory platform with atomics unit

Due to the NUMA properties of distributed shared memory architectures, different aspects of synchronization get a new weight. If, for example, an application loops over a CAS until it is successful, the retry penalty/NoC travel time for a failed CAS is much higher for remote than for local operations. Even though a purely lock-based or lock-free software implementation might be favorable for a given concurrent data structure in a conventional bus-based system, totally different results might be true for distributed shared memory architectures.

In this paper, we therefore investigate the effects of lock-based and lock-free software synchronization primitives on a distributed shared memory architecture. We further propose special-purpose hardware implementations for efficient remote atomic operations. We couple the advantages of both lock-based and lock-free primitives with remote execution of the critical section in dedicated hardware to tackle the challenge of NUMA operations on distributed shared memory platforms. We call this combination complex and compositional atomic operations (CaCAO). We compare our dedicated hardware implementation to lock-based and lock-free software based variants that use partial hardware support.

The rest of the paper is organized as follows. We describe the related work in Sect. 2. In Sect. 3, we analyze and compare existing synchronization primitives and propose the use of complex and compositional atomic operations.

Architectural details of our implemented hardware prototype are given in Sect. 4. In Sect. 5, we present and discuss our experimental results, before we finally conclude this paper and give an outlook to future work in Sect. 6.

2   Related Work

On the one hand, the trend of lock-based synchronization leads towards efficient lock implementations [1, 7–9] without support for general purpose atomic primitives. On the other hand, many - but not all - multicore platforms provide lock-free synchronization capabilities [2–4, 6, 10]. For example Mellanox, earlier Tilera, - who provides one of the modern tile-based architectures - supports the CAS primitive only for their GX platform [2], not for the Pro platform [11].

Authors in [12] developed the MCS-lock to overcome the performance bottleneck and other limitations of simple, ticket and various queue based spinlocks [4, 7, 10, 13]. Through spinning on local variables only, they require $\mathcal{O}(1)$ network operations for acquiring a remote lock. The MCS-lock can be efficiently implemented in software, but needs an atomic swap operation for basic functionality and the CAS primitive to provide full features like FIFO ordering and starvation freedom. This was adopted by the authors of [7, 8] in their two consecutive works on efficient lock-based synchronization for NoC-based distributed shared memory systems. They transitioned from optimized simple and ticket spinlocks [8] to MCS-locks [7]. Their lock implementations use a hardware loop for local polling until acquisition. An atomic fetch-and-inc/dec unit is used to integrate the ticket spinlock and semaphores. They purely focus on optimizing locks by performing these atomic operations exclusively on special globally addressable registers in their synchronization unit and not on arbitrary memory locations. Apart from the swap instruction, they do not support atomic operations on memory, especially no lock-free primitives. Authors in [9] basically adopt the same idea of just optimizing lock implementations for distributed memory. Through optimized lock queue handling, they avoid head-of-line blocking of independent synchronization requests.

With the lock-free universal primitives CAS and LL/SC, it is possible to emulate all other atomic primitives or transform lock-based mechanisms into lock-free ones [3–6]. Authors in [4] convert operations into purely lock-free variants using the universal primitive LL/SC and the fetch-and-op primitives, that are common in modern multicore systems. However, they admit that in general many lock-free mechanisms can get quite complex. Authors in [3] use a standard 2D-mesh NoC interconnect with one core per tile. They suggest a rather complex combination of CAS as in-cache implementation together with a write-invalidate coherence policy and a load-exclusive coherence policy extension to minimize the CAS operations on memory. Furthermore, they recommend a hardware based serial number extension for the CAS primitive to tackle the ABA problem and also suggest a fetch-and-add primitive for efficient counters.

To our knowledge, the related work either optimizes lock-based synchronization with efficient lock implementation or investigates purely lock-free variants [14, 15]. Few provide the special purpose fetch-and-increment primitive for remote operations on NoC-based systems [1,3]. However, no dedicated hardware support for more complex special purpose atomic operations are provided by state-of-the-art distributed shared memory systems.

3   Complex and Compositional Atomic Operations

We classify synchronization primitives into three main categories, that use different amounts and kinds of hardware support:

- (α) Software lock-based: using (efficient) hardware lock support
- (β) Software lock-free: using hardware CAS or LL/SC
- (γ) Dedicated hardware for whole critical section (wait-free)

In this paper, we first describe and compare (α) and (β). Then we propose to combine their conceptual advantages by using dedicated hardware support (γ) for complex and compositional atomic operations (CaCAO approach).

A main attribute of synchronization primitives is the number of retries. An operation has zero retries, if the read-modify-write cycle is non-conditional. This means, if there is no interfering concurrency on the data structure that makes a retry of the operation necessary. This holds true, e.g. for the fetch-and-ops, but not for the CAS, since the latter only writes back if the read value did not change in the meantime.

3.1   Comparison of the Synchronization Primitives (α) and (β)

(α) A **lock-based software** implementation of a given function locks the critical section (CS) that has to be performed atomically. It uses hardware support like test-and-set to acquire the lock. Whereas - by design - the critical section inside the lock has zero retries, the lock acquisition itself does not and is not even wait-free, since no upper bound for the number of retries until lock acquisition can be given. However, much research has already been done to provide efficient lock implementations [1, 7–9]. In the following, when we refer to lock-based software primitives, we therefore use a variant with efficient hardware look support.

(β) **Lock-free software** implementations of a given function can be achieved with the lock-free universal primitives CAS or LL/SC, that need to be provided by the hardware. As their names already suggest, their read-modify-write cycle is conditional and they therefore are not retry-free. A software loop is needed to repeat the operation until it is successful. The best-case execution time of a lock-free software primitive can be one try, if no other party interfered in the meantime. However, the average execution time is heavily dependent on the concurrency and the worst-case can even lead to starvation. Therefore, these lock-free implementations are not guaranteed to be wait-free.

A theoretical comparison between (α) and (β) shows that the best-case execution time of a lock-free software variant is approximately equal to the execution time of the critical section of a lock-based variant without the time for acquiring and releasing the lock. The average time of the lock-free variant is dependent on the interfering concurrency and the thereby necessary retries (as well as other factors like run-time background traffic). Whereas for the lock-free variant the average execution time is linear in the number of retries, the average lock-based execution time is linear in the number of concurrent contenders for the lock.

This comparison shows that - whereas in the best-case a lock-free implementation is always better - in the average case there can be a cross-over point between the lock-based and lock-free implementations. If the concurrency dependent retry rate is greater than a threshold, the lock-based implementation yields better performance and vice versa. A design time decision between (α) and (β) would be necessary by the programmer. In Sect. 6 we talk about a more dynamic decision making as future work.

3.2   CaCAO Approach (γ)

If one only has (α) and (β), no one-fits-all solution would be available. But we overcome the deficiencies of both software lock-based (α) as well as software lock-free (β) implementations by combining their conceptual advantages: zero retries and lock-freeness.

We propose a **dedicated hardware** (γ) implementation that outsources and atomically executes the whole critical section in a dedicated hardware module (near the memory where the shared data is stored), thereby guaranteeing zero retries by design. Since an upper bound for the execution time can be given, this approach is not only lock-free, but also wait-free.

In the best-case, the whole execution (NoC travel time plus atomic read-modify-write cycles) of the lock-free primitives (β and γ) is approximately as small as the minimal time for lock acquisition of the lock-based variant (α). More importantly, the average and worst case times for the proposed dedicated hardware solution (γ) do not rise much, since no interfering concurrency is possible and therefore no retries are necessary. Especially for remote accesses the atomic read-modify-write cycles with constant duration after bus grant are much shorter than the travel time over the NoC. Even if there are several concurrent contenders, they cannot interfere one another due to the atomic read-modify-write cycles in hardware, thereby guaranteeing wait-free operation.

This approach has general validity and outperforms the software lock-based as well as lock-free variants by design. This local or remote site execution in a dedicated hardware module (CaCAO approach) helps to tackle the data-to-task locality problem of distributed shared memory architectures.

In contrast to software based lock-free implementations that might get quite complex [4], CaCAO does not need atomic operations inside the critical section, since the atomicity is intrinsically provided by the dedicated hardware module.

However, the disadvantage of this approach is its very application specific nature due to the need of implementing each needed functionality in dedicated hardware.

In future work, we plan to further extend the functionality and complexity of CaCAO. Because of the compositional nature of this approach, various already

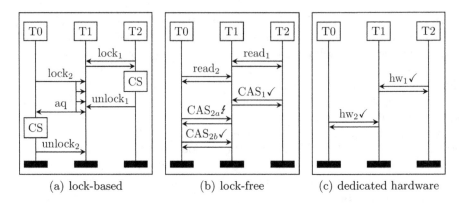

(a) lock-based   (b) lock-free   (c) dedicated hardware

Fig. 2. Message sequence charts for three types of shared counter implementations

implemented as well as future functionalities of our dedicated hardware module do and can reuse the same hardware blocks.

For the validation of the concept, we implemented and investigated the widely used fetch-and-add operation in the use case scenario of a shared counter as well as dedicated hardware implementations of atomic linked-queue enqueue/dequeue operations. For both scenarios, we implemented and evaluated all three variants (α), (β) and (γ) on our FPGA prototype as described in Sect. 5. In the following, these scenarios are briefly explained and used to show the key differences of the three synchronization variants.

Shared Counter Scenario. The pseudo source codes for the three synchronization types for the shared counter for N cores on several tiles are given in Fig. 3. In Fig. 2 the message sequence charts are given.

(α) The lock-based software implementation first acquires a lock (line 1 in Fig. 3) over the NoC, then remote reads the counter value (2), increments it (3) locally and writes the value back to memory (4) before unlocking (5) the critical section. As can be seen in Fig. 2(a), the critical section (CS) inside the lock has zero retries, whereas the lock acquisition itself may require several retries. An efficient lock implementation, as shown for $lock_2$, lowers these through local polling in hardware at remote site. For (α), hardware support is only provided for efficient locks.

```
shared_counter_locked(*lck,*cnt)
// HW support for lock
1   lock(lck);
2   tmp = *cnt
3   tmp++;
4   *cnt = tmp;
5   unlock(lck);

shared_counter_lock_free(*cnt)
// HW support for CAS
1   tmp = *cnt;
2   do{
3       old = tmp;
4       tmp = CAS(cnt, old, old+1);
5   }while(tmp != old);

shared_counter_HW(*cnt)
// HW support for whole CS
1   fetch_and_inc(cnt);
```

Fig. 3. Pseudo code of shared counter implementation for the three synchronization types

(β) The lock-free software based implementation reads the counter value non-atomically (1). Then it performs a compare-and-swap on the counter with the incremented old value (4). It is successful if the counter value did not change in the meantime (5). Otherwise, the compare-and-swap is reissued with the updated old value (2–4). This can be seen in Fig. 2(b). Between the $read_2$ (1) and the CAS_{2a} (4) from T0 to T1, another CAS_1 from T2 to T1 happens and updates the shared value, so that the CAS_{2a} fails and needs a retry (CAS_{2b}).

(γ) The dedicated hardware implementation uses the atomic fetch-and-increment mechanism. It is retry-free by definition since the read-modify-write operation is performed atomically in hardware at remote site by sending the whole operation there (Fig. 2(c)). It is clear that the fetch-and-add operation is standard in many CPU ISAs. However, these mostly support only local and no remote memory operations.

Linked Queue Scenario. A more advanced example is the enqueue and dequeue operation of a linked-list queue. Without loss of generality, we limit this scenario to tail-enqueue and head-dequeue operations. The tail-enqueue operation has to atomically update the tail.next pointer only if the read value of tail.next is still NULL, meaning no other enqueue operation happened in the meantime. The second step is to set the tail pointer to the new element non-atomically. Until this operation is finished, all other enqueue attempts result in a fail and retry.

The head-dequeue operation has to atomically update the head pointer, which is successful if no other dequeue operation happened in the meantime.

Analog to the shared counter example, (α) only uses hardware support for efficient lock implementation. (β) is in need for hardware CAS support and (γ) needs dedicated hardware for the whole enqueue/dequeue operation.

4   Implementation Aspects

We implemented a configurable, resource reusing hardware module for local and remote atomic operations. As depicted in Fig. 1, it is inside of a modular network adapter connected to the tile local bus. Besides the atomics unit, the network adapter provides several other functionalities, like e.g. remote reads and writes, direct memory accesses, etc. The extension towards atomic operations of the network adapter consists of submodules for sending (TX) and receiving (RX) atomic operation requests and the atomics unit containing several operations.

Architectural details. As we use a hybrid NoC-bus-based architecture, the atomics unit is - as part of the network adapter - connected to the bus. To perform any atomic operation on memory, it (1) first blocks the bus for any other accesses, (2) executes the (conditional) read-modify-write cycle on the memory connected to the bus, before (3) unlocking the bus again. The modify or conditional write operations of step (2) are performed or evaluated in the hardware unit to minimize calculation and network time by processing at the remote tile. This approach basically allows for arbitrary complex operations in step (2), that are completely atomic through the exclusive bus usage between (1) and (3). However, in this paper, we limit ourselves to the set of atomic primitives described below.

These network triggered atomic operations concur with atomic operations triggered by local processors and are sequentialized through exclusive usage of the bus. This modular design with standard interfaces therefore ensures high adaptability and integrability into existing systems. On our platform as described in Sect. 5, only support for local atomic swap and CAS is given as ISA of the cores. However - as for most systems - no support for inter-tile remote atomic operations is given.

As the atomic primitives described in the next paragraph require a response or acknowledgement, we implemented them in a synchronous manner. Therefore each CPU can have one pending request. However, since we have several CPUs per tile, several pending requests per tile are possible. The maximum number of pending requests per atomics unit is therefore the total number of CPUs in the system. These are buffered in the FIFOs of the virtual channel based packet-switched NoC which are served in a round-robin fashion.

Atomic Primitives. To support the three types of synchronization primitives (α, β and γ), we implemented the following set of atomic operations:

    (a) efficient spinlock implementation
    (b) fetch-and-op operations, with op = {Add, Sub, And, Or}
    (c) compare-and-swap primitive
    (d) CaCAO: linked queue enqueue/dequeue

(a) The efficient spinlock has an integrated hardware loop until lock acquisition to ensure an $\mathcal{O}(1)$ network utilization. Although acquiring a spinlock is in itself not retry-free and has to be repeated until it is successful, outsourcing the retry attempts into a remote site hardware loop minimizes the retry-penalty. Instead of going back and forth over the NoC, even up into system software - costing several hundreds of clock cycles - the retry penalty of the hardware loop is only a few cycles due to bus arbitration. A back-off retry threshold with accompanying "lock not acquired" response is also implemented.

(b) The fetch-and-op primitives follow the same (1)(2)(3) steps. Between (1) locking the bus and (3) unlocking the bus, the hardware unit performs the (2) step by (2a) reading/fetching data, (2b) executing the {op}-operation in hardware (2c) writing back the modified data and finally (2d) sending the fetched data back to the requesting processor. The fetch-and-op primitive has zero retries since the write-back is non-conditional. Strictly speaking, this primitive can already be classified as CaCAO, even though the critical section in step (2) is not very complex.

(c) The compare-and-swap instruction is similar to (b) with the difference of a conditional write-back, only if the read value is equal to the old value argument of the CAS. This additional comparison is handled in the hardware module, whilst reusing the read and write logic already present for (a) and (b).

The CAS can be in need of retries, since between reading the old value by the CPU (which then issues the CAS) and checking the read value against the old value inside of the CAS unit. An interfering write accesses can happen, which would lead to a unsuccessful CAS. Therefore, the CPU will have to repeat the procedure until it is eventually successful, leading to increasing network load.

A solution to this problem can be given in hardware, if the operation to be performed on the data can be outsourced to some dedicated logic in hardware. This possibility is function specific, but we show, that it well serves for certain frequently used methods, especially for remote atomic operations. We call these complex and composed atomic operations, as discussed in (d).

(d) CaCAO: Complex and compositional atomic operations. The same (1) (2) (3) steps are followed. However, step (2) basically could be of arbitrary complexity and functionality, even though in this paper we only provide enqueue/dequeue operations into a linked queue. But also the fetch-and-op primitive as discussed in (b) could be classified into this category, since the whole critical section is outsourced into dedicated hardware.

The proposed dedicated hardware module has a compositional nature since the various atomic primitives reuse the same building blocks. The memory read (1) and write (3) step is part of every primitive and there is therefore no waste of resources. E.g. the spinlock reuses the CAS building block with hard-coded old and new values 0 and 1, respectively. These building blocks compose the whole module and a future extension to more functionality can build upon them.

5 Experimental Setup and Results

Our measurements were carried out on our distributed shared memory architecture synthesized onto a FPGA prototype. We used a 2×2 tile design with up to 8 Leon3 cores per tile and a tile local memory, which are connected by a shared bus. The tiles are interconnected with a 2D-Mesh NoC. The timing analysis of our design with the tool Xilinx Vivado revealed, that the proposed atomics unit itself is able to operate at 419 MHz. Together with its TX and RX interface, it still reaches 285 MHz. It is integrated into the network adapter, which is currently able to run at 100 MHz. The complete design with CPUs, NoC, Bus and other modules of our complete project limits the frequency to 50 MHz, since one single clock domain is used so far. Further, due to resource constraints our FPGA prototype limits us to a 2×2 tile design. We tried to compensate this by increasing the core count to 8 cores per tile.

Before running actual stress tests, we first obtained cycle accurate minimal duration simulations using an RTL simulator. The results are shown in Fig. 4(a) for the various atomic primitives implemented in our atomics unit. The whole duration is split into trigger-time (triggering the network adapter by the cores), NoC-time (time for flit generation on sender side, reception on receiver side and travel time over the NoC for both request and response messages) and atomics-time (actual time for carrying out the atomic operation in the atomics unit). It is made clear, that while the trigger-time only depends on the bus arbitration, the NoC-time can increase drastically for higher network load. However, the atomics-time is constant after bus grant.

function	$T_{trigger}$	T_{NoC}	$T_{atomics}$
spinlock	7	47	10
spinlock retry	0	0	10
CAS	14	50	10
Fetch-and-op	11	49	10
hw_enqueue	14	49	37
hw_dequeue	7	48	30

(a) Cycle accurate minimal duration of individual and standalone atomic operations in number of clock cycles

Module	LUTs	Register
Atomics	501	316
TX & RX	1031	687
$\sum$	1532	1003
% NA	11.85%	12.35%
% Tile	1.44%	2.00%

(b) Resource utilization of the atomics unit

Fig. 4. Minimal duration simulations and synthesis results

Further, the synthesis of our module has the resource usage given in Fig. 4(b). It is part of a network adapter that additionally has load/store, DMA as well as task spawning support. The overall resource utilization of the atomics unit with around 12% of the network adapter and only maximally 2% of the whole tile, is comparatively low.

Besides these minimal duration simulations, we investigated several stress test measurements on our FPGA platform using the scenarios described earlier. In all the following micro benchmarks, each used core performs 10k iterations of the given scenarios, i.e. either 10k increments to the shared counter (SC) or 10k enqueue/dequeue operations to the linked queue (LQ). The tests are always done for all three synchronization types (lock-based, lock-free or dedicated hardware). We want to note, that for x cores, the overall workload is x-times as high. Alternatively, if the overall workload was kept constant with increasing core counts, the resulting graphs - from a purely visual perspective - would not be as easily distinguishable as shown in Fig. 5.

The results for the first stress test are depicted in Fig. 5(a) and show the execution time for both the shared counter (SC, solid lines) and the linked-queue update (LQ, dashed lines) for all three types of synchronization classes each. In this scenario, we investigate remote accesses to one tile from three other tiles with 1 to 8 cores each, totaling to up to 24 cores. Due to the higher complexity and therefore longer iteration duration of the linked-queue scenario, the dashed lines are always above the corresponding solid lines. Apart from that, the two scenarios behave similar. We make four key observations: (1) For no and low concurrency on the data structure, the lock-free variant is preferable over the lock-based one, since it does not suffer from (many) retries and the corresponding re-execution of the critical section. (2) Although not shown in the graphs, but underlined by our measurements, the retry rate rises with increasing concurrency, i.e. core count. We further did not depict but measured, that the execution time of the lock-based variants is linear in the number of cores, while the execution time for the lock-free variants is linear in the number of retries. (3) There is a concurrency depended cross-over point between the lock-based and lock-free variants (intersection of the lines). A concurrency depended decision

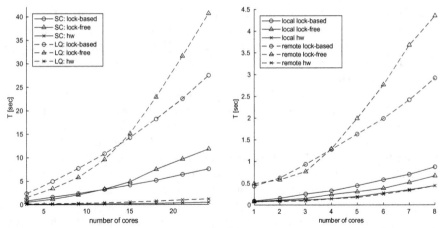

(a) Execution time for the three synchronization variants (lock-based, lock-free, hw) for the shared counter (SC) and the linked queue (LQ) for different core counts

(b) Comparison of purely local vs. purely remote execution of the linked queue (LQ) scenario for variable core counts per tile

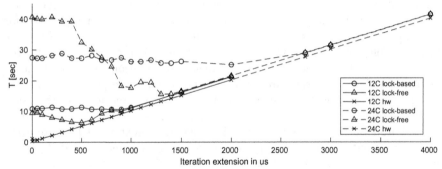

(c) Variable iteration duration for fixed critical section size for the three variants for a 12 and 24 core scenario, respectively

Fig. 5. Stress test measurement results

for one or the other could be investigated and made at design and/or run-time as possible performance optimization. (4) In all cases, the dedicated hardware implementation fetch-and-inc/CaCAO outperforms the other two variants by far. For the list-queue, the speedup rises from 9.5 (3×1 core) to 35.4 (3×8 cores) and from 14.6 to 23.9 compared to the lock-free and lock-based variant, respectively. The dedicated hardware implementation almost does not suffer from rising concurrency. The additional time is due to serialized execution in the atomics unit.

In the second stress test, we compare the execution time of LQ for purely local vs. purely remote access to the shared data structure. The results are depicted in Fig. 5(b) for varying core count between 1 and 8. We make 3 further key observations: (5) As expected, the purely local execution outperforms the remote operation in general. (6) Whereas for remote operation, there again is a cross-over point between the lock-based and lock-free variants (intersection of dashed lines), for local operations this behavior is not observed. The concurrency in combination with the much lower retry penalty explains this. (7) The relative advantage of the dedicated hardware implementation is much higher for remote than for local operations due to the higher retry penalty of the lock-free and the higher iteration duration of the lock-based variant. The advantage of the dedicated hardware over the lock-free variant is 6.5 times higher for remote compared to local operations. The advantage over the lock-based variant is 3.3 times higher. In both cases, we considered 8 local vs. 8 remote cores.

In our final measurements, we mimic different ratios of the non-critical part to the critical section of an application. This is done by keeping the critical section size constant, whereas we extend the whole base iteration by some iteration extension (iteration = base iteration + iteration extension). In Fig. 5(c), the results are depicted for the three variants of the linked-queue scenario for 12 and 24 cores. For an extension of 0 μs, the critical section in our scenarios is e.g. around 5% of the unextended base iteration for the SC in the 24 core variant. With this said, we make further key observations: (8) The lower the percentage of the critical section compared to the whole iteration, the lower the retries for the lock-free version and the corresponding total time. (9) A minimum can be found at a delay of around 1400 μs for the 24 core variant and at 500 μs for the 12 core variant (these times equal the average base iteration times for the lock-free variant). The retry rate drops to almost zero at these points. From then on, the execution time is dominated by the iteration extension, i.e. the additional time of the non-critical section. Similarly the lock-based variants start to be dominated by this extension after their average unextended base iteration times are reached, which are 800 μs and 2700 μs, respectively. (10) If the iteration extension dominates the whole iteration, i.e. if the percentage of the critical section gets very small, all variants converge. Even the dedicated hardware variants are dominated by the non-critical part. (11) At 500 μs, were the 12 core variant reaches the zero retry point, shows that the higher concurrency of 24 cores still has a high number of retries. An extrapolation of this principle would yield similar behavior for more than 24 cores at the 1400 μs mark, etc.

6   Conclusion and Future Work

To tackle the scalability issue of future manycore platforms, efficient remote operations and synchronization primitives are a key.

Our investigated scenarios show that there are application specific usecases for lock-based, as well as lock-free synchronization. Modern distributed shared memory platforms should therefore provide both types of synchronization (efficient inter-tile lock implementation, as well as general purpose atomic primitives like CAS or LL/SC) to allow flexibility for the programmer.

We further showed, that especially remote operation highly profit from dedicated hardware implementations to overcome the disadvantages of both lock-based and lock-free software implementations. Future systems should implement often used and highly concurrent tasks as dedicated hardware. Near memory acceleration could be a further improvement.

As future work, for systems without CaCAO support, one could explore the potential of situation based usage of the lock-based or lock-free variants, which would require a concurrency dependent decision. A heuristic, with which the runtime system could choose between the lock-based and lock-free variant would be needed.

Further, we plan to extend the CaCAO approach to more complex functionalities based on its compositional nature. We want to identify useful functions and investigate their potential in real applications.

Acknowledgement. This work was partly supported by the German Research Foundation (DFG) as part of the Transregional Collaborative Research Center Invasive Computing [SFB/TR 89]. The authors would also like to thank Christoph Erhardt, Sebastian Maier and Florian Schmaus from FAU Erlangen, as well as Dirk Gabriel from our chair for the helpful discussions.

References

1. Lenoski, D., Laudon, J., Gharachorloo, K., Weber, W.D., Gupta, A., Hennessy, J., Horowitz, M., Lam, M.S.: The stanford dash multiprocessor. Computer **25**(3), 63–79 (1992)
2. Mellanox: Ug130-archoverview-tile-gx. http://www.mellanox.com/repository/solutions/tile-scm/docs/UG130-ArchOverview-TILE-Gx.pdf
3. Michael, M.M., Scott, M.L.: Implementation of atomic primitives on distributed shared memory multiprocessors. In: 1995 Proceedings of First IEEE Symposium on High-Performance Computer Architecture, pp. 222–231. IEEE (1995)
4. Tsigas, P., Zhang, Y.: Integrating non-blocking synchronisation in parallel applications: performance advantages and methodologies. In: Proceedings of the 3rd International Workshop on Software and Performance, pp. 55–67. ACM (2002)
5. Herlihy, M.: Wait-free synchronization. ACM Trans. Program. Lang. Syst. (TOPLAS) **13**(1), 124–149 (1991)
6. Herlihy, M.: A methodology for implementing highly concurrent data objects. ACM Trans. Program. Lang. Syst. (TOPLAS) **15**(5), 745–770 (1993)
7. Wei, Z., Liu, P., Sun, R., Ying, R.: High-efficient queue-based spin locks for Network-on-Chip processors. In: 2014 IEEE Asia Pacific Conference on Circuits and Systems (APCCAS), pp. 260–263. IEEE (2014)
8. Wei, Z., Liu, P., Zeng, Z., Xu, J., Ying, R.: Instruction-based high-efficient synchronization in a many-core Network-on-Chip processor. In: 2014 IEEE International Symposium on Circuits and Systems (ISCAS), pp. 2193–2196. IEEE (2014)
9. Chen, X., Lu, Z., Jantsch, A., Chen, S.: Handling shared variable synchronization in multi-core Network-on-Chips with distributed memory. In: 2010 IEEE International on SOC Conference (SOCC), pp. 467–472. IEEE (2010)
10. Schweizer, H., Besta, M., Hoefler, T.: Evaluating the cost of atomic operations on modern architectures. In: 2015 International Conference on Parallel Architecture and Compilation (PACT), pp. 445–456. IEEE (2015)

11. Mellanox: Ug101-user-architecture-reference.pdf.   http://www.mellanox.com/repository/solutions/tile-scm/docs/UG101-User-Architecture-Reference.pdf

12. Mellor-Crummey, J.M., Scott, M.L.: Algorithms for scalable synchronization on shared-memory multiprocessors. ACM Trans. Comput. Syst. (TOCS) **9**(1), 21–65 (1991)

13. Herlihy, M., Shavit, N.: The Art of Multiprocessor Programming. Morgan Kaufmann, Burlington (2011)

14. Michael, M.M., Scott, M.L.: Nonblocking algorithms and preemption-safe locking on multiprogrammed shared memory multiprocessors. J. Parallel Distrib. Comput. **51**(1), 1–26 (1998)

15. Tian, G., Hammami, O.: Performance measurements of synchronization mechanisms on 16PE NoC based multi-core with dedicated synchronization and data NoC. In: 16th IEEE International Conference on Electronics, Circuits, and Systems, ICECS 2009, pp. 988–991. IEEE (2009)

Memory Models and Systems

Redundant Execution on Heterogeneous Multi-cores Utilizing Transactional Memory

Rico Amslinger[(✉)], Sebastian Weis, Christian Piatka, Florian Haas, and Theo Ungerer

University of Augsburg, Augsburg, Germany
{rico.amslinger,sebastian.weis,christian.piatka,
florian.haas,theo.ungerer}@informatik.uni-augsburg.de

Abstract. Cycle-by-cycle lockstep execution as implemented by current embedded processors is unsuitable for energy-efficient heterogeneous multi-cores, because the different cores are not cycle synchronous. Furthermore, current and future safety-critical applications demand fail-operational execution, which requires mechanisms for error recovery.

In this paper, we propose a loosely-coupled redundancy approach which combines an in-order with an out-of-order core and utilizes transactional memory for error recovery. The critical program is run in dual-modular redundancy on the out-of-order and the in-order core. The memory accesses of the out-of-order core are used to prefetch for the in-order core. The transactional memory system's checkpointing mechanism is leveraged to recover from errors. The resulting system runs up to 2.9 times faster than a lockstep system consisting of two in-order cores and consumes up to 35% less energy at the same performance than a lockstep system consisting of two out-of-order cores.

Keywords: Fault tolerance · Multi-core · Heterogeneous system
Transactional memory · Cache

1 Introduction

Heterogeneous multi-cores like ARM big.LITTLE^{TM}-systems [2] combine fast and complex (i.e. out-of-order) cores with slow and simple (i.e. in-order) cores to achieve both high peak performance and long battery life. While these architectures are mainly designed for mobile devices, modern embedded applications, e.g. those used for autonomous driving, also require high performance and power efficiency.

Additionally, these applications require high safety levels, as they are supported by current safety-critical lockstep processors [1,8,12]. However, cycle-by-cycle lockstep execution requires determinism at cycle granularity, because the core states are compared after every cycle. This strict determinism complicates

© Springer International Publishing AG, part of Springer Nature 2018
M. Berekovic et al. (Eds.): ARCS 2018, LNCS 10793, pp. 155–167, 2018.
https://doi.org/10.1007/978-3-319-77610-1_12

the use of modern out-of-order pipelines, limits dynamic power management mechanisms [5], and also prevents the combination of a fast out-of-order core with an energy-efficient in-order core, even if both execute the same instruction set. In contrast to lockstep execution, loosely-coupled redundant execution approaches [14–16], where the cores are not synchronized every cycle, allow the cores to execute more independently. As a cycle-based synchronization between the redundant cores is not necessary, resource sharing of parts of the memory hierarchy becomes possible. In that case, a heterogeneous dual-core may benefit from synergies between the cores, where a slower in-order core checks the results of a faster out-of-order core. In case an application does not need result verification, the redundant core can be switched off for energy savings or used as a separate unit for parallel execution.

Furthermore, current safety-critical lockstep cores only support fail-safe execution, since they are only able to detect errors. However, future safety-critical applications may additionally demand a fail-operational execution, which requires the implementation of recovery mechanisms. In this paper, we present a loosely-coupled fault-tolerance approach, combining a heterogeneous multi-core with hardware transactional memory for error isolation and recovery. Its advantages are a more energy efficient execution than an out-of-order lockstep system, more performance than an in-order lockstep system, and less hardware and energy consumption than a triple modular redundant system.

Due to the loose coupling it is possible to combine different cores and to employ fault-tolerance on a heterogeneous dual-core. In this case, the out-of-order core can run ahead of the in-order core. This enables the leading (out-of-order) core to forward its information about memory accesses and branch outcomes to the trailing (in-order) core to increase its performance. Therefore, the approach provides a desirable trade-off between a homogeneous lockstep system consisting of either out-of-order or in-order cores as it is more power efficient or faster, respectively. The hardware cost for the implementation can be reduced by utilizing existing hardware transactional memory (HTM) structures. The HTM system provides rollback capabilities, which enable the system to make progress even if faults occur. The affected transactions are re-executed, until they succeed. No additional main memory is required, as the HTM system isolates speculative values in the caches. If a parallel workload does not require a fault-tolerant execution, the loose coupling can be switched off at run-time to benefit from the multi-core CPU and the transactional memory for multi-threading.

The contributions of this paper are: (1) A mechanism to couple heterogeneous cores for redundancy that speeds up the trailing core by forwarding data cache accesses and branch outcomes. (2) A design of a HTM for embedded multi-cores to support loosely-coupled redundancy with implicit checkpoints. (3) An evaluation of throughput and power consumption of our proposed heterogeneous redundant system compared to a lockstep processor.

The remainder of this paper is structured as follows. Related work is discussed in Sect. 2. Section 3 describes our redundant execution implementation. The baseline system is depicted first. Then our loose coupling and the rollback mechanism are explained. The following subsection describes the necessary changes to the HTM system. The last subsection specifies the advantages for heterogeneous systems. Section 4 contains a performance evaluation of several microbenchmarks. Our approach is compared to a lockstep system and a stride prefetching mechanism. The paper is concluded in Sect. 5.

2   Related Work

Reinhardt and Mukherjee [15] propose to use the simultaneous multithreading capabilities of modern processors for error detection. The program is executed twice on the same core. The executions are shifted and can use different execution units for the same instruction. It is proposed to maintain a constant slack to minimize memory stalls.

AR-SMT [16] is a time redundant fault-tolerance approach. An SMT-processor executes the same program twice with some delay. The execution state of the second thread is used to restore the first thread to a safe state if an error occurs.

The Slipstream Processor [18] is a concept which does not only provide fault tolerance, but also higher performance by executing a second, slimmer version of the program on either the same or another core. The second version of the program is generated by leaving out instructions which are predicted to be ineffective. The resulting branch outcomes and prefetches are used to accelerate the full version of the program. Errors are detected by comparing stores.

LBRA [17] is a loosely-coupled redundant architecture extending the transaction system LogTM-SE [20]. The old value for every memory location accessed by the leading thread is stored in a log. For writes the new value is immediately stored in memory. The trailing thread uses the log values for input duplication. Both cores calculate signatures for every transaction. If an error is detected, the log is traversed backwards to restore the old memory state.

FaulTM [19] is a fault-tolerance system utilizing transactional memory. Their approach differs from ours in that it executes redundant transactions synchronously. The write-sets and registers of both transactions are compared simultaneously, with one transaction committing to memory. This prohibits one thread to run ahead of the other and thus suppresses possible cache-related performance benefits.

Haas et al. [9,10] use the existing Intel HTM system (TSX) for error detection and recovery. As Intel TSX does not support automatic transaction creation or write set comparison, the protected software is instrumented to provide those features itself. Transactional blocks are executed with an offset in the trailing process, as TSX does not allow checksum transfer within active transactions. As the redundant processes use the same virtual addresses, but different physical memory locations, no speedups due to positive cache effects occur in the trailing process.

3   Transaction-Based Redundant Execution Model

The baseline multi-core architecture with HTM is shown in Fig. 1 as an abstraction of a state-of-the-art heterogeneous multi-core. The architecture consists, similar to ARM big.LITTLE, of two different cores with private L1 data and instruction caches that are connected to a private L2 cache. Cache coherence is guaranteed by hardware.

Hardware facilities support the execution of transactions. As the ARM-architecture does not offer HTM yet, a design comparable to Intel Haswell [11] is used. The register sets of the cores are extended to provide snapshot capabilities. The data caches and the coherence protocol are enhanced to manage the read and write sets. The affected cache blocks cannot be evicted during the transaction. The instruction caches do not require read and write sets since self-modifying code is not supported. Transactional conflicts are detected by an extended cache-coherence protocol. Additional enhancements to support redundant execution are described in Sect. 3.2.

3.1   Loosely-Coupled Redundancy with Checkpoints

The proposed fault-tolerance mechanisms can detect and recover from faults that occur in the pipelines of the cores, which is shown by the Sphere of Replication in Fig. 1. While there are multiple instances of every cache and register set, a distinct fault-tolerance mechanism like an error correction code (ECC) is still required for all caches and register sets to ensure the consistency of the generated checkpoints.

Figure 2 shows the redundant execution approach. The redundant system proposed in this paper executes the same code on both cores. The execution on the cores is shifted by a dynamic time offset, called slack. Both cores will start

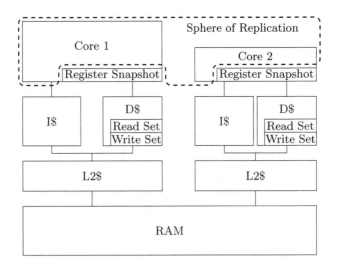

Fig. 1. Baseline multi-core architecture, enhanced to support hardware transactions.

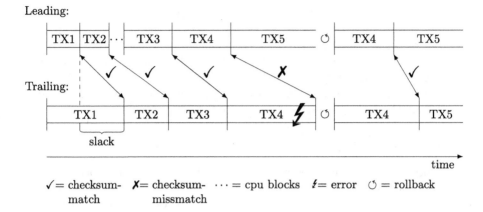

Fig. 2. Redundant execution with transactions.

execution at the same instruction, when redundancy is enabled. Later the out-of-order core is running ahead of the in-order core, except for I/O operations or error recovery, that require synchronization of the cores to be resolved. As the leading core usually runs faster, the slack increases. For implementation reasons like buffer sizes the slack is limited to a certain number of instructions. This hard limit will not be hit often, as accelerating effects for the trailing core like forwarding memory accesses will become more effective with increasing slack.

To enable recoverability, checkpoints are automatically created by the cores, when a transaction is started. The cores will automatically start and commit transactions in a way that minimizes transaction and comparison overhead, while ensuring that they fit in the cache. Instrumentation of the program with explicit transaction instructions is not required.

While the trailing core only keeps the last checkpoint, the leading core must retain two. This enables the rollback after an error, regardless of the core it occurs on. If the leading core gets more than two checkpoints ahead (e. g. after TX2), it has to wait. It is also necessary for the trailing core to wait at the checkpoint if it overtakes the leading core. As the HTM system uses the caches to hold unverified data, the cache size also limits the slack. When the trailing core reaches a checkpoint, the current state is compared to the corresponding checkpoint of the leading core. The new checkpoint for the trailing core is only created after a successful comparison. The leading core on the other hand can speculatively progress as long as it keeps at least one confirmed checkpoint.

Unconfirmed data is never written back to memory or transferred to another cache. Only after confirming correct execution, the trailing core writes modified data back to memory or marks it as valid for the cache coherence protocol. The leading core's cache silently evicts modified cache lines that were already verified instead of writing them back. It relies on getting their data back from memory or by cache to cache transfer from the trailing core. As none of the caches can evict data written after active checkpoints, the cache size clearly limits the distance between subsequent checkpoints.

Figure 2 also shows the handling of an error. After the error occurs, the next comparison after TX4 results in a mismatch. The leading core has already advanced past the potential erroneous checkpoint, but is still keeping an older confirmed checkpoint at the start of TX4. Thus both cores rollback to the start of TX4. As all changes after the confirmed checkpoint are confined in the cores and their L1 caches, the rollback is fast. If the fault was transient, the next comparison will succeed and the execution resumes regularly.

3.2   Extension of HTM to Support Fault Tolerance

If the processor already includes support for HTM to speculatively speed up parallel execution, the implementation of the redundant system can be simplified. The assumed HTM system has to provide support for isolation and checkpointing. Thus those components can simply be reused. As the leading core requires multiple checkpoints, the checkpointing capabilities of some simple transaction systems may be insufficient.

The conflict detection component of HTM is unnecessary for redundant execution on a dual-core, as both cores execute the same thread. The obvious approach is to disable it completely, in order to avoid detection of false conflicts between the leading and trailing core. The commit logic of the leading core can be simplified, as writeback of confirmed data is handled by the trailing core.

Some additions are still required to support full fault tolerance. First, HTM usually relies on special instructions to start and end transactions. For fault tolerance another approach is preferred: The transaction boundaries should be determined automatically at run-time, as it is hard to predict exact cache usage at compile time. The first transaction is started, when fault tolerance is enabled. The transaction is committed, once the checkpoint's capacity is exhausted or another limit (e. g. execution time or instruction count) is reached. The trailing core commits at the same instruction as the leading core. The next transaction is started directly after the commit.

Second, regular HTM systems do not care about the content of written cache blocks. Only their addresses need to be compared for conflict detection. It is thus necessary to implement an additional unit to compare registers and cache block content. Depending on the employed conflict detection mechanism, different implementations are feasible. If the transaction system uses a lazy conflict detection mechanism, which already transfers all cache lines and their content while committing, the comparison can be extended to include this data. Register values can be stored in a cache line with a special address. This does not only allow for their comparison, but will also store them in main memory for checkpoint creation. If the transaction system does not already transfer all cache lines while committing, the use of a checksum is favored, as this minimizes additional overhead at commit time. The checksum is updated whenever a cache line is written in a transaction. At commit the register values are also included in the checksum. The checksum has to be transferred to the other core. If a mismatch is detected, this information is broadcasted to restart both cores at the correct checkpoints.

3.3   Heterogeneous Redundant Systems

Tightly-coupled redundancy approaches like lockstep execution are not applicable when heterogeneous cores are employed. Once a core executes an instruction faster than the other core, a false error will be detected, causing the abort of the application or a costly recovery attempt. Loosely-coupled redundant execution does not suffer from the disadvantage of false positives caused by different microarchitectural implementations.

If the slack is sufficiently large, a cache miss is detected in the leading core before the trailing core even reaches the instruction that causes the fetch. Thus the leading core's memory access addresses can be forwarded to the trailing core, so it can prefetch them. This increases the performance, as cache misses are often more expensive for simpler cores. Since the total run-time of the system is determined by the slower core, this optimization improves total system performance. The trailing core still performs full address calculation, as an error could occur in the leading core's address calculation. The trailing core always uses its own address calculation for memory access and thus a cache miss can occur if the calculated addresses differ. If the loaded values also differ, the next comparison will detect the mismatch and cause a rollback.

The trailing core can also benefit from other information. Even simple in-order cores like the ARM Cortex-A7 feature branch prediction. As the cores' data structures used for branch prediction are smaller than those of complex cores, mispredictions are more common. These mispredictions can be eliminated by forwarding branch outcomes from the leading core to the trailing core by using a branch outcome queue [15]. This requires the leading core to stay far enough ahead, so that it can retire the branch before the trailing core decodes it. If the leading core is sufficiently fast, all branches in the trailing core are predicted correctly. Thus, the performance improves in programs with many data dependent branches. Error detection is not impacted, as the trailing core will interpret different branch outcomes as mispredict.

With increasing differences between the cores, the implementation of such enhancements becomes more difficult. For instance, a complex core may replace short branches with predicated execution [13]. Thus the branch will not reach the core's commit stage. As a result the trailing core will not find a corresponding entry in the branch outcome queue, when it reaches the branch. Such problems can cause the cores to lose synchronization and therefore decrease performance, as shifted branch outcomes can be more inaccurate than the trailing core's regular branch prediction.

4   Evaluation

The suggested approach was modeled in Gem5 [6]. Based on Butko et al. [7], the fast and slow cores were configured to match the ARM Cortex-A15 and ARM Cortex-A7, respectively. The per core 32 kB L1 caches are split into data and instruction caches, while the per core 512 kB L2 caches are unified. Power consumption was approximated as the product of the simulated benchmark runtime and the average power consumption of an Exynos 5430 SoC. It was assumed that a lockstep system runs as fast as a corresponding single-core machine, but consumes twice the energy. For our approach, a limit was put in place to prevent the leading core from running too far ahead. The leading core stalls when it has committed 1,000 instructions more than the trailing core, or if it tries to evict a modified cache line that the trailing core has not written yet.

We implemented several sequential microbenchmarks with different memory access patterns. The following microbenchmarks were used to assess the performance of the approach:

- The *breadth-first* benchmark calculates the size of a tree by traversing it in breadth-first order. Each node has a random number of children.
- The *heapsort* benchmark sorts an array using heapsort. The array is initialized with random positive integers.
- The *matrixmul* benchmark calculates the product of two dense matrices.
- The *quicksort* benchmark sorts an array using quicksort. The array is initialized with random positive integers.
- The *red-black tree* benchmark inserts random entries into a red-black tree.
- The *shuffle* benchmark shuffles an array using the Fisher-Yates shuffle.

The seed of the random number generator was constant for all runs.

Figure 3 shows the microbenchmarks' throughput on the y-axis and the corresponding energy consumption per run on the x-axis. The microbenchmarks were executed on a lockstep system consisting of two Cortex-A7, another lockstep system consisting of two Cortex-A15 and our approach, using a Cortex-A15 as leading core and a Cortex-A7 as trailing core. The cores' clock frequency were varied in their frequency ranges (Cortex-A7: 500–1300 MHz, Cortex-A15: 700–1900 MHz) in 100 MHz steps. For our approach the trailing core's frequency was fixed at 1300 MHz, while the leading core's frequency was varied from 700 MHz to 1900 MHz.

All systems were evaluated with and without a hardware prefetcher. The Cortex-A7 utilizes early issue of memory operations [3] in all variants. A stride prefetcher [4], which tries to detect regular access patterns on a per-instruction basis, was used in the corresponding variants. If an instruction accesses memory locations with a constant distance, the prefetcher will predict the next addresses and preload them into the L1 cache. As the stride prefetcher works on physical addresses, a detected stream will be terminated at the page boundary. For this evaluation the prefetcher was configured to observe 32 distinct instructions on a least recently used basis and prefetch up to 4 cache lines ahead of the last actual access.

At first only a small increase in voltage per 100 MHz step is required to allow the core to run stable. Thus for the lockstep systems, a large increase in throughput can be achieved at low frequencies by a small increase in power consumption. Note that the frequency itself has only minor influence on the results, as power consumption is measured per benchmark run and not per time unit.

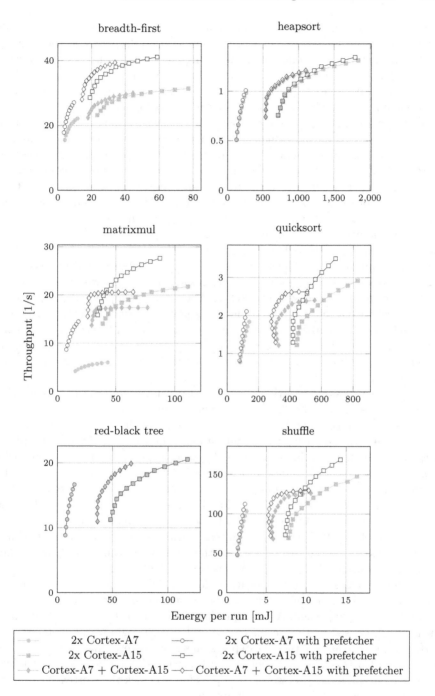

Fig. 3. Trade-off between throughput and power consumption (Color figure online)

When the cores approach their maximum frequency, the required increase in voltage raises. At the same time the achieved acceleration decreases, as the memory clock frequency remains constant. Thus for high frequencies only a small increase in throughput can be achieved by a large increase in power consumption. The effect is more pronounced on the Cortex-A15, as it performs more instructions per cycle on average and its maximum frequency is higher.

Our approach shows a different pattern. For the frequency range, in which the out-of-order core's performance does not exceed the in-order core's performance at maximum frequency, the leading core slows down the entire system. Increasing the leading core's frequency, can reduce total power consumption (e. g. in *quicksort* or *shuffle*), as the task finishes quicker, thus reducing the time the trailing core is running at maximum voltage. After the leading core's performance exceeds the trailing core's, there is a phase in which the trailing core can be accelerated to the leading core's level by prefetching. This area is the most interesting as it offers higher performance than the trailing core, at a lower power consumption than a lockstep system of two out-of-order cores. If the leading core's frequency is increased further, eventually a point will be reached, at which every memory access is prefetched. The graph asymptotically approaches this performance level. As the leading core's power consumption still raises, the combination will eventually consume more energy than a lockstep system consisting of two out-of-order cores would at the same performance level (apparent in *matrixmul*). Thus further increasing the frequency of the leading core should be avoided.

The effectiveness of the stride prefetcher varies depending on the benchmark's memory access pattern. For benchmarks with regular access pattern like *matrixmul* most cache misses can be eliminated by the prefetcher. This leads to a huge performance increase during the initialization of the source matrices. This phase does not profit from an increase in clock frequency, as it is entirely limited by the memory accesses. Out-of-order execution does not help much as well, as the reorder buffer can not hold enough loop iterations to reach the next cache line but one. The prefetcher on the other hand can fetch 4 cache lines ahead. If the prefetcher is enabled, all variants profit from a performance increase, which is independent of the clock frequency. The calculation phase still hits the same limit in the Cortex-A7, as the variant without the stride-prefetcher already prefetches all memory accesses if the Cortex-A15 is clocked high enough.

Shuffle accesses one of the locations for the swap operand at random. As consequence, the stride prefetcher is unable to predict this access. The other swap operand can be prefetched. As multiple values fit in a cache line, the amount of cache misses caused by this access is already lower to begin with. Therefore, the performance increase for the lockstep systems is relatively small. Our approach reaches the Cortex-A7's peak performance even without the stride prefetcher. With a stride prefetcher, however, it is possible, to clock the Cortex-A15 slower and thus decrease total power consumption.

Tree-based benchmarks like *breadth-first* or *red-black tree* show a very irregular memory access pattern. They do not benefit as much from a stride prefetcher, as it will rarely detect consistent strides when traversing the tree. Therefore, the performance is exactly the same for *red-black tree*. However, the stride prefetcher can improve performance for the queue used in *breadth-first*, as it shows a regular access pattern. An overly aggressive prefetcher may reduce performance for such algorithms, as it evicts cache lines that will be reused for false prefetches. Our approach on the other hand can eliminate all cache misses even for such irregular patterns, as long as the leading core runs fast enough. The resulting speedup exceeds, what is achievable with a simple prefetcher.

Our approach can achieve higher speedups than the stride prefetcher alone for both sorting algorithms. However the reasons differ. *Heapsort* shows an irregular access pattern, as the heap is tree-based. Thus, our approach can benefit from its superior prefetching performance, while enabling the stride prefetcher results only in minor performance improvements. *Quicksort* on the other hand shows a very regular access pattern, as it linearly accesses elements from both directions. However, *quicksort* uses data dependent comparisons as loop condition in the Hoare partition scheme. Regular branch predictors can not predict those branches, as they are essentially random for random data. However, in our approach the trailing core can use the forwarded branch outcomes from the leading core to further increase performance. Combining our approach with the stride prefetcher increases the throughput even further.

5   Conclusion

Loosely-coupled redundant execution with transactional memory to support checkpointing has the potential to be an alternative to current lockstep systems. As the HTM system already provides mechanisms like isolation and checkpointing, the required hardware enhancements are small. The isolation allows both cores to operate on the same memory region, while the checkpointing mechanism enables error recovery even with just two cores. The loose coupling makes it possible to use the approach in heterogeneous multi-cores.

The evaluation of the proposed approach showed that a slower in-order core is able to keep up with a faster out-of-order core to provide redundancy. This requires a near-optimal data prefetching in the trailing core, which is achieved by forwarding the memory accesses of the leading core. Supplying branch outcomes further increases the throughput of the slower core. The combination of heterogeneous cores for redundant execution results in a good trade-off between performance and power consumption. It offers up to 2.9 times the performance and up to 35% less power consumption than comparable lockstep systems consisting of only slow or fast cores, respectively. It is also possible to decrease power consumption by lowering the leading core's clock frequency, but this also slightly decreases performance. In some applications it is possible to achieve both a higher performance and a lower power consumption than a lockstep system consisting of slow cores, when an appropriate clock frequency is selected. Additionally, flexible coupling of cores improves the flexibility for parallel applications with varying fault-tolerance requirements.

As future work, we plan to extend our approach to larger heterogeneous multi-cores, which will enable to change the coupling of cores dynamically at run-time. Programs that exhibit a sufficient amount of cache misses benefit from a heterogeneous coupling, since the in-order trailing core will be accelerated by the cached data of the leading core. Otherwise, homogeneous coupling is preferred for compute intensive programs to deliver better performance. Further, we plan to extend the approach to support multi-threaded applications, regardless of the synchronization mechanism they use.

References

1. ARM Ltd.: Cortex-R5 and Cortex-R5F - Technical Reference Manual (2011). http://infocenter.arm.com/help/topic/com.arm.doc.ddi0460c/DDI0460C_cortexr5_trm.pdf. Revision r1p1
2. ARM Ltd.: big.LITTLE Technology: The Future of Mobile (2013). https://www.arm.com/files/pdf/big_LITTLE_Technology_the_Futue_of_Mobile.pdf
3. Austin, T.M., Sohi, G.S.: Zero-cycle loads: microarchitecture support for reducing load latency. In: Proceedings of the 28th Annual International Symposium on Microarchitecture, pp. 82–92 (1995)
4. Baer, J.L., Chen, T.F.: An effective on-chip preloading scheme to reduce data access penalty. In: Proceedings of the 1991 ACM/IEEE Conference on Supercomputing, Supercomputing 1991, pp. 176–186. ACM (1991)
5. Bernick, D., Bruckert, B., Vigna, P., Garcia, D., Jardine, R., Klecka, J., Smullen, J.: NonStop® advanced architecture. In: International Conference on Dependable Systems and Networks (DSN), pp. 12–21 (2005)
6. Binkert, N., Beckmann, B., Black, G., Reinhardt, S.K., Saidi, A., Basu, A., Hestness, J., Hower, D.R., Krishna, T., Sardashti, S., et al.: The gem5 simulator. ACM SIGARCH Comput. Archit. News **39**(2), 1–7 (2011)
7. Butko, A., Bruguier, F., Gamatié, A., Sassatelli, G., Novo, D., Torres, L., Robert, M.: Full-system simulation of big.LITTLE multicore architecture for performance and energy exploration. In: IEEE 10th International Symposium on Embedded Multicore/Many-Core Systems-on-Chip (MCSoC), pp. 201–208. IEEE (2016)
8. Freescale Semiconductor: Safety Manual for Qorivva MPC5643L (2013). https://www.nxp.com/docs/en/user-guide/MPC5643LSM.pdf
9. Haas, F., Weis, S., Metzlaff, S., Ungerer, T.: Exploiting Intel TSX for fault-tolerant execution in safety-critical systems. In: IEEE International Symposium on Defect and Fault Tolerance in VLSI and Nanotechnology Systems (DFT), pp. 197–202 (2014)
10. Haas, F., Weis, S., Ungerer, T., Pokam, G., Wu, Y.: Fault-tolerant execution on COTS multi-core processors with hardware transactional memory support. In: Knoop, J., Karl, W., Schulz, M., Inoue, K., Pionteck, T. (eds.) ARCS 2017. LNCS, vol. 10172, pp. 16–30. Springer, Cham (2017). https://doi.org/10.1007/978-3-319-54999-6_2
11. Hammarlund, P., Martinez, A.J., Bajwa, A.A., Hill, D.L., Hallnor, E., Jiang, H., Dixon, M., Derr, M., Hunsaker, M., Kumar, R., et al.: Haswell: the fourth-generation Intel core processor. IEEE Micro **34**(2), 6–20 (2014)
12. Infineon Technologies AG: Highly integrated and performance optimized 32-bit microcontrollers for automotive and industrial applications (2017). https://www.infineon.com/dgdl/Infineon-TriCore-Family_2017-BC-v02_00-EN.pdf?fileId=5546d4625d5945ed015dc81f47b436c7

13. Klauser, A., Austin, T., Grunwald, D., Calder, B.: Dynamic hammock predication for non-predicated instruction set architectures. In: International Conference on Parallel Architectures and Compilation Techniques (PACT), pp. 278–285 (1998)

14. LaFrieda, C., Ipek, E., Martinez, J., Manohar, R.: Utilizing dynamically coupled cores to form a resilient chip multiprocessor. In: 37th International Conference on Dependable Systems and Networks (DSN), pp. 317–326 (2007)

15. Reinhardt, S.K., Mukherjee, S.S.: Transient fault detection via simultaneous multithreading. In: 27th Annual International Symposium on Computer Architecture (ISCA), pp. 25–36. ACM (2000)

16. Rotenberg, E.: AR-SMT: a microarchitectural approach to fault tolerance in microprocessors. In: 29th International Symposium on Fault-Tolerant Computing (FTCS), pp. 84–91 (1999)

17. Sánchez, D., Aragón, J., Garcıa, J.: A log-based redundant architecture for reliable parallel computation. In: International Conference on High Performance Computing (HiPC) (2010)

18. Sundaramoorthy, K., Purser, Z., Rotenberg, E.: Slipstream processors: improving both performance and fault tolerance. ACM SIGPLAN Not. **35**(11), 257–268 (2000)

19. Yalcin, G., Unsal, O., Cristal, A.: FaulTM: error detection and recovery using hardware transactional memory. In: Conference on Design, Automation and Test in Europe (DATE), pp. 220–225 (2013)

20. Yen, L., Bobba, J., Marty, M.R., Moore, K.E., Volos, H., Hill, M.D., Swift, M.M., Wood, D.A.: LogTM-SE: decoupling hardware transactional memory from caches. In: IEEE 13th International Symposium on High Performance Computer Architecture (HPCA), pp. 261–272 (2007)

Improving the Performance of STT-MRAM LLC Through Enhanced Cache Replacement Policy

Pierre-Yves Péneau$^{(\boxtimes)}$, David Novo, Florent Bruguier, Lionel Torres, Gilles Sassatelli, and Abdoulaye Gamatié

LIRMM, CNRS and University of Montpellier,
161 rue Ada, 34095 Montpellier, France
{peneau,novo,bruguier,torres,sassatelli,gamatie}@lirmm.fr

Abstract. Modern architectures adopt large on-chip cache memory hierarchies with more than two levels. While this improves performance, it has a certain cost in area and power consumption. In this paper, we consider an emerging non volatile memory technology, namely the Spin-Transfer Torque Magnetic RAM (STT-MRAM), with a powerful cache replacement policy in order to design an efficient STT-MRAM Last-Level Cache (LLC) in terms of performance. Well-known benefits of STT-MRAM are their near-zero static power and high density compared to volatile memories. Nonetheless, their high write latency may be detrimental to system performance. In order to mitigate this issue, we combine STT-MRAM with a recent cache The benefit of this combination is evaluated through experiments on SPEC CPU2006 benchmark suite, showing performance improvements of up to 10% compared to SRAM cache with LRU on a single core system.

1 Introduction

Energy consumption has become an important concern of computer architecture design for the last decades. While the demand for more computing resources is growing every year, much effort has been put on finding the best trade-off between performance and power consumption in order to build *energy-efficient* architectures. Current design trends show that the memory speed is not growing as fast as cores computing capacity, leading to the so-called *memory-wall* issue. Caching techniques, which have been pushed in the past for mitigating the memory-wall, are facing the silicon area constraints. Typically, up to 40% of the total area of processors [9] is occupied by the caches hierarchy. As a consequence, the energy consumed by this part of the CPU is important. As an example, it constitutes up to 30% of the total energy of a StrongARM chip [11]. In particular, as the technology scaling continues, the static power consumption is becoming predominant over the dynamic power consumption [4].

Data accesses that occur beyond the Last-Level Cache (LLC) are usually time and energy-consuming as they have to reach the off-chip main memory. An

© Springer International Publishing AG, part of Springer Nature 2018
M. Berekovic et al. (Eds.): ARCS 2018, LNCS 10793, pp. 168–180, 2018.
https://doi.org/10.1007/978-3-319-77610-1_13

intelligent design of the LLC reducing such accesses can save power and increase the overall performance. An usual technique adopted in the past consists in increasing the cache storage capacity so as to reduce the cache miss rate. This approach is no longer desired due to area and energy constraints. Increasing the cache size has a negative impact on the financial cost and increases the static power consumption.

In this paper, we consider an emerging memory technology, the Spin-Torque Transfer Magnetic RAM (STT-MRAM), a Non-Volatile Memory (NVM) that has a near-zero leakage consumption. This memory has a higher density than SRAM, providing more storage capacity for the same area. While STT-MRAM read latency is close to SRAM read latency, the gap for write access is currently one obstacle to a wide STT-MRAM adoption. In the present work, we study the impact in write reduction of cache replacement policies. Each read request leading to a cache miss eventually triggers a write. Upon this cache miss, the request is forwarded to an upper level in the memory hierarchy.[1] When the response is received, the corresponding data is written into the cache. Hence, the cache replacement policy has indirectly an important impact on the number of writes that occur upon cache misses. We carry out a fine-grained analysis on the actual sequence of read/write transactions taking place in the cache management strategy. On the basis of this study, we propose and evaluate the combined use of STT-MRAM and *state-of-the-art* Hawkeye cache replacement policy [8]. Thanks to Hawkeye, the number of writes due to cache misses is reduced, while benefiting from STT-MRAM density for larger LLC. Since STT-MRAM integration is known to provide energy savings [17], we put the focus on its impact on system performance so as to avoid a degradation of the overall energy-efficiency.

This paper is organized as follows: Sect. 2 presents related work; Sect. 3 introduces a motivational example and our proposed approach; Sect. 4 describes the experimental results validating our proposal; finally, Sect. 5 gives some concluding remarks and perspectives.

2   Related Work

The use of hybrid caches has been a recurrent approach to address write asymmetry in NVMs. A hybrid cache mixes SRAM and NVM memories to achieve the best of each technology. Most existing techniques rely on a combination of hardware and software techniques.

Wu et al. [18] proposed a hybrid memory hierarchy based on a larger LLC thanks to NVM density. They evaluated different memory technologies and identified eDRAM as the best choice for performance improvement, while STT-MRAM is the best choice for energy saving. Sun et al. [16] designed a hybrid L2 cache with STT-MRAM and SRAM, and employed migration based policy to mitigate the latency drawbacks of STT-MRAM. The idea is to keep as many write intensive data in the SRAM part as possible. Senni et al. [14] proposed a hybrid cache design where the cache tag uses SRAM while cache data array

---

[1] The first cache level (L1), the closest to the CPU, is the lowest level.

uses STT-MRAM. The cache reacts at the speed of SRAM for hits and misses, which slightly mitigate the overall latency, while power is saved on the data array thanks to low leakage. Migration techniques for hybrid memories are expensive and may suffer from inaccurate predictions, inducing extra write operations.

Zhou et al. [19] proposed another technique called early-write-termination: upon a write, if the value to write is already in the cell, i.e., a redundant write, the operation is canceled. This technique, implemented at circuit level, does not require an extra read before writing and saves dynamic writing energy. Nevertheless, it is mainly relevant to applications with many redundant writes.

Software techniques to mitigate NVMs drawbacks have been also proposed. Li et al. [10] proposed a compilation method called migration-aware code motion. The goal is to change the data access patterns in cache blocks so as to minimize the extra cost due to migrations. Instructions that access the same cache block with the same operation are scheduled by the CPU close to each other. Péneau et al. [13] proposed to integrate STT-MRAM-based cache at L1 and L2 level and to apply aggressive code optimizations to reduce the number of writes.

Smullen et al. [15] redesigned the STT-MRAM memory cells to reduce the high dynamic energy and write latency. They decreased the data retention time (i.e., the non-volatility period) and reduce the current required for writing. While this approach shows promising results, it relies on an aggressive retention reduction that incurs the introduction of a costly refresh policy to avoid data loss.

In this work, we take a complementary approach and evaluate the impact of cache replacement policies coupled with variations on LLC capacity in the reduction of critical writes. We basically re-evaluate the gap in performance between STT-MRAM and SRAM-based LLC given the latest advances in cache replacement policies.

3   Motivation and Approach

In this work, we use the ChampSim [1] simulator with a subset of applications from the SPEC CPU2006 benchmark suite [7] for motivating our approach. Timing and energy results are obtained from CACTI [12] for the LLC and from datasheet information for the main memory [2]. More details of the experimental setup are given in Sect. 4.1. A common metric used to assess LLC performance is the *Miss Per Kilo Instructions* (MPKI), defined as the total number of cache misses divided by the total number of executed instructions. One possibility to reduce the MPKI is to increase the cache size. The cache contains more data and reduces the probability for a cache miss to occur. This results in penalties in terms of cache latency, energy and area.

3.1   Motivational Example

Let us evaluate the execution of two SPEC CPU2006 applications, namely *soplex* and *libquantum*. These applications have different memory access patterns. Figure 1a depicts the impact of 4 MB versus 2 MB LLC cache designs on the MPKI, the Instruction Per Cycle (IPC) and the energy consumption of LLC and the main memory. For *soplex*, the MPKI is decreased by 27.6%, leading to a faster execution by 9.7%, while the energy consumption of the LLC and the main memory is respectively degraded by 33% and improved by 23%. While the performance for *soplex* application benefits from a larger cache, this induces a negative impact on the LLC energy consumption. On the other hand, the outcome is different for the *libquantum* application. As shown in Fig. 1a, the MPKI is unchanged (i.e., no improvement), while the IPC is slightly degraded by 0.6%. The energy consumption of the LLC and the main memory is also degraded, due to more expensive read/write transactions on the LLC. Moreover, a lower IPC, i.e., a longer execution time, increases the static energy. Here, the energy consumption of the LLC drastically grows by up to 47% with larger cache. The breakdown in static and dynamic energy consumption of the LLC is detailed in Fig. 1b: 80% of the energy comes from the static part.

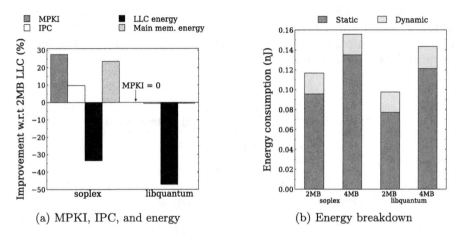

(a) MPKI, IPC, and energy   (b) Energy breakdown

Fig. 1. Evaluation of 2 MB and 4 MB LLC for *soplex* and *libquantum*

Increasing the cache size shows interesting results for performance but faces two obstacles. Firstly, the LLC energy consumption is increased. Moreover, depending of the memory access pattern of the application, it may degrade the LLC energy while offering no gain in performance. Secondly, doubling the LLC size increases the silicon area on the chip. This aspect is crucial in design and larger caches are often not realistic due to area budget constraints. To tackle these two aspects, we consider STT-MRAM, which is considered as a future candidate for SRAM replacement [17]. NVMs offer near-zero leakage and are denser than SRAM (a STT-MRAM cell is composed of one transistor versus six transistors for a SRAM cell). But, they suffer from higher memory access latency and energy per access, especially for write operation. STT-MRAM offers a near-zero leakage consumption, eliminating the high static energy consumption observed with SRAM (see Fig. 1b). This is even relevant for applications that do not benefit from larger cache such as *libquantum* (see Fig. 1b) In such a case, even though the execution time is longer, the energy consumption would not dramatically increase thanks to the low static energy of STT-MRAM.

3.2   Writes Operations at Last-Level Cache

At last-level cache, write operations are divided into two categories: *(a) write-back*, i.e., a write operation coming from a lower cache level, and *(b) write-fill*, i.e., a write operation that occurs when the LLC receives an answer from the main memory. These schemes are illustrated in Fig. 2. Let us consider L3 cache as LLC. Transaction (1) is a *write-back* coming from the L2 for data X. In this case, X is immediately written in the cache line (transaction (2a)). Possibly, a *write-back* could be generated by the LLC towards the main memory (transaction (2b)) if data D has been modified and needs to be saved. For the request (3) and (4), corresponding respectively to a *read* and a *prefetch*, the requested Y data is not in the cache. This cache miss triggers a transaction to the main memory to fetch Y, and upon receiving the response, Y data is written in the cache. This operation represents a *write-fill*. As with transaction (2b), a *write-back* is generated if data L replaced in the LLC must be saved.

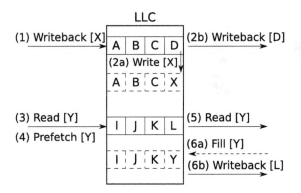

Fig. 2. Write transactions on the Last-Level Cache

Then, an important question that arises is to know whether or not *write-back* and *write-fill* have an equivalent impact on the overall system performance? For illustration, we consider five SPEC CPU2006 applications with different writes distributions to answer this question. Figure 3a reports the normalized IPC for different write latencies. Here, WF and WB respectively denote *write-fill* latency and *write-back* latency. We define the reference configuration as a 2 MB STT-MRAM LLC with $WF = WB = 38\,cycles$. Results are normalized to this reference. We also compare with a 2 MB SRAM LLC where $WF = WB = 20\,cycles$.

First, we set $WF = 0\,cycle$ in order to assess the impact of the *write-fill* operation on system performance. Then, we apply the same for WB for evaluating the impact of *write-back*. We also compare to the specific configuration where both WF and WB are set to zero. For all configurations, the write-buffer contains up to 16 elements. Moreover, bypassing is disabled for *write-back*.

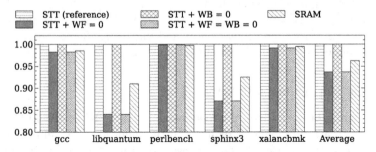

(a) *Write-back* (WB) and *write-fill* (WF) effects on performances normalized to baseline STT-MRAM

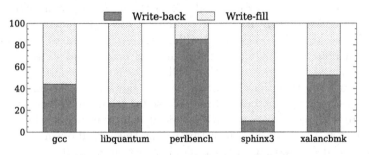

(b) *Write-back* and *write-fill* distribution

Fig. 3. Write operations performance and distribution

When $WF = 0\,cycle$, i.e., *write-fill* has no impact on performance, results show a reduced execution time by 0.93× on average and up to 0.84× for *libquantum*. When $WB = 0\,cycle$, i.e., *write-back* has no impact on performance, the execution time is the same as for the reference STT-MRAM configuration. Finally, when both WF and WB are set to zero, the execution time is the same as the case where only *write-fill* latency is set to zero. Performance gains are particularly visible for applications that have a higher number of *write-fill* than *write-back* requests, such as *libquantum* or *sphinx3*. Nevertheless, even for an application with more *write-back* requests such as *perlbench* (see Fig. 3b), results show that $WB = 0\,cycle$ has no impact on performance. These results show that only *write-fill* have a high impact on performance. Indeed, a *write-back* operation coming from a lower level of the memory does not require an immediate response from the LLC. Hence, it does not stall the CPU. Conversely, a *write-fill* occurs upon a cache miss, meaning that the CPU needs a data to continue the execution of an application. Unless the data becomes available, the CPU could be stalled if further instructions depend on this data.

The above analysis shows that one should primarily focus on *write-fill* operations for reducing the number of writes on the LLC and improving system performance. Let us define A the performance improvement with $WF = 0$, B the performance improvement with $WB = 0$ and C the performance improvement with $WF = WB = 0$. Figure 3a shows that $A + B = C$ for all applications. Hence, A does not have an impact on B and vice versa. Therefore, one could reduce the number of *write-fill* without a side effect on *write-back*.

3.3   Cache Replacement Policy

Write-fill operations are directly dependent on the MPKI of the LLC. A low MPKI leads to a low amount of requests to the main memory, and then a low amount of *write-fill* operations. Thus, one way to mitigate the STT-MRAM write latency is to reduce the MPKI to decrease the number of *write-fill* requests.

The cache replacement policy is responsible for data eviction when a cache line is full. For example, in Fig. 2, data X of the *write-back* transaction erases data D. It means that D has been chosen by the replacement policy to be evicted. Hence, the next access to D will generate a cache miss. Therefore, the replacement policy directly affects the number of misses, and so the MPKI. An efficient policy should evict data that will not be re-used in the future, or at least be re-used further than the other data in the same cache line. The most common used policy is the Least-Recently Used (LRU), which is cheap in terms of hardware resources. However, LRU is less efficient than advanced replacement policies such as Hawkeye [8], which targets the theoretical optimal in terms of cache eviction decision. Hawkeye identifies instructions that often generate cache misses. For each cache access, a data structure called a *predictor* keeps in memory the result of this access, i.e., hit or miss. The instruction that has generated the access is also saved. Hence, the memory of the predictor contains instructions that generate hits or misses. Predictions are made upon each access. Cache blocks, which are accessed by instructions generating cache misses have higher priority for eviction. The policy is based on the MIN algorithm [5]. To the best of our knowledge, this is the most advanced replacement policy [3].

4   Experimental Results

4.1   Environment Setup

We describe the timing and area models used in the sequel for the LLC and the main memory. Then, we introduce the used simulation infrastructure and we explain its calibration with considered timing information.

Memory Model. We first optimized SRAM and STT-MRAM cache memories respectively for low leakage with CACTI [12] and read energy-delay-product with NVSim [6]. For both LLC models, we used 32 nm technology with a temperature of 350 K. The considered STT-MRAM model is provided with NVSim and assumes optimizations for cell area, set/reset pulse duration and energy. The obtained parameter values are summarized in Table 1. The considered main memory model is based on a publicly available datasheet from Micron Technology [2]. We modeled a 4 GB DDR3 with 1 DIMM, 8 ranks, 8 banks per ranks, organized with 16×65536 columns with 64 B on each row. Thus, each bank contains 64 MB of data, each rank 512 MB, and the total is 4 GB. The extracted latency parameters are as follows: $tRP = tRCD = tCAS = 11\,cycles$, $tRAS = 28\,cycles$, $tRFC = 208\,cycles$ and $tCK = 1.25$ ns.

Table 1. SRAM and STT-MRAM timing and area results configurations

	SRAM			STT-MRAM		
	2 MB	4 MB	8 MB	2 MB	4 MB	8 MB
Read latency [ns]	1.34	1.47	1.66	1.90	2.06	2.53
Write latency [ns]	1.34	1.47	1.66	5.75	5.83	6.07
Area [mm^2]	5.32	10.88	20.49	1.19	2.19	4.00

Simulation Environment. Our evaluation is conducted with the ChampSim simulator [1] used for the Cache Replacement Championship at ISCA'17 conference [3]. The simulator executes application traces. The modeled architecture is based on an Intel Core i7 system. Cores are Out-of-Order with a 3-level on chip cache hierarchy plus a main memory. The setup is specified in Table 2. We use a set of 20 SPEC CPU2006 traces available with ChampSim. The cache warm-up period is 200 millions instructions. Reported statistics concern a period of 800 millions instructions. We calculate the average performance, i.e., IPC, by applying a geometric mean on the IPCs measured for all applications, as in [8].

Eight configurations are addressed in this study: 2 MB LLC cache with SRAM and STT-MRAM; 4 MB and 8 MB LLC caches only with STT-MRAM; and each of these four caches is combined with either LRU or Hawkeye. For the sake of simplicity, we associate the prefixes M (for Medium), B (for Big) and H (for Huge) together with technology names in order to denote respectively the 2 MB, 4 MB and 8 MB LLC configurations. The name of considered replacement policies, i.e., LRU and Hawkeye, are used as a suffix. For instance, M_stt_hawk denotes a 2 MB STT cache, using the Hawkeye policy.

Latency Calibration. The reference LLC latency in ChampSim is 20 cycles for a 2 MB 16-way associative cache, based on an Intel i7 processor. This corresponds to a latency of 5 ns at 4 GHz. Hence, we define the following latency relation: $L_T = L_C + L_W = 5$ ns, where L_T is the total latency for LLC to process a

Table 2. Experimental setup configuration

L1 (I/D)	32 KB, 8-way, LRU, private, 4 cycles		
L2	256 KB, 8-way, LRU, unified, 8 cycles		
L3	Varying size/policy, 16-way, shared		
L3 size	2 MB	4 MB	8 MB
L3 SRAM latency	20	21	22
L3 STT latency (R/W)	22/38	23/38	23/38
Hawkeye budget	28.2 KB	58.7 KB	114.7 KB
CPU	1core, Out-of-order, 4 GHz		
Main mem. size/latency	4 GB, hit: 55 cycles, miss: 165 cycles		

request from L2 cache, L_C is the LLC access latency and L_W is the wire latency between L2 cache and LLC. Thus, the effective latency is the sum of the wire latency and the cache latency. Thanks to CACTI, we extract $L_C = 1.34$ ns for the LLC reference configuration. Then, $L_W = L_T - L_C = 3.66$ ns. We set L_W to this value and use it as an offset to calculate each cache latency with the previous latency relation, where L_C is extracted from either CACTI or NVSim.

4.2   Results

This section presents our results as follows: firstly, we assess the impact of the LLC size in SRAM and STT-MRAM, by exploiting density to enlarge the cache capacity. Secondly, we report results when taking the Hawkeye cache replacement policy into account. Finally, we discuss this policy w.r.t. LRU. Except when it is explicitly mentioned, all results are normalized to the reference setup, i.e., *M_sram_lru*.

Impact of Cache Size and Technology. Here, all configurations use the LRU replacement policy. The top of Fig. 4 shows the MPKI improvement w.r.t. the reference configuration. We observe that the *M_stt_lru* configuration does not influence the MPKI since the cache size remains unchanged. Conversely, a reduction of MPKI is clearly visible with *B_stt_lru* and *H_stt_lru* configurations. Some applications are not sensitive to cache size, like *bwaves*, *libquantum* or *milc*. Conversely, the *lbm* application is very sensitive to cache size from 8 MB. For this application, the MPKI is decreased by a factor of 0.56× (i.e., 56%). This indicates that a large part of the working set now fits into the LLC.

The bottom part of Fig. 4 shows the normalized IPC achieved by STT-MRAM configurations w.r.t the reference configuration. The *M_stt_lru* config-uration, i.e., a direct replacement of SRAM by STT-MRAM, is slower than the reference. This is due to the higher latency of STT-MRAM. The *B_stt_lru* and *H_stt_lru* configurations outperform the reference on average by 1.03× and 1.09× respectively. With *B_stt_lru*, the IPC is degraded for nine applications, while it is only for five applications with *H_stt_lru*. The performance for the *soplex* application is correlated to the MPKI. Indeed, there is a linear trend between MPKI reduction and IPC improvement. Conversely, the following applications, *gobmk*, *gromacs* and *perlbench* exhibit a significant MPKI reduction with no visible impact on performance. This is due to the very low amount of requests received by the LLC compared to the other applications. Hence, reducing this activity is not significant enough to improve the overall performance.

On average, increasing the LLC size shows that STT-MRAM could achieve the same performance as SRAM under area constraint.

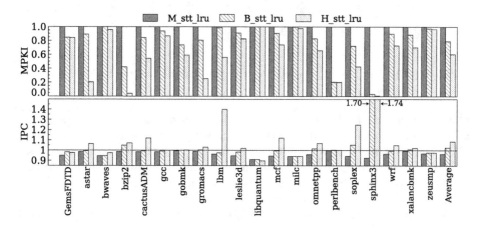

Fig. 4. MPKI (top) and IPC (bottom) with LRU normalized to *M_sram_lru*

Impact of Cache Replacement Policy. Here, all configurations use the Hawkeye replacement policy. Performance results are presented in Fig. 5. We observe the gains on the *M_sram_hawk* configuration, i.e., the Hawkeye reference. This configuration never degrades performances and achieves an average speedup of 1.05×. Larger STT-MRAM configurations, *B_stt_hawk* and *H_stt_hawk*, perform better than *M_sram_hawk* on average. Thanks to the Hawkeye policy, *M_stt_hawk* and *B_stt_hawk* outperform the reference for *lbm* or *mcf*. This was not the case with LRU, as depicted in Fig. 4. Note that for a few applications such as *bwaves*, *GemsFDTD* or *zeusmp*, the *M_sram_hawk* configuration achieves a higher speedup than larger configurations with the same MPKI. This shows that performance is still constrained by STT-MRAM latency, even with an enhanced replacement policy.

Nevertheless, Hawkeye improves performance where a larger cache only cannot. For example, all STT-MRAM configurations achieve the same IPC for the *milc* application with LRU, considering the LLC size. When Hawkeye is used, the performance is linearly increased with the cache size. As a matter of fact, Hawkeye can deal with some memory patterns not exploited by larger LLCs.

The best configuration is *H_stt_hawk*, which achieves a performance improvement of 1.1× (i.e., 10%) on average over the *M_sram_lru* baseline.

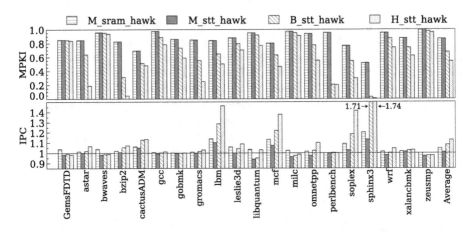

Fig. 5. MPKI (top) and IPC (bottom) with Hawkeye normalized to *M_sram_lru*

Hawkeye versus LRU. Figure 6 shows the effect of the Hawkeye policy over LRU. Results are normalized for each configuration to its counterpart with LRU. For example, *H_stt_hawk* is normalized to *H_stt_lru*. For this experiment, we also run SRAM configuration that do not fit into area constraint to illustrate the effect of Hawkeye on SRAM and STT-MRAM for the same cache size. Both SRAM and STT-MRAM configurations follow the same trend regarding the MPKI reduction over LRU since the Hawkeye policy is not impacted by cache latency. Moreover, we use a single core platform where parallel events cannot occur. Hence, eviction decision remains identical for a given cache size, regardless of the cache size. However, the average gain obtained with Hawkeye is slightly better with STT-MRAM. The performance gap between SRAM and STT-MRAM is 3.3% and 3.1%, respectively with LRU and Hawkeye. Hence, reducing the amount of *write-fill* has higher impact on STT-MRAM where writes are penalizing.

Figure 6 shows that the 8 MB configuration is not as efficient as the 4 MB configuration in terms of performance improvement. The average gain for the IPC for *H_sram_hawk* and *H_stt_hawk* is lower than *B_sram_hawk* and *B_stt_hawk*. This suggests an issue that can be due to either a larger LLC, or the Hawkeye policy, or both. Even if the overall performance improvement reported in Fig. 5 shows that the 8 MB configuration is faster, we note that there may be a limit to the performance improvement provided by the Hawkeye policy. This behavior is visible with *bzip2*, *wrf* and *sphinx3*. In Fig. 4, results show that the MPKI is reduced for *B_stt_lru* and *H_stt_lru*. Hence, increasing the cache size is efficient. Similarly, in Fig. 5, the MPKI is also reduced for the same configurations while replacing LRU by Hawkeye. However, the gains observed in Fig. 6 show that Hawkeye increases the MPKI compared to LRU for a 8 MB LLC. The reason is that Hawkeye made wrong eviction decisions. Indeed, the Hawkeye predictor exploits all cache accesses to identify the instructions that generate cache misses. Since a large cache size reduces the number of cache misses, it becomes more difficult for the predictor to learn accurately from a small set of miss events. Note that the performance for *H_stt_hawk* is still better than other configurations despite these inaccurate decisions.

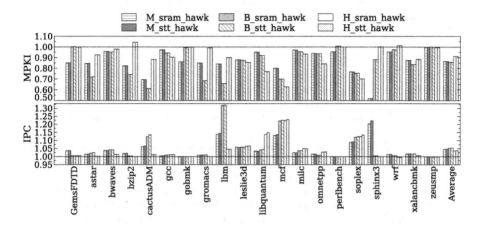

Fig. 6. Performance impact of Hawkeye normalized to LRU

5 Conclusion and Perspectives

This paper evaluates the mitigation of STT-MRAM performance obstacle by exploiting its density to increase LLC cache size and by applying an enhanced cache replacement policy to reduce the LLC *write-fill* activity due to cache misses.

We showed that *write-fill* are a side-effect of read misses and they are more important than *write-back* for performance improvement since they are on the *critical path* to main memory access. Thus, we applied the Hawkeye replacement policy which is designed for reducing cache read misses. Moreover, we showed that using such policy with STT-MRAM is more beneficial than with SRAM. Indeed, the read/write latency asymmetry of this technology allows a higher gap of improvement in terms of performance than with SRAM. However, with a large cache that drastically reduces the number of misses, the small amount of accesses makes the training of the Hawkeye predictor longer. Thus, it leads to wrong eviction decisions. The evaluation results showed that performance can be improved up to 10%. This gain, combined with the drastic static energy reduction enabled by STT-MRAM, leads to increased energy-efficiency.

Future work will focus on a deeper study of the Hawkeye policy to improve its accuracy under low LLC activity. A multicore design will be also investigated to confirm the benefits of large STT-MRAM LLC with this replacement policy.

Acknowledgements. This work has been funded by the French ANR agency under the grant ANR-15-CE25-0007-01, within the framework of the CONTINUUM project.

References

1. The ChampSim simulator. https://github.com/ChampSim/ChampSim
2. DDR3-Micron MT41K512M8DA-125 datasheet, October 2017. https://www.micron.com/~/media/documents/products/data-sheet/dram/ddr3/4gb_ddr3l.pdf
3. ISCA 2017 Cache Replacement Championship. http://crc2.ece.tamu.edu
4. International Technology Roadmap for Semiconductors (ITRS) (2015)
5. Belady, L.A.: A study of replacement algorithms for a virtual-storage computer. IBM Syst. J. **5**(2), 78–101 (1966)
6. Dong, X., Xu, C., Xie, Y., Jouppi, N.P.: NVSim: a circuit-level performance, energy, and area model for emerging nonvolatile memory. IEEE Trans. Comput.-Aided Des. Integr. Circ. Syst. **31**(7), 994–1007 (2012)
7. Henning, J.L.: SPEC CPU2006 benchmark descriptions. ACM SIGARCH Comput. Archit. News **34**(4), 1–17 (2006)
8. Jain, A., Lin, C.: Back to the future: leveraging Belady's algorithm for improved cache replacement. In: 2016 ACM/IEEE 43rd Annual International Symposium on Computer Architecture (ISCA), pp. 78–89. IEEE (2016)
9. Kommaraju, A.V.: Designing energy-aware optimization techniques through program behavior analysis. Ph.D. thesis, Indian Institute of Science, Bangalore (2014)
10. Li, Q., Shi, L., Li, J., Xue, C.J., He, Y.: Code motion for migration minimization in STT-RAM based hybrid cache. In: 2012 IEEE Computer Society Annual Symposium on VLSI (ISVLSI), pp. 410–415. IEEE (2012)
11. Mittal, S.: A survey of architectural techniques for improving cache power efficiency. Sustain. Comput.: Inform. Syst. **4**(1), 33–43 (2014)
12. Muralimanohar, N., Balasubramonian, R., Jouppi, N.P.: CACTI 6.0: a tool to model large caches. HP Laboratories, pp. 22–31 (2009)
13. Péneau, P.Y., Bouziane, R., Gamatié, A., Rohou, E., Bruguier, F., Sassatelli, G., Torres, L., Senni, S.: Loop optimization in presence of STT-MRAM caches: a study of performance-energy tradeoffs. In: 2016 26th International Workshop on Power and Timing Modeling, Optimization and Simulation (PATMOS), pp. 162–169. IEEE (2016)
14. Senni, S., Delobelle, T., Coi, O., Péneau, P.Y., Torres, L., Gamatié, A., Benoit, P., Sassatelli, G.: Embedded systems to high performance computing using STT-MRAM. In: 2017 Design, Automation and Test in Europe Conference and Exhibition (DATE), pp. 536–541. IEEE (2017)
15. Smullen, C.W., Mohan, V., Nigam, A., Gurumurthi, S., Stan, M.R.: Relaxing nonvolatility for fast and energy-efficient STT-RAM caches. In: 2011 IEEE 17th International Symposium on High Performance Computer Architecture (HPCA), pp. 50–61. IEEE (2011)
16. Sun, G., Dong, X., Xie, Y., Li, J., Chen, Y.: A novel architecture of the 3D stacked MRAM L2 cache for CMPs. In: IEEE 15th International Symposium on High Performance Computer Architecture, HPCA 2009, pp. 239–249. IEEE (2009)
17. Vetter, J.S., Mittal, S.: Opportunities for nonvolatile memory systems in extreme-scale high-performance computing. Comput. Sci. Eng. **17**(2), 73–82 (2015)
18. Wu, X., Li, J., Zhang, L., Speight, E., Rajamony, R., Xie, Y.: Hybrid cache architecture with disparate memory technologies. In: ACM SIGARCH Computer Architecture News, vol. 37, pp. 34–45. ACM (2009)
19. Zhou, P., Zhao, B., Yang, J., Zhang, Y.: Energy reduction for STT-RAM using early write termination. In: IEEE/ACM International Conference on Computer-Aided Design-Digest of Technical Papers, ICCAD 2009, pp. 264–268. IEEE (2009)

On Automated Feedback-Driven Data Placement in Multi-tiered Memory

T. Chad Effler[1], Adam P. Howard[1], Tong Zhou[1], Michael R. Jantz[1(✉)],
Kshitij A. Doshi[2], and Prasad A. Kulkarni[3]

[1] University of Tennessee, Knoxville, USA
{teffler,ahoward,tzhou9,mrjantz}@utk.edu
[2] Intel Corporation, Santa Clara, USA
kshitij.a.doshi@intel.com
[3] University of Kansas, Lawrence, USA
kulkarni@ittc.ku.edu

Abstract. Recent emergence of systems with multiple performance and capacity tiers of memory invites a fresh consideration of strategies for optimal placement of data into the various tiers. This work explores a variety of cross-layer strategies for managing application data in multi-tiered memory. We propose new profiling techniques based on the automatic classification of program allocation sites, with the goal of using those classifications to guide memory tier assignments. We evaluate our approach with different profiling inputs and application strategies, and show that it outperforms other state-of-the-art management techniques.

1 Introduction

Systems with multiple tiers of memory that are directly accessible via processor-memory buses are emerging. These tiers include (i) a limited capacity high-performance MCDRAM or HBM tier, (ii) a traditional DDR3/4 DRAM tier, and (iii) a large capacity (∼terabytes) tier [1] whose performance may lag current DDR technologies by only a small factor. For a virtuous blend of capacity and performance from the multiple tiers, memory allocation needs to match different categories of data to the performance characteristics of the tiers into which they are placed, within the capacity constraints of each tier.

One approach is to exercise the faster, lower capacity tier(s) as a large, hardware-managed cache. While this approach has the immediate advantage of being backwards compatible and software transparent, it is not flexible and imposes unpalatable architectural costs that are difficult to scale in line with capacity increases [2]. An alternative approach is for application and-or operating system (OS) software to assign data into different memory tiers with facilities to allow migration of data between those tiers as needed. Monitoring of per-page accesses has been proposed recently [3,4] with the goal of letting an OS (re)assign tiers. While this approach preserves application transparency, it is strictly reactive and relies on non-standard hardware. A third approach is annotation of source code [5–7] by which developers take control of, and coordinate

© Springer International Publishing AG, part of Springer Nature 2018
M. Berekovic et al. (Eds.): ARCS 2018, LNCS 10793, pp. 181–194, 2018.
https://doi.org/10.1007/978-3-319-77610-1_14

tier assignments at the finer-grain of program objects. This approach requires expert knowledge, manual modifications to source code, and risks making such guidance stale as programs and configurations evolve.

Our work aims to combine the power and control of profile-guided and application-directed management with the transparency of OS-based approaches without relying on non-standard hardware. Allocation code paths are grouped into various sets on the basis of prior profiling, and the sets are preference-tied to different tiers in the underlying memory hardware. During execution, these preferences guide the placement of data. This approach does not require source code modifications and permits adapting to memory usage guidance for different program inputs and alternating phases of execution. In this paper, we describe the design and implementation of our automated application guidance framework, and then compare its performance to other hardware- and software-based hybrid memory management strategies using SPEC CPU2006 as workload.

This work makes the following important contributions: (1) We propose, design, implement and evaluate a multi-tiered allocation strategy that uses prior information to group sites for automatic tier selection, (2) We build an open-source simulation-based framework for instrumenting and evaluating it, including a custom Pin binary instrumentation tool [8], as well as extensions to the jemalloc arena allocator [9] and to Ramulator [10], (3) We show that a guidance-based approach has the potential, even when guidance has some inaccuracy, to outperform precise information based reactive placement of data, and (4) We find that adapting to individual program phases has limited benefit, suggesting that a simpler, static policy based on prior profiling is likely to be good enough.

2   Related Work

New frameworks, techniques, and strategies for managing heterogeneous memory systems [3–7,11–14] have emerged recently. Of these, several works [6,7,13,14] employ profiling to find frequently accessed data structures, and translate their findings into tiering hints that can be inserted into program source code. Our approach combines runtime allocation site detection with a custom arena allocator to enable memory usage guidance without altering source, and is the first to explore impacts from variation in profiling inputs and from adapting tiering to individual program phases.

Cross-layer management techniques have also been used to optimize data placement across NUMA or other parts of the (single-tier) memory hierarchy [15–18]. Some of these works [17,18] rely on program profiling and analysis to guide placement decisions. While this work employs similar techniques, the goals, application, and effects of our proposed management strategies are very different.

3   Feedback-Driven Data Placement for Hybrid Memories

Our approach uses a capacity normalized access metric to generate guidance: informally, it seeks to favor placing smaller and hotter objects for allocation into a higher performance tier. This metric is generated on the basis of prior profiling, and is associated with the code paths (also called allocation sites[1]) by which objects are allocated. Since the number of allocation sites can be much larger than the number of memory tiers, allocation sites are further grouped into sets (as described shortly in Sect. 3.2) and this partitioning guides the placements at run time.[2] To bound evaluation scope, each application is assumed to execute within a container with fixed upper tier capacity.

3.1 Allocation Site Partitioning

We propose two simple alternatives for partitioning program sites into groups. The first alternative is called knapsack. Inspired by [17], it uses a classical 0/1 knapsack formulation to produce groupings that collectively fit into a knapsack (of any capacity by which we want to represent the upper tier) while maximizing aggregate access into it. The second alternative is called hotset. It avoids a weakness of knapsack, namely, that knapsack may exclude an allocation site based on the raw capacity of that site, even if allocations from it exhibit a high access count. In the hotset approach, we sort allocation sites by accesses-per-byte scores and then select those with highest scores until we exceed an alternate soft capacity. The limiting capacity for inducing the hot-cold split in each case is taken as a fraction of an applications total dynamic footprint, D. Thus, if this fraction is 12.5%, then the knapsack approach selects allocation sites such that the aggregate size is just below $D/8$, while the hotset approaches stops after $D/8$ is crossed.

3.2 Profile-Guided Management

During a guided run, the application address space is divided into arenas, each of which is page-aligned and therefore can be independently assigned to a memory tier. Using a system interface, such as the NUMA API or memory coloring [16], the application or runtime can instruct the OS memory manager about preferred arena-to-tier assignments. Our framework supports two schemes for using prior guidance: *static arena allocation* and *per-phase arena allocation*. In the static scheme, the application creates two arenas: hot and cold, and guides allocations from the hotset/knapsack partitions into the hot (and all else into the cold) arena, with the guidance remaining fixed across the run. The per-phase scheme is designed to adjust with changes of behavior during the run. It uses per-phase guidance for grouping sites into arenas such that phase by phase, an arena can (optionally) swap tiers, but may never be in more than one tier at a time.

---

[1] This allocation site-based strategy for optimizing accesses-per-byte is designed to obviate tracing or sampling on an object-by-object basis.

[2] The primary goal of this work is to study the potential benefits of automated application guidance. While our simulation-based evaluation neglects overhead of profiling, Sect. 4 covers how in practice, allocation site based guidance can be generated (either online or offline) and applied in direct execution with negligible overhead.

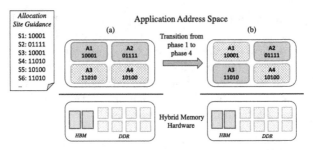

Fig. 1. Per-phase strategy for managing hybrid memories. (a) In phase 1, A1 and A2 correspond to hot allocation sites and are originally mapped to the HBM tier. (b) On transition to phase 4, the guidance indicates A3 will become hot, and A1 is now cold. The application communicates this guidance to the lower-level memory manager, which may now attempt to remap the data in A1 to DDR and the data in A3 to HBM.

Figure 1 illustrates the per-phase scheme. Program execution is divided into phases. For N phases, an N bit vector per allocation site describes the sites hot/cold classification phase by phase. For instance, if a site has a vector '10100', the vector indicates it is hot in phases 3 and 5, and cold in phases 1, 2, and 4, across 5 phases. The total number of unique vectors determines the total number of arenas created at application startup time. During execution, sites with matching bit vectors allocate data to the same arena. Upon a phase transition[3], the OS adjusts the hot/cold tier classification of each arena and migrates data accordingly. This arena-based coarse-grained remapping of tiers to virtual ranges permits efficiently amortized and application transparent migration.

4   Implementation Details

4.1   Associating Memory Usage Profiles with Program Allocation Sites

To collect access profiles, we instrumented using the Pin framework (v. 2.14) [8]. Our custom Pintool[4] intercepts all of the application's allocation and deallocation requests (specifically, all calls to `malloc`, `calloc`, `realloc`, and `free`). The arguments to these routines are then used to build a shadow structure mapping each allocated region to its allocation site with context. The tool captures the estimated capacity (in peak resident set size, accounting for dynamic allocations and unmaps) allocated at each allocation site; and, it computes an estimated aggregate post-cache memory access counts over those allocations by filtering the accessed addresses through an in-band cache simulator. At the end of application execution, the tool outputs the allocation site profiles to a file.

---

[3] Phase transitions may be detected online by several means, including through models of instruction and data access behaviors, hardware event ratios, etc.

[4] For direct execution, an alternative to Pin based instrumentation is to use LLVM inserted wrappers (as described in Sect. 4.2.1), and to sample access rates through hardware-based counters (e.g., using the PEBS facility on modern Intel processors).

4.2   Hybrid Memory Management

Evaluation requires two major components: (1) an allocator that uses the above profiles to partition allocation sites into arenas, and (2) a manager that models the effect of, and which applies, guidance-based management strategies.

4.2.1   Arena Allocation

We employ shared library preloading to dynamically link each evaluation run to a custom allocator that overrides allocation requests with our own arena allocation routines based off of jemalloc [9]. Some calls to `realloc` may request a different arena from that used for the original data, and for those, the overriding call transfers the resized data into the new arena.

To identify allocation sites during execution, our evaluation framework currently collects up to seven layers of call stack context using the `backtrace` routine from the C standard library. While straightforward and easy to implement, this approach can incur substantial overhead if there are too many allocation requests. In a set of native execution runs on an Intel Xeon-based server machine, we found that using backtrace for context detection incurs an average overhead of 3.6% for the 14 benchmarks listed in Table 1, with a maximum slowdown of more than 40% for *gcc*.

To eliminate these overheads, we developed a static compilation pass in the LLVM compiler infrastructure [19] that automatically creates a separate code path for each hot call site and its context. Preliminary tests show that this static pass completely eliminates the overhead of context detection for our benchmark set, and is still able to identify the same set of hot data as the `backtrace` technique.[5] Since the primary goal of this work is to study the potential benefits of automated application guidance during hybrid memory management, we leave full evaluation of the accuracy and performance of static context detection as future work. The simulation-based experiments in Sect. 6 assume no additional overhead for context detection.

4.2.2   Simulation of Hybrid Memory Architectures

Our framework for modeling the behavior and performance of hybrid memory systems adopts and extends the Ramulator DRAM simulator [10]. Ramulator is a trace-based simulator that provides cycle accurate performance models for a variety of DRAM standards, including: conventional (DDR3/4), low-power (LPDDR3/4), graphics (GDDR5), and die-stacked (HBM, WIO2) memories, as well as a number of other academic and emerging memory technologies. For this work, we modified Ramulator's memory controller to support multiple tiers with distinct DRAM standards simultaneously. This extended simulator maintains a map of which physical pages correspond to each tier, and sends each request

---

[5] Other, more compact encodings of the allocation sites may also be employed – e.g., a low-overhead approximate method in direct execution is to use a hash over (call-return) last branch records (LBR) recorded by a processor's monitoring unit.

Table 1. Benchmarks with usage statistics.

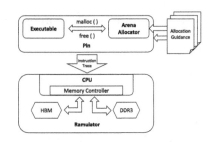

Benchmark	MB	Sites	Allocs	LLCPKI	
				512 KB	8 MB
bzip2	853	10	174	15.43	-
gcc	901	19.6K	28.46M	32.18	-
mcf	1,683	5	6	95.26	46.17
milc	711	56	6.52M	47.77	23.72
cactusADM	668	5.3K	0.13M	15.46	5.07
leslie3d	146	101	0.31M	65.23	22.59
gobmk	39	175	0.66M	4.27	-
soplex	604	363	0.31M	57.30	22.07
hmmer	45	188	2.47M	46.31	-
GemsFDTD	884	509	0.75M	31.42	17.26
libquantum	105	10	180	40.95	29.06
h264ref	83	260	0.18M	7.39	-
lbm	415	4	5	66.72	38.75
sphinx3	72	281	14.22M	18.18	-
Average	514	1.9K	3.39M	38.85	25.59

Fig. 2. Framework for simulating hybrid memory management.

to the appropriate DRAM model depending on its address. It also accepts an alternative instruction trace format with annotations describing the preferred tier of each memory request. When a page is first accessed, the simulator uses the annotations to map the page to the appropriate tier, depending on the current policy and system configuration.

Figure 2 illustrates our approach. At startup, the application connects to a custom Pintool, which filters each load/store through an online cache model and emits a post-cache instruction trace into the extended Ramulator. At the same time, the custom allocator automatically partitions the allocation sites into arenas according to the pre-computed guidance files, and the Pintool inserts the preferred tier into the trace. Ramulator interprets the trace, one request at a time, mapping new data to the appropriate memory tier, until completion.

5   Experimental Framework

5.1   Simulation Platform

Ramulators execution model includes a 3.2 GHz, 4-wide issue CPU with 128-entry re-order buffer, and assumes one cycle for each non-memory instruction. To estimate the impact of various hybrid memory strategies we simulated with two processor cache configurations: (1) a single-level, 512 KB, 32-way cache, which would be suitable for embedded devices, and (2) a two-level cache with 32 KB, 32-way L1, and an 8 MB, 16-way L2, which is more typical for desktop and server machines.

We added logic to Ramulator for simulating a hybrid memory architecture with two tiers: a high-performance tier with configurable, limited capacity, and a slower tier with no capacity bound. We experimented with a range of capacities for the upper tier, and opted to use 12.5% of peak resident set size (RSS) (i.e., 1:8 ratio across tiers) in our evaluations. The choice of 1:8 reasonably approximates the expected capacity ratios of typical (current [20] and expected [1]) hybrid memory systems.

All experiments use the (unmodified) HBM standard included with Ramulator to simulate the fast tier, and use either the DDR3 or DDR4 standard to simulate the slow tier. Detailed statistics about each standard, including rate, timing, bus width, and bandwidth, are listed in Table 4 of [10]. Although we evaluate all of the proposed strategies with an HBM-DDR4 configuration, our detailed experimental results use HBM-DDR3 to model a wider asymmetry between the upper and lower tiers. A summary of our performance results for both platform configurations is presented in Sect. 6.5.

Some of our studies include migration of data between memory tiers. To model the cost of data movement, we folded penalties for migration into our simulations experiments as described in [3], which are as follows. Page faults and TLB shootdowns incur fixed penalties of $5\,\mu s$ and $3\,\mu s$, respectively. The experimental framework further adds execution time for data migrations, which is a function of the bandwidth of the lower tier.

For a faithful reflection of the effects that guidance-based strategies have on allocation behavior and heap layout, each experiment executes the entire program run from start to finish. However, detailed cache and memory simulations are limited to only a representative portion of the run using Simpoints [21]. Unless stated otherwise, all of the experiments simulate a single, large, contiguous slice of 64 billion program instructions. With our simulation framework, this volume of instructions corresponds to at least 5 full seconds of execution time (measured in CPU cycles), and a typical execution time of 20 to 30 s.

5.2   Benchmarks Description

For our evaluation, we used the standard SPEC CPU2006 benchmark suite [22]. We compiled the benchmarks using gcc (version 4.8.5) with -O2. Profile guidance is collected using both the *train* and *ref* inputs, and all evaluation is performed using the *ref* input. In cases where the benchmark-input pair requires multiple invocations of the application, we conduct independent experiments for each invocation and aggregate the results to compute a single score for each benchmark.

To identify applications where efficient utilization of the upper-level memory can have a significant impact on program performance, we conducted pilot measurements using shorter simulations of up to 10 program phases and 1 billion instructions per phase for each program run.[6] For these experiments, we evaluated each benchmark against the two cache configurations and against Ramulators default memory model with (1) a single-tier of (unlimited capacity) HBM (HBM-only) and (2) a single-tier of DDR3 (DDR3-only).

The results of the pilot measurements showed that there is significant potential to improve performance with HBM. 14 (of 28) benchmarks exhibited more

---

[6] We had to omit *zeusmp* due to an incompatibility with our adopted basic block vector collection tool [23].

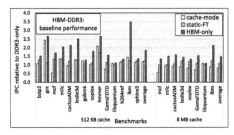 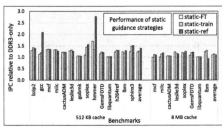

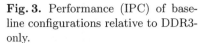

Fig. 3. Performance (IPC) of baseline configurations relative to DDR3-only.

Fig. 4. Performance (IPC) with static guidance strategies relative to DDR3-only.

than 10% IPC improvement with HBM relative to DDR3 with the 512 KB cache, while 8 benchmarks show similar improvements with the 8 MB cache. The remainder of this work focuses on this limited set of benchmark-cache pairs. Table 1 lists our selected benchmarks along with their memory usage information.

6 Evaluation

6.1 Baseline Configurations

For baseline comparison, we implement two strategies that have been common in hybrid memory systems. The first uses the upper tier as a large direct-mapped cache to hold data brought in from an even larger lower tier [20]. We refer to this type of hardware based tiering as *cache mode* (not to be confused with processor caches). The other baseline strategy is the *static first touch (FT)* [3] policy. Under static FT, when a page is first touched, it is instantiated in HBM if possible and in DDR (the lower tier) otherwise; and, remains there until unmapped.

Figure 3 shows the performance (IPC) of the two baseline policies– cache mode and static FT in a hybrid HBM-DDR3 system where the capacity of the HBM tier is 12.5% of the DDR3 tier. For each benchmark, the IPC in Fig. 3 is shown relative to the IPC of the DDR3-only configuration. Hence, while cache mode outperforms static FT for a few benchmarks (e.g., *gcc* and *hmmer*) static FT is the superior choice. On average, static FT allocation improves IPC (over DDR3-only) by 22% and 9% for the 512 KB and 8 MB CPU cache sizes, respectively. In cache mode, the average IPC change is 17% better for the 512 KB CPU cache but 17% worse for the 8 MB CPU cache. Our simulation diagnostics show that the degradation in cache mode occurs due to a high miss rate (over 67% for the 8 MB cache) resulting in higher overheads for memory traffic. A third bar in Fig. 3 also shows that in the idealized HBM-only case, the average IPC is better by 61.9% and 30.1% respectively for the small and large CPU caches.

6.2   Static Application Guidance

We next introduce a *static guidance* hybrid management policy that uses prior profiling to partition allocation sites into hot and cold subsets, and then applies the static arena allocation scheme to separate hot and cold data in the evaluation run. The hot space places data in the HBM tier on a first touch basis, while cold data is always assigned to DDR.

We conducted an initial set of shorter simulations (10 phases, 1B instructions per phase) to assess the impact of different strategies for selecting hot subsets. For these experiments, we compute profiling with the *ref* and *train* program inputs and construct hot subsets using the knapsack and hotset strategies with capacities of 3.125%, 6.25%, 12.5%, 25.0%, and 50.0%. We find that the best size for each approach varies depending on the benchmark and profile input. Knapsack achieves its best performance with the largest capacity (50.0%), while hotset does best with sizes similar or smaller than the upper tier capacity limit (of 12.5%). Across all benchmarks, the best hotset outperforms the best knapsack by 4.4% with the *train* profile and by 4.2% with the *ref* profile, on average. This outcome lends strength to the idea that being too conservative in cases where an allocation site with very hot data does not fit entirely in the upper tier is less effective than allowing a portion of the site's data to map to the faster device. We therefore continue using only the hotset strategy and select the hotset capacity that performs best on average, as follows: 12.5% for *train* and 6.25% for *ref* with the smaller cache, and 25% for both *train* and *ref* with the larger cache.

Figure 4 shows the IPC of the benchmarks with the static hotset guidance approaches with *train* and *ref* profiling inputs (respectively labeled as *static-train* and *static-ref*) relative to single-tier DDR3. Thus, application guidance, whether based on profiles of the *train* or *ref* input, does better than static FT during the evaluation run. On average, the more accurate *ref* profile enables static-ref to outperform static-train by more than 12%, when the CPU cache is small (512 KB), but the difference is negligible when the cache is larger (8 MB). Surprisingly, with the 8 MB cache, static-train performs slightly better due to a skewed result from the *lbm* benchmark. Further analysis shows that *lbm* produces about the same amount of traffic into the upper tier with both static-ref and static-train, but the disparity is primarily due to an effect on spatial locality caused by different data layouts. We plan to fully evaluate the impact of our technique on spatial locality in future work.

6.3   Adaptive Application Guidance

We next introduce the *adaptive-ref* policy to examine the potential benefit of adapting guidance to changing access patterns, as described below.

For each benchmark, we use Simpoints to divide the evaluation (*ref* input) run into slices of dynamic instructions (of length l), and then classify each slice into one of up to k program phases. We then conduct profiling and compute hotsets for each program phase, and use this guidance to apply the per-phase arena allocation scheme during the evaluation run. When the application enters a new

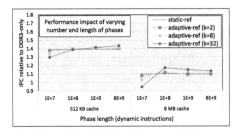 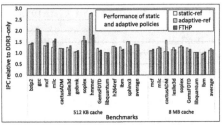

Fig. 5. Performance (IPC) of adaptive-ref with different # and length of phases.

Fig. 6. Performance (IPC) with adaptive strategies on relative to DDR3-only.

phase, it suspends execution, and attempts to migrate data in each arena to the appropriate tier using the guidance for the *upcoming* program phase. Since our goal is to investigate the potential advantages of this approach, our experiments assume the application is always able to detect program phase changes accurately and immediately.

We conducted a series of experiments with the adaptive-ref policy varying the length (l) and maximum number of program phases (k). For k values of 2, 8, and 32, Fig. 5 plots a line showing the average performance (IPC) of the adaptive-ref policy, relative to DDR3-only, with phase lengths of 10 million (M), 100M, 1 billion (B), and 8B dynamic instructions. Additionally, we plot dashed lines to show the average IPC of the static-ref policy with each cache size. Detailed results comparing the static-ref and best adaptive-ref configuration (with $k = 8$, $l =$ 100M) for each benchmark are shown in Fig. 6.

In most cases, we find that adaptive-ref exhibits similar performance as static-ref, even with the idealistic assumption of accurate phase detection. Different phase lengths have little impact on the proportion of accesses to the HBM tier, but selecting a length that is too short will incur significant data migration overheads, and result in worse overall performance. For a few workloads, such as *milc* and *cactusADM*, increasing the number of program phases does produce benefits, but on average the impact is small. Additionally, we find that the best adaptive-ref configuration drives only slightly ($<2\%$) more traffic to the HBM tier than the static approach, as shown in Table 2. Thus, static-ref makes nearly as-good placement decisions across phases as adaptive-ref, even though it is not capable of adapting to the individual program phases.

6.4   Comparison with OS/Architectural Reactive Profiling

Using our simulation framework, we implemented the *first-touch-hot-page (FTHP)* reactive profiling approach from Meswani et al. [3]. FTHP uses non-standard page access counters in hardware to identify recently hot physical pages and migrate them at epoch boundaries. We evaluate FTHP using two epoch lengths of 1 s and 100 ms. For our comparisons, we chose the 1 s epoch because it achieves slightly (1.2%) better performance with our benchmarks.

Table 2. % of accesses to upper-level memory and data migrated (in GB).

Benchmark	% of accesses to upper-level memory						GBs migrated		
	Cache-mode	Static FT	Static train	Static ref	Adaptive ref	FTHP 1s	Cache-mode	FTHP 1s	Adaptive ref
512 KB cache									
bzip2	80.92	69.03	77.08	70.59	81.06	94.09	207.44	0.99	16.94
gcc	96.17	16.78	24.61	80.57	70.14	69.24	68.70	3.73	16.99
mcf	20.04	48.80	48.50	48.48	48.50	63.39	256.59	6.15	0.00
milc	80.97	31.58	32.54	27.16	53.80	56.98	55.36	0.50	19.75
cactusADM	79.27	46.89	46.70	46.69	46.54	44.37	57.24	0.66	0.00
leslie3d	76.12	28.21	27.83	28.76	18.10	37.17	106.71	0.15	0.00
gobmk	95.39	27.84	13.78	14.90	14.18	37.53	13.19	0.04	0.00
soplex	59.65	15.87	46.37	52.92	61.66	51.52	137.88	0.12	0.13
hmmer	96.04	63.31	34.41	75.00	75.79	71.08	59.20	0.01	0.00
GemsFDTD	11.05	13.46	15.56	21.55	12.93	17.70	79.66	2.02	63.95
libquantum	99.53	11.55	11.54	11.54	11.54	13.53	1.04	0.02	0.00
h264ref	95.63	72.13	85.55	86.84	88.21	77.83	32.04	0.02	0.75
lbm	94.97	12.77	12.72	12.72	12.51	10.64	145.82	0.55	29.81
sphinx3	62.65	45.66	59.33	61.83	57.25	69.18	29.74	0.01	0.17
Average	74.88	35.99	38.32	45.68	46.59	51.02	89.33	1.07	10.61
8 MB cache									
mcf	17.77	24.78	24.88	25.22	24.88	43.24	137.19	5.60	0.00
milc	57.89	15.48	16.09	21.58	32.42	29.44	43.87	0.58	20.92
cactusADM	30.58	29.74	29.74	29.69	32.66	27.31	13.69	0.52	0.00
leslie3d	43.66	20.81	20.96	20.75	20.04	14.74	52.86	0.10	0.00
soplex	43.93	30.85	19.64	30.39	35.40	30.16	80.07	0.11	2.17
GemsFDTD	4.72	14.40	15.00	14.99	11.87	9.60	62.14	1.38	61.97
libquantum	99.97	12.50	0.00	12.49	12.49	11.33	0.03	0.01	0.00
lbm	84.00	12.71	12.79	12.79	12.47	11.73	50.37	0.10	30.01
Average	47.82	20.16	17.39	20.99	22.78	22.19	55.03	1.05	14.38

Referring again to Fig. 6, a third bar shows the results for FTHP relative to DDR3-only, on an identical HBM-DDR3 platform with 12.5% HBM capacity. Thus, even though they do not have the benefit of dynamic feedback from specialized hardware, the application guidance policies often achieve similar performance as FTHP. With the 512 KB cache, static-ref and adaptive-ref respectively outperform FTHP by 2.8% and 2.9%, while with the 8 MB cache, static-ref performs slightly (1.9%) worse, and adaptive-ref performs 5.3% better. Even static-train (shown in Fig. 4) performs slightly (1.5%) better than FTHP with the larger cache, but does exhibit some slowdown (9.6%) with the smaller cache.

Both adaptive-ref and FTHP limit the frequency of data migration to amortize the cost of page faults and TLB synchronization. The final three columns of Table 2 show the amount of data migrated (in GB) for each adaptive policy.

Note also that the amount of migration for both FTHP and adaptive-ref depends on the length of each epoch/phase. For instance, compared to the adaptive-ref configuration in the table (with $k = 8$, $l = 100M$), adaptive-ref with $l = 10M$ migrates almost $2.4x$ more data over the course of each run, on average. Considering these results with the performance results in Fig. 6 and HBM traffic comparison in Table 2, we conclude that, although more frequent migration can steer a higher portion of traffic to the HBM, the additional costs often outweigh the performance benefits for our selected benchmarks.

6.5   Performance Summary

Table 3 presents the average IPC of all of the management policies for both HBM-DDR3 and HBM-DDR4 platforms with 12.5% capacity in the HBM tier. Each set of results uses the corresponding DDR3/4-only configuration as its baseline. As expected, the policies on the HBM-DDR4 platform exhibit similar performance trends as on the HBM-DDR3 platform. On average, the application-guided policies achieve the best performance on HBM-

Table 3. Performance (IPC) summary of different allocation strategies.

Policy	512 KB cache		8 MB cache	
	HBM-DDR3	HBM-DDR4	HBM-DDR3	HBM-DDR4
Cache-mode	1.173	1.173	0.833	0.907
Static-FT	1.223	1.165	1.094	1.045
Static-train	1.269	1.226	1.136	1.115
Static-ref	1.393	1.325	1.102	1.113
Adaptive-ref	1.393	1.323	1.173	1.099
FTHP	1.347	1.272	1.107	1.084
HBM-only	1.838	1.568	1.466	1.255

DDR4, boosting performance with the small and large caches by more than 15% and 20% compared to cache mode, by 16% and 7% compared to static FT, and by 5% and 3% compared to FTHP.

7   Conclusions and Future Work

This work demonstrates that emerging hybrid memory systems will not be able to rely solely on conventional hardware-based caching or coarse-grained software approaches, such as static NUMA assignments, and stand to benefit greatly from fine-grained, application-level guidance. The results point to a need for developing new source, binary, and run-time capabilities to make application guided memory tiering practical. While the current evaluation uses simulation, our goal is to adapt our automated guidance framework for direct execution on real hybrid memory hardware. The immediate next steps include development of hardware-based sampling to profile memory accesses during native execution and low-overhead context detection techniques as described in Sect. 4.

Other findings in this study warrant additional investigation. In many cases, we found that tailoring application guidance to each program phase has a relatively small impact on performance. Further research is necessary to understand the relationship between program phases and memory behavior, and whether this result is specific to our selected benchmarks and experimental configuration, or if it reflects a more fundamental property of hybrid memory systems.

While investigating these issues, we also plan to explore the feasibility of using pure static analysis, without program profiling, to guide hybrid memory management. Finally, we plan to evaluate the potential of extending guidance to other parts of the memory hierarchy, such as caching or prefetching.

Acknowledgements. This research is supported in part by the National Science Foundation under CCF-1619140, CCF-1617954, and CNS-1464288, as well as a grant from the Software and Services Group (SSG) at Intel®.

References

1. Intel: 3D XPoint (2016). http://www.intel.com/content/www/us/en/architecture-and-technology/3d-xpoint-unveiled-video.html
2. Mittal, S., Vetter, J.S.: A survey of techniques for architecting DRAM caches. IEEE Trans. Parallel Distrib. Syst. **27**(6), 1852–1863 (2016)
3. Meswani, M., Blagodurov, S., Roberts, D., Slice, J., Ignatowski, M., Loh, G.: Heterogeneous memory architectures: a HW/SW approach for mixing die-stacked and off-package memories. In: HPCA, 2015 (February 2015)
4. Li, Y., Ghose, S., Choi, J., Sun, J., Wang, H., Mutlu, O.: Utility-based hybrid memory management. In: IEEE CLUSTER (September 2017)
5. Cantalupo, C., Venkatesan, V., Hammond, J.R.: User extensible heap manager for heterogeneous memory platforms and mixed memory policies (2015). http://memkind.github.io/memkind/memkind_arch_20150318.pdf
6. Dulloor, S.R., et al.: Data tiering in heterogeneous memory systems. In: Eleventh European Conference on Computer Systems, p. 15. ACM (2016)
7. Agarwal, N., et al.: Page placement strategies for GPUs within heterogeneous memory systems. SIGPLAN Not. **50**(4), 607–618 (2015)
8. Luk, C.K., et al.: Pin: building customized program analysis tools with dynamic instrumentation. SIGPLAN Not. **40**(6), 190–200 (2005)
9. Evans, J.: A scalable concurrent malloc (3) implementation for FreeBSD (2006)
10. Kim, Y., Yang, W., Mutlu, O.: Ramulator: a fast and extensible DRAM simulator. IEEE Comput. Archit. Lett. **15**(1), 45–49 (2016). https://doi.org/10.1109/LCA.2015.2414456
11. Giardino, M., Doshi, K., Ferri, B.H.: Soft2LM: application guided heterogeneous memory management. In: IEEE International Conference on Networking, Architecture and Storage (NAS), USA, pp. 1–10 (2016)
12. Agarwal, N., Wenisch, T.F.: Thermostat: application-transparent page management for two-tiered main memory. In: ASPLOS. ASPLOS 2017, pp. 631–644. ACM, New York (2017)
13. Peng, I.B., Gioiosa, R., Kestor, G., Cicotti, P., Laure, E., Markidis, S.: RTHMS: a tool for data placement on hybrid memory system. In: ISMM (2017)
14. Servat, H., Pea, A.J., Llort, G., Mercadal, E., Hoppe, H., Labarta, J.: Automating the application data placement in hybrid memory systems. In: 2017 IEEE International Conference on Cluster Computing (CLUSTER) (September 2017)
15. Dashti, M., Fedorova, A., Funston, J., Gaud, F., Lachaize, R., Lepers, B., Quema, V., Roth, M.: Traffic management: a holistic approach to memory placement on NUMA systems. SIGPLAN Not. **48**(4), 381–394 (2013)
16. Jantz, M.R., et al.: A framework for application guidance in virtual memory systems. In: Virtual Execution Environments. VEE 2013, pp. 155–166 (2013)

17. Jantz, M.R., et al.: Cross-layer memory management for managed language applications. In: ACM/SIGPLAN OOPSLA. ACM, New York (2015)
18. Guo, R., Liao, X., Jin, H., Yue, J., Tan, G.: NightWatch: integrating lightweight and transparent cache pollution control into dynamic memory allocation systems. In: 2015 USENIX Annual Technical Conference (USENIX ATC 15), pp. 307–318 (2015)
19. Lattner, C., Adve, V.: LLVM: a compilation framework for lifelong program analysis & transformation. In: Code Generation and Optimization (2004)
20. Sodani, A.: Knights Landing (KNL): 2nd generation Intel® Xeon Phi processor. In: 2015 IEEE Hot Chips 27 Symposium (HCS), pp. 1–24. IEEE (2015)
21. Hamerly, G., Perelman, E., Lau, J., Calder, B.: Simpoint 3.0. J. Instr. Level Parallelism **7**(4), 1–28 (2005)
22. Henning, J.L.: SPEC CPU2006 benchmark descriptions. ACM SIGARCH Comput. Archit. News **34**(4), 1–17 (2006)
23. Nethercote, N., Seward, J.: Valgrind: a framework for heavyweight dynamic binary instrumentation. In: PLDI (2007)

Operational Characterization of Weak Memory Consistency Models

M. Senftleben[(✉)] and K. Schneider

TU Kaiserslautern, 67653 Kaiserslautern, Germany
{senftleben,schneider}@cs.uni-kl.de

Abstract. To improve their overall performance, all current multicore and multiprocessor systems are based on memory architectures that allow behaviors that do not exist in interleaved (sequential) memory systems. The possible behaviors of such systems can be described by so-called weak memory consistency models. Several of these models have been introduced so far, and different ways to specify these models have been considered like axiomatic or view-based formalizations which have their particular advantages and disadvantages. In this paper, we propose the use of operational/architectural models to describe the semantics of weak memory consistency models in an operational, i.e., executable way. The operational semantics allow a more intuitive understanding of the possible behaviors and clearly point out the differences of these models. Furthermore, they can be used for simulation, formal verification, and even to automatically synthesize such memory systems.

Keywords: Memory models · Weak memory consistency
Processor architecture · Memory architecture

1 Introduction

Historically, computer architectures were considered to consist of a single processor that is connected with a single memory via a bus (von Neumann architecture; 1945). The sequentialization of the read and write operations via the single bus ensured that each read operation returns the value most recently written to the corresponding memory location and that we can at all define *the most recently written value*. Even if the processor of such a computer architecture would be used to execute multiple processes by interleaving their executions, the memory operations would still take place one after the other and will therefore form a sequence where all memory operations are totally ordered.

Nowadays, essentially all computer architectures consist of multicore processors or even multiple processors which share a common main memory. Early multiprocessor systems still connected multiple processors via a single bus with the shared memory. This way, processors had to compete for bus access that still enforced an ordering of the memory operations in a linear sequence. Modern multiprocessor systems, however, are based on much more complex memory

© Springer International Publishing AG, part of Springer Nature 2018
M. Berekovic et al. (Eds.): ARCS 2018, LNCS 10793, pp. 195–208, 2018.
https://doi.org/10.1007/978-3-319-77610-1_15

architectures that do not only make use of caches with cache coherence protocols, but also add further local memories to improve their performance. In particular, the use of local store buffers between the processor cores and the caches allows a significantly faster execution: Using store buffers, processors simply 'execute' store operations by putting a pair consisting of an address and a value to be stored at that address in a FIFO buffer. The processor can then continue with the execution of its next instruction and may consult its own store buffer in case a later load operation is executed. The store buffer will execute its store operations as soon as it is given access to the main memory. This avoids idle times due to waiting for the bus access for each store operation and allows a faster execution in general. However, since processors cannot see the store buffers of other processors, they will temporarily have different views on the shared memory. Note that after the store buffers were finally emptied, the cache coherence protocol ensures a coherent view on the shared memory, but before that point of time, the different views that exist due to the contents of the local store buffers allow executions that are otherwise impossible. For this reason, one speaks about weakly consistent memory models that do not impose as strong constraints as the traditional sequential memory models that just interleaved the memory operations of different processors.

Store buffers are one – but not the only – reason that lead to the introduction of weak memory consistency models [1,12,15,27]. For example, in distributed computer systems, the single memory is replaced by multiple distributed memories which can be specific to single processors or can be shared with all or some other processors. Depending on the implemented memory architecture, very different weak memory models were developed through the past decades, and some of them may lead to behaviors that are really unexpected by the programmers. It is therefore very important that the designers of modern computer systems are able to describe the potential memory behaviors of their systems in a precise but yet comprehensive way so that the programmers are able to determine when memory synchronization is required in their programs.

Memory consistency models have been defined in different ways: First descriptions of weak memory models were just given in natural language and were therefore often ambiguous. In fact, such ambiguous descriptions lead to non-equivalent versions of the processor consistency model [3,10].

Another way to define a memory consistency model is the so-called view-based approach where the different views processors may have during the execution of a multithreaded program are formally specified. From the viewpoint of a particular processor, this is usually done in that one has to determine which of the memory operations of other threads have to be interleaved with the memory operations of the own thread to define its local view. For example, for PRAM consistency, one would have to consider all store operations of all other threads, but not their load operations, while for other memory models other sets of store operations may be considered. The view-based approach can also be defined from the viewpoint of the memory, providing rules for the ordering of all operations as observed by the main memory. View-based definitions are quite popular, and

[27] showed how most of the existing weak memory models can be defined in this way. The authors of [27] even managed to organize many weak memory models in a hierarchy regarding their weakness, and they could describe most of the weak memory models systematically as combinations of four basic constraints.

However, the view-based approach remains quite abstract and formal, and while being precise for a formal analysis [9], it is not comprehensive enough to serve as a general description for programmers. A slightly different approach has been followed by the SPARC memory models TSO and PSO that are described in an axiomatic way [28]. Also being view-based in principle, these weak memory models were specified by just a few axioms that can be directly used for formal reasoning about the potential executions of a multithreaded system. While also lacking of comprehensiveness, these descriptions are much more succinct, and allow one to directly make use of formal verification that is not that directly applicable when the views are defined by a couple of total or partial orders.

More recent efforts made use of theorem provers to specify weak memory models, using e.g., higher order logic [18,22] or temporal logic [25]. The motivation for this choice is to ensure the well-definedness of the given non-trivial formalization, and to directly reason about properties of the specified memory models with verification tools. However, also these approaches tend to be too difficult to be used as a reference for programmers.

From programming languages, it is well-known that besides the axiomatic and denotational semantics, the operational semantics is often preferred for defining simulators or virtual machines [6]. Usually, programmers also prefer operational semantics, obviously since that kind of semantics directly determines how the programs are executed. Operational semantics are therefore usually the best means to define programming models.

In this paper, we therefore advocate the use of operational semantics for the specification of weak memory consistency models. We believe that operational semantics may also lead to formally precise, but still comprehensive specifications of weak memory consistency models that might be preferable for programmers. To specify such an operational description, one has to define for each weak memory model an abstract memory architecture with load/store ports for the processors. These operational/architectural models can be described using modern system-level languages to obtain precise and executable models. Using these operational models in teaching, we found that students were able to much better and quicker understand the subtle differences between the memory models. Moreover, our operational models can be directly used for simulation, formal verification, and also for synthesis. In particular, we will list such operational/architectural models for the important memory consistency models described in literature [5,10,14,16]. These reference architectures are obtained by directly deriving implementations of memory systems from the definitions of their memory consistency model. The resulting reference machines do not claim to be efficient (for synthesis), but minimal in terms of different components and structures to simplify verification of correctness and completeness of the implementation.

The outline of the paper is as follows: In the next section, we briefly review related work and then define some weak memory models according to [27]. Section 4 contains the core of this paper where we present operational architectures for the models considered before. Finally, we discuss future work with preliminary conclusions.

2   Related Work

Comprehensive introductions to memory consistency models are [1,19]. Reference [20] provides a good overview over many of the models known at that time and compares these with each other.

The formalism and some of the definitions used in this publication are based on [27] which introduced a systematic framework for view-based definitions for many common memory consistency models and revealed the relations between different memory models. In the next section, we list four of the many weak memory models of [27] which are described in an operational way afterwards. Similarly, [2,4] provided unified formalizations for multiple memory models. Other work on view-based definitions include [3,5]. Reference [26], on the other hand, introduces a framework for axiomatic definitions.

In our own previous work, we analyzed in [8,9] the complexity of testing whether given execution traces comply with a certain memory model. Similar to this publication, [13] provided definitions and comparisons of several consistency models and defined machines for the models.

The only previous works we are aware of that made also use of operational semantics were Lipton and Sandberg [16] who provided an implementation for PRAM by defining its structure and communication rules. Recently, [7] described the semantics of the ARMv8 multiprocessor architecture with an operational approach. Our approach is more general, and claims to have the potential to be used to describe most known weak memory models in an operational, and thus comprehensive way.

3   View-Based Definitions of Memory Consistency Models

In this section, we adapt the terminology introduced by Steinke and Nutt in [27] to provide formal definitions of four weak memory consistency models. Note that this formalism does not describe the multithreaded system in an executable/operational way. Instead, it just determines the set of possible executions in terms of possible traces of memory operations, but does not explain how or why these were generated. In the next section, we will then provide operational models for the memory models considered in this section.

In this setting, a memory operation is expressed as a quadruple (o, p, l, v) where o is either a read or write operation, p is the process id of the process executing the operation o, l is the memory location (address), and v is the value read or written. The local order relation $<_i$ reflects the execution order of all memory operations of process P_i in that it orders the operations according to the program code of the process. The process order $<_P$ is the conjunction $\bigwedge_{i \in P} <_i$ of all local order relations. Definitions of memory models can then be given in the following form:

$$\forall_{i \in P} \exists SerialView \left(< | \; (*, i, *, *) \cup (w, *, *, *) \right)$$

which means that for each process P_i, there must exist a serial view on all its own operations (using wildcards $(*, i, *, *)$) and all write operations of all processes $((w, *, *, *))$ which respects the ordering $<$. A serial view is thereby a total order $\lhd$ over the given set of operations and a superset of the provided relation $<$. Furthermore, in a serial view $\lhd$, the memory value of each read operation has to correspond to the most recent write operation to that location with respect to $\lhd$. This implicitly defines the writes-to order $w \mapsto r$ which maps each read operation r to the write operation it reads from.

3.1 Local Consistency

Local consistency was first defined by Heddaya and Sinha [11] as the weakest constraint that could be required of a shared memory system. In a locally consistent system, each process observes its own operations in local order while all other operations may be observed in an arbitrary order. Different processes' orders are not related at all in this memory model. Local consistency [5,11] can be expressed in the introduced formalism as follows [27]:

$$\forall_{i \in P} \exists SerialView \left(<_i | \; (*, i, *, *) \cup (w, *, *, *) \right).$$

3.2 Cache Consistency (CC)

In 1989, Goodman [10] provided a definition for cache consistency, which he called weak consistency since he assumed that it is the weakest form of memory consistency. Furthermore, he expected that no synchronization guarantees could be given in cache consistency. Meanwhile, both assumptions have been proven wrong by the existence of weaker models and algorithms that can ensure mutual exclusion in weaker models like slow consistency. Cache consistency [10] can be defined as follows, which means that each process observes the same ordering on memory operations regarding the same memory location, but processes may see operations regarding different memory locations in different orders:

$$\forall_{x \in V} \exists SerialView \left(<_P | \; (*, *, x, *) \right)$$

3.3 Pipelined-RAM (PRAM) Consistency

One of the first well known weak memory models described was PRAM (Pipelined RAM) which was presented 1988 by Lipton and Sandberg [16,17].

They show that their shared memory system PRAM scales better than sequentially consistent systems as it is immune to high network latency. Additionally, synchronization costs remain low while performance increases significantly. Due to its informal textual definition, there exists an interpretation of Ahamad et al. [3], and another slightly different one by Mosberger [21] as shown in [24]. PRAM consistency based on Ahamad et al. [3] can be expressed as follows:

$$\forall_{i \in P} \exists SerialView \left(<_P \, | (*, i, *, *) \cup (w, *, *, *) \right)$$

In a PRAM consistent execution, every process observes all the writes of all other processes in the order they were issued. However, different processes may see the writes of the other processes in a different order. A system implementing PRAM consistency therefore only has to ensure that the communication from one process to another does not reorder or lose writes, while the transmission delay between processors is arbitrary.

3.4   Sequential Consistency (SC)

While technically not a weak model, we include sequential consistency as defined by Lamport [14] as a base reference. Sequential consistency has been the preferred memory model for programmers since it just considers the interleaving of the single thread executions. The definition of sequential consistency [14] as expressed by [27] is:

$$\exists SerialView \left(<_P \, | (*, *, *, *) \right)$$

which means that a system is sequentially consistent if for all executions, there exists a corresponding sequential order for all operations which respects the process order.

4   Operational Definitions of Memory Consistency Models

This section contains the main contribution of our paper, i.e., the operational/ architectural characterizations of the four weak memory models described in the previous section. To this end, we provide reference machines for each one of these memory models, and discuss then their correctness and completeness, i.e., that these reference machines can only execute computations that belong to the considered memory model (correctness), and that the reference machine can execute *all* computations that belong to the considered memory model (completeness). We have also developed reference machines for other memory models during our research [24] but these cannot be included in this paper due to lack of space.

In order to discuss these reference machines, we first introduce some common basic components in the next section. Then, the reference machines are presented and their correctness and completeness are briefly discussed. Finally, further details on the actual implementation in the synchronous language Quartz [23] are given.

4.1   Basic Components

The reference machines in this section are constructed with the basic components described in this section.

FIFO: The FIFO component is a First-In-First-Out Buffer which buffers memory operations as tuples. It holds the operation type (read or write), the issuing process' id, the memory address, and in case of a write operation the value to be written. The component's interface is defined as follows:

```
module FIFO(
    event ?pop,
    event ?push,
    event !isempty,
    event isfull,
    // input : writeCommand & target & value
    event (bool * nat{ProcessCount} * nat{MemSize} * bv{DataWidth}) ?inp,
    // output : writeCommand & target & value
    event (bool * nat{ProcessCount} * nat{MemSize} * bv{DataWidth}) !outp
)
```

The outputs `isempty` and `isfull` signal the current state of the buffer. Both data channels `inp` and `outp` consist of a valid flag, the id of the originating processor, the memory location to write to and the actual value to write. Adding an entry to the buffer is handled by input signal `push` while providing the data to `inp`. Similarly, removing the first entry of the buffer is handled by input signal `pop` and reading data from `outp`.

BAG: The BAG component shares the same interface as the FIFO component but slightly differs in its semantics: While the FIFO component will always return and remove the oldest entry when signal `pop` is set, the BAG component may non-deterministically return and remove any stored entry.

MEM: The memory unit MEM stores the latest write to a location and returns for read operations the most recently written value of a location.

In the next subsections, we discuss reference machines for local consistency, cache consistency, PRAM consistency, and sequential consistency. To that end, we will first describe the architecture of the reference machine using the above mentioned basic components. After this, we briefly discuss the correctness and completeness of the given reference machine, where *correctness means that all computations of our reference machine belong to the considered weak memory consistency model*, and conversely, *completeness means that our reference machine can simulate all possible executions of the considered weak memory consistency model*. Hence, the reference machines exactly characterize the weak memory consistency model in an operational/architectural manner.

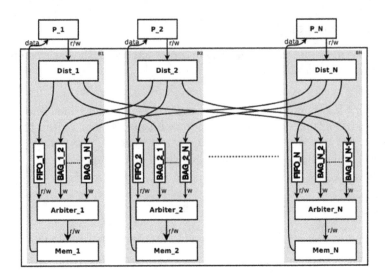

Fig. 1. Reference machine for local consistency

4.2 Reference Machine for Local Consistency

Architecture: The implementation of the reference machine for local consistency is shown in Fig. 1 for a given set P of n processes and m memory locations. For each process $P_i \in P$, the memory system has a distributor $Dist_i$, an arbiter $Arbiter_i$, a memory unit Mem_i, a FIFO buffer $FIFO_i$, and $n-1$ different BAG structures $BAG_{i,j}$ with $j \in \{1, \ldots, n\}, j \neq i$. A distributor $Dist_i$ broadcasts received writes to its $FIFO_i$, and all corresponding $BAG_{j,i}, j \in \{1, \ldots, n\}, j \neq i$, and sends all received reads to its $FIFO_i$. The arbiters nondeterministically decide to idle or to nondeterministically choose a read from the connected FIFO and BAG structures. Any operation read from the selected FIFO or BAG is forwarded to the memory unit.

Correctness: By construction, a process' own memory operations are kept in order in the FIFO maintaining $<_i$. The arbiters generate a serial view covering all own ordered operations and all others' write operations.

Completeness: Consider now an arbitrary locally consistent execution. According to its definition, a serial view exists for each process. Now, the arbiter can choose to read from the BAG/FIFO structures as the order of the serial view suggests, or to idle as long as the next required value is not yet available. The given architecture allows to wait until the required values are available and therefore covers the required behavior.

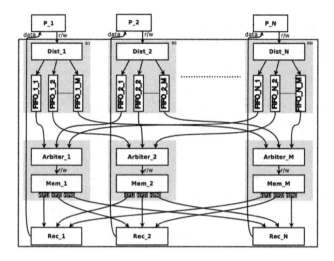

Fig. 2. Reference machine for cache consistency

4.3   Reference Machine for Cache Consistency

Architecture: The implementation of the reference machine for cache consistency is shown in Fig. 2 for a given set P of n processes. For each process $P_i \in P$, the memory system has a distributor $Dist_i$, a receiver Rec_i, and m different FIFO buffers $FIFO_{i,j}$ for $j \in \{1, \dots, m\}$. For each memory cell M_j, the memory system provides a memory unit Mem_j and an arbiter $Arbiter_j$. A distributor $Dist_i$ passes the received memory command for memory cell M_j to the corresponding $FIFO_{i,j}$. The arbiters choose nondeterministically from the connected FIFOs to read from. The memory unit returns the result of a read operation to the receiver Rec_i of process P_i. The receiver Rec_i receives reads for its process and returns them to the process' data interface.

Correctness: The use of FIFO buffers ensures by construction that the read and write operations regarding a specific memory location of each process are kept in order (maintains $\leq_{PO}$ per variable). Therefore, each arbiter $Arbiter_j$ constructs a serial view on all read and write operations regarding its memory location j.

Completeness: Consider now an arbitrary cache consistent execution. If each arbiter selects its action according to the executions' serial view corresponding to its memory location, then the resulting writes-to order $\mapsto$ is the same as the one of the assumed execution. As no memory operations are lost, and the serial views adhere to the process order, it cannot be the case that the next required value is stuck behind another value in one of the FIFOs. Therefore, each arbiter can idle until eventually the next required operation will be available at the head of one of the connected FIFOs.

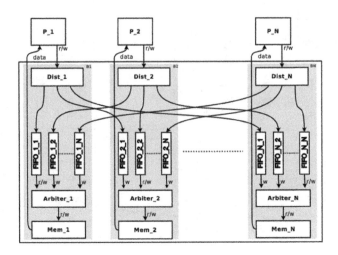

Fig. 3. Reference machine for PRAM consistency

4.4   Reference Machine for PRAM Consistency

As can be seen in Fig. 3, the reference machine for PRAM consistency provides a single memory for every process, so that this kind of memory model is typically found in distributed computing.

Architecture: The implementation of the reference machine for PRAM consistency is shown in Fig. 3 for a given set P of n processes. For each process $P_i \in P$, the memory system has a distributor $Dist_i$, an arbiter $Arbiter_i$, a memory unit Mem_i, and n different buffers $FIFO_{i,j}$ for $j \in \{1, \ldots, n\}$. A distributor $Dist_i$ broadcasts received writes to all corresponding $FIFO_{i,j}$ for $j \in \{1, \ldots, n\}$, and sends all received reads to its $FIFO_{i,i}$. The arbiters choose nondeterministically from the connected FIFOs.

Correctness: Using FIFO buffers ensures by construction that the read and write operations of each process are kept in order (maintaining $\leq_{PO}$). The arbiter takes elements from the top of a FIFO buffer and issues the operation to the memory unit. Therefore, the arbiter constructs a serial view on write operations of all processes and the read operations of its corresponding process.

Completeness: Consider now an arbitrary PRAM execution. If each arbiter selects its actions according to the execution's serial view corresponding to its process, then the resulting writes-to order $\mapsto$ is the same as the one of the assumed execution. As said before, as no writes are lost and an arbiter can always wait until the required value is available, every PRAM consistent execution is covered by the reference machine.

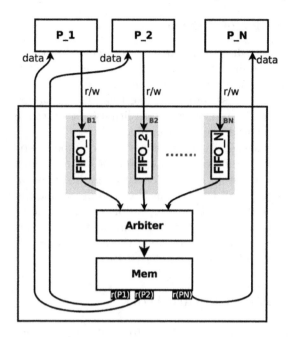

Fig. 4. Reference machine for sequential consistency

4.5   Reference Machine for Sequential Consistency

Architecture: Figure 4 shows an implementation of a reference machine for a sequential consistency. It consists of a FIFO buffer for each connected process, which are directly connected to their process interface, an arbiter which selects nondeterministically from all FIFOs and passes the operations to the memory unit or otherwise idles. The memory unit passes processed reads to the process that issued the read operation.

Correctness: Using FIFO buffers ensures by construction that the read and write operations of each process are kept in order (maintaining $\leq_{PO}$). The arbiter generates a serialization of all memory operations while maintaining the process order and therefore satisfies sequential consistency.

Completeness: If an arbitrary execution is sequentially consistent, then a serial view exists for all memory operations which respects $<_P$. If the arbiter uses this view to make its nondeterministic choices, then the resulting behavior is equivalent to the considered execution. Consequently, all sequentially consistent executions are covered by the given reference machine.

4.6   Implementation of Reference Machines

We have implemented all reference machines discussed in the previous sections as well as many others in the synchronous programming language Quartz [23]. The complete implementations can be found in [24].

To test their correctness, programs like Dekkers mutual exclusion protocol and programs derived from memory model litmus test suites have been successfully run on the presented reference machines.

While the introduced reference machines require unbounded buffers and true nondeterminism to guarantee the completeness of the memory model, their implementations in a system description language like Quartz have to specify bounds for such structures. Clearly, since we can determine the required buffer sizes for each finite execution, it is still possible to ensure the completeness. For simulation purposes, we can resort to randomizing the nondeterministic choices, and for verification or coverage checking, those have to be handled by oracle inputs which are controlled by the underlying tools.

5   Conclusions and Future Work

This paper presents reference machines to characterize weak memory consistency models in an operational manner. We have implemented these reference machines in the synchronous language Quartz so that their behaviors are precisely determined by the formal semantics of Quartz. All reference machines were implemented by means of some basic components that clearly reflect the intention of the considered memory model. The resulting reference machines are useful for simulation and verification, and can serve as a comprehensive specification that can be used as a programming model.

We have proved the correctness and completeness of our reference machines, i.e., that the reference machines can only perform computations that belong to the weak memory model (correctness), and that all possible computations of the memory model can also be performed by our reference machines (completeness). Hence, our reference machines characterize the memory models in an operational manner.

In our future work, we would like to develop reference machines closer to real implementations. As stated before, the provided implementations aimed to be both correct and complete following the corresponding definitions. As a result, their structure is more complex as a real implementation would be, including both unboundedness and nondeterminism which are not wanted in real implementations.

Furthermore, as we want to observe the behavior of programs developed for sequential machines on weak memory models, the memory models were all analyzed and defined without synchronization operations. Multicore processors offer synchronization operations for enforcing a desired behavior if needed. Therefore, it might be of interest to include in future also synchronization operations like fences in our architectures.

References

1. Adve, S., Gharachorloo, K.: Shared memory consistency models: a tutorial. IEEE Comput. **29**(12), 66–76 (1996)
2. Adve, S., Hill, M.: A unified formalization of four shared-memory models. IEEE Trans. Parallel Distrib. Syst. (TPDS) **4**(6), 613–624 (1993)
3. Ahamad, M., Bazzi, R., John, R., Kohli, P., Neiger, G.: The power of processor consistency. In: Snyder, L. (ed.) Symposium on Parallel Algorithms and Architectures (SPAA), pp. 251–260. ACM, Velen (1993)
4. Alglave, J.: A formal hierarchy of weak memory models. Form. Methods Syst. Des. (FMSD) **41**(2), 178–210 (2012)
5. Bataller, J., Bernabeu, J.: Synchronized DSM models. In: Lengauer, C., Griebl, M., Gorlatch, S. (eds.) Euro-Par 1997. LNCS, vol. 1300, pp. 468–475. Springer, Heidelberg (1997). https://doi.org/10.1007/BFb0002771
6. Bruni, R., Montanari, U.: Models of Computation. Texts in Theoretical Computer Science. Springer, Cham (2017). https://doi.org/10.1007/978-3-319-42900-7
7. Flur, S., Gray, K., Pulte, C., Sarkar, S., Sezgin, A., Maranget, L., Deacon, W., Sewell, P.: Modelling the ARMv8 architecture, operationally: concurrency and ISA. In: Principles of Programming Languages (POPL), pp. 608–621. ACM (2016)
8. Furbach, F., Meyer, R., Schneider, K., Senftleben, M.: Memory model-aware testing - a unified complexity analysis. In: Application of Concurrency to System Design (ACSD), pp. 92–101. IEEE Computer Society, Tunis La Marsa (2014)
9. Furbach, F., Meyer, R., Schneider, K., Senftleben, M.: Memory-model-aware testing – a unified complexity analysis. Trans. Embed. Comput. Syst. (TECS) **14**(4), 63:1–63:25 (2015)
10. Goodman, J.: Cache consistency and sequential consistency. Technical report 1006, Computer Sciences Department, University of Wisconsin-Madison, February 1991
11. Heddaya, A., Sinha, H.: Coherence, non-coherence and local consistency in distributed shared memory for parallel computing. Technical report BU-CS-92-004, Department of Computer Science, Boston University (1992)
12. Hennessy, J., Patterson, D.: Computer Architecture: A Quantitative Approach, 3rd edn. Morgan Kaufmann, Burlington (2003)
13. Higham, L., Kawash, J., Verwaal, N.: Weak memory consistency models - part I: definitions and comparisons. Technical report 98/612/03, Department of Computer Science, University of Calgary (1998)
14. Lamport, L.: How to make a multiprocessor computer that correctly executes multiprocess programs. IEEE Trans. Comput. (T-C) **28**(9), 690–691 (1979)
15. Lawrence, R.: A survey of cache coherence mechanisms in shared memory multiprocessors (1998)
16. Lipton, R., Sandberg, J.: PRAM: a scalable shared memory. Technical report CS-TR-180-88, Princeton University (1988)
17. Lipton, R., Sandberg, J.: Oblivious memory computer networking. Patent US 5276806, January 1994
18. Mador-Haim, S., et al.: An axiomatic memory model for POWER multiprocessors. In: Madhusudan, P., Seshia, S.A. (eds.) CAV 2012. LNCS, vol. 7358, pp. 495–512. Springer, Heidelberg (2012). https://doi.org/10.1007/978-3-642-31424-7_36
19. McKenney, P.: Memory barriers: a hardware view for software hackers, June 2010. http://www.rdrop.com/users/paulmck
20. Mosberger, D.: Memory consistency models. ACM SIGOPS: Oper. Syst. Rev. **27**(1), 18–26 (1993)

21. Mosberger, D.: Memory consistency models. Technical report TR 93/11, Department of Computer Science, The University of Arizona, Tucson, Arizona, USA (1993)
22. Owens, S., Sarkar, S., Sewell, P.: A better x86 memory model: x86-TSO. In: Berghofer, S., Nipkow, T., Urban, C., Wenzel, M. (eds.) TPHOLs 2009. LNCS, vol. 5674, pp. 391–407. Springer, Heidelberg (2009). https://doi.org/10.1007/978-3-642-03359-9_27
23. Schneider, K.: The synchronous programming language Quartz. Internal report 375, Department of Computer Science, University of Kaiserslautern, Kaiserslautern, Germany, December 2009
24. Senftleben, M.: Operational characterization of weak memory consistency models. Master's thesis, Department of Computer Science, University of Kaiserslautern, Germany, March 2013
25. Senftleben, M., Schneider, K.: Specifying weak memory consistency with temporal logic. In: Ghazel, M., Jmaiel, M. (eds.) Verification and Evaluation of Computer and Communication Systems (VECoS). CEUR Workshop Proceedings, vol. 1689, pp. 107–122. Sun SITE Central Europe, Tunis (2016). http://ceur-ws.org/Vol-1689/
26. Sindhu, P., Frailong, J.M., Cekleov, M.: Formal specification of memory models. In: Dubois, M., Thakkar, S. (eds.) Scalable Shared Memory Multiprocessors, pp. 25–41. Kluwer, Dordrecht (1992)
27. Steinke, R., Nutt, G.: A unified theory of shared memory consistency. J. ACM (JACM) **51**(5), 800–849 (2004)
28. Weaver, D., Germond, T. (eds.): The SPARC Architecture Manual-Version 9. Prentice-Hall Inc., Upper Saddle River (1994)

Energy Efficient Systems

A Tightly Coupled Heterogeneous Core with Highly Efficient Low-Power Mode

Yasumasa Chidai[1]([✉]), Kojiro Izuoka[1], Ryota Shioya[1], Masahiro Goshima[2], and Hideki Ando[1]

[1] Nagoya University, Nagoya, Aichi, Japan
{chidai,izuoka}@ando.nuee.nagoya-u.ac.jp,
{shioya,ando}@nuee.nagoya-u.ac.jp
[2] National Institute of Informatics, Tokyo, Japan
goshima@nii.ac.jp

Abstract. A tightly coupled heterogeneous core (TCHC) has heterogeneous execution units with different characteristics inside the core. The composite core (CC) and the front-end execution architecture (FXA) are examples of state-of-the-art TCHCs. These TCHCs have in-order and out-of-order execution units in the core. They selectively execute instructions in-order and it improves the energy efficiency without significant performance degradation compared to out-of-order execution. However, these TCHCs cannot improve the energy efficiency sufficiently. CC has a large switching penalty of the execution units, and thus, CC cannot sufficiently execute instructions in-order. FXA cannot suspend energy consuming out-of-order execution units when it executes instructions in-order. We propose a dual-mode frontend execution architecture (DM-FXA), which is based on the FXA. DM-FXA has our proposed low-power execution mode, which completely suspends the out-of-order execution unit on in-order execution, and thus, DM-FXA consumes less energy than does the FXA. In addition, DM-FXA has a smaller switching penalty than CC. In our evaluation, the proposed methods reduce energy consumption by 34.7% compared with a conventional out-of-order processor, and performance degradation is within 3.2%.

1 Introduction

A *heterogeneous multicore (HMC)* is an effective method for improving the energy efficiency of processors [1–5]. HMCs consist of multiple cores with different performance and energy-efficiency characteristics. HMCs execute each program phase using the most energy-efficient core by switching the active core. ARM big.LITTLE [5] is a commercialized example of an HMC.

However, because each core has dedicated caches and predictors, core switching causes significant penalty cycles. As a result, core switching granularity is restricted to be long intervals (e.g., 100M instructions) [1].

To reduce the switching penalty, a *tightly coupled heterogeneous core (TCHC)* was proposed [6–12]. A typical TCHC has two execution units, in-order (InO)

© Springer International Publishing AG, part of Springer Nature 2018
M. Berekovic et al. (Eds.): ARCS 2018, LNCS 10793, pp. 211–224, 2018.
https://doi.org/10.1007/978-3-319-77610-1_16

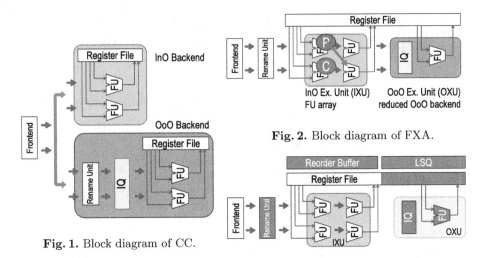

Fig. 1. Block diagram of CC.

Fig. 2. Block diagram of FXA.

Fig. 3. LP mode in DM-FXA.

and out-of-order (OoO), in a single core. Because the caches and predictors are shared by the units in the core, the TCHC enables the fine-grained switching of execution units, and thus, it improves energy efficiency.

The *composite core (CC)* [6,7] is an example of state-of-the-art TCHCs. CC [6,7] has an InO and an OoO backend, as shown in Fig. 1. CC has two execution modes: a *low-power (LP)* mode, using the InO backend and a *high-performance (HP)* mode, using the OoO backend. CC shares the frontend and L1D/I cache between the backends, thereby reducing the penalty for mode switching.

However, because CC has the independent backends, there is always a penalty when switching modes. Although this switching penalty is much shorter than those of the HMCs, it has a non-negligible effect on fine-grained mode switching in CC (e.g., 500 instructions interval). As a result, the switching penalty significantly reduces opportunities for LP mode execution in CC.

The *front-end execution architecture (FXA)* [8] is a TCHC contrasting to CC. FXA has two execution units: an in-order execution unit (IXU) and an OoO execution unit (OXU), as shown in Fig. 2 [8]. The difference between FXA and CC is that the IXU and OXU are connected serially, and the IXU serves as a filter for the OXU. The IXU is placed in the processor frontend and executes instructions that can fetch all their source operands in the frontend. The instructions executed in the IXU are not dispatched to the OXU, which reduces the energy consumption of the OXU. As a result, FXA does not have the mode switching penalty and can execute instructions in-order at instruction granularity.

In addition, the IXU has a higher capability than an InO processor. An InO processor usually stalls the pipeline when dependent instructions are decoded at the same cycle. In contrast, the IXU can execute such instructions without pipeline stall. As a result, the IXU can execute many instructions (approximately 50% [8]).

However, FXA cannot sufficiently reduce the energy consumption compared to CC. This is because it is necessary for FXA to keep to operate some OoO components such as a rename unit and a re-order buffer (ROB) even if instructions are executed in the IXU. As a result, the in-order execution in FXA is less energy efficient than the LP mode in CC, because the LP mode in CC completely stops the OoO components.

As described above, CC and FXA have the following problems: (1) the mode-switching penalty of CC is still large, and (2) the in-order execution in FXA is not energy efficient. In order to resolve these problems, we propose a *dual-mode frontend execution architecture (DM-FXA)*, which is based on FXA and has LP and HP modes. The LP mode executes all instructions in-order using the IXU only and suspends the OXU, whereas the HP mode executes instructions in the same way as in FXA. Similarly to CC, DM-FXA executes instructions by switching between these modes and improves the energy efficiency.

The contributions of DM-FXA are as follows:

1. DM-FXA can switch from LP to HP mode without incurring a penalty. This is because the switching from in-order (LP) to OoO (HP) execution can be realized only by resuming dispatch to the OXU since the IXU and OXU are connected serially. Consequently, it mitigates the large switching penalty of CC, and thus, it improves an LP mode use rate.
2. The LP mode in DM-FXA completely omits the processes required by OoO execution, and consequently, it solves the inefficient energy reduction of the in-order execution in FXA.
3. Since the LP mode of DM-FXA leverages the IXU, the LP mode of DM-FXA has higher performance than LP mode of CC using a normal InO processor. As a result, DM-FXA can get more opportunities to perform LP mode execution than CC without performance degradation.
4. Our evaluation shows that the performance-energy ratio (the inverse of the energy-delay product) of DM-FXA is 24.1% and 12.1% higher than those of CC and FXA, respectively.

The rest of the paper is organized as follows. Section 2 describes CC and FXA. In Sect. 3, we propose DM-FXA, and in Sect. 4, we evaluate our proposed method. Then, Sect. 5 summarizes related work.

2 Existing TCHC Architecture

2.1 Composite Core

CC [6,7] has *InO* and *OoO backends* (Fig. 1), which are used in LP and HP mode, respectively. The two backends share some units, such as the branch predictor and L1D/I caches, to avoid a cold start on switching. This allows CC to perform fast execution-mode switching. Other latency-critical components, such as a register file (RF), are independent for each backend.

Execution Mode Selection. CC basically selects the execution mode as follows. In execution mode selection, CC controls the (estimated) increase of execution cycles from the HP mode within a user-configured range (e.g., 5%). That is, supposing that a part of a program is executed by both HP and LP modes, and if the increase in cycles of LP mode execution is estimated to be smaller than that of the HP mode execution, then CC switches its mode to LP mode. We call such a part an *LP-friendly interval* when LP mode effectively improves energy efficiency.

The authors of CC found that the LP-friendliness fluctuates wildly in fine granularity (e.g., 500 instructions) [6,7], and CC improves energy efficiency by exploiting such fine-grained LP-friendly intervals. In their evaluation, the use rate of LP mode in CC is approximately 30% while the performance degradation is within 5% [7].

Execution Mode Switching. CC switches its execution mode as follows. (1) CC stops the instruction fetch and waits until all instructions are retired from the active backend. (2) In parallel with the fetch stop, CC speculatively starts to migrate register values between the dedicated RFs. (3) After the retirement of instructions from the active backend, the values for which speculative migration failed are remigrated. (4) When the remigration is completed, the switching destination backend starts instruction execution. The cycles required for this retirement and migration is the switching penalty.

Although the penalty cycles are significantly shorter (about 37 cycles in our evaluation) than those in conventional heterogeneous multicore processors (approximately $20\,\mu s$ [13]), the penalty has non-negligible negative effects because CC switches modes with a considerably fine granularity. As a result, CC's switching granularity is restricted to more than hundreds of instructions [7].

2.2 Front-End Execution Architecture

Structure and Behavior. FXA also has two execution units: OXU and IXU (Fig. 2). While the OXU is a reduced backend of a conventional OoO processor, the IXU consists of an array of functional units (FUs). The IXU is placed after the rename stage in the frontend and executes instructions in order. FXA has additional register ports for the IXU; however, the total number of register ports is not significantly increased because the OXU size is reduced as shown in Figs. 1 and 2.

FXA handles instructions as follows (assuming integer instructions with one-cycle latency). (1) FXA attempts to obtain source operands at the register read stage in the frontend by (1-a) reading from RF or (1-b) bypassing from the FUs in the IXU (not from the OXU). Operands are bypassed between FUs on different stages, e.g., a result calculated on the first stage is received by the second stage. FXA then checks whether all the operands are obtained, that is, whether instructions are ready to be executed. (2) A ready instruction is executed in the IXU and is not dispatched to the IQ. (3) A non-ready instruction goes through the IXU as a NOP and is then dispatched to the IQ in OXU and executed. Note that an InO processor stalls its pipeline until its readiness is resolved; however non-ready instructions in FXA go through the IXU pipeline as a NOP without stalling the pipeline.

IXU Capability. The IXU has a higher capability than an InO processor. An InO processor usually stalls the pipeline when dependent instructions are decoded at the same cycle. In contrast, the FU array in the IXU can execute such instructions without pipeline stall. For example, in Fig. 2, when the producer instruction ⓟ is executed in the first stage of the IXU, its consumer ⓒ decoded at the same cycle goes through the first stage as a NOP and then is executed in the second stage. As a result, the IXU can execute many instructions (approximately 50% [8]).

IXU executes not only integer instructions but also load/store and branch instructions. Other instructions such as floating-point (FP) instructions are not executed in IXU because the resource overhead for additional FPUs is large.

Merits and Demerits. FXA has the following merits:

– The energy consumption is reduced. IXU has no instruction-scheduling hardware and thus it can execute instructions with high energy efficiency. Moreover, IXU filters many instructions (e.g. 50%); thus, the size of OXU can be reduced without performance degradation.
– The performance is improved because the number of FUs is increased as shown in Figs. 1 and 2. CC can execute up to two instructions, while FXA can execute up to five instructions per cycle.

However, the IXU execution in FXA cannot sufficiently reduce energy consumption compared with the LP mode in CC, which can completely omit OoO execution. In FXA, OXU must execute instructions not filtered by IXU, and thus FXA must keep operating OoO execution components such as a rename unit, ROB, and load/store queue (LSQ).

3   Dual-Mode Front-End Execution Architecture

As described before, CC and FXA have the following problems:

1. CC: The switching penalty is large (Sect. 2.1).
2. FXA: The reduction in energy consumption is not sufficient (Sect. 2.2).

In order to solve these problems, we propose a **dual-mode front-end execution architecture (DM-FXA)**, based on FXA, with LP and HP modes.

3.1   Implementation of LP Mode

The LP mode in DM-FXA executes all instructions using the IXU only, whereas the HP mode executes instructions in the same way as in FXA. The execution mode selection is performed in the same way of CC (Sect. 2.1).

Figure 3 shows DM-FXA in the LP mode. DM-FXA has a similar physical architecture to FXA. In this figure, the shadowed units, such as IQ, are stopped in the LP mode. Note that power gating is not applied to the deactivated units as in the prior work of CC [6, 7] because recovery from power gating requires significant time.

The LP mode stalls the pipeline when its source operands cannot be obtained and waits for resolving dependencies as in an InO processor. When decoding complex instructions not supported by the IXU (Sect. 2.2) in the LP mode, DM-FXA immediately switches to the HP mode.

The LP mode completely omits OoO execution as follows:

1. It deactivates the OXU including IQ, LSQ, and ROB.
2. It stops register renaming, and RF is accessed using logical register numbers.
3. Only a partial region in RF is accessed when accessing RF with the logical numbers; thus, the other region of RF can be deactivated. We call active partial region *head region*. If the number of logical registers is 32, the head region is from register 0 to 31. In modern processors, RFs generally consist of hierarchical SRAMs [14, 15]; thus, the LP mode deactivates not accessed SRAMs.

Thus, the LP mode resolves the problem of inefficient energy reduction in FXA (Sect. 2.2).

3.2   Switching from HP to LP Mode

The switching from the HP to LP mode occurs as follows.

1. The fetch instruction is stopped, and DM-FXA waits for the retirement of all instructions in a similar way to the as CC.
2. DM-FXA rearranges the values in the RF in the order of the logical register numbers so that the RF is accessed using logical numbers. In this rearrangement, live values in the head region are temporally migrated to the other region in order to clean out the head region, and then all values are migrated to the head region.

Additional cycles for this temporal migration are small because the number of live registers is equal to that of logical registers after the retirement of all instructions; thus, there is a low probability of live values in the head region (e.g., 32 logical regs/160 physical regs = 0.2). In addition, the required cycles for this rearrangement are shorter (maximally 20 cycles in our evaluation) than those required for the retirement of instructions, and thus, does not cause serious problems.

3.3   Switching from LP to HP Mode

The switching from the LP to HP mode is performed by (1) initializing a register alias table (RAT), and (2) restarting OoO execution. Unlike CC, DM-FXA does not incur a penalty when switching from the LP to HP mode.

The RAT must be initialized before returning to the HP mode because the register values are rearranged when switching modes. In this case, the RAT is initialized because each logical register number points to the same number of a physical register entry. This initialization can be performed in parallel with execution in the LP mode because the LP mode does not use the RAT.

3.4   Execution Correctness

When switching from the LP to HP mode, unlike CC, it is not necessary for DM-FXA to wait for the instructions to retire from the pipeline. In this behavior, the execution correctness in DM-FXA is still maintained. For describing the reason, we refer to instructions fetched in LP and HP mode as LP and HP instructions, respectively.

In the LP mode of DM-FXA, ROB and LSQ entries are not allocated to LP instructions; consequently, if HP instructions are executed before the execution of all LP instructions, the correctness of execution is not maintained.

However, HP instructions do not overtake LP instructions in execution. Figure 4 shows the switching of an execution mode from the LP to HP mode, and both LP and HP instructions simultaneously exist in the pipeline. The ovals labeled as LP and HP show LP and HP instructions respectively, and the instructions are arranged from right to left in the program order.

The left-sided HP instructions cannot be dispatched to IQ in OXU before all the right-sided LP instructions are executed because all the instructions must proceed in order in the frontend pipeline including IXU. As a result, when HP instructions are dispatched to IQ in OXU, all the LP instructions have been completed to maintain execution correctness.

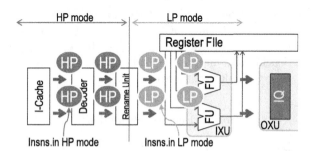

Fig. 4. Switching from LP to HP mode.

3.5   LP Mode Utilization

DM-FXA can get more opportunities to perform LP mode execution than CC without performance degradation for the following reasons:

1. As described above, DM-FXA can switch from the LP to HP mode without incurring the switching penalty. As a result, compared with CC, execution cycles in which the core is stopped due to the switching penalty are reduced, and more instructions can be executed by LP mode.
2. As described in Sect. 2.2, the IXU has the higher capability than an InO processor. Since the LP mode of DM-FXA leverages the IXU, the LP mode of DM-FXA has higher performance than LP mode of CC using a normal InO processor.

The evaluation results in Sect. 4.2 show that DM-FXA can execute about 3 times more instructions in LP mode than CC with the same performance.

3.6   Hardware Cost

The additional hardware cost of DM-FXA compared with FXA is mainly composed of switching control hardware that is almost the same as that for CC. The circuit area and energy consumption of this additional hardware are negligible compared with those of the whole processor [6,7].

4   Evaluation

4.1   Evaluation Environment

We evaluate the IPCs using an in-house cycle-accurate processor simulator. Similar to gem5 [16], this simulator is execution driven, but it more accurately simulates dynamic scheduling in OoO processors, such as a replay mechanism on cache misses. We evaluate the energy consumption using the McPAT simulator [17], with the parameters shown in Table 1.

We use the programs from the SPEC CPU 2006 INT benchmark suite [18]. The programs were compiled using GCC 4.5.3 with "-O3" option. We skipped the first 2G instructions, and evaluate the next 100M instructions using *ref* data sets. These benchmarks and evaluated instructions are basically the same as those used in prior CC-related studies [6,7].

Table 1. Device configurations

Technology	22 nm, Fin-FET
Temperature, VDD	320 K, 0.8 V
Device type (core)	High performance (I_off: 127 nA/um)
Device type (L2)	Low standby power (I_off: 0.0968 nA/um)

Table 2. Processor configurations.

	BASE/CC(OoO)	FXA/DM-FXA	CC(InO)
Fetch width	3	←	←
Issue width	4	2	3
Retire width	3	←	N/A
Function unit	ALU:2, FPU:2, MEM:2	←	ALU:2, FPU:1, MEM:1
IQ	64 entries	32 entries	N/A
Ld./St. queue	32/32 entries	←	N/A
ROB	128 entries	←	N/A
I/D TLB	64/64 entries	←	←
u-op cache	4 KB, one cycle	←	←
L1 I-cache	48 KB, two cycles	←	←
L1 D-cache	32 KB, two cycles	←	←
L2 cache	512 KB, 12 cycles	←	←
L2 prefetcher	Stream prefetcher	←	←
Main memory	200 cycles	←	←
IXU	N/A	5 FUs, 3 stages [8]	N/A
ISA	Alpha	←	←

We evaluate the following models:

BASE: A baseline model for an OoO superscalar processor.

CC5: A CC model with an execution mode selection algorithm proposed in [7]. As in previous studies, we use a trace-based phase predictor with a 9-bit index and the corresponding 512-entry PHT. The switching length [7] is set to 500 instructions. In this model, the allowable increase rate for the execution cycles is set to 1.05 (5% slowdown) from BASE, as in previous studies [6,7].

CC10: This model is CC5 with an allowable increase rate of 1.1 (10% slowdown).

FXA: An FXA model with an IQ with issue width and half the capacity of those in BASE because the IXU filters instructions to the IQ without performance degradation, as described in Sect. 2.2.

DMFXA5: A DM-FXA model with the same mode selection algorithm of the CC models. The length of the switching interval is set to 500 instructions. In this model, the allowable increase rate is set to 1.05 (5% slowdown), not from BASE, but from FXA. This model has a comparable IPC to that of BASE because the IPC for FXA is 6.8% higher than that for BASE, as described in Sect. 2.2. The IQ in this model is also half that in BASE.

DMFXA10: This model is DMFXA5 with an allowable increase rate of 1.1 (10% slowdown). For the same reason as in DMFXA5, this model has almost same IPC as CC5.

Table 2 lists the configurations for these models. The parameters are based on those in ARM big.LITTLE architecture, which consists of ARM Cortex-A57 [19] and A53 [20]. The InO backend used in CC5 is a three-issue in-order superscalar processor. These configurations are similar to those used in prior FXA studies [8].

4.2   Evaluation Results

Control Accuracy and Performance. First, we evaluate the performance control accuracy for each model. The average error rates for CC5, CC10, DMFXA5, and DMFXA10 are 0.35%, 0.15%, 0.28%, and 0.55%, respectively. Thus, the performance follows each target performance with high accuracy. These results show that the mode selection algorithm for CC can be also applicable to DM-FXA with high control accuracy.

Figure 5 shows the performance of all models, normalized by that of BASE. As mentioned above, the performance of FXA is 6.8% higher than BASE, on average. Therefore, DMFXA5 has almost the same performance as BASE, and DMFXA10 has almost the same performance as CC5. Compared to BASE, the performance levels of CC5 and DMFXA10 are 95.2% and 96.8%, respectively.

LP Mode Utilization. Figure 6 shows the rate of instructions executed in LP mode. The use rate in CC5 is 21.7%, on average, whereas that of DMFXA5, which has the same 5% slowdown rate as CC5, is 38.0%, on average. Moreover, the use rate for DMFXA10, the performance of which is nearly equal to that of CC5,

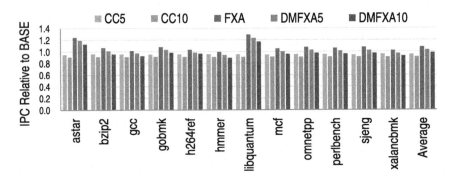

Fig. 5. IPC relative to BASE.

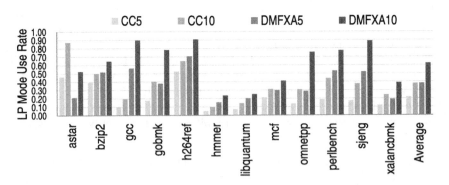

Fig. 6. LP mode use rate.

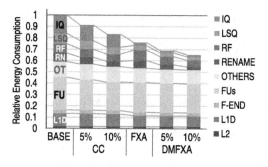

Fig. 7. Energy consumption relative to BASE.

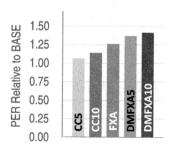

Fig. 8. PER relative to BASE.

is 60.0%. Such improvements are achieved by the following reasons: (1) DM-FXA can reduce the switching penalty compared to CC and (2) since IXU has better performance than normal in-order execution, it gives more opportunities to execute LP mode than CC (Sect. 3).

Energy Consumption. Figure 7 shows the energy consumption of each model relative to that of BASE, on average. These results include static and dynamic energy consumption.

DMFXA10 reduces the energy consumption by 34.7% compared with BASE because the energy consumption of the units for OoO execution, such as IQ, LSQ, RF and a rename logic, is significantly reduced. DMFXA10 reduces energy consumption by 28.5% compared with CC5, which has almost the same performance as DMFXA10. This is because the use rate of LP mode increases significantly, as described before. DMFXA10 reduces energy consumption by 14.2% compared with FXA, because the energy consumption of the components that the FXA must continue activating, such as the rename logic (Sect. 3.1), is reduced in the LP mode of DM-FXA.

Note that the breakdown of BASE is very similar to that in AMD Steamroller [21] and ARM Cortex A15 [22]. The energy consumption of the L2 cache is very small in all the models. This is because we use Fin-FET technology [23] and low-standby-power transistors for the L2 caches (Table 1), and consequently, the static energy consumption of the L2 caches is very small.

Performance Energy Ratio. This section shows the performance-energy ratio (PER) of each model, which is equal to the inverse of the energy-delay product (EDP)[1]. The PER shows how each model reduces energy consumption with respect to its performance degradation. Figure 8 shows the PER of each model relative to that of BASE. In the figure, DMFXA10 improves the PER compared to BASE, CC10, and FXA by 41.5%, 24.1%, and 12.1%, respectively. This high

---

[1] We use a PER instead of an EDP because it is easy to understand. That is, a larger PER shows better energy efficiency.

PER is achieved because DMFXA10 significantly reduces the energy consumption compared to its performance degradation. Noted that FXA has the better PER than its reduced energy consumption, because FXA does not degrade but improves performance [8].

Switching Penalty. In the DM-FXA, there is no penalty for switching from LP to HP mode; thus, the number of penalty cycles per switch is smaller than that of the CC. The number of average penalty cycles per switch is 56 cycles for the CC and 32 cycles for the DM-FXA, respectively. As described in Sect. 3.5, DM-FXA takes advantage of this short penalty and increases the number of instructions executed in the LP mode

5   Related Work

Typical HMCs include heterogeneity based on the difference in the microarchitecture between the cores, such as InO and OoO cores [1–5]. Other methods have also been proposed with heterogeneity based on the DVFS control [3,24].

Unlike the naive HMCs, TCHCs have tightly coupled heterogeneous execution units within a single core. Therefore, TCHCs perform energy-efficient execution at a finer granularity. We summarize this research in the following paragraphs.

The heterogeneous block architecture (HBA) [9] improves energy efficiency by caching dynamically scheduled instructions and executing the cached instructions InO. DynaMOS [10] also caches scheduled instructions and executes them InO. DynaMOS is based on the CC architecture and improves the InO backend execution ratio by executing the *scheduled* instructions in the InO backend. Compared with our proposed method, these methods require special mechanisms, such as a special trace cache for storing scheduled instructions and additional renaming logic.

Early OoO late execution (EOLE) [12] is similar to the FXA in that EOLE executes instructions InO using FUs added to the frontend. EOLE must also continue activating components for OoO execution for the same reason as the FXA, and consequently, the reduction of consumed energy is restricted compared with that of the DM-FXA.

6   Conclusion

The CC and FXA introduce heterogeneity within a single core and were previously proposed for to improve energy efficiency. However, these TCHCs have problems with their switching latency hardware, and the amount of energy consumption reduction is insufficient. In order to resolve these problems, we proposed the DM-FXA, which is based on the FXA and has an LP mode. In our evaluation, our proposed method achieved a reduction in energy consumption by 34.7%, with a 3.2% performance overhead in comparison with a conventional superscalar processor.

Acknowledgment. This work was supported by JSPS KAKENHI Grant Number 16H05855.

References

1. Kumar, R., Farkas, K.I., Jouppi, N.P., Ranganathan, P., Tullsen, D.M.: Single-ISA heterogeneous multi-core architectures: the potential for processor power reduction. In: Proceedings of the 36th Annual International Symposium on Microarchitecture (MICRO), pp. 81–92, December 2003
2. Becchi, M., Crowley, P.: Dynamic thread assignment on heterogeneous multiprocessor architectures. In: Proceedings of the 3rd Conference on Computing Frontiers, pp. 29–40, May 2006
3. Rangan, K.K., Wei, G.Y., Brooks, D.: Thread motion: fine-grained power management for multi-core systems. In: Proceedings of the 36th Annual International Symposium on Computer Architecture, pp. 302–313, June 2009
4. Joao, J.A., Suleman, M.A., Mutlu, O., Patt, Y.N.: Bottleneck identification and scheduling in multithreaded applications. In: Proceedings of the International Conference on Architectural Support for Programming Languages and Operating Systems (ASPLOS), pp. 223–234, April 2012
5. Greenhalgh, P.: Big.LITTLE Processing with ARM Cortex-A15 and Cortex-A7. Whitepaper, September 2011
6. Lukefahr, A., Padmanabha, S., Das, R., Sleiman, F.M., Dreslinski, R., Wenisch, T.F., Mahlke, S.: Composite cores: pushing heterogeneity into a core. In: Proceedings of the 45th Annual International Symposium on Microarchitecture, pp. 317–328, December 2012
7. Padmanabha, S., Lukefahr, A., Das, R., Mahlke, S.: Trace based phase prediction for tightly-coupled heterogeneous cores. In: Proceedings of the 46th Annual International Symposium on Microarchitecture, pp. 445–456, December 2009
8. Shioya, R., Goshima, M., Ando, H.: A front-end execution architecture for high energy efficiency. In: Proceedings of the 47th Annual International Symposium on Microarchitecture, pp. 419–431, December 2014
9. Fallin, C., Wilkerson, C., Mutlu, O.: The heterogeneous block architecture. In: Proceedings of the International Conference on Computer Design (ICCD), pp. 386–393, October 2014
10. Padmanabha, S., Lukefahr, A., Das, R., Mahlke, S.: DynaMOS: dynamic schedule migration for heterogeneous cores. In: Proceedings of the 48th International Symposium on Microarchitecture, December 2015
11. Khubaib, Suleman, M.A., Hashemi, M., Wilkerson, C., Patt, Y.N.: MorphCore: an energy-efficient microarchitecture for high performance ILP and high throughput TLP. In: Proceedings of the 45th Annual International Symposium on Microarchitecture, pp. 305–316, December 2012
12. Perais, A., Seznec, A.: EOLE: paving the way for an effective implementation of value prediction. In: Proceeding of the 41st Annual International Symposium on Computer Architecture, pp. 481–492, June 2014
13. ARM: ARM Unveils its Most Energy Efficient Application Processor Ever; Redefines Traditional Power And Performance Relationship With big.LITTLE Processing (2011)
14. Weste, N.H.E., Harris, D.M.: CMOS VLSI Design: A Circuits and Systems Perspective, 4th edn. Pearson/Addison-Wesley, Boston (2011)

15. Golden, M., Arekapudi, S., Vinh, J.: 40-Entry unified out-of-order scheduler and integer execution unit for the AMD Bulldozer x86-64 core. In: Proceedings of the International Solid-State Circuits Conference (ISSCC), pp. 80–82, February 2011

16. Binkert, N.: The gem5 simulator. SIGARCH Comput. Archit. News **39**(2), 1–7 (2011)

17. Li, S., Ahn, J.H., Strong, R.D., Brockman, J.B., Tullsen, D.M., Jouppi, N.P.: McPAT: an integrated power, area, and timing modeling framework for multi-core and manycore architectures. In: Proceedings of the 42nd Annual International Symposium on Microarchitecture, pp. 469–480, December 2009

18. The Standard Performance Evaluation Corporation: SPEC CPU 2006 Suite. http://www.spec.org/cpu2006/

19. Bolaria, J.: Cortex-A57 Extends ARM's Reach. Microprocessor Report 11/5/12-1, November 2012

20. Krewell, K.: Cortex-A53 Is ARM's Next Little Thing. Microprocessor Report 11/5/12-2, November 2012

21. Gillespie, K., et al.: Steamroller: an x86-64 core implemented in 28nm bulk CMOS. In: International Solid-State Circuits Conference (ISSCC). Presentation Slides (2014)

22. NVIDIA: NVIDIA Tegra 4 Family CPU Architecture. Whitepaper (2013)

23. Auth, C., et al.: A 22 nm high performance and low-power CMOS technology featuring fully-depleted tri-gate transistors, self-aligned contacts and high density MIM capacitors. In: Symposium on VLSI Technology (VLSIT), pp. 131–132 (2012)

24. Lukefahr, A., Padmanabha, S., Das, R., Dreslinski Jr., R., Wenisch, T.F., Mahlke, S.: Heterogeneous microarchitectures trump voltage scaling for low-power cores. In: Proceedings of the International Conference on Parallel Architectures and Compilation Techniques (PACT), pp. 237–250, July 2014

Performance-Energy Trade-off in CMPs with Per-Core DVFS

Solomon Abera$^{(\boxtimes)}$, M. Balakrishnan, and Anshul Kumar

Indian Institute of Technology Delhi, New Delhi, India
{solomon,mbala,anshul}@cse.iitd.ac.in

Abstract. In recent years, energy consumption of multicores has been a critical research agenda as chip multiprocessors (CMPs) have emerged as the leading architectural choice of computing systems. Unlike the uniprocessor environment, the energy consumption of an application running on a CMP depends not only on the characteristics of the application but also the behavior of its co-runners (applications running on other cores). In this paper, we model the energy-performance trade-off using machine learning. We use the model to sacrifice a certain user-specified percentage of the maximum achievable performance of an application to save energy. The input to the model is the isolated memory behavior of the application and each of its co-runners, as well as the performance constraint. The output of the model is the minimum core frequency at which the application should run to guarantee the given performance constraint in the influence of the co-runners. We show that, in a quad-core processor, we can save up to 51% core energy by allowing 16% degradation of performance.

Keywords: CMP · Shared resource · DVFS · Machine learning

1 Introduction

Over the last couple of decades, CMPs have been the leading architectural choice for computing systems ranging from high-end servers to battery-operated devices. Energy efficiency has been an issue for multicores due to battery life in portable devices, and cooling and energy costs in server class systems and compute clusters. Despite the fact that CMPs improve performance through concurrency, the contention for shared resources makes their performance and energy consumption unpredictable and inefficient [7,8]. These depend greatly on the nature of the co-runners.

Dynamic voltage and frequency scaling (DVFS) is used to reduce the power consumption of a processor by trading-off performance. In recent years, modern processors (Intel Haswell, IBM Power8, ...) provide support for per-core DVFS where each core can run at different frequency, resulting in a vast configuration space for the applications running on these cores.

© Springer International Publishing AG, part of Springer Nature 2018
M. Berekovic et al. (Eds.): ARCS 2018, LNCS 10793, pp. 225–238, 2018.
https://doi.org/10.1007/978-3-319-77610-1_17

Compute-bound applications, which make very few accesses to LLC, benefit from a higher core frequency as their performance is determined by the processing speed of the cores.

On the other hand, memory-bound applications, which make a lot of accesses to the LLC, behave differently and can be divided into two classes. The first class consists of those applications whose performance has a high dependence on the shared cache space (applications with high data reuse, or "cache-friendly" applications). These show higher performance when they run alone or with compute-bound applications. With such co-runners, their performance is determined by the core frequency as their memory transaction latency is hidden by the cache. However, in the wake of competition for shared cache space from other memory-bound co-runners, their performance hugely drops. In such situations, the core frequency is not a big factor, and it can be lowered without impacting the performance much.

The second class of memory-bound applications are those whose performance does not depend on the amount of shared cache space (applications with low data reuse), like streaming applications. However, the performance of such applications is affected by the available memory bandwidth when they run with memory-bound co-runners. Regarding core frequency, varying it has little impact on the performance of these applications, regardless of the nature of the co-runners.

Any DVFS policy should take these determining factors into account before choosing the optimal frequency at which any workload should run. Consider the two SPEC2006 benchmarks calculix and bzip2. Calculix is a compute-intensive benchmark, whereas bzip2 is a cache-friendly one. We simulated the execution of each of the two benchmarks running on a quad-core CMP sharing 2 MB L2 cache with other three co-runner benchmarks. We prepared five different sets of co-runners, each posing a different cumulative pressure on the shared L2 cache. We quantify the pressure posed by an application with the metric "aggressiveness" (see Sect. 3.1). The cumulative pressure of the three co-runners is termed "global-aggressiveness" (GA). The higher the GA, the greater the pressure on the L2 by the co-runners. When calculix runs with different competing benchmarks (Fig. 1a), its performance shows little degradation. Rather its performance is severely affected by the reduction of its core frequency. On the other hand, bzip2 (Fig. 1b) shows different levels of performance degradation with different co-runners. When it runs with memory-intensive co-runners ($GA = 53$), its execution time increased by only 40% when the core frequency changed from 2.4 GHz to 1.0 GHz. However, when it runs with compute-intensive workloads ($GA = 8.92$), it slowed down by 120% for the same change in frequency. Therefore, any proposed model to select the appropriate frequency should take into account the application's characteristics and the global stress on the shared resources.

Furthermore, there are cases in which we may need a DVFS policy that enables us to trade-off certain percentage of the maximum achievable performance for energy savings. For example, let us say the user is willing to sacrifice

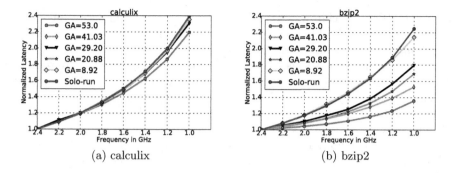

Fig. 1. Effect of DVFS and resource contention on performance

10% of the maximum possible performance of an application (when it runs with a given set of co-runners) in exchange for energy savings. As we discussed earlier, this 10% of application's performance is determined by its behavior as well as the nature of the co-runners. When that application runs with memory-intensive workloads, surrendering 10% of its performance might allow significant lowering of the core frequency as the application will slow down due to the cache and bandwidth contention. On the other hand, the same application, when it runs with less memory hungry applications, even a small reduction in the core frequency may reduce the performance beyond the allowed 10% limit. In this paper, we model the performance-energy trade-off using a learning-based algorithm. In order to capture the contention among the co-runners, we chose a lightweight contention metric that can efficiently convey the potential contention that will be faced by the workload. The model takes individual LLC aggressiveness, the global LLC intensity that emanates from the other cores and the performance constraint as input and generates the optimal frequency setting for that core. We assume that the underlying architecture to be a CMP architecture consisting of multiple symmetric cores, where all the cores share the LLC. We also consider the applications to be single threaded, with no data sharing among them.

The rest of the paper is organized as follows: Sect. 2 describes previous work in the domain of CMP energy efficiency. Section 3 discusses the overview of the model construction, Sect. 4 compares different machine learning algorithms, Sect. 5 describes the evaluation of the described scheme, for different performance constraints, and shows the efficiency of the developed model. Finally, Sect. 6 concludes the paper.

2   Related Work

Energy consumption has become an important optimization metric for CMP based computational platforms. Since its proposal by Weiser et al. [1], DVFS has been used to minimize the processor energy consumption while limiting the reduction of the overall system performance. DVFS can be applied in CMPs on a per-chip, per-core or per-cluster basis. Most of the previous works are directed towards CMPs with chip-wise DVFS. There have been a significant amount of DVFS based works [2–6] focused on real-time systems that try to reduce energy consumption by utilizing the slack time for frequency scaling.

A lot of solutions have been proposed in the form of energy-aware scheduling that try to minimize the effect of contention, and apply DVFS to decrease the energy consumption. Merkel et al. [9] used task activity vectors (L2 and memory accesses) to capture the resource utilization of each task. When they schedule tasks, they try to pair memory-intensive tasks with compute-intensive ones to improve performance. When there are only memory intensive tasks in the workload, they scale down the chip frequency to save energy. Dhiman et al. [10] proposed a learning-based algorithm for a multi-tasking environment that suggests the optimal frequency based on tasks' degree of memory-boundedness. They used CPI stacks to quantify this behavior.

In recent years, machine learning algorithms have been applied to perform intelligent DVFS based energy saving [10–15]. The authors of [14] used reinforcement learning in which they took task characteristics and processor configuration to scale frequency for real-time systems. The task execution characteristics are derived from the execution time of the task (its CPU-time and stall-time). The proposal by Shen and Qiu [15] is the most related work to ours. In their work, they applied a machine learning technique to predict the performance degradation that would be faced by an application due to other applications in a CMP, and simultaneous application of DVFS. They define degradation with respect to a solitary run (solo-run) of the application on the CMP at the highest allowed frequency. They assumed global DVFS for all the cores. In this work, we assume that DVFS can be individually applied to each core. In addition to that, we argue that it would be difficult to guarantee a quality of service from the solo-run performance perspective as resource contention depends on the identity of the co-runner. Instead, the reference should be the maximum achievable performance with the given set of co-runners. In this work, we take this approach. For a given application, based on its memory behavior and that of its co-runners', the model can predict the correspondence between the performance loss and the discrete frequency steps.

3   Model Construction Methodology

The proposed machine learning based DVFS model attempts to predict the optimal core-frequency setting for a given user-specified acceptable loss in performance. The model is constructed offline by capturing the relationship between the nature of a benchmark, its operating frequency, the nature of its co-runners, and its performance. The model is then used online to find the optimal frequency that an application should run at, such that the given performance requirement is satisfied, and maximum energy savings are obtained.

Section 3.1 discusses the contention metrics that best capture the nature of a benchmark for the task at hand while Sect. 3.2 describes the data collection methodology. Section 3.3 then discusses the building process of the model and Sect. 3.4 covers the application of the model.

3.1   Contention Metrics

In order to construct a model that accurately captures the impact of frequency scaling and resource contention on performance, we need appropriate contention metrics. When applications are run in an isolated environment (solo-run), the amount of energy saved per percentage point of performance degradation varies based on their characteristics. Applications that are compute-intensive tend to save less energy for each percentage point of performance loss. Whereas, applications that are memory intensive tend to save much more energy for each percentage point of performance loss. This is because these applications take much time to progress as they wait for their data to arrive. Hence, in an isolated environment, the applications performance-energy trade-off balance can be modeled by its characteristics only.

As we mentioned earlier, shared resource contention in CMPs, particularly competition for shared cache space and memory bandwidth, severely harms performance and makes them energy inefficient. The slowdown encountered by individual applications hugely varies with the identities of the co-runners. The more the application slowed, the more insensitive it will be to frequency change and vice versa. Hence, the effect of frequency scaling also varies with the co-runners.

Therefore, when an application runs with other co-runners, they also prove to be a factor in the obtained energy savings through frequency scaling. If the application's performance does not depend on its usage of the shared resources, it does not incur any significant additional delay because of sharing. Hence, its own memory characteristics can be enough to drive the performance-energy trade-off and shows similar trade-off curve as its solo-run (Fig. 1a). If the application's performance does depend on the usage of the shared resources, it can show different behaviors based on the co-runners' characteristics. When the co-runners are not very shared resource hungry, the application might not incur much slowdown. Here, the performance-energy trade-off might not deviate much from its solo-run trade-off curve (see the curve in Fig. 1b with $GA = 8.92$). On the other hand, if its co-runners are resource hungry, the magnitude of their resource usage determines the slowdown suffered by the application. Accordingly, its energy saving per percentage point of performance loss varies with co-runners (see the curves in Fig. 1b with $GA = 53, GA = 41.03, GA = 29.20$ and $GA = 20.88$).

We desire a lightweight contention metric that conveys the resource hungriness of the application and helps in predicting slowdown that will be encountered by individual applications when they run together. This metric should be easy to collect online and the number of attributes should also be small as it reduces the sampling time. We have collected various performance metrics and tested their ability to predict the potential contention between the co-running applications. In our study, we run 275 combinations (each set of four) of SPEC2006 benchmark fragments on a quad-core environment sharing the LLC. We record the solo-run and co-run performance of the four co-running applications A_0, A_1, A_2 and A_3. The solo-run and co-run performance of each application is represented by its number of instructions per cycle as IPC_{solo} and IPC_{co} respectively. We computed the average slowdown as specified in Eq. 1.

$$Slowdown = \frac{\sum_{i=0}^{3} IPC_{solo}(A_i) - \sum_{i=0}^{3} IPC_{co}(A_i)}{\sum_{i=0}^{3} IPC_{solo}(A_i)} \times 100, \qquad (1)$$

We have analyzed parameters that present a high correlation with the observed slowdown. We chose three metrics: the solo-run IPC, number of LLC accesses (LLCA) and LLC misses per 1K cycles (MPKC). We also considered two methods of aggregating the parameters of the applications: *sum* and *product*. Table 1 presents the correlation between the six different candidates with the actual slowdown.

Table 1. Correlation between aggressiveness strategies and slowdown

Parameter	Correlation with slowdown
IPC_{sum}	−0.69469
$IPC_{product}$	−0.46521
$LLCA_{sum}$	0.73869
$LLCA_{product}$	0.48090
$MPKC_{sum}$	0.81011
$MPKC_{product}$	0.57714

As we can see from Table 1, $MPKC_{sum}$ shows the highest correlation with slowdown. The IPC based contention metrics show negative correlation with the slowdown, as high aggregate IPC implies lower contention, resulting in a lower slowdown. In this work, we represent the memory characteristics of applications by their aggressiveness scores (A_Score). A_Score is a metric that characterizes how aggressively an application competes for the shared cache space and memory bandwidth. We use MPKC as A_Score, and to model the global cache pressure emanating from the co-runners, define global-aggressiveness (GA) as the sum of the individual A_Scores of the co-runners.

We also perform experiment to demonstrate the correlation of the A_Score with performance loss, under the influence of frequency scaling. We run 20 single-threaded, single-phase (collected 250 million instructions fragments using Sim-Point) SPEC2006 benchmarks on sniper multicore simulator with quad-core configuration sharing a 2 MB L2 cache. In the experiment, we run the benchmarks without competing co-runners. We scaled the frequency from 2.4 GHz through 1.0 GHz and record the performance response of each benchmark to the frequency scaling. We present, in Fig. 2, the correlation between their A_Score and performance degradation. As we can observe from the figure, the compute-intensive benchmarks (low A_Score) show higher performance degradation when their frequency is scaled down. On the other hand, we can see memory-intensive

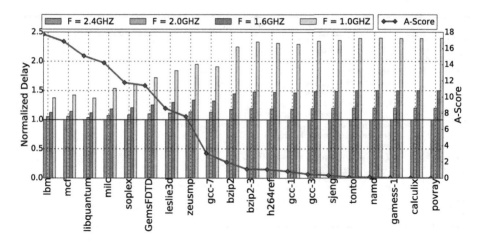

Fig. 2. Sensitivity of 20 SPEC2006 applications for frequency scaling and correlation with their A_Score

benchmarks are only marginally affected by frequency scaling as their performance is not determined by the core frequency.

In addition to its correlation with the slowdown (because of contention as well as frequency scaling), A_Score also can capture the impact of core-frequency changes on the aggressiveness of the application. Let us assume one application has x LLC misses when running at frequency f1. When the same application runs at f2 (f2 = 0.5f1), its LLC misses do not change but its cache pressure is minimized as its cache requests arrive at longer time intervals between them. This phenomenon is captured by the choice of LLC MPKC as a contention metric and makes it suitable for online DVFS modeling as every core might run at a different frequency. The cycles in our context are representation of time (elapsed time multiplied by the maximum core frequency).

3.2 Data Collection

Let us assume a processor having N_C cores. Let us also assume we have a set of N_A applications $A = \{A_0, A_1, \ldots, A_{N_A-1}\}$ that are to be run on this processor. We first collect the aggressiveness score of each application $A_{cur} \in A$ as $A\_Score_{A_{cur}}$ by running (or simulating) it alone on the given processor. We then construct a set of N_{CG} co-runner groups, $C = \{CG_0, CG_1, \ldots, CG_{N_{CG}-1}\}$, with each group having $N_C - 1$ applications from the set A. The global-aggressiveness of each co-runner group C_{cur} is given by $GA_{C_{cur}}$, and is computed by summing the individual A_Scores of the $N_C - 1$ applications in that group. We prepared the set C in such a way that their GA values are well spread over the entire spectrum of GA values ranging from maximum (all memory-bound) to the minimum (all compute-bound). We take only representative samples, not exhaustively, to construct the set C.

Algorithm 1. Data Collection Methodology

```
 1  for each application A_cur in A do
 2  │   schedule A_cur on core 0;
 3  │   for each co-runner group C_cur in C do
 4  │   │   schedule the applications in C_cur on cores 1 to N_C − 1;
 5  │   │   set the frequency of cores 1 to N_C − 1 to f_max;
 6  │   │   set the frequency of core 0 to f_max;
 7  │   │   execute / simulate;
 8  │   │   T_{f_max} = time taken to execute A_cur;
 9  │   │   for each frequency f_cur in F, other than f_max do
10  │   │   │   set the frequency of core 0 to f_cur;
11  │   │   │   execute / simulate;
12  │   │   │   T_cur = time taken to execute A_cur;
13  │   │   │   ΔP = (T_cur − T_{f_max})/T_{f_max} × 100;
14  │   │   │   save the tuple <A_Score_{A_cur}, GA_{C_cur}, ΔP, f_cur>;
15  │   │   end
16  │   end
17  end
```

Let us also assume that the processor is capable of operating at N_f different frequencies $F = \{f_0, f_1, \ldots, f_{N_f - 1}\}$, with the maximum frequency among these being labeled f_{max}. As discussed earlier, we assume the DVFS can be done on a per-core basis. Algorithm 1 describes how the data collection is done.

3.3 Building the Model

We desire a model that best captures the relationship between a benchmark's memory behavior, that of its co-runners, the frequency at which former is executed, and its performance. Therefore, in the training phase, we use $A\_Score, GA,$ ΔP (as defined in Algorithm 1) and frequency values, as collected in Sect. 3.2 to build the model, as shown in Fig. 3. In the testing phase, the model, given a benchmark, its co-runners, and a desired performance requirement, returns the minimum frequency that guarantees specified performance. There are a variety of machine learning algorithms that can be applied to capture the relationships

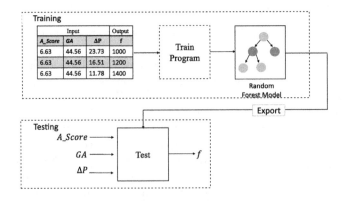

Fig. 3. Training and testing of the model

in different ways. Section 4 discusses the various machine learning algorithms considered, and their respective scores of predictions.

3.4 Application of the Model

The model can be used as a part of *batch* as well as *online* scheduler. In the case of *online* use, at each scheduling decision, for each of the runnable tasks running on the available cores, their previous epochs' performance metrics can be used for tuning each core's frequency. Here, the cost of DVFS transition as well as the time it takes to execute the prediction model should be taken into account to determine the time interval between two consecutive schedules. The input parameters that are collected from performance counters (A_score, GA) will be used along with the QoS policy imposed by the user, like $\Delta P = x$, for $x\%$ of performance loss that the user wants to let go to save energy. Then the model predicts the minimum frequency at which the core should run to satisfy the requested QoS.

4 Comparison of Machine Learning Algorithms

There are a variety of machine learning algorithms to choose from. We used the WEKA (Waikato Environment for Knowledge Analysis) [16] machine learning suite to study the efficacy of the different modeling alternatives. Table 2 shows the list of various machine learning algorithms with their respective correlation indexes when tested using 10 fold cross-validation and our test set data respectively. The experiment was performed on Intel i7-4770 (number of physical cores = 4, logical cores = 8) processor with a speed of 3.4 GHz. We found that the decision tree based `Random Forest (RF)` regression model best captures the relationship between the aggressiveness metrics, the core-frequency, and the performance degradation. In addition to that, the time taken for testing the model is short enough for an online application. `RF` [17] is ensemble of decision trees where each tree depends on the values of a random vector sampled independently and with the same distribution for all trees in the forest. The reason that the `RF` model performs well is that it alleviates the overfitting problem, which is common on other regression models.

Table 2. Algorithm comparison

Algorithms	Cross-validation (correlation index)	Test set (correlation index)	Testing time per data point (secs)	Training time (secs)
Linear regression	0.8273	0.8799	2.27 E−05	0.26
MLP regressor	0.9664	0.9815	3.97 E−05	0.17
SVM regressor	0.858	0.9054	2.84 E−05	2.34
REP tree	0.9764	0.9742	3.40 E−05	0.04
Random forest	0.9904	0.9815	3.96 E−05	0.28

5   Evaluation

5.1   Evaluation Setup

We use sniper multicore simulator [19] version 6.0 to validate the proposed model. To model the energy consumption, we use McPAT (Multicore Power, Area, and Timing) integrated power, area, and timing modeling framework [18].

Table 3. System configuration

Core		Caches	
Parameter	Value	Parameter	Value
ISA	X86	L1-D	32 KB, 8-way, WB, 4 cycles
Micro-architecture	Nehalem	L1-I	32 KB, 8-way, 4 cycles
N_C	4	L2(LLC)	2 MB, 16-way, WB, 30 cycles
F	$\{1000, +200, \dots, 2400\}$ MHz	Cache block size	64
V	$\{0.8, +0.1, \dots, 1.5\}$ v	Memory latency	45 ns
Technology	45 nm		

The architectural configuration of the simulated system is given in Table 3. We use 45 single-phase, single-threaded, 250 million instruction long SPEC2006 benchmark fragments. The SPEC2006 benchmark suite contains a mixture of compute and memory intensive workloads [21]. The fragments are collected using SimPoint [20].

Data Collection: We use 25 of these 45 benchmarks for the purpose of data collection, that is, set A as defined in Sect. 3.2 ($N_A = 25$). The 25 benchmarks used for the training are selected by their A_Score values covering the whole range of A_Score values. We construct the co-runner group C as explained in Sect. 3.2 with $N_{CG} = 10$.

Testing of the Model: We first performed 10-fold cross validation using the training set of 25 applications. We observed a high correlation index of 0.9904, providing a preliminary validation of the proposed model. We also performed online testing of the model. We use the remaining 20 applications for this purpose. We schedule each of the 20 applications on core 0. Let us call this application running on core 0 as the primary application. We randomly select 10 co-runner groups, each group containing 3 applications from this set of 20. These 3 co-runners are scheduled on cores 1–3, and the latter are made to run at the highest frequency setting, that is, 2400 MHz. We evaluate against four different *Quality of Service* (QoS) policies, that is, the maximum degradation in the performance of the primary application that the user is willing to accept. The four policies are: 5%, 10%, 15%, and 20%. Thus, there were a total of $20 \times 10 \times 4 = 800$ experiments. In each experiment, we use the constructed model to predict the lowest frequency at which core 0 must run such that the QoS policy is honored. Since the output of the model is a real number, we approximate the value to the nearest frequency setting. We then perform a reference run at different frequency settings and select the frequency setting which best satisfies the user QoS policy. We check that if the best frequency matches the predicted one or not. If not, we see by how many frequency steps it deviates. Based on the distribution of the inaccuracies, we calculate the average loss/gain in performance and energy. The results of the testing is presented next.

5.2   Analysis of the Results

Figure 4 shows the average energy saved through DVFS, and the associated average degradation in the performance of the primary application, for the four QoS policies. We see that up to 51% of energy can be saved when the user is willing to sacrifice 20% of the performance.

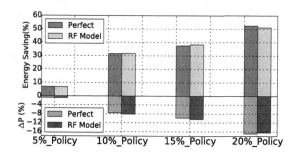

Fig. 4. Performance-energy trade-off for different QoS policies: perfect vs random forest model

We compare our proposed frequency predictor (RF model) against a perfect predictor (one that always predicts the optimal frequency). As can be seen, our predictor performs very close to the perfect predictor, with an accuracy of 1.3%, thereby validating our model – both the choice of the contention metric, as well as the machine learning algorithm. We see that, both with our predictor and the perfect one, in each of the four QoS policies, the observed average performance degradation is much lesser than that specified by the user. This is because of the coarse granularity of the DVFS regulator that allows us to scale the frequency only at steps of 200 MHz.

We further analyze the almost negligible inaccuracies of our model, and describe our findings in Fig. 5. In each of the four figures, the first row depicts the fraction of predictions that were correct (same as the perfect predictor), and the fraction of predictions that were incorrect by -200 MHz, $+200$ MHz, and $+400$ MHz. Note that there were no predictions that were incorrect by a greater

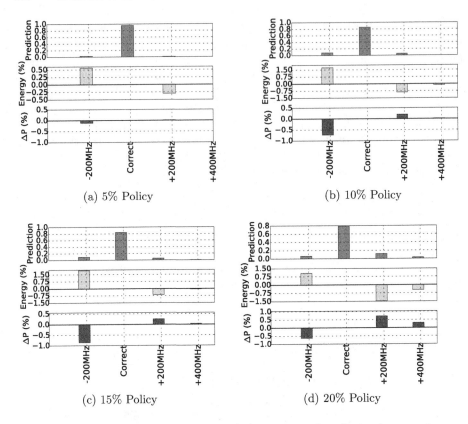

Fig. 5. Energy and performance loss/gain because of prediction inaccuracies

margin. The second row depicts the loss/gain in energy savings associated with the incorrect predictions, as compared to the perfect predictor. The third row depicts the associated loss/gain in performance.

We see that the percentage of correct predictions on average is 86%. Among the incorrect predictions, 94% are within one frequency step away from the optimal frequency. When the predicted frequency was higher than optimal, there is a loss in energy savings. Likewise, when the predicted frequency was lower, there is a gain. The net effect of these inaccuracies is negligible, as can be seen in Fig. 4. Additionally, when the predicted frequency is lower than optimal, the QoS policy is not honored. We see that this scenario occurred only in 6.7% of the test runs.

6   Conclusion

In this work, for chips with per-core DVFS capability, with the help of lightweight metrics, we showed that we can predict the application's performance response to shared resource contention and frequency scaling. We also demonstrated that, given application's and its co-runners' memory behavior just captured through a single parameter of Aggressiveness Score, we can accurately predict the optimal frequency for the given user QoS policy through machine learning. The results demonstrated that on an average, 86% of the predictions were accurate and out of the inaccurate predictions 94% were within a distance of one frequency step (200 MHz). In addition to that, only 6.7% of the total predictions violated the user QoS requirement. In the experiments, we observed that, by allowing 16% of performance degradation, we can save up to 51% core-energy saving. We believe that incorporating additional locality metrics to capture the behavior of the applications can further improve the accuracy of the model. In addition to that, the impact of the model from thermal perspective should also be studied.

References

1. Weiser, M., et al.: Scheduling for reduced CPU energy. USENIX (1994)
2. Zhu, D., Melhem, R., Childers, B.: Scheduling with dynamic voltage/speed adjustment using slack reclamation in multiprocessor real-time systems. IEEE TPDS **4**, 686–700 (2003)
3. Cong, J., Gururaj, K.: Energy efficient multiprocessor task scheduling under input-dependent variation. In: DATE 2009, Dresden, Germany (2010)
4. Yao, F., et al.: A scheduling model for reduced CPU energy. In: FOCS 1995 (1995)
5. Ishihara, T., Yasuura, H.: Voltage scheduling problem for dynamically variable voltage processors. In: ISLPED 1998 (1998)
6. Kim, S.I., Kim, H.T., Kang, G.S., Kim, J.-K.: Using DVFS and task scheduling algorithms for a hard real-time heterogeneous multicore processor environment. In: EEHPDC 2013 (2013)
7. Zhuravlev, S., Blagodurov, S., Fedorova, A.: Addressing shared resource contention in multicore processors via scheduling. In: ASPLOS 2010 (2010)
8. Abera, S., Balakrishnan, M., Kumar, A.: PLSS: a scheduler for multi-core embedded systems. In: Knoop, J., Karl, W., Schulz, M., Inoue, K., Pionteck, T. (eds.) ARCS 2017. LNCS, vol. 10172, pp. 164–176. Springer, Cham (2017). https://doi.org/10.1007/978-3-319-54999-6_13
9. Merkel, A., Stoess, J., Bellosa, F.: Resource-conscious scheduling for energy efficiency on multicore processors. In: EuroSys 2010 (2010)
10. Dhiman, G., Rosing, T.S.: Dynamic voltage frequency scaling for multi-tasking systems using online learning. In: ISLPED 2007 (2007)
11. Khan, U.A., Rinner, B.: Online learning of timeout policies for dynamic power management. ACM-TECS **13**(4), 1–25 (2014)
12. Otoom, M., et al.: Scalable and dynamic global power management for multicore chips. In: ACM 2015 (2015)
13. Ye, R., Xu, Q.: Learning-based power management for multicore processors via idle period manipulation. IEEE Trans. Comput.-Aided Des. Integr. Circuits Syst. **33**, 1043–1055 (2014)
14. Islam, F., Lin, M.: A framework for learning based DVFS technique selection and frequency scaling for multi-core real-time systems. In: HPCC 2015 (2015)
15. Shen, H., Qiu, Q.: Contention aware frequency scaling on CMPs with guaranteed quality of service. In: DATE 2014 (2014)
16. Hall, M., Frank, E., Holmes, G., Pfahringer, B., Reutemann, P., Witten, I.H.: The weka data mining software: an update. SIGKDD Explor. **11**, 10–18 (2009)

17. Breiman, L.: Random forest. Mach. Learn. **45**(1), 5–32 (2001)
18. Li, S., et al.: McPAT: an integrated power, area, and timing modeling framework for multicore and manycore architectures. In: MICRO 2009 (2009)
19. Sniper Multicore Simulator. http://snipersim.org
20. Calder, B., et al.: SimPoint: picking representative samples to guide simulation (Chap. 7). In: Performance Evaluation and Benchmarking (2005)
21. Jaleel, A.: Memory characterization of workloads using instrumentation-driven simulation. Technical report, VSSAD (2007)

Towards Fine-Grained DVFS
in Embedded Multi-core CPUs

Giuseppe Massari, Federico Terraneo(✉), Michele Zanella, and Davide Zoni

DEIB, Politecnico di Milano, Milan, Italy
{giuseppe.massari,federico.terraneo,michele.zanella,
davide.zoni}@polimi.it

Abstract. Dynamic Voltage and Frequency Scaling (DVFS) is the preferred actuator for power-performance policies, and its use is growing also for thermal management. DVFS implementations, especially for embedded platforms, have historically provided only few possible operating points, despite this may impair the optimality of the frequency selection for a given application. Moreover, with multiple policies making use of it, the rate at which frequency and voltage changes will occur in a given system is expected to increase. The work presented in this paper has a two-fold objective: first, to present a methodology to extend a DVFS driver with additional operating points and second, to measure the impact of DVFS transitions from the performance and energy consumption perspective. This contribution can thus help both operating system and run-time manager designers to implement more efficient policies, as well as device driver programmers and hardware designers to optimize the DVFS infrastructure. The proposed approach has been tested on a quad-core ARM Cortex-A9 CPU based development board.

1 Introduction

Despite the current well-know dark silicon issues [1], parallel processing architectures have found place also in power-constrained devices such as smart-phones and tablets, with System-on-chip featuring multi-core CPUs and GPUs. However, the end of Dennard scaling has introduced *energy efficiency* as the main issue in modern computing systems, in the mobile and HPC world alike.

Dedicated solutions have become widespread including heterogeneous architectures with specialized accelerators or single-ISA approaches such as the ARM big.LITTLE [2]. Regardless of the solution, one of the key mechanism to optimize energy efficiency is Dynamic Voltage and Frequency Scaling (DVFS) [3–5].

Looking at the DVFS implementations available in current embedded platforms, however, we can say that they still exhibit some limitations with respect to their desktop counterpart. More in detail, the overhead of DVFS transitions may have a higher weight [6]. Moreover, the software drivers provided by the vendors usually expose a limited number of nominal voltage-frequency operating points, despite the underlying hardware could operate on a wider set of points.

© Springer International Publishing AG, part of Springer Nature 2018
M. Berekovic et al. (Eds.): ARCS 2018, LNCS 10793, pp. 239–251, 2018.
https://doi.org/10.1007/978-3-319-77610-1_18

With multiple power-performance and thermal management frameworks [7,8] simultaneously triggering DVFS transitions, the availability of more operating points could increase power efficiency by selecting more accurate points [9,10] to save power without "over-performing".

To this aim, we propose a methodology to extend the DVFS support of existing embedded software platforms. This approach allows the operating system to access the entire set of operating points supported by the underlying hardware. This is a first step in our ongoing research to improve DVFS effectiveness for combined power/performance/thermal policies. The proposed methodology includes an interpolation step between the nominal operating points, thus it does not require input from the System-on-chip (SoC) manufacturer about the safe voltage margins of the new points, nor hardware modifications to the PLL or voltage regulator. The only requirement is the access to the source code of the kernel-level DVFS device driver and the data sheet of the SoC.

Another relevant issue is the efficiency of the DVFS, which becomes not negligible with policies that lead to operating point changes very frequently. By measuring this overhead, policy designers can be made aware of the costs of operating point changes, both in terms of latency and energy consumption. This allows to take into account the benefits-costs trade-off. In this regard, a second contribution of this paper is given by a method to characterize DVFS transition overhead and identify possible bottlenecks.

From the experimental point of view, the proposed approach has been tested on a NXP i.MX6 SABRE board, featuring an ARM Cortex A9 quad-core CPU – a common architecture among mobile and high-end embedded platforms –, but can be easily applied to any architecture for which documentation is available.

2   Related Works

DVFS implementations and policies making use of DVFS are subjects of significant research, with works spanning from electronic-level voltage regulators and PLL design, to dynamic power/performance and thermal policies, often implemented at software level.

From the electronic perspective, the problem of designing fast lock PLLs [11] that can reduce the DVFS switching overhead, as well as low power PLLs [12] to reduce the overall energy consumption has been well studied. For what concerns voltage regulators, attempts have been made to design on-chip voltage regulators [13] and assess their performance compared to traditional off-chip solutions. Another optimization considers the coupled control of the PLL and voltage regulator to reduce DVFS transition times [14].

The aforementioned works address the DVFS problem at hardware level, while targeting future System-on-chip designs. This is because the proposed solutions require the introduction of significant changes in the processor design. Regarding the DVFS overhead characterization, some models have been proposed [15] to get estimations from desktop, mobile and low-power processors. Some of them have been also integrated in hardware simulators, with the aim of taking it into account, when performing cycle accurate simulations of multi-core System-on-chips [16]. Compared to the state of the art, our approach derives overheads from measurements on real processors.

DVFS has been also compared to other solutions in terms of throughput/Watt. Srinivasan et al. [6] compared DVFS with dynamic reconfiguration in four different architectures. Begum et al. [17] illustrated the trade-off between CPU DVFS and memory DFS in energy-constrained devices such as smartphones.

Although DVFS exploitation is subject of plenty of works in the literature, this paper focuses on a methodology to extend the number of DVFS points of existing platforms, as well as to characterize their overhead from actual measurements, so as to enable a better exploitation at the software level. For instance, this should be advantageous for DVFS scheduling algorithms for computation and data intensive applications [18,19]. Moreover, recently introduced policies based, for example, on control theory [8,20,21] show that the policy overhead does not depend on the number of DVFS points, so having more DVFS points would be even more advantageous.

3 Fine-Grained DVFS

The proposed approach applies to the case where the hardware components that implement DVFS, the PLL and voltage regulator, can be programmed to obtain more DVFS points than the number supported by the vendor-supplied drivers.

3.1 DVFS Points Extension

The power consumption of CMOS digital logic, without considering the static contribution due to leakage, is governed by the well known expression $P = \alpha C V_{dd}^2 f$ where V_{dd} and f are the operating voltage and frequency, C the load capacitance, and α a coefficient summarizing the switching activity.

However, voltage and frequency cannot be set arbitrarily, as voltage influences the logic delays. In fact, given a certain target frequency, a minimum voltage is required to allows the device to operate without incurring in a critical path failure, leading to erroneous computations. A safety margin is usually added to account for process variability and the temperature dependence of gate delays. Figure 1 shows how DVFS points are located in the frequency-voltage plane. The filled area represents the critical path failure region, i.e. the area including voltage-frequency points for which we can experience system faults.

To extend the DVFS points set, the proposed approach assumes that the boundary of the critical path failure region, as well as the margins, are unknown, but can be identified through interpolation starting from the nominal DVFS points. It is important to remind that DVFS margins depend on temperature, running workload and process variability. The goal of our approach is not to fully explore this dependence, but rather to select new DVFS points with margins that are consistent with the ones selected by the manufacturer.

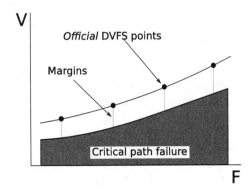

Fig. 1. Voltage and frequency plane showing the official DFVS points and their margin.

The approach starts from a study of the DVFS hardware support, in detail the PLL and voltage regulator. The data sheets provided by the vendor are used to understand the actual capabilities of the hardware. At high level, a PLL can be thought as a frequency multiplier that allows us to set the frequency of the processor to any multiple of a base frequency, within a given range. The number of frequency points that can be set are obtained from the data sheets, by dividing the range width by the base frequency. Similarly to the PLL, also the voltage regulator will have a minimum (voltage) step and a range.

We therefore obtain the entire DVFS space as the Cartesian product of voltage and frequency points. This space includes the optimal points, the points that cause a critical path failure and those characterized by a low energy efficiency. In order to find the optimal points, we start from observing the points provided by the vendor. Then we decide what kind of interpolation (linear, quadratic, ...) best fits them. The selected interpolation is then performed to obtain the extended set of points. For the validation of the set, we proceed as follows:

1. Computing the voltage margins of the official nominal DVFS points;
2. Verifying that the voltage margin of the new points is compatible with the nominal ones.

Each of the nominal points is indeed tested using suitable benchmarks and decreasing the voltage till a system failure is experienced. Typically such failures consist of software faults, e.g., unexpected program terminations, wrong results or operating system stuck due to kernel panics.

The difference between the nominal voltage and the highest voltage value causing a failure is the *voltage margin* of that DVFS point. The procedure is iterated for all the nominal points, and the iterated margins are again interpolated to compute the *expected* margins for the new DVFS points. For the validation procedure we used the same benchmarks, but applied to the new points, obtaining the *actual* margins. These are then compared against the expected ones computed earlier. For each new DVFS point, if the difference between the expected and actual margin is lower than a given threshold, in the order of a few units of the voltage regulator resolution, the voltage point is accepted. Otherwise, the highest of the two margins is taken.

3.2 Overhead Characterization

Power-performance and thermal policies relying on DVFS are often closed loop ones, meaning that they measure some quantity (system load or chip temperature), execute an algorithm to decide whether a change of operating point is needed, and in case, pick the best one according to a multi-objective function. Many different approaches exist, from PID control [22] to optimization techniques [23], and policies can be executed as either as periodic or event-based [21] tasks. Such policies often work better if the rate of DVFS point changes is increased, as they can better keep up with the variability introduced by the applications [9].

The rate of DVFS changes is thus a trade-off between the advantages of a fast rate control and the overhead of DVFS transitions. This overhead is limited by hardware factors, which are mainly the time the PLL takes to set a new frequency, and the time required by the voltage regulator to switch to a new voltage. Often these two actions are performed sequentially [14], to avoid transition through critical path failure regions.

The impact of switching to a new DVFS point can be evaluated from a *performance* and a *energy* perspective. In fact, a DVFS transition subtracts a certain amount of CPU time to useful computations, resulting in both performance and energy overhead. In most embedded DVFS implementations, voltage and frequency control are exposed to the operating system independently, and cannot be changed simultaneously. For example, in a scale-down transition the frequency must be changed before decreasing the voltage. The opposite happens in the scale-up transitions. In both cases for a certain amount of time in the middle of DVFS transitions, the voltage applied to the CPU is higher than the value expected by the operating point for the current frequency. This sequence is a further source of energy overhead.

The proposed solution for measuring time overheads makes use of on-board GPIO ports, or general purpose input/output on the SoC. The DVFS driver is instrumented in order to set the pin at the beginning of the code block to profile, and clear it at the end. An oscilloscope can be connected to the GPIO and used to measure the time. This technique allows to measure the full DVFS transition, as well as its individual parts such as the PLL lock and voltage regulator settling.

To measure the energy consumption the power supply line of the CPU cores should be cut, and the insertion of a shunt resistor is required. Using an oscilloscope, it is then possible to measure the CPU core voltage and the current drawn, from which it is possible to compute the DVFS energy consumption.

4   Experimental Results

The proposed approach has been applied to a NXP i.MX6Q SABRE development board, featuring an ARM Cortex A9 quad-core CPU, shown in Fig. 2.

Fig. 2. One of the boards used for the experimental evaluation, outlining the added connections. Voltage and current probe points (red circle), and GPIOs (yellow circle). (Color figure online)

The DVFS point extension was tested on two identical boards to account for process variability, while the overhead measurement has been performed on a single board, which has been instrumented by exposing two GPIOs for the time overhead profiling. For what concerns the energy overhead profiling, the on-board shunt resistor was used to measure the SoC current consumption. However, it is important to remark that no hardware modifications were needed for extending the number of DVFS points. The performed modifications were only necessary for the (optional) profiling phase.

4.1 DVFS Points Extension

The NXP SoC driver exposes only three nominal DVFS points for the ARM cores, as summarized in Table 1. Following the approach of Sect. 3, the data sheet was studied and it was found that the PLL has a 12 MHz resolution. Considering that the range from 396 to 996 MHz spans 600 MHz, it has been possible to extend the number of DVFS points from 3 to 51. The voltage regulator has instead a resolution of 25 mV. Looking at the official DVFS points, it can be easily seen that the points fit a line whose equation is:

$$V = 0.95 + 0.0005 * (f - 396). \tag{1}$$

For this reason, a linear interpolation was selected to generate the voltage values for the additional 48 DVFS points. The Linux DVFS driver has been extended by replacing the look-up table of DVFS points with a function that

Table 1. Nominal CPU DVFS points supported by the NXP SoC.

Frequency (MHz)	Voltage (V)
996	1.25
792	1.15
396	0.95

Table 2. Voltage margins for the official DVFS points and the benchmark applications

Frequency (MHz)	*cpuburn* margin (V)	*yes* margin (V)	*FFT* margin (V)
996	0.125	0.175	0.175
792	0.125	0.175	0.175
396	0.150	0.150	0.150

uses Eq. (1) to algorithmically compute the voltage starting from the frequency. Although we considered the possibility to extend the interpolation to values higher than the nominal range for overclocking, one of the boards that we tested had recurrent kernel panics above 1 GHz, while the other worked flawlessly up to 1.14 GHz. Due to the significant variability between boards, we do not recommend overclocking the i.MX6Q SoC.

The next step has been the evaluation of the voltage margins of the nominal DVFS points, to determine which was the voltage at which a fault may occur. This is done in order to evaluate the reliability of the new DVFS points.

Three applications were tested to identify critical path failures: the port of cpuburn for ARM, a simple ''yes>/dev/null'' on all the CPU cores and a multi-threaded application computing Fast-Fourier Transformations, properly instrumented to perform a consistency check of its data structures.

Table 2 reports the voltage margins computed as the nominal voltage minus the highest voltage at which a failure occurs. For cpuburn and yes, that do not produce an output, the observed failures were either a kernel panic or a board lock-up, requiring a power-cycle to be operational again. For whatever concerns the instrumented application, no consistency check failure has been observed, and in all cases the failure was again a kernel panic or board lock-up, hence the OS kernel was found to be more susceptible to failures than the applications.

The collected data shows that, given a certain application, the voltage margin is nearly constant. The only variation is by no more than one DVFS voltage step, which in this architecture is 25 mV. cpuburn stresses the CPU generating a higher load with respect to yes and the instrumented FFT application, causing failures also at voltage values at which the other two work. This is to be expected, as the critical path failure also depends on temperature, and an application that causes a higher current consumption causes a temperature increase in the SoC. Summarizing, the voltage margins were found to be constant for each application.

The validation procedure of the new DVFS points has been performed as follows: assuming that the fixed margins hypothesis is correct, and considering that a decrease in voltage for a given frequency of 125 ± 25 mV could cause a failure, a decrease in voltage by 75 mV should not cause any failure. This should hold true also for the intermediate DVFS points, not just the official ones. Now assuming that also the linear relation of frequency to voltage is correct, it would be possible to decrease the voltage computed through the linear interpolation by 75 mV, and the resulting (voltage, frequency) point should still not fail.

The performed test therefore consists of assigning a voltage value 75 mV lower than Eq. (1), testing all the 51 DVFS points with the execution of cpuburn and checking that no failure occurs. This test was performed, and as expected, no failures have been reported, confirming that each of the 48 new DVFS points has the same margin as the ones provided by the manufacturer.

A second test has been performed to assess the optimality of the obtained points, by decreased the voltage an additional 50 mV, for a total of 125 mV. As in this test the expected result is a failure, such as a kernel panic, it difficult to automate. For this reason, not all DVFS points were tested, but for all the DVFS points that have the same voltage (due to the voltage regulator granularity), only the one with the highest frequency was tested. The result is that for all the tested operating points, but two, we reported a failure. These two points are those with a frequency of 492 and 444 MHz, respectively. A further test with the voltage reduced by an additional 25 mV caused a kernel panic also in these two cases. This test shows that of the 48 new DVFS points, 46 have at most 125 mV of margin, and two have 150 mV, operating at ambient temperature. Finally, the test was repeated with the other two applications and the other board, with similar results.

4.2   Overhead Characterization

In this section we performed a set of measurements, aiming at characterizing the overhead of the DVFS activity in terms of both time and energy. All measurements were performed by toggling GPIO pins at the beginning and the end of the code fragment to profile, and using an oscilloscope to measure the time interval. We have also taken into account the overhead introduced by the experimental setup. Specifically, we estimated the number of CPU cycles lost due to the added GPIO toggling. It turned out that depending on the current operating point (396, 792, 900 MHz) this number is about 280, 475 and 600 respectively. Such values correspond to 0.6–0.7 µs, which means that this contribution can be considered negligible.

Time Overhead. Concerning the effective overhead in terms of time, we identified three main steps through which a change of operating point goes through. Therefore, we separated the overhead characterization into three contributions:

1. The context-switch time occurring in case the tool sending the DVFS request is located in user-space;
2. The time required to set the new frequency by properly configuring the PLL;
3. The time required to set the voltage, which in this architecture is dominated by the time required for writing to the off-chip voltage regulator through the I^2C bus.

This breakdown has been summarized in Table 3. The user/kernel-space context switch takes an almost constant value of 9 µs, marginally affected by the

Table 3. Time overhead breakdown for each of the nominal values of frequency supported by the CPU. Time values in (μs).

	396 MHz	792 MHz	900 MHz
U/K context-switch	9	9	9
Frequency setting (PLL)	see Table 4		
Voltage setting (I²C)	625	610	607

Table 4. Transition times matrix: the amount of time required to switch from one operating frequency (row) to another (column). The values reported are in μs.

Frequencies (MHz) From/To	396	504	600	792	900	996
396	45	30/125*				
504	8	27	121	122	121	122
600	7	125	27	123	122	122
792	7	124	123	27	123	123
900	7	123	122	123	27	121
996	7	122	122	123	122	27

* Switching time depending on previous frequency

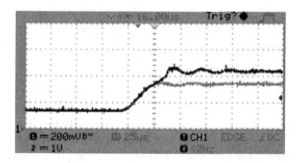

Fig. 3. Voltage regulator performance. Darker line shows the transition from 0.95 V to 1.25 V, while the lighter line shows the 0.95 V to 1.1 V transitions.

current operating point. The PLL lock time is instead operating point dependent. We detailed this point in Table 4. Finally, the voltage setting performance is limited by the I²C bus bandwidth, and is the dominating contribution. The penalty introduced by the I²C bus becomes more evident as we compare the values in Table 3 with the oscilloscope output in Fig. 3. What we observed is that the voltage regulator performs the two transitions (from 0.95 V to 1.25 through which a change of V and from 0.95 V to 1.1 V) in about 40 μs and 25 μs, respectively. This means that the I²C overhead is actually more than 10 times the voltage change time.

In Table 4 we can now give a detailed look at the time required to switch between operating frequencies. What we can see in the table is a regular pattern, with the exception given by the frequency changes involving the lowermost value, i.e. the 396 MHz frequency. The reason behind this has been discovered by reading the data sheet coming with the development board. We have seen indeed that the 396 MHz value comes from a secondary clock source which is not managed through the PLL. Excluding this case, an actual change of frequency requires 122 μs on average, while resetting the same frequency value takes 27 μs.

For the 396 MHz special case, scaling down the frequency is very fast (7–8 μs), since no PLL is involved, as already said. The scaling indeed is actually performed by simply multiplexing two different clock sources. When scaling up, we measured two different timings, depending on the frequency previously set. In one case, scaling up from 396 MHz took around 125 μs on average, which is in line with all the other cases. This happens when we made a transition of type $X \rightarrow 396 \rightarrow Y$. In another case, we experienced a switching time of only 30 μs, that is the case of a transition of type $X \rightarrow 396 \rightarrow X$. In such a case the PLL is already set for the frequency X, and the transition time is thus faster.

Summing up the two contributions at OS level, a DVFS transition requires $125 + 625 = 750$ μs in the worst case scenario. During this time the CPU does not perform any useful work, therefore this time represents a performance penalty.

Energy Overhead. In order to estimate the energy consumption occurring in DVFS transitions, we must keep in mind what happens at the operating system level. As we have seen, the driver in fact sets the PLL for the frequency change and then the off-chip voltage regulator via I^2C. In the former step, the OS must first switch the CPU clock to a frequency not controlled by the PLL, then set the new frequency and wait for the PLL to lock. Although the driver is implemented using busy waiting, thus consuming energy, the CPU is clocked at a very low frequency (24 MHz), so the energy consumption is negligible. Also the I^2C driver is implemented using busy waiting, but in this case the CPU is running at the full clock frequency. This fact, combined with the long time needed for the I^2C communication causes this energy contribution to be the highest one. Probably, a driver implementation exploiting DMA could have been a more efficient solution, since in such a case we could still use the CPU for useful processing while carrying out data transmission for the voltage regulator setting.

At this point, in order to proceed with the energy consumption estimation, we got the CPU current drawn by measuring the voltage on top of the shunt resistor connected to the CPU and dividing the value by the resistance value (0.02 Ω). We repeated the measurement with the CPU running a workload simulating the busy waiting worst case, setting first the frequency to 24 MHz, and then varying it over a range of points from 396 to 996 MHz, as summarized in Table 5.

Now, for the CPU power consumption estimation we must consider that the CPU operating voltage is comprised in the range [0.95–1.25] V. To simplify our analysis we approximated it to the mean value of 1.1 V. Given that, we can first estimate the power and energy consumption of the frequency (PLL) setting

Table 5. Current drawn by the CPU while spinning on a busy waiting.

Frequency (MHz)	24	396	504	600	792	900	996
Current (mA)	20	145	200	245	355	405	450

stage. As during this stage, the CPU operates at 24 MHz which means that the current drawn is approximately equal to 20 mA. By multiplying the current for the voltage value we obtained a power consumption value of 22 mW. Considering that this stage can last at most from $7\,\mu s$ to $125\,\mu s$, it turned out that the energy consumption of the frequency setting ranges from $0.15\,\mu J$ to $2.75\,\mu J$.

On the voltage setting side, we can say that the busy waiting of the CPU operating at a frequency value between 396 and 996 MHz leads to a current drawn in the range [145–450] mA, hence a power consumption contribution of 145*1.1 = 160 mW and 450*1.1 = 495 mW, respectively. We have shown how this voltage regulation stage dominates the DVFS time overhead, taking from $607\,\mu s$ to $625\,\mu s$, according to the power values computed above, this means an energy consumption contribution of about $100\,\mu J$ and $300\,\mu J$.

Summing up the average values of energy consumption found for the frequency setting and the voltage regulation, we can say that the overall energy required to perform a DVFS transition is $201.5\,\mu J$ on average.

5   Conclusions

To summarize, in this paper we provided an experimental methodology to extend the DVFS operating points supported by an embedded CPU beyond the nominal ones, and validating the new points. Moreover, our approach allows to measure the overheads occurring in DVFS transitions, both in terms of performance and energy consumption. The approach has been tested on a real embedded development platform, using CPU stressing workloads.

Overall, the outcome of this work aims at being a support for hardware designer and OS level developers, in order to optimize DVFS mechanisms and run-time management policies, taking into account both its advantages and costs.

Acknowledgments. This work was supported in part by the European Union funded project under the grant M2DC H2020-688201 (http://www.m2dc.eu/en/) and MANGO H2020-671668 (http://www.mango-project.eu/).

References

1. Taylor, M.: A landscape of the new dark silicon design regime. In: IEEE Micro, pp. 8–19, September 2013
2. Nikov, K., Nunez-Yanez, J.L., Horsnell, M.: Evaluation of hybrid run-time power models for the ARM Big.LITTLE architecture. In: IEEE International Conference on Embedded and Ubiquitous Computing (EUC), October 2015

3. Garcia, R.C., Chung, J.M., Jo, S.W., Ha, T., Kyong, T.: Response time performance estimation in smartphones applying dynamic voltage & frequency scaling and completely fair scheduler. In: IEEE International Symposium on Consumer Electronics (ISCE), pp. 1–2, June 2014

4. Kwak, J., Choi, O., Chong, S., Mohapatra, P.: Dynamic speed scaling for energy minimization in delay-tolerant smartphone applications. In: IEEE Conference on Computer Communications (INFOCOM), pp. 2292–2300, April 2014

5. Park, J.G., Hsieh, C.Y., Dutt, N., Lim, S.S.: Quality-aware mobile graphics workload characterization for energy-efficient DVFS design. In: IEEE Symposium on Embedded Systems for Real-time Multimedia (ESTIMedia), October 2014

6. Srinivasan, S., Kurella, N., Koren, I., Kundu, S.: Dynamic reconfiguration vs. DVFS: a comparative study on power efficiency of processors. In: International Conference on VLSI Design and International Conference on Embedded Systems (VLSID), pp. 563–564, January 2016

7. Egilmez, B., Memik, G., Ogrenci-Memik, S., Ergin, O.: User-specific skin temperature-aware DVFS for smartphones. In: Design, Automation Test in Europe Conference Exhibition (DATE), pp. 1217–1220, March 2015

8. Leva, A., Terraneo, F., Giacomello, I., Fornaciari, W.: Event-based power/performance-aware thermal management for high-density microprocessors. IEEE Trans. Control Syst. Technol. **26**, 535–550 (2017)

9. Eyerman, S., Eeckhout, L.: Fine-grained DVFS Using on-chip regulators. ACM Trans. Archit. Code Optim. **8**, 1:1–1:24 (2011)

10. Juan, D.C., Garg, S., Park, J., Marculescu, D.: Learning the optimal operating point for many-core systems with extended range voltage/frequency scaling. In: International Conference on Hardware/Software Codesign and System Synthesis (CODES + ISSS), pp. 1–10. IEEE (2013)

11. Pan, J., Yoshihara, T.: A fast lock phase-locked loop using a continuous-time phase frequency detector. In: IEEE Conference on Electron Devices and Solid-State Circuits, pp. 393–396, December 2007

12. Abadian, A., Lotfizad, M., Majd, N.E., Ghoushchi, M.B.G., Mirzaie, H.: A new low-power and low-complexity all digital PLL (ADPLL) in 180 nm and 32 nm. In: IEEE International Conference on Electronics, Circuits and Systems (2010)

13. Kim, W., Gupta, M.S., Wei, G.Y., Brooks, D.: System level analysis of fast, per-core DVFS using on-chip switching regulators. In: IEEE International Symposium on High Performance Computer Architecture, pp. 123–134, February 2008

14. Altieri, M., Lombardi, W., Puschini, D., Lesecq, S.: Coupled voltage and frequency control for DVFS management. In: International Workshop on Power and Timing Modeling, Optimization and Simulation (PATMOS), September 2013

15. Park, S., Park, J., Shin, D., Wang, Y., Xie, Q.: Accurate modeling of the delay and energy overhead of dynamic voltage and frequency scaling in modern microprocessors. IEEE Trans. Comput.-Aided Des. Integr. Circ. Syst. **32**, 695–708 (2013)

16. Terraneo, F., Zoni, D., Fornaciari, W.: A cycle accurate simulation framework for asynchronous NoC design. In: International Symposium on System-on-Chip, SoC 2013 (2013)

17. Begum, R., Werner, D., Hempstead, M., Prasad, G., Challen, G.: Energy-performance trade-offs on energy-constrained devices with multi-component DVFS. In: IEEE International Symposium on Workload Characterization (IISWC) (2015)

18. Tan, L., Chen, Z., Zong, Z., Li, D., Ge, R.: A2E: Adaptively aggressive energy efficient DVFS scheduling for data intensive applications. In: IEEE International Performance Computing and Communications Conference (IPCCC) (2013)

19. Ge, R., Feng, X., Feng, W.C., Cameron, K.W.: CPU MISER: a performance-directed, run-time system for power-aware clusters. In: International Conference on Parallel Processing (ICPP), p. 18, September 2007
20. https://www.kernel.org/doc/html/v4.13/admin-guide/pm/intel_pstate.html
21. Leva, A., Terraneo, F., Fornaciari, W.: Event-based control as an enabler for high power density processors. In: International Conference on Event-based Control, Communication, and Signal Processing (EBCCSP), June 2016
22. Rodopoulos, D., Catthoor, F., Soudris, D.: Tackling performance variability due to RAS mechanisms with PID-controlled DVFS. IEEE Comput. Architect. Lett. **14**, 156–159 (2015)
23. Liu, Y., Yang, H., Dick, R.P., Wang, H., Shang, L.: Thermal vs energy optimization for DVFS-enabled processors in embedded systems. In: International Symposium on Quality Electronic Design (ISQED), pp. 204–209 (2007)

Partial Reconfiguration

Evaluating Auto-adaptation Methods
for Fine-Grained Adaptable Processors

Joost Hoozemans[✉], Jeroen van Straten, Zaid Al-Ars, and Stephan Wong

Delft University of Technology, Mekelweg 4, 2628 CD Delft, The Netherlands
{j.j.hoozemans,j.vanstraten-1,z.al-ars,j.s.s.m.wong}@tudelft.nl

Abstract. To achieve energy savings while maintaining adequate performance, system designers and programmers wish to create the best possible match between program behavior and the underlying hardware. Well-known current approaches include DVFS and task migrations in heterogeneous platforms such as big.LITTLE processors. Additionally, processors have been proposed in literature that are able to adapt (parts of) their organization to the workload. These reconfigurations can be managed using hardware monitors, profiling and other compile-time information or a combination of both. Many current solutions are suitable for heterogeneous systems, as migration penalties pose a practical limit to the maximum adaptation frequency, but not for dynamic processors that can adapt much more fine-grained.

In this paper, we present two novel concepts to aid these low-penalty reconfigurable processors - one requiring an ISA extension and one without. Our experimental results show that our approaches enable a dynamic processor to reduce the energy-delay product by up to 25% and on average 10% to 18% compared to the best performing static setups.

1 Introduction

With energy utilization as a new critical metric for computing systems, designers have devised numerous ways of configuring systems to run in various performance/power modes. The most notable examples are Dynamic Voltage and Frequency Scaling (DVFS), Heterogeneous Multicore Processors (HMPs) such as big.LITTLE, and polymorphic processors such as MorphCore [1]. In turn, researchers try to match program behavior to processor configurations in order to minimize both the energy utilization and the performance penalty associated with low-power configurations.

The time it takes to move an ARM big.LITTLE core in or out of sleep modes lies in the order of *milliseconds* and changing DVFS involves a latency of tens of microseconds. Furthermore, migrating a task to another core will introduce an additional penalty because of cold resources (cache, predictors) [2]. Because of these properties, a granularity of context-switch level (10 ms) is adequate, as adapting to the workload any faster will only result in prohibitively large penalties.

© Springer International Publishing AG, part of Springer Nature 2018
M. Berekovic et al. (Eds.): ARCS 2018, LNCS 10793, pp. 255–268, 2018.
https://doi.org/10.1007/978-3-319-77610-1_19

In contrast to this, program characteristics can change at much higher frequencies [3]. Therefore, designs have been proposed that greatly reduce these penalties for heterogeneous systems [2,4], and adaptable processors have been proposed that have very low adaptation penalties [1,5]. These processing platforms have the potential of matching the program in a far more fine-grained way (in the time domain). However, currently used monitoring-based approaches are often based on measurement windows that are far too large to drive these high-frequency adaptations.

This work aims to determine what evaluation frequency is needed to profit from fine-grained adaptable processors. As sampling performance counters at this rate will create excessive overhead, we argue that an automatic evaluation circuit is required, moving the evaluation and adaptation control loop into hardware. Next to sampling performance counters, we propose two additional auto-adaptation approaches. In one approach, we modified the compiler to insert instructions in locations that are likely to correspond with a phase boundary. When encountering this instruction, the processor starts a measurement and stores the results in a dedicated field in the same instruction word. The second approach involves a branch target buffer. At every branch, a measurement is started and results are stored in the buffer. When branching to the same target address again, the code characteristics have already been measured and can be retrieved. These two approaches aim to make adaptations more proactive.

We have applied the approaches to the ρ-VEX dynamic VLIW (very long instruction word) processor that is able to change configurations with a penalty of only 5 cycles (a pipeline flush). Results show that the ρ-VEX processor benefits from monitoring windows of approximately 75 cycles. Using the auto-adaptation approaches, the energy consumption of the adaptable processor can be reduced by 10% to 18% on average compared to the best static setup. The branch-based proactive approach slightly outperforms window-based solutions.

2   Approach

2.1   Target Processor

In this work, we target the ρ-VEX processor, an open-source reconfigurable VLIW processor [6]. It can assign datapaths in pairs to one or multiple threads or disable them to conserve energy (see Fig. 1). It has a reconfiguration penalty of 5 cycles, because it needs to flush the pipeline. The processor can switch between a 2, 4, or 8-issue configuration without changing the binary it is executing, because it utilizes generic binaries [7]. In short, generic binaries work by ensuring that each VLIW bundle of 8 operations can also be executed in 2 or 4-issue mode, by removing intra-bundle dependencies (see Fig. 2 for a simplified depiction of this).

VLIW architectures are widely adopted in embedded media and DSP applications, providing high energy efficiency (for example, in modem, audio and image processing subsystems in mobile phone SoCs) [8]. Code for VLIWs is statically scheduled by the compiler, decreasing hardware complexity. Instruction-level

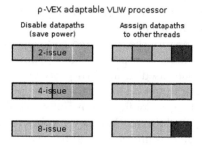

Fig. 1. Conceptual depiction of the fine-grained reconfigurable VLIW processor targeted in this work. It consists of 8 datapaths that can be split or merged in pairs (i.e., each sub-block represents a 2-issue VLIW processor). These can be assigned to a thread or powered down to conserve power (left-hand side). Multiple blocks can be assigned to a single thread to exploit as much ILP as possible, or each block can be assigned to its own thread to exploit thread-level parallelism (right-hand side - the colors represent different threads).

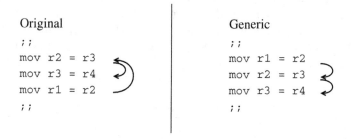

Fig. 2. The ρ-VEX is able to switch configurations at any time, because the toolchain makes sure the code can be executed in every possible configuration. It does this by 're-sequentializing' the code after it has been compiled for 8-issue. Each bundle is reordered such that the dependencies (shown as arrows) are met when executing the operations one by one.

parallelism (ILP) is explicitly encoded in the binary. This makes it possible to measure performance of different core configurations, as we will see in Sect. 3. This makes the chosen VLIW platform very suitable to evaluate the proposed techniques.

2.2   Proposed Auto-adapting Method

The main idea behind our approach is that program characteristics change during the course of execution, but characteristics of code itself is fixed. In other words, the changes are due to the control flow through the different code sections in the binary. We propose to measure these characteristics once for every code section, and store this information in such a way that we can easily retrieve it whenever we revisit that section. For each section, a measurement only needs to be performed once for each core type (for HMPs) or configuration (for adaptable processors), after which the results for both are stored in their own field.[1] We are proposing two ways to store the measured code characteristics.

The first approach utilizes a structure that is similar to the branch target buffer (BTB) that is widely used in modern processors. Normally, the BTB is used to predict the branch target address early in the pipeline to reduce branch penalties. Our 'Branch Target Configuration Buffer' (BTCB) is a cache that is indexed by branch target addresses. Whenever a branch occurs, the BTCB is accessed to determine if there is information about the code that is being jumped to. If there is not, a measurement is triggered. When the next branch occurs, the measurement results are stored in the buffer. If there is information in the buffer, it can be used during the branch to reconfigure the processor to the most energy efficient configuration.

Our second approach introduces a special instruction we named `pchg` (phase change) that is added to the program by the compiler at certain locations that are likely to correspond with a longer, more stable phase (compared to the first approach, that operates on a basic block level). When encountering this instruction, a lookup is performed in a configuration buffer similar to the BTCB. This lookup can use the least significant bits of the PC (program counter) as index, or the compiler can assign indexes to code sections and place their index in the instruction.

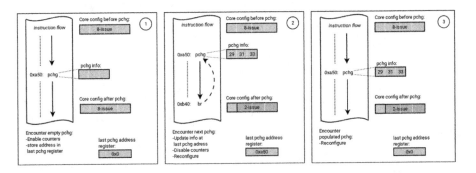

Fig. 3. Overview of the pchg approach when encountering a loop, using the PC address as configuration buffer index.

During runtime, when the processor encounters this instruction for the first time, it keeps track of the index and starts the performance counters to evaluate the program characteristics in that phase. When the measurement has completed (when encountering the next `pchg` instruction), the results of the measurement

---

[1] On HMPs, measuring performance on one core type does not provide information about the performance on the other core type (see [9, Sect. 6.3]). To monitor which core type is the most efficient, the program needs to be migrated back and forth continuously. The same holds for different configurations of an adaptable processor.

are written back into the configuration buffer. Each time the processor encounters the instruction again, the information is available and the processor can use it to perform a reconfiguration immediately. An overview of the pchg approach is depicted in Fig. 3. Both approaches have their merits. The first approach is the most fine-grained but may trigger adaptations too often. The second approach requires recompilation of binaries (note that, if this is not possible, old binaries will still execute correctly but not trigger any adaptations) and results in runtime overhead because of the added instructions.

3   Implementation

This section discusses the implementation of the different approaches in the target platform. We start with the elements that the different approaches have in common, then we discuss the window-based monitoring approach, followed by the BTCB approach, and concluding with the phase change annotations.

3.1   Common

The target processor has a controller that handles reconfiguration requests. These requests can be performed via a memory-mapped control register writable by software (user or OS). Although the platform reduces adaptation overhead to only 5 cycles, sampling and evaluating performance counters in software introduces additional overhead. At the frequencies we are proposing in this paper, this overhead becomes very significant. Therefore, we propose to use a hardware circuit to perform the evaluation and reconfiguration request directly. This section discusses this circuit.

We use a performance counter for each possible ρ-VEX core configuration. Using a scheme similar to [10], we increment these counters based on the location of a VLIW bundle marker. If a bundle is completely filled with 8 operations, the counter for the 2-issue configuration will increase by 4 and the counter for the 4-issue configuration will increase by 2 (see Fig. 4). This scheme is enough to measure the performance of the configurations. However, we propose to estimate energy utilization.

We have used the following energy estimation function:

$E = E_{static} + E_{dynamic}$ where
$E_{dynamic} = (SYL * E_{syl}) + (NOP * E_{nop})$ and
$E_{static} = (CYC_2 * E_{cyc2}) + (CYC_4 * E_{cyc4}) + (CYS_8 * E_{cyc8}).$

Here, SYL is the number of execution syllables (individual operations of a VLIW bundle), NOP is the number of unfilled syllable slots, and CYC represents the number of executed cycles in 2-issue, 4-issue and 8-issue mode. The energy values depend on the hardware characteristics and should be set by the designer based on power estimations or measurements. For our evaluation we have used the values listed in Table 1. The dynamic part of the function is largely the same between configurations, so we can use a single cost value for each configuration.

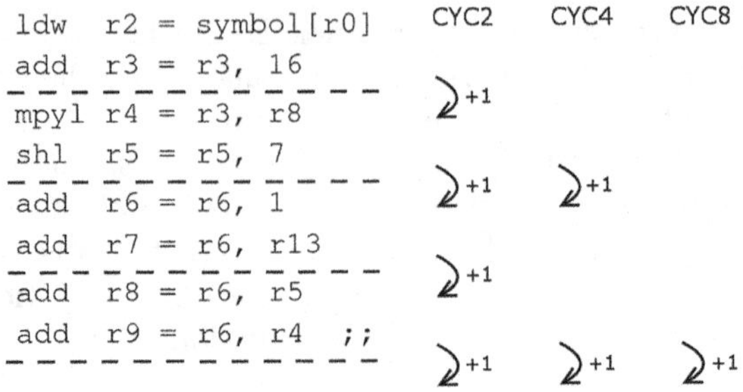

```
ldw   r2 = symbol[r0]    CYC2    CYC4    CYC8
add   r3 = r3, 16
- - - - - - - - - - - -
mpyl  r4 = r3, r8
shl   r5 = r5, 7
- - - - - - - - - - - -
add   r6 = r6, 1
add   r7 = r6, r13
- - - - - - - - - - - -
add   r8 = r6, r5
add   r9 = r6, r4  ;;
- - - - - - - - - - - -
```

Fig. 4. Measuring the performance for different configurations is done by decoding the location of the stop bit (VLIW bundle boundaries shown as ';;'). This bundle requires 4 cycles to execute on the 2-issue configuration and 2 cycles on the 4-issue. The 8-issue counter is equivalent to the bundle counter.

Table 1. Used values for the energy estimation function in the simulator

E_{syl}	E_{nop}	E_{cyc2}	E_{cyc4}	E_{cyc8}
4	1	2	3	4

Instead of multiplying the counter values with the energy estimation values (which would be expensive in hardware), we propose to use prescaler counters. The prescaler is increased using the configuration cycle count of the bundle (as depicted in Fig. 4). When a configuration's prescaler exceeds its cost value, its energy estimation counter is increased by 1 and the prescaler is reset. The prescaler only needs enough precision to express the ratios between the cost values. The final energy estimation counters also needs limited precision, because (1) we are measuring relatively short sections of code and (2) if two estimations are very close to each other, both choices are equally suitable. In our current implementation, we are using 7 bits per configuration for the energy estimation counters. When any one of the counters overflows, all of them are right shifted by 1 position (the ratios between them stay intact). The required storage for the configuration buffer entries is 7×3 bits (one for each possible ρ-VEX configuration).

3.2   Window-Based Monitoring

Window-based monitoring is not a novel approach proposed in this paper but rather the current art to which we will compare. Using the hardware circuit from the previous section, our window-based implementation evaluates the energy estimation using a fixed period. The configuration with the lowest value is forwarded to the reconfiguration request register, and the counters are reset.

3.3   BTCB

For this approach we propose to add a buffer, the Branch Target Configuration Buffer (BTCB) that stores code information about branch targets. In case the processor already features a BTB, such as the Philips TriMedia VLIW [11], this structure can be widened to include the desired information.[2] When the processor executes a branch (conditional branches are only considered when taken), it will perform a lookup in the buffer to see if there is an entry with valid code information. If that is the case, it will perform a core adaptation.

If no such entry is found, the processor will start the performance counters. A register keeps track of the index of the entry. When a new branch is taken, this register is used to update the BTCB using the measured values. This can be done one cycle later than the new branch's BTCB lookup, to avoid requiring an additional access port. In our implementation, the BTCB is direct-mapped. Therefore, any collision (two branch addresses that map to the same BTCB entry) results in an eviction.

3.4   Phase Change Annotations

In this approach, the compiler identifies locations that are likely to correspond to a phase. In these locations, it adds an instruction, named pchg (phase change). The processor performs a lookup in the configuration buffer when encountering this instruction, instead of at every branch. We have modified the ρ-VEX compiler to add a pchg instruction at the top of every loop and every leaf function. The compiler can choose to skip loops and functions that it estimates to have a total execution time lower than a certain threshold.

4   Evaluation

4.1   Experimental Setup

To evaluate our approach, we have used the open source ρ-VEX polymorphic processor as discussed in Sect. 2.1. We have implemented our pchg approach in the compiler as discussed in Sect. 3 and modeled the monitoring hardware in the simulator. To measure only the behavior of the processor core, caches were disabled. Using this setup, the simulator is cycle-accurate regarding a ρ-VEX core attached to single-cycle instruction and data memories, as the code is completely statically scheduled. We will use MiBench [12] and SPECINT 2006 for our measurements. Not all programs could be used, as some are not supported by the ρ-VEX toolchain or libraries. We will use the modes listed in Table 2.

Here, the static setups represent the supported ρ-VEX configuration modes, without any runtime adaptations. The windowed modes utilize performance

---

[2] Note that in that case, it is no longer indexed by the branch *target* but rather the PC of the branch itself; the buffer will return the predicted branch target and we propose to add the code information for that branch target to the entry.

Table 2. Evaluated modes of execution.

Type	Modes
Static core	2-issue, 4-issue, 8-issue
Dynamic core, windowed	10,000, 1,000, 500, 250, 100, 75, 50
Dynamic core, pchg	pchg-0, pchg-100
Dynamic core, BTCB	BTCB-inf, BTCB-2048

monitoring with fixed windows of various sizes to perform core adaptations. The pchg modes utilize the proposed phase change annotations, with loop annotation thresholds of 0 and 100 cycles. BTCB uses the proposed branch target configuration buffer. We have evaluated a buffer with infinite entries and one with 2048 entries.

We will use the Energy-Delay Product (EDP) as metric and normalize to a static 8-issue configuration which represents the highest performing setup. Note that, due to the chosen values for the energy estimation function (see Table 1), the outcome for all measurements cannot be lower than 0.5, because no setup can execute faster than the 8-issue and the 2-issue energy estimation is $0.5\times$ that of the 8-issue.

4.2 Results

Overhead. Adding the pchg instructions into the programs results in runtime overhead. We have measured this overhead by running all 3 version of the binaries (not annotated, threshold 0, threshold 100 cycles) on a static 2-issue core. The results are plotted in Fig. 5. On average, the runtime overhead is quite acceptable at approximately 0.5% on average.

Window sizes. We evaluate windowed monitoring setups using various window sizes between 50 and 10,000 cycles. The results are plotted in Fig. 6. For both benchmark suites, the disadvantage (overhead) surpasses the advantage of higher frequency adaptations at approximately 75 cycles. Our measurements reveal that using a window size of 75 compared to 1000 cycles improves EDP up to 20% (for specrand and rijndael) and on average 6%, supporting our claim that code can change very frequently and a fine-grained reconfigurable processor is able to match these changes more closely.

Runlength thresholds. The energy estimation counters can use a minimum runlength threshold for a measured code section. If this threshold is not reached when the measurement is finished (because of a new pchg instruction, or because of a branch), the core will not perform an adaptation. We have evaluated different threshold values and the results are depicted in Fig. 7. In case the BTCB is limited in size to 2048 entries, there is a clear optimal threshold for MiBench of

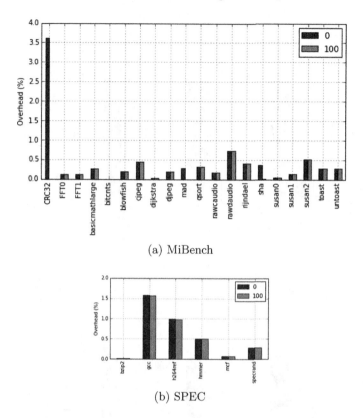

(a) MiBench

(b) SPEC

Fig. 5. Overhead of adding the phase change instructions.

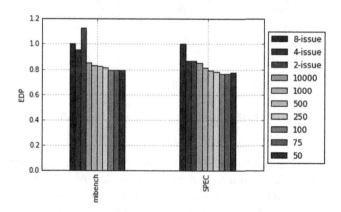

Fig. 6. EDP for different window sizes. For both benchmark suites, 75 instructions performs best.

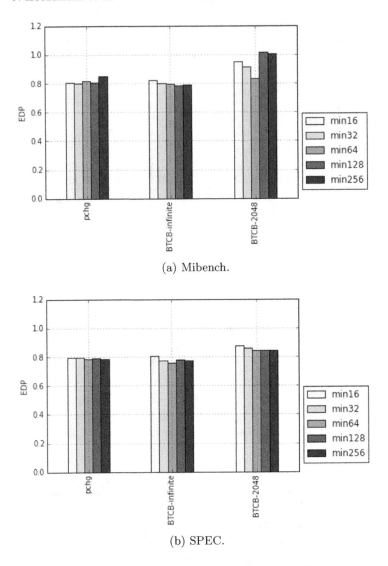

(a) Mibench.

(b) SPEC.

Fig. 7. EDP for different runlength thresholds.

64 instruction bundles and the relative loss in performance (compared to the best performing setup with an infinite buffer) is in this case 6%. The other setups, as well as the SPEC benchmarks, are not as strongly influenced by the threshold. The loss can be attributed mostly to two outliers in the form of basicmath in MiBench and specrand in SPEC, that may suffer from a high number of collisions.

Comparing the approaches. Using the best results for each approach as reported in previous sections, we have plotted the averages of the different techniques in Fig. 8. The dynamic setups perform considerably better compared to the static cores. The first observation is that the window-75 setup performs relatively well, achieving 10% and 17% better EDP on average (for SPEC and MiBench, respectively), compared to the best performing 4-issue static core. The BTCB approach performs best, with on average 12% and 18% better EDP. The pchg annotations perform up to 26% and on average 10% (SPEC) and 16% (MiBench) better than the best performing static core.

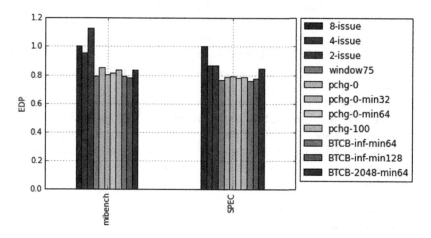

Fig. 8. EDP for the best performing setups for each approach.

For many programs, ILP variability is quite low, and the EDP for the dynamic approaches is not significantly lower than that of the best performing static setup. The largest gains are measured for the program rawcaudio with all approaches achieving approximately 25% better EDP than static setups. However, the window-1000 approach performs similarly for this program (indicating that fine-grained approaches do not provide an advantage) In contrast, rijndael does not show any improvement when using a 1000 cycle monitoring window, while our proposed BTCB approach provides 20% lower EDP compared to the best static core and 8% over the best window approach (75 cycles).

5   Related Work

The polymorphic processor used in our evaluations is discussed in more detail in [5]. Other dynamic processors that could make use of our proposed scheme are MorphCore [1], TRIPS [13] and CoreFusion [14]. Rodrigues et al. [15] propose a dynamic processor that morphs by allowing one core to take control over a functional unit residing in a neighboring core. They introduce a dynamic phase classification scheme that uses a table to store and lookup phases. Guo et al. [10] built a windowed counter scheme for the ρ-VEX that predicts program phases and reconfigures the processor accordingly. Similarly, [16] tries to predict phases using statistical and table-based predictors. Chi et al. [17] show the advantage of combining static and dynamic profiling techniques to improve performance/energy tuning, focusing on disabling some processor resources and fetch throttling. Our approach uses compiler analysis instead of profiling as the static component.

In addition to dynamic processors, the scheme can be used by single-ISA heterogeneous multicore systems [18] such as ARM big.LITTLE processors [19], particularly, systems that were designed to have low migration penalties such as [2,4]. For schemes with similar objectives on HMPs see for example [3,9,20]. Related work in autotuning are for example [21,22], where hardware modules are introduced that perform evaluation of power and performance on a softcore processor. However, the purpose is to perform dynamic partial reconfiguration, which is very different from how the ρ-VEX works.

Sherwood et al. [23] propose a similar technique of using an on-chip buffer to store detected phases based on branches, but focusing on long, stable phases. In addition, they evaluate "Dynamic Processor Width Adaptation" similar to the ρ-VEX (but supporting only a 2-issue and 8-issue configuration). They perform a short measurement in both configurations at every phase change, which is one of the problems that our proposed solution aims to solve (see Sect. 2.2).

6   Conclusions

When targeting a highly dynamic processor that has a low reconfiguration penalty (in this work, the ρ-VEX with a penalty of 5 cycles), improvements in energy efficiency can be gained by using very fine-grained automatic adaptations. Evaluations of window-based autotuning of the configuration show that using a window of 75 cycles results in the best EDP (up to 20% better than a 1000 cycle window). This confirms that code characteristics can change very rapidly, and that the dynamic processor is able to follow the changes more closely than traditional autotuning schemes that use relatively large window sizes. Not all programs show this highly dynamic behavior.

The proposed approaches open up the possibility of superscalar-based, single-ISA heterogeneous or adaptable processors with low penalties. Using a window-based approach is not possible in this case, because it would need continuous migrations between core types to evaluate the code characteristics, negating the advantages. Using our proposed methods to store information about code sections, measurements need to be performed once in every configuration, after which the information is stored and can be retrieved when revisiting the section.

Overall, the approaches enable the reconfigurable processor to achieve up to 25% and between 10% and 18% on average better EDP compared to the best static platform. The proposed BTCB approach achieves the best results, slightly outperforming window-based autotuning.

Acknowledgements. This work has been supported by the ALMARVI European Artemis project nr. 621439.

References

1. Khubaib, Suleman, M.A., Hashemi, M., Wilkerson, C., Patt, Y.N.: MorphCore: an energy-efficient microarchitecture for high performance ILP and high throughput TLP. In: 2012 45th Annual IEEE/ACM International Symposium on Microarchitecture (MICRO), pp. 305–316, December 2012
2. Brown, J.A., Porter, L., Tullsen, D.M.: Fast thread migration via cache working set prediction. In: 2011 IEEE 17th International Symposium on High Performance Computer Architecture (HPCA), pp. 193–204. IEEE (2011)
3. Rangan, K.K., Wei, G.-Y., Brooks, D.: Thread motion: fine-grained power management for multi-core systems. In: Proceedings of the 36th Annual International Symposium on Computer Architecture, ser. ISCA 2009, pp. 302–313. ACM, New York (2009). http://doi.acm.org/10.1145/1555754.1555793
4. Rodrigues, M., Roma, N., Tomás, P.: Fast and scalable thread migration for multi-core architectures. In: 2015 IEEE 13th International Conference on Embedded and Ubiquitous Computing, pp. 9–16, October 2015
5. Brandon, A., Hoozemans, J., van Straten, J., Wong, S.: Exploring ILP and TLP on a polymorphic VLIW processor. In: Knoop, J., Karl, W., Schulz, M., Inoue, K., Pionteck, T. (eds.) ARCS 2017. LNCS, vol. 10172, pp. 177–189. Springer, Cham (2017). https://doi.org/10.1007/978-3-319-54999-6_14
6. Wong, S., van As, T., Brown, G.: ρ-VEX: a reconfigurable and extensible softcore VLIW processor. In: International Conference on Field-Programmable Technology (ICFPT), December 2008
7. Brandon, A., Wong, S.: Support for dynamic issue width in VLIW processors using generic binaries. In: Design, Automation Test in Europe Conference Exhibition (DATE), pp. 827–832, March 2013
8. Codrescu, L., Anderson, W., Venkumanhanti, S., Zeng, M., Plondke, E., Koob, C., Ingle, A., Tabony, C., Maule, R.: Hexagon DSP: an architecture optimized for mobile multimedia and communications. IEEE Micro **34**(2), 34–43 (2014)
9. Becchi, M., Crowley, P.: Dynamic thread assignment on heterogeneous multiprocessor architectures. In: Proceedings of the 3rd Conference on Computing Frontiers, ser. CF 2006, pp. 29–40. ACM, New York (2006)
10. Guo, Q., Sartor, A., Brandon, A., Beck, A.C., Zhou, X., Wong, S.: Run-time phase prediction for a reconfigurable VLIW processor. In: 2016 Design, Automation and Test in Europe Conference and Exhibition (DATE), pp. 1634–1639. IEEE (2016)
11. Hoogerbrugge, J.: Dynamic branch prediction for a VLIW processor. In: Proceedings of the International Conference on Parallel Architectures and Compilation Techniques, (PACT), pp. 207–214. IEEE (2000)
12. Guthaus, M.R., Ringenberg, J.S., Ernst, D., Austin, T.M., Mudge, T., Brown, R.B.: MiBench: a free, commercially representative embedded benchmark suite. In: 2001 IEEE International Workshop on Workload Characterization: WWC-4, pp. 3–14. IEEE (2001)
13. Sankaralingam, K., Nagarajan, R., Liu, H., Kim, C., Huh, J., Burger, D., Keckler, S.W., Moore, C.R.: Exploiting ILP, TLP, and DLP with the polymorphous TRIPS architecture. In: Proceedings of the 30th Annual International Symposium on Computer Architecture, pp. 422–433. IEEE (2003)

14. Ipek, E., Kirman, M., Kirman, N., Martinez, J.F.: Core fusion: accommodating software diversity in chip multiprocessors. In: Proceedings of the 34th Annual International Symposium on Computer Architecture, ser. ISCA 2007, pp. 186–197. ACM, New York (2007). http://doi.acm.org/10.1145/1250662.1250686

15. Rodrigues, R., Annamalai, A., Koren, I., Kundu, S.: Improving performance per watt of asymmetric multi-core processors via online program phase classification and adaptive core morphing. ACM Trans. Des. Autom. Electron. Syst. **18**(1), 5:1–5:23 (2013). http://doi.acm.org/10.1145/2390191.2390196

16. Duesterwald, E., Cascaval, C., Dwarkadas, S.: Characterizing and predicting program behavior and its variability. In: Proceedings of the 12th International Conference on Parallel Architectures and Compilation Techniques, PACT 2003, pp. 220–231, September 2003

17. Chi, E., Salem, A.M., Bahar, R.I., Weiss, R.: Combining software and hardware monitoring for improved power and performance tuning. In: Proceedings of the Seventh Workshop on Interaction Between Compilers and Computer Architectures: INTERACT-7, pp. 57–64. IEEE (2003)

18. Kumar, R., Farkas, K.I., Jouppi, N.P., Ranganathan, P., Tullsen, D.M.: Single-ISA heterogeneous multi-core architectures: the potential for processor power reduction. In: Proceedings of the 36th Annual IEEE/ACM International Symposium on Microarchitecture: MICRO-36, pp. 81–92. IEEE (2003)

19. Greenhalgh, P.: big.LITTLE processing with ARM cortex-A15 & Cortex-A7. ARM White Paper, pp. 1–8 (2011)

20. Van Craeynest, K., Jaleel, A., Eeckhout, L., Narvaez, P., Emer, J.: Scheduling heterogeneous multi-cores through performance impact estimation (PIE). In: Proceedings of the 39th Annual International Symposium on Computer Architecture, ser. ISCA 2012, pp. 213–224. IEEE Computer Society, Washington, DC (2012). http://dl.acm.org/citation.cfm?id=2337159.2337184

21. Otero, A., Morales-Cas, A., Portilla, J., de la Torre, E., Riesgo, T.: A modular peripheral to support self-reconfiguration in SoCs. In: 2010 13th Euromicro Conference on Digital System Design: Architectures, Methods and Tools, pp. 88–95 (2010)

22. Aldham, M., Anderson, J., Brown, S., Canis, A.: Low-cost hardware profiling of run-time and energy in FPGA embedded processors. In: ASAP 2011–22nd IEEE International Conference on Application-specific Systems, Architectures and Processors, pp. 61–68, September 2011

23. Sherwood, T., Sair, S., Calder, B.: Phase tracking and prediction. In: ACM SIGARCH Computer Architecture News, vol. 31, no. 2, pp. 336–349. ACM (2003)

HLS Enabled Partially Reconfigurable Module Implementation

Nicolae Bogdan Grigore, Charalampos Kritikakis[(✉)], and Dirk Koch

The University of Manchester, Manchester, UK
{nicolae.grigore,charalampos.kritikakis,dirk.koch}@manchester.ac.uk

Abstract. Making full use of the capabilities of the FPGA as an accelerator is difficult for non hardware experts, especially if partial reconfiguration is to be employed. One of the issues that arise is to physically implement modules into bounding boxes of minimum size for improving fragmentation cost and reconfiguration time. In this paper we present a method which automates the modules designing step, fulfilling module resource requirements and architectural FPGA constraints. We present a case study that shows how our automatic module implementation flow can be used to generate run-time reconfigurable bitstreams that are suited for stitching together processing pipelines directly from a Maxeler MaxJ HLS specification. This takes into consideration design alternatives, fragmentation, and routing failure mitigation strategies.

1 Introduction

HLS has made tremendous progress in recent years in improving design productivity of hardware systems. In particular for FPGA acceleration in datacenters, HLS and domain specific languages are commonly considered to be key technologies for succeeding with widespread FPGA deployment. However, one concern against this approach is the effect of *logic explosion* which expresses the situation that every line of (extra) HLS code translates somehow into extra logic on the FPGA and consequently in extra cost and more power. This situation gets crucial if major parts of the FPGA will remain idle for longer periods of time. For example: let us consider a driver assistance system with entire different object classifiers that were optimized for day and night modes. Then parts of the system (and correspondingly the FPGA) may not be used depending on the present mode. In this situation, partial reconfiguration at run-time is a viable option to optimize the module layout for optimizing resource utilization (e.g., by using reconfiguration to change between day and night object classification in our example). In general, whenever a system provides periods in time where functions are used mutual exclusively to each other, this is an opportunity for applying partial reconfiguration. This holds in particular if these periods are long enough in order to amortize the overhead induced for the reconfiguration.

© Springer International Publishing AG, part of Springer Nature 2018
M. Berekovic et al. (Eds.): ARCS 2018, LNCS 10793, pp. 269–282, 2018.
https://doi.org/10.1007/978-3-319-77610-1_20

The FPGA vendors Xilinx [1] and Altera [2] provide frameworks that allow developing run-time reconfigurable systems using HLS. In particular for the OpenCL language, industry reached a maturity level that allows software engineers and domain experts to build run-time reconfigurable systems without the need for extensive FPGA knowledge. This allows for non-FPGA experts to develop systems that can adapt to different requirements or workloads with the help of partial reconfiguration.

However, while this fundamentally is a strong achievement, present design methodologies and corresponding reconfigurable FPGA-based systems have important shortcomings that are not sufficiently addressed by the FPGA vendors. This includes in particular the flexibility in which partial reconfiguration can be used in a system. For example, present OpenCL frameworks support multiple reconfigurable regions that could host an accelerator module. However, a module is always only working at the position it was physically implemented and it is not possible to run a module implementation (given as a configuration bitstream) at another position. Moreover, the physical partially reconfigurable module implementation is needed to be executed again whenever something changes in the static system (i.e. the part of the system providing I/O access to DDR memory etc.). Furthermore, the vendor flow does not foresee to use reconfigurable regions by multiple independently reconfigured and operated modules. Luckily, there are academic frameworks that allow the implementation of more flexible reconfigurable systems (e.g., OpenPR [3] and GoAhead [4]).

While such tools allow implementing reconfigurable systems with more capabilities, these tools are still designed to be used by FPGA experts. The goal of this paper is to provide a frontend for such tools (in this paper, we are building a frontend for GoAhead) that allows implementing partially reconfigurable modules directly from HLS descriptions by designers that do not need to be FPGA experts. In detail, this paper provides an automatic compilation framework for stream processing applications starting from HLS all the way down to a partial reconfiguration bitstream that supports flexible module placement, module relocation and multi module instantiation. We will provide a solution for compilation of MaxJ (Java) specifications to relocatable and stitchable stream processing modules (Sect. 5) in a dynamic dataflow system. We assume that an expert is providing a static system. For this, HLS compilers are used to retrieve module primitive requirements. With this, we will show how bounding boxes for modules can be automatically computed and implemented all the way to reconfigurable modules.

2 Related Work

As mentioned in the introduction, the major FPGA vendors are already providing solutions that allow building applications in HDLs for FPGAs that rudimentary use partial reconfiguration [1,2]. Building partially reconfigurable systems introduces some extra level of complexity that commonly needs dealing with some low-level FPGA specific issues. In order to deal with such issues, design automation for partial reconfiguration has been researched.

With OpenPR [3] and GoAhead [4], tools have been developed that allow FPGA experts building reconfigurable systems with distinct features like module relocation and direct module to module communication. However, using these tools needs significant FPGA experience and a specific way of floorplanning for partitioning FPGA resources into static and run-time reconfigurable sections as well as for providing interfaces for integrating reconfigurable parts of a system. The work in [5] is focusing on automating the interface design using simulated annealing while in [6–9] the whole floorplanning process for the static system and/or partial modules was automated for RTL designs and demonstrated for a small number of modules. Static system only floorplanning was presented in [10,11]. The problem of physically designing relocatable modules was addressed, for example, in [12–14]. There is a large body of rather theoretical related work (commonly without a system that is actually working on an FPGA) on automated floorplanning that is not listed here due to space limitations.

Physically implementing relocatable modules adds more constraints to be obeyed by design tools, and consequently, more potential points of failure for successfully completing the process all the way to the bitstream level. While related work marks important automation steps, in this work we do not only provide a holistic solution to automatic floorplanning and interface synthesis for implementing relocatable modules, we in addition provide automatic mitigation strategies for the case that the physical FPGA implementation fails. This makes the whole backend flow that robust that it can be coupled with an HLS frontend such that reconfigurable modules can be implemented fully automated directly from high-level languages.

3   Model

Our goal is to build a design flow that can be used by non FPGA experts to take advantage of partial dynamic reconfiguration. For this, we assume that an expert must first design a static system that defines a reconfigurable area to test the modules (representing the actual application). These modules will then be implemented by a non FPGA expert using HLS.

To do this, we must first define a model for the FPGA's reconfigurable resources and reconfigurable modules. All modern FPGAs from the vendor Xilinx contain a set number of resource slice types. These are usually SliceL, SliceM, BRAM and DSP (with some variations depending on the FPGA family). We can model the FPGA as a set of these resources or, in order to also express the exact sequential order of resource columns, as a resource string. This allows for modeling of the module placement process as a string matching problem.

Our automatic bounding box generation tool is generic in that it can work on any device as long as the following generic parameters are provided:

– Number of CLBs in a clock region
– Number of LUTs in a CLB
– Number of BRAMs in a clock region
– Number of DSPs in a clock region

– Total number of clock regions in the reconfigurable area
– Resource string of the reconfigurable area.

This model fits directly to all Xilinx FPGA families including all 7-series devices.

Each module requires a number of resources in order to perform the task required, thus our initial representation has to provide at least the minimum requirements for each: number of BRAMs, LUTs and DSPs.

Using these two string representations for the FPGA and modules, as well as the number of primitives per resource column, we can find bounding boxes (as discussed later). Bounding boxes are represented in two complimentary ways: a set of three parameters specifying start position, width and height, as well as the resource string of the bounding box and number of clock regions required. Using string representations for the reconfigurable area and the reconfigurable modules allows for checking for feasible placement positions using simple string compare. The bounding box information can be used to build partially reconfigurable modules as shown in Fig. 5. The example shows how MaxJ specifications are divided into a static part that is separated from the actual application (here the partial modules). Further details about this process will be given later in Sect. 5.

4   Bounding Box Generation

4.1   Overview

Our algorithm generates bounding boxes for a module based on the FPGA resource string modeling of the available resources in the reconfigurable region, the device specific primitive allocation to slices, and module primitive requirements.

During the generation phase we add more and more slices to the module string specification from the FPGA representation until all primitive requirements have been met. With this, we ensure to only implement modules for feasible module bounding boxes and that we identify all possible minimal design alternatives. Our system also takes into consideration multiple clock regions. The generated bounding boxes can span anywhere between one clock region and the entire height of the device (or reconfigurable region). This adds even further flexibility to the placement phase, making sure that the modules come with more possible placement positions, for allowing a much tighter overall packing.

In this work we assume scenarios that benefit from small module sizes as both examples will allow using multiple modules in a shared reconfigurable region. In both case studies we build modules to allow stitching together processing pipelines, while supporting direct communication.

4.2   Generation

Let us assume that we need to find placement positions for the module in Fig. 1 inside the shown reconfigurable region. Firstly, we must know the number of primitives provided in each column. These values are device specific and

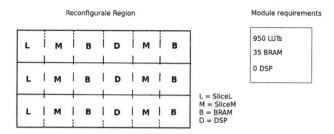

Fig. 1. Example of a reconfigurable region, spanning 3 clock regions, and some module requirements. The region is modeled with the shown alphabet, and a module is presented as a set of primitive requirements.

must be fed into our bounding box generator. In this example we will use a Zynq FPGA. On this device, we have the following number of resources for each column:

- SliceL: 40 * 8 LUTs
- SliceM: 40 * 8 LUTs
- BRAM: 20 RAM primitives (10 36 Kbit or 20 18 Kbit)
- DSP: 20 DSP primitives.

The algorithm (illustrated in Fig. 2) begins at the first available resource in the reconfigurable region. It checks if this resource contains primitives needed by the module. If so, it adds the slice to the module string and updates the module requirements to reflect that the primitive in the added slice have already been take into consideration. This step is repeated until all primitive requirements have been met, and the resulting module string represents a design alternative.

As stated before, in order to give the user as much choice as possible and to allow for fine grained and flexible module placement, our system looks for bounding boxes spanning from one to as many clock regions as the reconfigurable area has available. As such the steps above are repeated using incrementally more clock regions (i.e. increasing the height of the modules). Considering our example, we are looking at the bounding boxes starting with the first resource slice we can determine 3 placement positions as can be seen in Fig. 3.

The bounding box generator exploits the fact that the smallest module (i.e. the module variant with the shortest resource string) that fulfills the resource requirements will result in the lowest internal fragmentation. As such, only the smallest design alternatives are considered at the end of this computation. This allows for the reduction of the run-time search space, whilst still providing high placement flexibility. For example, we will consider only two of the three module design alternatives for the first g position in the reconfigurable region provided:

- (LMBDMB) * 1 row
- (LMB) * 2 rows
- (LMB) * 3 rows (discarded as the two row variant has lower internal fragmentation).

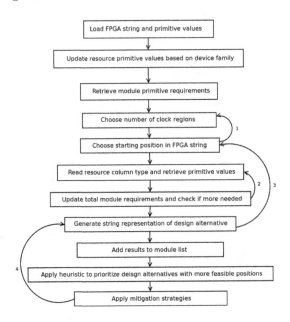

Fig. 2. Algorithm applied to each module specification. Transition 1 happens when all bounding boxes for the current number of clock regions were found. Transition 2 happens at every step until all resource requirements for the module are met. Transition 3 occurs once the bounding boxes starting at the current start position were found. Transition 4 allows for mitigation strategies to be employed if routing fails.

All module bounding boxes generated will be continuous and rectangle. This means that unnecessary resources cannot be skipped. In our example, we see that the 1 row module generated contains a DSP resource slice even though DSPs were not necessary for the correct run of the module. Similarly the 3 row implementation uses more resources than the 2 row one, even though it only needs just as many. This means that there is a need for a step after the bounding box generation to determine which bounding boxes should be used for physical implementation.

In order to further reduce the search space and still provide the user with flexibility, we employ a heuristic. Once the total number of design alternative is computed we sort the resulting list of bounding boxes in such a way that the alternatives with the most possible placement positions are at the start. Typically, a relatively small number of alternatives is sufficient to allow placement with little external fragmentation (i.e. unused resources between placed modules). This heuristic increases the chance that run-time placement results in better resource utilization.

One of the problems that can occur when creating bounding boxes is that, if they are defined aggressively small, there might not be enough resources left over for routing. Because our bounding boxes are rectangles and because we use resource columns as our placement atoms, the bounding box will likely leave

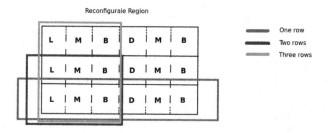

Fig. 3. Bounding boxes for the defined module in the reconfigurable region, starting only at the first resource slice.

some resources unused. Seeing as how routing a particular module can be difficult [15], the excess resources can improve the chance that routing will succeed and timing will be met.

As an extra precaution, we have implemented a method by which the module string can be updated to contain more resource columns as needed. Since routing requires the switch matrix only within a column, the extra resource (which we refer to as a slack variable) can be seen as a wild card (meaning any resource type can be used to ensure routing). This can be added before a placement method is applied. Finally, if timing still isn't met, we also allow for a "fail" message to be fed back to the generator in order to further increase the number of resources assigned for a module (i.e. one extra slice to the left and one to the right will most definitely solve the problem, but would be wasteful if not necessary).

Furthermore, our tool flow implements mitigation strategies that apply physical constraints that will be tried out to improve routability and performance (achieved clock frequency). This includes using switch matrices only at places of high possible congestion (e.g. the corner of the bounding box), as described in Sect. 5.4.

5   Case Study

This section focuses on applying an automatic partial module implementation flow on a Maxeler Max3 system using its dataflow model. The case study will include creating the static part in our design, as well as injecting a reconfigurable region amongst the automatically generated RTL code from an HLS tool. Moreover, we will focus on the extraction of HLS generated accelerators and the final mapping using the bounding box generator.

5.1   Maxeler System and Dataflow

Maxeler Workstations [16] are hybrid computing platforms that are using both a CPU and an FPGA to implement complex functions. The FPGA device is programmed by a Java dialect, which is called MaxJ, in order to be more design friendly to non-FPGA experts, without having knowledge of HDLs.

The system uses an automatically generated interface infrastructure between the FPGAs and the rest of the system and, depending on the input interface, our system needs for example, PCI-e and/or memory. Moreover, Maxeler has a large userbase in academia and industry. Common applications domains include databases, medical applications, image/video processing, networking and so on [17].

We are currently using a Max3 Workstation, which provides a Virtex-6 XC6VSX475T FPGA from Xilinx, connected to the mother-board via PCI-e. The FPGA is surrounded by 24 GB of DDR-3 memory and the host CPU is an Intel(R) Core(TM) i7-2600S CPU clocked at 2.80 GHz CPU.

In order to use Maxeler, the designer has to focus on three basic parts, the CPU interface code, the main Kernel and the Manager. When all these three parts are developed, the MaxJ code is compiled to a corresponding RTL VHDL description, which is compiled by the ISE toolchain, until the final bitfile generation. The tool creates the Maxfile, which is a monolithic binary that contains the full static configuration of the FPGA and the host machine binary file. In order to run the system, Maxeler combines the CPU interface code and the Maxfile to run the computation and to retrieve the final result. Figure 4 is showing an overview of the whole design flow. It should be mentioned that Maxeler is offering a custom HDL interface, in order to allow the integration of hand-crafted RTL code to be used within Maxeler's framework.

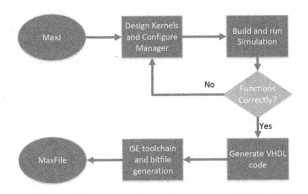

Fig. 4. Maxeler design flow from MaxJ to Maxfile.

5.2   Static System

Our system consists of a Maxeler interface that transfers data from the CPU to and from the FPGA, a custom HDL implementation or an HLS generated accelerator and a connection to the internal configuration access port (ICAP). The input to ICAP is needed to load the partial bitstreams of our partial modules. Inside the wrapper of our accelerator, we can replace the automatically generated accelerator with our reconfigurable region, which will host the partial modules.

In order to split the accelerator from the static part, we can use Xilinx tools to set the accelerator as a top level entity and extract the netlist of the kernel. Then, we can use this netlist to have the full functionality of the kernel and create a partial module. We will focus more on the partial module creation in Sect. 5.3. The interface of the reconfigurable region is currently implemented entirely as a loopback device for a 512-bit wide datapath. In total, Maxeler's automatically generated modules around the accelerator, plus our reconfigurable region as an entity, are defined as the final fully static part of our system. Figure 5 shows a detailed overview of the steps we follow to generate the full static system of the dynamic part and the reconfigurable region.

For integrating a reconfigurable region into the design, we manually floor-planned the static system, by taking into consideration where Maxeler maps the rest of its system. That includes the placement of I/O cells for the PCI-e and DDR3 memory connections and the surrounding modules. Given these constraints, the Maxeler implementation is not using the corners of the device. Hence, our reconfigurable region is constrained to be placed in the upper right corner of the FPGA, which is not used by the surrounding Maxeler system.

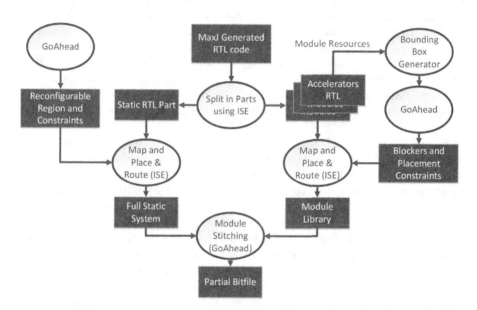

Fig. 5. Proposed design approach: MaxJ generated system split into a static system with reconfigurable area and a module library.

The reconfigurable region is entirely generated by GoAhead and placed and routed with ISE tools. The final reconfigurable region is depicted in Fig. 6a. To create the reconfigurable region, we define a bounding box in GoAhead. Then, inside the reconfigurable region, we place a series of registers in vertical fashion on the left side, middle and right side of our region, that help us route in a specific way across our defined area. Additionally, placement and routing constraints are generated that prevent the Xilinx place and route tool to use any resources within the reconfigurable region.

5.3 Implemented Modules

For the whole process we follow a standard pattern which is depicted in the right side of Fig. 5. For each one of our modules, we programmed our kernel in MaxJ and went through the Maxeler compilation flow, until the HDL code is generated. Then, we automatically analyze the generated HDL code, in order to identify and separate the kernel hierarchy from the surrounding Maxeler system (Fig. 5). More specifically, we set the kernel as a top-level module and compile the entire kernel hierarchy into one netlist file. This will also report resource requirements to the automatic bounding box generator, which will in turn return the starting point, the width and a resource string of the module. For each module we get a different resource string or a set of resource strings, that refer to different positions, depending on the requirements of the implemented module.

Subsequently, we use GoAhead to generate placement constraints and to create a blocker around the module, such that the module routing will never cross the module borders. With the generated constraints we can use the Xilinx toolchain to fully map and route the module. One of our main challenges is to route through and back of our module, precisely as we did in our reconfigurable region. In order to ensure this routing, we place a vertical series of registers before and after the module, that we call connection macros, that act as the interface of our partial module. It should be mentioned that the clock signals to ensure the routing will exactly match the routing used in the reconfigurable region.

Finally, we can cut off only the module and save it in a netlist file format in a module library. Again, the cutting of the module from the final routed file is done by GoAhead. This tool allows to select a specific area, by given constraints like height and width and a starting point, in order to extract only the module. This module can now be placed into the reconfigurable region of the static system. We use string matching to find module placement positions, following the module presented in Sect. 4. This placement allows us to stitch together different stream processing modules (that are generated by MaxJ). After each stitching process, we generate a partial bitstream for the design. In order to place the module in the Maxeler system, we need to have an input in our device, that targets the ICAP port. More specifically, we can generate a partial bitfile, containing the position and the configuration of a partial module. This bitfile can then be used for reconfiguration through the ICAP port.

Our current module library consists of 6 image processing functions. Those are a Sobel filter, brightness correction, a gaussian filter, an RGB to greyscale filter, a skin color detection and a mean filter. All of those functions are generated entirely by Maxeler and MaxJ code.

It is possible to place more than one reconfigurable module in the reconfigurable region. An example of fully placed modules is shown in Fig. 6. More specifically, Fig. 6(a) illustrates an empty state of our reconfigurable region using

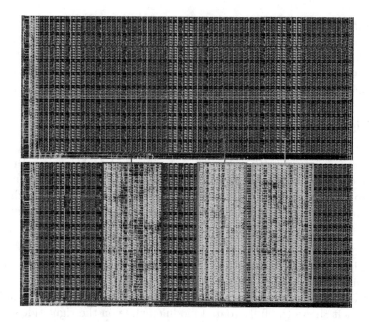

Fig. 6. (Top) Empty reconfigurable region. (Bottom) Placed partial modules in reconfigurable region. (Color figure online)

the resource string model of this region, the placer can calculate positions for each module. Figure 6(b) shows the final placing of 3 distinct modules in the same reconfigurable region. In that way, we can stitch a parallel pipeline of modules, that can take an input stream and apply different functions on it.

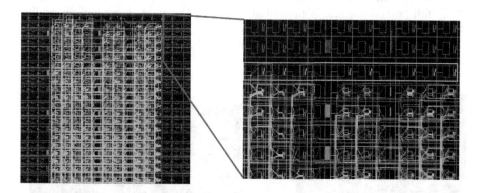

Fig. 7. Mitigation strategy 2: we leave the top and bottom of the partial module unmapped and we just use the switch matrices. (Color figure online)

At this point, we should point out that some parts of the modules are underutilized. The restricting factor is practically the internal design of the Virtex 6 FPGAs. To be more precise, if a module needs more than 4 rows of CLBs, then, by definition, the design will have a row of either BRAMs or DSPs. This will result in internal and external fragmentation, in order to fulfill the CLB resource requirement. An example is shown in Fig. 6b, where the first module (red boxed module) has two columns in the middle which are a row of DSPs and a row of BRAMs. However, we can observe that the rest of the rows, which consist of CLBs, are almost fully populated, thus a smaller bounding box could not be chosen.

5.4   Mitigation Strategies

As an additional function, our physical implementation flow is able to handle failures during mapping or routing. For example, if a module does not get mapped, we will extend the bounding box left or right by an additional column. In the case of a routing failure, the tool can relax the routing inside the bounding box, using 3 different strategies, that are tried out in the following consecutive order.

- The tool can block the placement in the corners of the bounding box, because the design tends to be heavily congested in the corners. So we are leaving them unused but, by taking advantage of their routing resources (switch matrices), we provide locally a higher ratio of routing logic.
- We are leaving the top and bottom side unmapped, as it can be seen in Fig. 7. Figure 7 left shows the fully routed module, while on the right side of Fig. 7, the unmapped CLBs on the top row are depicted, inside the gray box. This solution can solve a rather small unroutable situation, without spreading the design in more rows.
- The last, most efficient but also expensive strategy, occurs by using an additional layer as a frame around the module, in which we will only take advantage of the routing resources. Figure 8 depicts that kind of situation. In this case, the mapping will be done entirely in the inner side of the frame, while we will use only the routing resources of the frame. In the left side of Fig. 8, the full partial module is presented, while on the right, a zoomed in representation of the partial module is presented. The above solutions can offer significant design alternatives for our modules, without the risk of having external fragmentation.

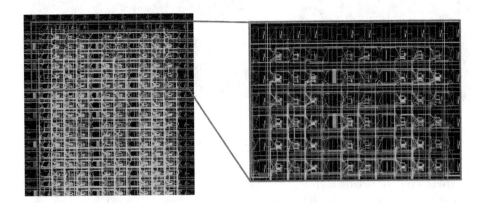

Fig. 8. Mitigation strategy 3: unplaced, but routed frame around the module, to relax routing if necessary.

Implementing modules in bounding boxes includes more constrains on the physical implementation. However, in some cases, routing is not possible, for a module with the given constraints. As an example, in the four corners of the bounding box, the router has only available about half of the available routing wires. This situation may result in an unroutable situation and that is why mitigation strategies are vital for such kind of implementations.

6 Conclusion

In this work we presented a tool flow that automates the generation of partially reconfigurable stream processing accelerator modules directly from HLS using minimum feasible module bounding boxes. We have discussed in detail how our bounding box generator incorporates the heterogeneous resource layout of FPGAs using a string model for reconfigurable regions as well as for the reconfigurable modules. We are able to generate physical implementation alternatives for enhancing module packing at run-time. Furthermore we incorporated automatic mitigation strategies to get even highly congested modules physically implemented.

We demonstrated our approach using a case study that centers on a Maxeler Max-3 Dataflow processing system. Our flow allows it to automatically generate relocatable partial bitstreams directly from MaxJ. We also showed how these bitstreams can be used at run-time. The here presented methodology is quite universal and can be applied to other (Xilinx) FPGAs and other HLS tools (e.g., Vivado HLS).

With the proposed flow we allow for non FPGA experts to make better use of FPGAs including powerful tools such as dynamic partial reconfiguration. This provides also means to close a semantic gap that is that commonly a few functions out of a larger library are called dynamically in software and the here presented tool provides an important piece to translate this approach into FPGA acceleration.

Acknowledgements. This work is kindly supported by the European Commission under the H2020 Programme with the project ECOSCALE (grant agreement 671632) and with the project Reconfigurable Tera Stream Computing, funded by the Defence Science and Technology Laboratory under grant DSTLX10000092266.

References

1. Wirbel, L.: Xilinx SDAccel (2014)
2. Stone, J.E., Gohara, D., Shi, G.: OpenCL: a parallel programming standard for heterogeneous computing systems. Comput. Sci. Eng. **12**(3), 66–73 (2010)
3. Sohanghpurwala, A.A., Athanas, P., Frangieh, T., Wood, A.: OpenPR: an open-source partial-reconfiguration toolkit for Xilinx FPGAs. In: 2011 IEEE International Symposium on Parallel and Distributed Processing Workshops and Ph.D. Forum (IPDPSW), pp. 228–235. IEEE (2011)

4. GoAhead Project (2017). http://www.mn.uio.no/ifi/english/research/projects/cosrecos/goahead/

5. Carver, J.M., Pittman, R.N., Forin, A.: Automatic bus macro placement for partially reconfigurable FPGA designs. In: Proceedings of the ACM/SIGDA International Symposium on Field Programmable Gate Arrays, pp. 269–272. ACM (2009)

6. Vipin, K., Fahmy, S.A.: Mapping adaptive hardware systems with partial reconfiguration using CoPR for Zynq. In: 2015 NASA/ESA Conference on Adaptive Hardware and Systems (AHS), pp. 1–8. IEEE (2015)

7. Beckhoff, C., Koch, D., Torreson, J.: Automatic floorplanning and interface synthesis of island style reconfigurable systems with GoAHEAD. In: Kubátová, H., Hochberger, C., Daněk, M., Sick, B. (eds.) ARCS 2013. LNCS, vol. 7767, pp. 303–316. Springer, Heidelberg (2013). https://doi.org/10.1007/978-3-642-36424-2_26

8. Beckhoff, C., Koch, D., Torresen, J.: GoAhead: a partial reconfiguration framework. In: IEEE 20th Annual International Symposium on Field-Programmable Custom Computing Machines (FCCM), pp. 37–44. IEEE (2012)

9. Rabozzi, M., Durelli, G.C., Miele, A., Lillis, J., Santambrogio, M.D.: Floorplanning automation for partial-reconfigurable FPGAs via feasible placements generation. IEEE Trans. Very Large Scale Integr. VLSI Syst. **25**(1), 151–164 (2017)

10. Mao, F., Chen, Y.-C., Zhang, W., Li, H.H., He, B.: Library-based placement and routing in FPGAs with support of partial reconfiguration. ACM Trans. Des. Autom. Electron. Syst. (TODAES) **21**(4), 71 (2016)

11. Otero, A., Morales-Cas, A., Portilla, J., de la Torre, E., Riesgo, T.: A modular peripheral to support self-reconfiguration in SoCs. In: 2010 13th Euromicro Conference on Digital System Design: Architectures, Methods and Tools (DSD), pp. 88–95. IEEE (2010)

12. Lalevee, A., Horrein, P.-H., Arzel, M., Hübner, M., Vaton, S.: AutoReloc: automated design flow for bitstream relocation on Xilinx FPGAs. In: 2016 Euromicro Conference on Digital System Design (DSD), pp. 14–21. IEEE (2016)

13. Ferrandi, F., Novati, M., Morandi, M., Santambrogio, M.D., Sciuto, D.: Dynamic reconfiguration: core relocation via partial bitstreams filtering with minimal overhead. In: International Symposium on System-on-Chip, pp. 1–4. IEEE (2006)

14. Kalte, H., Lee, G., Porrmann, M., Ruckert, U.: Replica: a bitstream manipulation filter for module relocation in partial reconfigurable systems. In: Proceedings of the 19th IEEE International Parallel and Distributed Processing Symposium, pp. 8–pp. IEEE (2005)

15. DeHon, A.: Balancing interconnect and computation in a reconfigurable computing array (or, why you don't really want 100% LUT utilization). In: Proceedings of the 1999 ACM/SIGDA Seventh International Symposium on Field Programmable Gate Arrays, pp. 69–78. ACM (1999)

16. Maxeler Technologies: Multiscale dataflow programing (2014)

17. Maxeler App Gallery (2017). http://appgallery.maxeler.com/

Hardware Acceleration in Genode OS Using Dynamic Partial Reconfiguration

Alexander Dörflinger$^{(\boxtimes)}$, Mark Albers, Björn Fiethe, and Harald Michalik

Institute of Computer and Network Engineering (IDA), TU Braunschweig,
Braunschweig, Germany
{doerflinger,albers,fiethe,michalik}@ida.ing.tu-bs.de

Abstract. Algorithms with operations on large regular data structures such as image processing can be highly accelerated when executed as hardware tasks in an FPGA fabric. The Dynamic Partial Reconfiguration (DPR) feature of new SRAM-based FPGA families allows a dynamic swapping and replacement of hardware tasks during runtime. Particularly embedded systems with processing chains that change over time or that are too large to be implemented in an FPGA fabric in parallel, benefit from DPR. In this paper we present a complete framework for hardware acceleration using DPR in the microkernel based Genode OS. This makes the DPR feature available not only for the high-performance computing field, but also for safety-critical applications. The new framework is evaluated for an exemplary imaging application running on a Xilinx Zynq-7000 SoC.

1 Introduction

Dynamic Partial Reconfiguration (DPR) is a promising feature of new SRAM-based FPGAs to increase the overall processing power of a system. It allows to offload software tasks and process them as hardware tasks within the FPGA fabric. Computation-intensive algorithms as needed e.g. for computer vision systems yield high acceleration rates when executed in hardware [1]. Without DPR, all hardware tasks needed at some point during runtime, have to be instantiated concurrently in a static FPGA design. Due to limited resources available, only a few tasks could be migrated to hardware. DPR now allows to time-share resources of the FPGA by swapping hardware tasks in reconfigurable regions. Therefore, it combines the performance gain of hardware acceleration with the flexibility of software tasks. Furthermore, complex processing pipelines that would not fit in one static FPGA design can now be implemented for sequential execution.

Robotic applications and embedded systems in general have strict requirements regarding the utilized operating system in matters of real-time, safety and reliability. The Genode OS [2] targets safety-critical applications because it enforces a strong isolation between software components. For that reason, it has been decided to use Genode OS in various research projects. Specifically, the Controlling Concurrent Change (CCC) project [3] investigates mechanisms for

© Springer International Publishing AG, part of Springer Nature 2018
M. Berekovic et al. (Eds.): ARCS 2018, LNCS 10793, pp. 283–293, 2018.
https://doi.org/10.1007/978-3-319-77610-1_21

an automated integration of embedded systems. In this context, the stringent fault isolation and separation of concerns provided by Genode OS is used to border the effects of each sub-component on the overall system.

The DPR feature has been investigated in CCC for adapting a given platform to different operation scenarios, e.g. a car driving on a highway/in a city/parking. Hardware accelerators suitable for the current scenario are loaded into the FPGA fabric during runtime. This extends the utilization of DPR to mixed-critical systems. So far, the utilization of DPR has been limited to the high-performance computing field, and therefore safety- and reliability requirements have not been covered yet. Safety-critical applications require the reconfiguration process to be controlled from within an OS with appropriate real-time and reliability features, for which Genode OS might be suitable in future. In this paper we present, how the DPR feature can be made available for Genode OS running on a hybrid CPU-FPGA SoC device. A framework has been developed to dispatch tasks from software and execute them hardware-accelerated in the FPGA fabric of the SoC. Real-time aspects of DPR are discussed.

The rest of this paper is organized as follows: the principles of Genode OS are introduced in Sect. 2. Section 3 gives an overview of DPR support in other operating systems. Subsequently the hardware- (Sect. 4) and software architecture (Sect. 5) for using DPR in Genode OS are described. In Sect. 6, the newly developed framework is evaluated for an exemplary imaging application running on a Xilinx Zynq-7000 SoC.

2   Genode OS

The Genode OS framework [2] is a novel operating system approach, which is able to master complexity by applying a strict organizational structure to all software components including device drivers, system services and applications. Its continuing development takes place as a community-driven open source project.

2.1   Microkernel Based System Policy

A kernel of a modern operating system, such as the Linux kernel, manages resources, accesses the hardware, controls user processes, and more. Hence, it requires the privilege to control the whole machine. The high functional requirements and the broad range of existing hardware causes such a kernel to grow huge, by which it is impossible to fully avoid safety and security leaks that could corrupt the proper operation of the whole system. An isolation of concurrently running user applications can be provided by executing them within a dedicated address space and allowing interaction with other user applications only via mechanisms provided by the kernel. Microkernel-based systems use this technique also for device drivers, file systems, and other typical kernel-level services. Therefore, the effect of a bug-prone component is locally restricted. Furthermore, a microkernel enforces CPU time scheduling and can grant guaranteed processing time to user processes. No unprivileged system component is able to violate such guarantees. Therefore, a microkernel can safely execute sensitive applications, unprivileged system services, and large untrusted applications side by side on one machine.

To make the approach of fault isolation and separation of concerns effective, all those unprivileged components must be appropriately organized. A policy must be provided by some instance because typical microkernels implement only mechanisms. This would be possible with a central policy management component controlled by a specially-privileged administrator. The complexity and manageability of a centralized policy, however, depends on the scale of the system. To overcome this problem, Genode OS extends the microkernel idea by decomposing also the system policy and imposes a strict organizational structure onto each part of the system. Processes are organized as a tree and child processes are created out of the resources of their respective parent. When creating a child process, a parent fully defines the virtual environment in which the new process gets executed. The child, in turn, can further create children from its assigned resources, thereby creating an arbitrary structured subsystem. Each parent maintains full control over the subsystems it created and defines their inter-relationship, for example by selectively permitting communication between them or by assigning physical resources. The parent-child interface is the same at each hierarchy level, which makes this organizational approach recursively applicable.

2.2 Component Communication

The basic communication between components takes place via services using Remote Procedure Call (RPC). In order to provide a service, a component needs to create an RPC object implementing the so-called root interface, which offers functions for creating and destroying sessions of the service. Then, the component has to inform its parent about it by an announce function, which takes the service name and the capability for the service's root interface as arguments. The counterpart of the service announcement is the creation of a session by a client which issues a session request to its parent. Along with the session call, the client specifies the type of the service and a number of session arguments. As a result of the session request, the client expects to obtain a capability to an RPC object that implements the session interface of the requested service.

3   Related Work

The approach of developing efficient embedded CPU-FPGA based systems with DPR has already been studied in some researches. [4] discusses the reconfiguration management on the Xilinx Zynq-7000 platform at application level without the use of any operating system. Another approach used a custom ARM-specified microkernel on a partial reconfigurable FPGA platform to dynamically manage reconfigurable HW accelerators and SW tasks by developing a specific scheduling mechanism [5]. Based on this, the ability to dispatch hardware tasks to virtual machines hosted by the microkernel was integrated [6]. In [7], a PowerPC was used to exchange reconfigurable engines representing different image processing algorithms for driving assistant systems. There are also approaches to design new interface structures to either increase the performance [8] or reduce the resource requirements [9]. Another work describes a dynamic and partial reconfigurable system using a Zynq-7000 SoC with Linux and demonstrates, that acceptable delays for the configuration process can be achieved in that constellation [10]. In spite of all investigation efforts on DPR for CPU-FPGA based systems, there is no solution for doing this in Genode OS, yet. By implementing DPR for Genode OS, hardware acceleration can be applied for safety-critical applications which require strong isolation of software components.

4   Reconfigurable Hardware

Hardware tasks are hosted and run within separate reconfigurable regions of the FPGA fabric. These regions need to be embedded in a static logic that provides the infrastructure for communication etc. While the static logic is configured at startup and remains unchanged thereafter, the configuration of hardware tasks can be written into reconfigurable regions through the Processor Configuration Access Port (PCAP) during runtime. Other alternative configuration ports (such as ICAP, SelectMAP, Serial, and JTAG) are available in the Zynq-7000 SoC, but have drawbacks regarding bandwidth or accessibility. With a bandwidth of up to 3.2Gb/s, the PCAP allows fast reconfiguration times.

The resulting architecture for a hardware accelerated CPU-FPGA SoC design is depicted in Fig. 1. The architecture targets Xilinx Zynq-7000 or Zynq-UltraScale+ devices with a Processing System (PS) and Programmable Logic (PL). Hardware accelerated algorithms are implemented for the FPGA fabric and can be placed in one or more available reconfigurable regions. Configuration- and status data is communicated over the AXI Lite Interconnect and attached to a general purpose AXI port (AXI GP).

Each reconfigurable region connects to an AXI Stream Interconnect network which allows flexible streaming of data to any endpoint. This allows to stream the output of one reconfigurable region directly to the input of another region, and datapaths with multiple hardware tasks to be executed sequentially can be set up. DMA (or Video DMA for image processing applications) IP-cores translate between the streaming- and memory mapped communication. For a fast transfer of processing data, a high performance AXI port (AXI HP) is used between the PS and PL.

As different hardware tasks generally have very diverse demands of FPGA resources, the definition of appropriate reconfigurable region sizes is a sophisticated problem. In order to distribute the FPGA resources between all reconfigurable regions for a given set of hardware tasks efficiently, we use an algorithm introduced by us in [11].

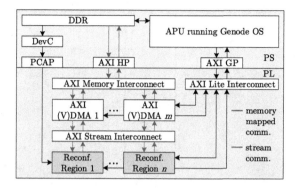

Fig. 1. Hardware accelerated CPU-FPGA SoC design.

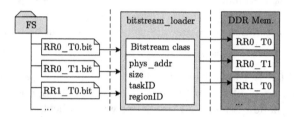

Fig. 2. Loading bitstreams from a file system to DDR memory.

5   Reconfiguration Software

5.1   Loading Partial Bitstreams

For an autonomous operation of an embedded system, all partial bitstreams need to be stored in non-volatile memory. Similar to [12], all bitstreams are copied from non-volatile memory to DDR memory during the boot sequence. Hence, partial bitstreams can be accessed rapidly and reconfiguration times are kept short. This task is executed by the *bitstream_loader* component in Genode OS. For each partial bitstream, it requests a read-only dataspace (ROM session) which is served by a file system containing the corresponding *.bit* files. Once the ROM session is created, Genode OS maps the bitstream to the private memory of the *bitstream_loader* component. The *bitstream_loader* also keeps track of metadata for each bitstream, such as its physical address, size, region, and contained hardware task. Figure 2 depicts the principle process of loading bitstreams to DDR memory.

5.2   Accessing the Configuration Port

Once a reconfiguration process is triggered, the partial bitstream needs to be written into the FPGA fabric. This is handled by the *device configuration interface* (DevC, [13]), which moves the bitstream data from DDR memory to the

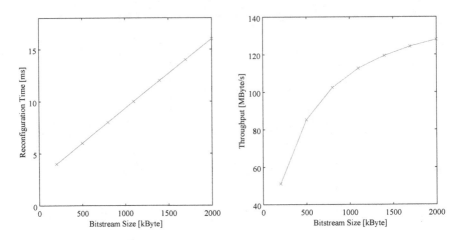

Fig. 3. Reconfiguration times and throughput for different bitstream sizes.

PCAP using DMA. A DevC driver has been developed for Genode OS. It provides address and size of the bitstream to the DevC component, enables the PCAP port, and handles the PCAP interrupt which indicates the completion of a bitstream transfer.

Important performance metrics of the DevC driver are reconfiguration times, which are measured for various bitstream sizes ranging from 100 kByte to 2 MByte. As depicted in Fig. 3, the reconfiguration time scales accurately with the bitstream size. The slope of reconfiguration time to bitstream size is limited by DDR memory and the PCAP bandwidth. The initialization time of the DevC component for each reconfiguration process is independent of bitstream size and causes the throughput to drop for small bitstreams copied to the PL. The throughput saturates at about 130 MByte/s for large bitstreams, which is below the PCAP bandwidth. Still, when compared to a Linux-based reference design provided by Xilinx [14] using the same FPGA device and identical PCAP clock, the reconfiguration speed achieved with the new Genode OS DevC driver is about twice as fast for a bitstream of a medium size of 734 kByte.

5.3 Hardware Scheduler

The *hardware_scheduler* knows which hardware task can be placed in which reconfigurable region. Once it receives an incoming request for a hardware task, it checks if the task is already configured in any reconfigurable region and suspended. If true, it returns access to the corresponding region to the requesting software component. If the task is not configured in any region yet, it tries to place it in a free region. For Genode OS, such a *hardware_scheduler* has been developed. Up to now, it serves incoming requests in FCFS order. In future it is planned to implement an intelligent scheduling strategy and algorithm. Depending on well predictable reconfiguration times, execution times, and deadlines,

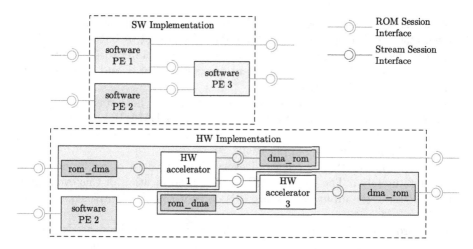

Fig. 4. SW component instantiation graphs for a processing chain fully implemented in SW and HW accelerated.

the *hardware_scheduler* can select a requested hardware task which fits best for the next reconfiguration.

The reconfiguration time of a task can be accurately predicted as it is a function of bitstream size. No other dependencies such as interfering memory access have been observed. Hence, the reconfiguration time can be upper bounded when considered in a real-time application. However, a task might get blocked once its region is occupied. In order to meet given real-time requirements, the scheduler is responsible for guaranteeing an upper bound for blocking times. The currently implemented FCFS scheduler does not satisfy this requirement and further work needs to be done on this topic.

5.4   Hardware Acceleration

The top part of Fig. 4 depicts the software component instantiation graph of a processing chain with three Processing Elements (PEs) implemented in software. Such a processing chain could be part of an image processing application. Each PE may require $1..n$ data inputs and generate $1..m$ data outputs. Multiple tasks can be connected in parallel or serially. In Genode OS, a software component can access its source data by reading from one ore more read-only dataspace(s) or ROM session(s). Respectively, the software component writes the already processed destination data to one or more RAM dataspace(s), which can be accessed by the following component as a ROM session again.

Now some computation intensive PEs are identified and should be accelerated in hardware. In the example given, PE 1 and PE 3 can be accelerated and the resulting software component instantiation graph is given in the bottom part of Fig. 4. Hardware tasks receive their source data from a network on chip and also transmit their results over the same communication medium. Therefore each input dataspace needs to be converted into a stream before passing it to the hardware task. This is handled by the *rom_dma* component. It initializes a DMA engine that moves the input data from DDR memory to a network on chip, e.g. the AXI stream. The *dma_rom* component works analogously and copies stream data to a dataspace in DDR memory.

The *rom_dma* and *dma_rom* software components have been developed together with Genode OS drivers for the Xilinx AXI DMA IP-core [15]. Also, its variants *rom_vdma* and *vdma_rom* using the Xilinx AXI Video DMA IP-Core [16] are available for imaging applications.

The execution of PEs is triggered every time the data of an input ROM session gets updated. The software PE receives a notification of this event and starts processing the input data. Once it is done, it signals a notification to the proceeding PE.

For hardware accelerated designs, this forward signaling needs to be extended, because hardware modules need to be reconfigured and initialized before starting execution. The following signaling policy, as depicted in Fig. 5, is implemented:

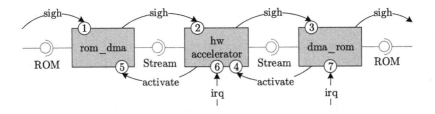

Fig. 5. Signaling policy.

1. The first component in line (here *rom_dma*) receives a notification that its input ROM has been updated. It forwards the notification to the next component in line.
2. All intermediate components in line (here *hw_accelerator*) forward the notification.
3. The last component in line (here *dma_rom*) initializes itself and signals *activate* to the preceding component. By doing this, it informs the preceding component that it is ready to stream data.
4. All intermediate components in line initialize themselves, which includes reconfiguration of hardware modules, and forward the *activate* notification. They are now ready to process data.
5. The *rom_dma* component initializes itself and starts streaming data by executing a DMA transaction.
6. On a hardware interrupt indicating the end of data processing, all hardware accelerators release their reconfigurable region.
7. On the same hardware interrupt, the next component is notified that newly processed data is available.

6   Exemplary Use Case and Evaluation

In order to verify the proper functionality of the new hardware acceleration framework for Genode OS and to produce realistic benchmark results, we set up the following exemplary use case. A stereo-vision system offers two operation modes in order to satisfy the requirements of different applications such as object recognition. Firstly, a high frame rate mode can be selected that is capable of providing images with a frame rate of up to 60 fps. Secondly, the high-quality mode runs additionally a rectification algorithm on each image. However, in this mode only a frame rate of 30 fps can be achieved. In both operation modes, a debayering algorithm converts the camera sensor data to RGB format. Both the debayering- and the rectification algorithm have been implemented as IP-cores for hardware acceleration.

Two reconfigurable regions are available for hosting hardware acceleration modules. The high frame rate requires a debayering IP-core to be placed in each region, so that sensor data from the left- and right camera eye may be processed in parallel. This operation mode emphasizes the advantage of hardware acceleration, as two debayering tasks can be executed in parallel, while an execution in software would force the tasks to be scheduled one after the other. The high-quality mode configures one debayering and one rectification IP-core; sensor data from the left- and right camera eye are processed sequentially in each hardware component. Figure 6 depicts the hardware task graph for both operation modes.

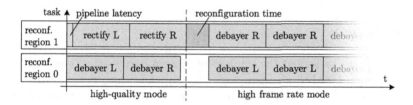

Fig. 6. Hardware task graph for high-quality and high frame rate operation modes.

For comparison, both algorithms are executed in software using the OpenCV implementation and run on one ARM Cortex-A9 core of the Zynq-7000 clocked with 667 MHz. Execution times for the tasks accelerated in hardware are measured for a 100 MHz clocking of the hardware modules in the FPGA fabric. Table 1 shows the results for the software- and hardware implementation of both algorithms executed stand-alone and serially one after the other. As the debayering- and rectification algorithms have no input-dependent branches, the measured execution times are very deterministic with a scatter of less than 0.2 ms. All tests process images with a resolution of 1280 × 960 pixels.

The hardware acceleration of the debayering algorithm yields a speedup factor of about 2; the more complex rectification algorithm of about 14. When executed one after the other, the performance gain is increased even more.

Table 1. Execution times

Task	SW impl.	HW impl.	Bitstream size	Reconf. time
Debayer	28 ms	14 ms	521 kByte	6 ms
Rectify	212 ms	15 ms	1992 kByte	16 ms
Debayer + rectify	241 ms	15 ms	2513 kByte	22 ms

In software, both algorithms are executed sequentially, hence the execution times of debayering and rectification add up. In hardware, a stream of pixels is processed in a pipelined manner and therefore the overall execution time does not increase compared to a stand-alone execution of the debayering- or rectification algorithm.

The cost for switching the operation mode correlates to the reconfiguration time of one debayering or rectification module. As the debayering module has a quite small footprint in the FPGA fabric and therefore fits into a reconfigurable region with smaller bitstream size, its reconfiguration time is shorter. In this presented use case, exchanging a hardware module requires a reconfiguration time on a scale of its hardware execution time. To be still efficient, the number of reconfigurations needs to be minimized by a smart scheduling algorithm. The given use case drops one image when switching between one operation mode and the other, however only a few occurrences of these operation mode change are expected.

7 Conclusion

In this paper, we presented the implementation of hardware acceleration using DPR in Genode OS. For an exemplary imaging algorithm, the performance of the new framework has been evaluated. It has been showed, that the hardware acceleration yields high speedup factors while reconfiguration times are kept low. The new availability of DPR for Genode OS allows this feature to be used in safety-critical applications with strict requirements for real-time and isolation. Computation intensive algorithms implemented in Genode OS, such as in the Controlling Concurrent Change project, can now easily be accelerated in hardware.

So far, the functionality of the DPR feature in Genode OS has been verified using simple application examples. In future, we will add an intelligent hardware task scheduling for arbitrary complex applications and further performance increase.

Acknowledgment. This work is part of the DFG Research Group FOR 1800 "Controlling Concurrent Change". Funding for the Institute of Computer and Network Engineering (IDA) was provided under grant number MI 1172/3-1.

References

1. Lomuscio, A., Cardarilli, G.C., Nannarelli, A., Re, M.: A hardware framework for on-chip FPGA acceleration. In: 2016 International Symposium on Integrated Circuits (ISIC), pp. 1–4, December 2016
2. Genode Labs: Genode OS framework. http://genode.org/. Accessed 12 October 2017
3. TUBS.digital: Controlling concurrent change. http://ccc-project.org/. Accessed 26 October 2017
4. Vipin, K., Fahmy, S.A.: A high speed open source controller for FPGA partial reconfiguration. In: 2012 International Conference on Field-Programmable Technology, pp. 61–66, December 2012
5. Xia, T., Prévotet, J.C., Nouvel, F.: Microkernel dedicated for dynamic partial reconfiguration on ARM-FPGA platform. ACM SIGBED Rev. **11**(4), 31–36 (2015)
6. Xia, T., Prévotet, J.C., Nouvel, F.: Mini-nova: a lightweight ARM-based virtualization microkernel supporting dynamic partial reconfiguration. In: 2015 IEEE International Parallel and Distributed Processing Symposium Workshops, pp. 71–80, May 2015
7. Claus, C., Stechele, W., Herkersdorf, A.: Autovision - a run-time reconfigurable MPSoC architecture for future driver assistance systems. IT Inf. Technol. **49**, 181–187 (2007)
8. Claus, C., Zhang, B., Stechele, W., Braun, L., Hubner, M., Becker, J.: A multi-platform controller allowing for maximum dynamic partial reconfiguration throughput. In: 2008 International Conference on Field Programmable Logic and Applications, pp. 535–538, September 2008
9. Hübner, M., Göhringer, D., Noguera, J., Becker, J.: Fast dynamic and partial reconfiguration data path with low hardware overhead on Xilinx FPGAs. In: IEEE International Symposium on Parallel Distributed Processing, Workshops and Ph.D. Forum (IPDPSW), pp. 1–8, April 2010
10. Kadi, M.A., Rudolph, P., Göhringer, D., Hübner, M.: Dynamic and partial reconfiguration of Zynq 7000 under Linux. In: International Conference on Reconfigurable Computing and FPGAs (ReConFig), pp. 1–5, December 2013
11. Dörflinger, A., Fiethe, B., Michalik, H., Fekete, S.P., Keldenich, P., Scheffer, C.: Resource-efficient dynamic partial reconfiguration on FPGAs for space instruments. In: 2017 NASA/ESA Conference on Adaptive Hardware and Systems (AHS), pp. 24–31, July 2017
12. Xilinx Inc.: Partial reconfiguration of a hardware accelerator on Zynq-7000 All programmable SoC devices, XAPP1159. v1.0 edn (2013)
13. Xilinx Inc.: Zynq-7000 all programmable SoC TRM, UG585. v1.11 edn (2016)
14. Kohn, C.: Partial reconfiguration of a hardware accelerator with Vivado design suite for Zynq-7000 AP SoC processor. Xilinx Inc. v1.1 edn (2015)
15. Xilinx Inc.: AXI DMA LogiCORE IP Product Guide, PG021. v7.1 edn (2017)
16. Xilinx Inc.: AXI Video Direct Memory Access LogiCORE IP Product Guide, PG020. v6.2 edn (2016)

Large Scale Computing

Do Iterative Solvers Benefit from Approximate Computing? An Evaluation Study Considering Orthogonal Approximation Methods

Michael Bromberger[1]([✉]), Markus Hoffmann[1], and Robin Rehrmann[2]

[1] Computer Architecture and Parallel Processing,
Karlsruhe Institute of Technology, Karlsruhe, Germany
`bromberger@kit.edu`
[2] Database Technology Group, Technische Universität Dresden,
Dresden, Germany

Abstract. Employing algorithms of scientific computing often comes in hand with finding a trade-off between accuracy and performance. Novel parallel hardware and algorithms only slightly improve these issues due to the increasing size of the problems. While high accuracy is inevitable for most problems, there are parts in scientific computing that allow us to introduce approximation. Therefore, in this paper we give answers to the following questions: (1) Can we exploit different approximate computing strategies in scientific computing? (2) Is there a strategy to combine approaches? To answer these questions, we apply different approximation strategies to a widely used iterative solver for linear systems of equations. We show the advantages and the limits of each strategy and a way to configure a combination of strategies according to a given relative error. Combining orthogonal strategies as an overall concept gives us significant opportunities to increase the performance.

1 Introduction

Scientific computing poses a difficult challenge for people from different domains, especially in order to find a suitable trade-off between desired solution quality and computational effort. Even the high parallel capabilities of todays hardware and novel parallel algorithms do not lead to a significant reduction of these challenges because of the increasing dimensions of current problems. Hence, we rely on new ways to find suitable methods to overcome the aforementioned issues.

In recent years, the idea of an approximate computing (AC) paradigm has been gaining high attention in computer science [11]. A consideration of current applications, such as Recognition, Mining, and Synthesis (RMS) concludes that these applications have an inherent resilience against computational errors [8]. Trading off internal or external accuracy of an application allows the hardware, the programmer, or the user to improve other design goals like performance or energy consumption [3]. There already exists a wide variety of AC approaches

M. Berekovic et al. (Eds.): ARCS 2018, LNCS 10793, pp. 297–310, 2018.
https://doi.org/10.1007/978-3-319-77610-1_22

on different layers of the compute stack [11, 21]. Additionally, there is quite some effort to control the degree of approximation according to given constraints [3].

In contrast, high accuracy is often inevitable for scientific computing. Hence, at first glance, it seems counterproductive to marry AC with scientific computing. However, there is already some successful work that introduces AC into scientific computing [2, 17–19, 22, 23]. They mostly analyze the influence of data type precision on the accuracy. Asynchronous parallelization methods, which can be compared with relaxed synchronization, are well-known in numerics and show a high efficiency on GPUs [1]. But these works lack a schematic evaluation of AC on different parts inside a scientific application. Therefore, this paper is a first step to apply a holistic evaluation of AC on a widely used algorithm in scientific computing. This gives us the knowledge, where it is possible to apply AC and how we can combine orthogonal methods.

1.1 Current Status

AC approaches can be grouped according to the compute stack. Here, we order the approaches in the following:

- *Task Layer* approaches comprise skipping tasks, relaxing synchronization points [13], or exploiting approximate parallel patterns [15]. There exist runtime approaches that select a task from different approximate versions [3].
- *Algorithmic Layer* methods use the concept of loop perforation [21] or loop tiling [15]. Others rely on an automatic transformation of the code into a neural network. Sampling the input data offers a further way. Additionally, there are automatic ways to reason about the required data type.
- *Architecture Layer* approaches introduce AC into the hardware architecture. This includes neural processing units, approximated memory components [10], or entire designs that integrated dynamic accuracy and voltage scaling. Programmers can use such components through an extended ISA.
- *Hardware Layer* approaches [11] often deal with approximating processing units. This also includes providing different hardware-supported data types [6], i.e. exploit precision scaling.

Previous work shows that considering various levels and introducing different AC methods result in an enormous benefit [12]. However, such an orthogonal view is missing for scientific applications.

1.2 Methodology of the Evaluation

As previous work shows that AC can be beneficial for scientific computation, we analyze the usage of orthogonal AC methods for the Jacobi method. Firstly, we assemble representative input data for our evaluation (see Sect. 2). Then, we select suitable and promising AC approaches for our evaluation in Sect. 3. To note, we analyze the applicability and combination of orthogonal AC approaches, but we do not provide a run-time approach that controls the quality. However, there already exist such approaches that can be used to control a combination of AC methods [11]. Our systematic evaluation compares the different approaches regarding their execution times and the relative error as described in Sect. 4. This evaluation aims to answer the following questions: How big is the influence of well-known AC methods on the accuracy of a scientific algorithm? Is it possible to combine AC methods to improve other design parameters while keeping an acceptable accuracy?

1.3 Main Findings

Based on the outcome of our experiments, the following conclusions can be drawn:

- **Conclusion 1:** There exist further AC approaches besides precision scaling which are useful for scientific computing. Loop tiling and loop truncation enable a programmer to trade-off accuracy for performance for the synchronous and parallelized Jacobi algorithm. Additionally, an approximation parameter that specifies the degree of relaxed synchronization poses an opportunity to find an optimal configuration point for accuracy and performance.
- **Conclusion 2:** Combining orthogonal AC methods leads to configuration points that cannot not be reached by a single method. Hence, this combination outperforms single methods regarding accuracy and performance. We show that coupling up to five AC methods is possible for the Jacobi method.
- **Conclusion 3:** Using a simple greedy-based algorithm, we can find suitable parameter values for the orthogonal AC methods. A user can state a desired relative error that is tolerable for the solution of the Jacobi method. Then, the algorithm finds the best possible performance for that given error by tuning the AC parameter.

2 Mathematical Background and Data Generation

A common task within scientific computing is numerically solving partial differential equations (PDEs). This is typically done by transforming the basic problem into a large scaled system of (linear) equations [9]. The finite element method, for example, transfers a weak formulation of the PDE directly into a system of linear equations:

$$Ax = b, \tag{1}$$

where x_i are the coefficients of a linear combination of basis functions for an appropriate function space, which approximate the solution of the PDE. Depending on the set of basis functions, the original problem, and the given approximation of the observed area, A has different characteristics including high dimensionality. Wisely selecting the basis functions leads to a sparse A. Hence, Krylow subspace methods are ideal candidates for solving the problem (1) [14]. Lowering the conditional number of A results in a higher convergence for those methods. This is accomplished by multiplying a suitable matrix B with A [20]. One method to find a suitable B, the so-called preconditioning matrix, is a factorization of A based on its characteristics. A widely usable factorization is the incomplete LU-factorization [5]:

$$A \approx LU = B^{-1}, \tag{2}$$

where L and U are lower and upper triangle matrices, respectively. As for performance reasons B is embedded within the Krylow subspace method by multiplying it with a basis vector v_m of the actual Krylow subspace V_m, new systems of equations have to be computed:

$$Bv_m = y \quad \Leftrightarrow \quad LUy = v_m \quad \Leftrightarrow \quad L\tilde{y} = v_m, \quad Uy = \tilde{y}. \tag{3}$$

Because L and U are sparse but triangle matrices, typically solvers based on splitting methods like the Jacobi method are used to solve the inner systems [5].

The main challenge now is to solve these inner systems (3) very efficiently to keep the performance benefit due to fewer iterations of the Krylow subspace method. An important fact to note is that the accuracy of the solution of the inner systems only affects the convergence rate, hence it does not affect the solution of the outer method. To note, there are some important mathematical properties for solvers and preconditioning methods. First of all, the preconditioning operator B has to be invariable over the whole iteration process for most Krylow subspace methods [14]. Manipulating the updating process of the inner solver may change the operator from one iteration to another. However, methods such as FGMRES allow us to adapt the preconditioners per iteration [14].

The second problem is the convergence of the inner solver. Having a spectral radius ρ of L and U smaller than unity results in a secured convergence [4]. Although this requirement on ρ might not be fulfilled for all matrices assembled from discretization of PDEs and incomplete factorization, there are large and relevant classes of problems with resulting triangular matrices that can be solved by matrix splitting based solving methods.

Now, we take a look at the generation of the test data. The basic problem that we use is an inhomogeneous Poisson's problem with homogeneous boundary conditions on the unit square. The discretization is done with a five-point-stencil and the finite difference method. The resulting system of equations is diagonally dominant, irreducible, and can be easily scaled to any useful dimension. A is also sparse, symmetric, and positive definite. We use the Jacobi method as inner solver. The right side v_m of (3) is a set of vectors that are created as residuals within a performed CG method. To avoid misunderstandings, we would like to emphasize that we are only investigating the influence of AC on the Jacobi method. Therefore, we are only solving the resulting inner systems for evaluation purposes, but we are not trying to precondition the CG method. As mentioned before, the CG method needs an invariable preconditioning operator which is violated by our methods. Considering the influence on the preconditioning quality, for instance using FGMRES is left for future work.

3   Approximation Computing Methods

The selection of the considered approximation methods is inspired by two things. Firstly, we want to evaluate orthogonal methods which can be applied concurrently. Secondly, we decide to use approaches that seem promising and have a high standing in the approximate computing domain. Moreover, each of them have shown great success on different applications. Our selection of methods is shown in Table 1. Each of these methods offers different parameters that influence the trade-off between different design goals like accuracy and performance. We describe the meaning of each parameter in this section. Moreover, we state the useful approximation parameters.

Table 1. Overview about the considered approximation methods.

Level	Approaches	Description	Evaluation
Thread	Relaxed synchronisation	Section 3.1	Section 4.4
Data	Loop perforation, Loop tiling, and Loop skipping	Section 3.2	Section 4.3
Data type	Precision scaling and approximate memory	Section 3.3	Section 4.2
Input approximation	Input data approximation	Section 3.4	Section 4.5

3.1   Relaxed Synchronization

Relaxed synchronization is a way to reduce the synchronization overhead introduced for a parallel execution [13]. It means that some synchronization points are intentionally violated to improve performance. However, relaxed synchronization can hamper the accuracy of the result. Hence, programmers have to take care where relaxed synchronization is viable. Barriers or synchronizations that assure to read the most recent data are good points to introduce relaxation.

For our evaluation, we use an algorithmic-specific relaxation, which are often called asynchronous methods in numerics. The used relaxation is based on a work of Anzt et al. [1]. Normally, a given starting vector is updated within each step of the Jacobi method which can be done in parallel but needs synchronization at the end of the iteration. The idea behind the relaxation is to subdivide entries of the vector in groups of a given size. Only all members of the same group are synchronized at the end of the iteration step but synchronizations between two different groups are relaxed. Anzt showed that this relaxation may lead to great speedups on GPUs. Additionally, convergence is proven for the asynchronous Jacobi method [7]. The number of groups present the approximation parameter.

3.2   Sampling

Here, we present approaches that influence the loop behavior of an algorithm. On one side, there are approaches on this level that can be considered as sampling approaches. They decide which items of the input data are used for the

```
for i ← 0 to n − 1,
  i+=steps do
  | result = do_work();
end
```

(a) Loop perforation.

```
for i ← 0 to
  (n − steps), i++ do
  | result = do_work();
end
```

(b) Loop truncation.

```
for i ← 0 to n − 1, i+=steps do
    result[i] = do_work(input[i]);
    for j ← 1 to steps − 1, j++ do
    | result[i+j] = result[i];
    end
end
```

(c) Loop tiling.

Fig. 1. Used approximation methods on the data level (sampling approaches).

computation. On the other side, we count approaches to this level that earlier stops the execution of an iterative algorithm. Figure 1 shows the schematic of these approaches.

Loop perforation (see Fig. 1a) is a well-known technique of AC on the software level [21]. The idea is to reduce the execution time of a loop by skipping iterations in between. Depending on the actual loop this essentially results in sampling the input or output. In addition, it is sometimes worth to adapt the final result, for instance using scaling for a summation of an array. Let us assume, that we only use half of the values of the sum, then multiplying the result with two can be useful. The perforation rate is the approximation parameter.

Loop truncation (see Fig. 1b) is a method that drops the last iterations of a loop. Here, the approximation parameter specifies the number of dropped iterations. Such an approach is especially useful for iterative methods. Iterative methods are commonly used in numerical mathematics. They perform a computation in such a way that they calculate a sequence of approximate solutions that ideally converge to the exact solution.

Loop tiling (see Fig. 1c) assumes that near located elements of an input have similar values [15]. Hence, it only calculates some iterations of the loop and assigns nearby outputs to the already calculated value. This actually forms a tile structure of the output. The tile size presents the approximation parameter.

3.3   On the Data Type Level

Typically, numerical algorithms rely on floating-point operations performed on the executing hardware. Many approaches in AC present designs that deal with arithmetic units, which also includes floating-point units. These approaches can be roughly grouped into two general approaches.

One deals with the precision of the operations itself [11]. This is achieved by precision scaling or by redesigning a processing unit in an approximate way. This leads to more efficient hardware designs regarding power consumption, latency, or area. The other approaches deal with approximate memory which may affect the accuracy of involved operands [10]. In general, approximate memories can lead to indeterministic stored data.

To include those approaches in our evaluation, we adapt floating-point operations within the algorithm. The first group is simulated by truncating bits of the significand (called `precision scaling`). The approximation parameter states the number of truncated bits. For the second, we introduce random bits for those less significant bits. However, this means that each memory access is affected. Therefore, we perform additional experiments, where we introduce errors according to different realistic error rates of an approximate memory [10].

3.4 Input Data Approximation

We consider a method that approximates the input data. In our test case, this can be done by taking influence to the ILU factorization as this specifies the resulting system of equations, hence the input data of the Jacobi method.

Using a sparsity pattern it is possible to specify entries of L or U that are set to zero. Therefore, the operations within the Jacobi method are reduced. The challenge is to decide which entry has the least impact on the accuracy of the Jacobi method as this is most likely the best entry to remove next.

Taking a look at the updating process of the Jacobi method it is obvious that for us the best element of L or U to remove is either the one matching to the entry of y from (3) closest to zero or the one which is closest to zero itself, both with the restriction not to remove the diagonals of the matrices. As y is unknown while computing the ILU factorization, the latter method is the one of choice. To keep the original structure of the matrices as long as possible, we additionally decide to give removing priority to the leftmost (rightmost) element of a row. Hence, it results in removing these elements first. We exploit the number of removed entries as the approximation parameter.

4 Experiments

We apply the described methods above to an iterative and parallel Jacobi solver individually. Additionally, we consider a combination of several AC methods. We run all the experiments on a AMD Opteron 6128 processor providing 64 GB of main memory. A synchronous and parallel version of the Jacobi solver executed using 32 threads is our base line. We parallelize over matrix rows. The parallel algorithm requires 130.1 ms for a matrix dimension of 1024^2 and 631.2 ms for a dimension of 2048^2. If not otherwise mentioned, we set the iteration count to 10. Stopping the iterative method after 10 iterations results in a relative error of roughly 10^{-4} compared to the exact solution independent from the matrix dimension d.

4.1   Evaluation Metrics

For the accuracy, we calculate the relative error

$$E_{rel} = \frac{||\boldsymbol{x} - \tilde{\boldsymbol{x}}||_2}{||\boldsymbol{x}||_2},$$

where $\boldsymbol{x}$ is the solution vector of the base line and $\tilde{\boldsymbol{x}}$ the solution of the approximate version. Moreover, we measure the performance stated as execution time if possible. In other cases, we include realistic numbers from the literature.

4.2   Influence of Approximate Computing on the Data Type Level

In this section, we investigate how the internal data type precision impacts the accuracy of the solution vector. Since we cannot perform these experiments on current hardware, we use an emulation scheme to evaluate the influence of precision. The reason is that current hardware does not provide other floating-point data types apart from float or double in general. We consider two well-known AC methods: precision scaling and approximate memory. Figure 2a shows the impact of these methods on the relative error. We vary the number of influenced precision bits of the significands from 53 to 0. We can see that for the given linear system, the most of the least significant bits of the significand play a minor role for the accuracy. Moreover, the results are more or less independent from the matrix dimension d and the way how we influence the data type precision. 13 bits are enough to have almost no additional error compared to the base line. Having less than roughly 8 correct bits leads to an exponential increase in the relative error. However, according to literature it is not very likely that all memory reads are affected by approximation. It actually depends on how this approximation method is implemented. A common way is to increase the refresh cycle time of a DDR memory bank, which can significantly save energy. Depending on this

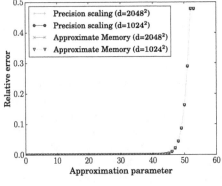

Error rate	Relative error	
	$d = 1024^2$	$d = 2048^2$
1.3×10^{-4}	0.00234583	0.0026825
2.0×10^{-5}	0.00221096	0.0010068
3.8×10^{-6}	0	0
2.6×10^{-7}	0	0

(a) Precision scaling.   (b) Approximate Memory.

Fig. 2. Influence of the data type precision on the accuracy.

increase the error rate of getting wrong results from the memory also raises. For some realistic values, we consider how this error rate impacts the accuracy of the Jacobi solver, see Fig. 2b. Even if we have relatively high error rates, for instance 1.3×10^{-4}, the influence on the accuracy is not drastic. Such an approximate memory approach decreases the power required for refresh up to 25% having an error rate of 1.3×10^{-4} [10]. Getting the actual performance or energy gain is very difficult, since it would require to build such a hardware and to evaluate the wanted metrics. Here, we show the potential of the reduction in precision bits.

4.3 Analysis of Approximate Computing Loop Strategies

A common method in AC is to adapt the execution of iterations for a loop. This essentially leads to skipping iterations or a sampling scheme on the input data. Figure 3 shows the impact of loop perforation and loop tiling for different approximation parameters (called `steps` in Fig. 1). The method `loop perforation` is not applicable at all for the considered algorithm, since the error exponentially increases with the approximation parameter. In contrast, `loop tiling` works quite well. Especially, small values for the approximation parameter still lead to small errors. We can see an influence of the dimension on the accuracy for `loop tiling`. A smaller dimension shows a higher error behavior.

Fortunately, the execution time significantly decreases for small parameter values. Larger values have no further considerable benefit regarding the execution time. The rationale behind is that at a certain point the synchronization overhead of the parallelization and other parts of the algorithm, where the AC methods have no effect, have the main impact on the execution time.

`loop truncation` is a natural way to approximate iterative methods. It just stops the iterative method before it converges. Figure 4 shows the accuracy and

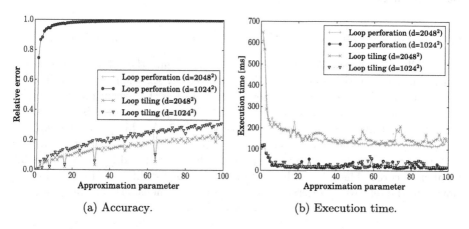

(a) Accuracy.   (b) Execution time.

Fig. 3. Influence of loop perforation and loop tiling (Measurements are overlapping for loop perforation).

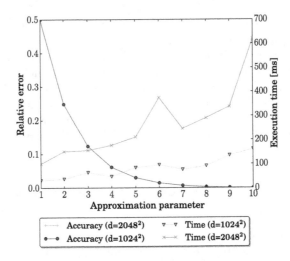

Fig. 4. Influence of loop truncation regarding accuracy and performance (Measurements for accuracy are overlapping).

execution time for different stop points. A stop point specifies the number of allowed iterations. Again the relative error is almost independent from the matrix dimension. The error exponentially decreases with the iterations at the beginning and then requires some time to converge. The execution time for large dimensions scales roughly linearly with the number of iterations. For small dimensions, the synchronization overhead is quite high.

To sum up, `loop perforation` is not a useful approach for the Jacobi method. Regarding the error and performance, `loop truncation` provides the best solution in general. However, `loop tiling` can be a useful method for larger allowed relative errors.

4.4 Accuracy Degradation Caused by Relaxed Synchronization

In the following experiment (see Fig. 5a), we investigate the influence of relaxed synchronization on the accuracy of the result vector. A higher number of blocks states that more synchronizations are relaxed during the execution. The relaxation method introduces a small error until the number of blocks is larger than the number of available cores, in our case $2^5 = 32$. At this point, we can see a high increase of the relative error. In contrast, the optimal point regarding performance is reached when the number of blocks is roughly eight times the number of cores. The curves show similar behavior for different matrix dimensions, but the relative error is smaller for the larger dimensions. The performance gain is more significant for larger matrix dimensions.

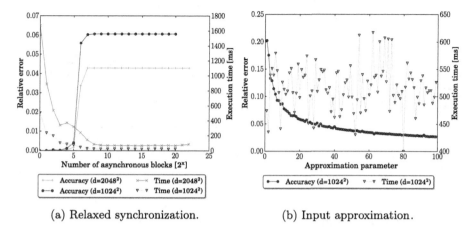

(a) Relaxed synchronization.   (b) Input approximation.

Fig. 5. Consideration of relaxed synchronization and input approximation on the Jacobi method (We are aware of the strange time measurements but unfortunately it is unclear where the oscillation comes from. However, they are reproduceable).

4.5   Input Approximation

Instead of using approximation in the algorithm itself, one can adapt the input data. Therefore, we remove certain inputs according to a method described in Sect. 3.4. The approximation parameter presents an offset which specifies the rows of the input matrix that will be affected. For instance, 20 means that we influence each 20th row. In general, affecting fewer rows leads to a reduction of the error. Until a parameter value of 20, this reduction is exponential (see Fig. 5b). Afterwards, the error decreases slowly.

However, we cannot see that removing certain inputs have a clear influence on the execution time. There are strong variations in the execution time which means that they are independent from the approximation parameter. According to these results, we draw the conclusion that input approximation is not useful for our test case.

4.6   Putting Everything Together

Now, we are able to combine multiple and orthogonal AC methods. According to the results so far, we include `loop truncation`, `loop tiling`, relaxed synchronization and precision scaling. All of them have an approximation parameter that can be tuned. We set these approximation parameter values according to a given relative error, which represents our constraint. To find a good configuration of parameter values that satisfies these constraints, we exploit a known greedy algorithm [16] based on steepest ascent hill climbing. For the first test, we exclude precision scaling, since we cannot make performance measurements for this method. Then, the task of the greedy algorithm is to find the parameter values which offers the best performance under the given error constraint. We adapt

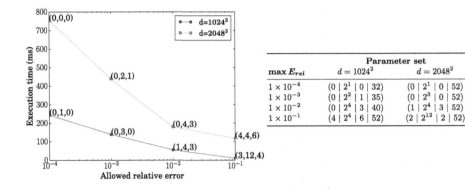

(a) Three approximation methods.   (b) Four approximation methods.

Fig. 6. Considering multiple orthogonal approximation methods for the Jacobi method. Parameter set $(TI|RS|TR|PS)$ TI: loop tiling, RS: relaxed synchronization, TR: loop truncation, PS: precision scaling

approximation parameters in a way that higher values present a more aggressive approximation level. The results are shown for different error constraints in Fig. 6a. As we can see, the configuration algorithm tunes the parameter of all three orthogonal methods. Hence, the combination of methods is beneficial to reach good performance points for different error constraints. Allowing a relative error of 1%, we get a performance improvement of roughly 300% compared to the 32 threaded basis version. Moreover, a 10% allowed error leads to almost a speed-up of 6.

For the found configuration points, we further consider the potential of precision scaling, see Fig. 6b. All configurations enable us to further introduce AC on the data type level. This allows a hardware designer to approximate hardware arithmetic units for the algorithm under test. Additionally, another possibility is to include approximate DRAM according to Sect. 4.2 as fifth parameter.

4.7   Discussion

Taking a look on our results, we see that not only a single AC strategy can be useful in terms of scientific computing, but also a combination of strategies, especially in the context of preconditioning, where high accuracy is unnecessary in most cases. Moreover, it is possible to estimate tolerable computing errors. Hence, we are sure, that it is possible to reduce computation times for the inner solver dramatically by reducing accuracy to a reasonable degree. Of course, we are aware that accompanying quality loss of the preconditioning method can result in lower convergence rates for the Krylow subspace method. But the results of the combined AC strategies show that remarkable speed-ups can be gained with careful accuracy reductions.

Based on our results we want to use a flexible Krylow subspace method, like FGMRES, in combination with a set of AC strategies for the preconditioning method adjusted with a tunable accuracy parameter. Although we have not measured the quality of the preconditioning method yet, we think that this setting will lead to great speed-ups for the whole preconditioned solver. Additionally, further AC strategies, like reformulating the ILU solver into an iterative method and skipping iterations, which does not influence the speed of the Jacobi method but the quality of the preconditioning method, can be added easily.

5   Conclusion and Future Directions

In this paper, we considered orthogonal approximate computing (AC) methods and how they influence the accuracy and performance trade-off of a scientific computing algorithm. All methods were experimentally investigated for the Jacobi method performing on realistic data. Hence, we applied the first extensive, holistic, and schematic evaluation of AC on a scientific algorithm. While single methods already can be seen as useful, a combination of them results in a much higher gain. For instance, allowing 1% relative error we achieve an acceleration of 3 compared to the parallel version of Jacobi (32 threads).

For future work it is mandatory to extend the test setting to the complete Krylow subspace method to measure the effects of AC methods on the quality of the preconditioning. With this enlarged setting, the usefulness of the presented methods can be considered in a broader spectrum.

References

1. Anzt, H., Chow, E., Dongarra, J.: Iterative sparse triangular solves for preconditioning. In: Träff, J.L., Hunold, S., Versaci, F. (eds.) Euro-Par 2015. LNCS, vol. 9233, pp. 650–661. Springer, Heidelberg (2015). https://doi.org/10.1007/978-3-662-48096-0_50
2. Anzt, H., Dongarra, J., Quintana-Ortí, E.S.: Adaptive precision solvers for sparse linear systems. In: Proceedings of the 3rd International Workshop on Energy Efficient Supercomputing, p. 2. ACM (2015)
3. Baek, W., Chilimbi, T.: Green: a framework for supporting energy-conscious programming using controlled approximation. In: ACM SIGPLAN Conference on Programming Language Design and Implementation (2010)
4. Bagnara, R.: A unified proof for the convergence of Jacobi and Gauss Seidel methods. SIAM Rev. **37**, 93–97 (1995)
5. Benzi, M.: Preconditioning techniques for large linear systems: a survey. J. Comput. Phys. **182**, 418–477 (2002)
6. Bromberger, M., Heuveline, V., Karl, W.: Reducing energy consumption of data transfers using runtime data type conversion. In: Hannig, F., Cardoso, J.M.P., Pionteck, T., Fey, D., Schröder-Preikschat, W., Teich, J. (eds.) ARCS 2016. LNCS, vol. 9637, pp. 239–250. Springer, Cham (2016). https://doi.org/10.1007/978-3-319-30695-7_18
7. Chazan, D., Miranker, W.: Chaotic relaxation. Linear Algebra Appl. **2**, 199–222 (1969)

8. Chippa, V., Chakradhar, S., Roy, K., Raghunathan, A.: Analysis and characterization of inherent application resilience for approximate computing. In: Proceedings of the 50th Annual Design Automation Conference, DAC 2013, pp. 113:1–113:9. ACM, New York (2013)

9. Larsson, S., Thomee, V.: Partial Differential Equations with Numerical Methods. Springer, Heidelberg (2003). https://doi.org/10.1007/978-3-540-88706-5

10. Liu, S., Pattabiraman, K., Moscibroda, T., Zorn, B.G.: Flikker: saving DRAM refresh-power through critical data partitioning. ACM SIGPLAN Not. **47**(4), 213–224 (2012)

11. Mittal, S.: A survey of techniques for approximate computing. ACM Comput. Surv. (CSUR) **48**, 62:1–62:33 (2016)

12. Raha, A., Venkataramani, S., Raghunathan, V., Raghunathan, A.: Energy-efficient reduce-and-rank using input-adaptive approximations. IEEE Trans. Very Large Scale Integr. (VLSI) Syst. **25**(2), 462–475 (2017)

13. Renganarayana, L., Srinivasan, V., Nair, R., Prener, D.: Programming with relaxed synchronization. In: Proceedings of the 2012 ACM Workshop on Relaxing Synchronization for Multicore and Manycore Scalability, pp. 41–50. ACM (2012)

14. Saad, Y.: Iterative Methods for Sparse Linear Systems. PWS, Boston (1996)

15. Samadi, M., Jamshidi, D.A., Lee, J., Mahlke, S.: Paraprox: pattern-based approximation for data parallel applications. ACM SIGARCH Comput. Archit. News **42**, 35–50 (2014)

16. Samadi, M., Lee, J., Jamshidi, D.A., Hormati, A., Mahlke, S.: SAGE: self-tuning approximation for graphics engines. In: Proceedings of the 46th Annual IEEE/ACM International Symposium on Microarchitecture, pp. 13–24. ACM (2013)

17. Schaffner, M., Gurkaynak, F.K., Smolic, A., Kaeslin, H., Benini, L.: An approximate computing technique for reducing the complexity of a direct-solver for sparse linear systems in real-time video processing. In: 2014 51st ACM/EDAC/IEEE Design Automation Conference (DAC), pp. 1–6. IEEE (2014)

18. Schöll, A., Braun, C., Wunderlich, H.J.: Applying efficient fault tolerance to enable the preconditioned conjugate gradient solver on approximate computing hardware. In: 2016 IEEE International Symposium on Defect and Fault Tolerance in VLSI and Nanotechnology Systems (DFT), pp. 21–26. IEEE (2016)

19. Schöll, A., Braun, C., Wunderlich, H.J.: Energy-efficient and error-resilient iterative solvers for approximate computing. In: Proceedings of the 23rd IEEE International Symposium on On-Line Testing and Robust System Design (IOLTS 2017), pp. 237–239 (2017)

20. Shewchuk, J.R.: An Introduction to the Conjugate Gradient Method Without the Agonizing Pain. School of Computer Science, Carnegie Mellon University, Pittsburgh, August 1994

21. Sidiroglou-Douskos, S., Misailovic, S., Hoffmann, H., Rinard, M.: Managing performance vs. accuracy trade-offs with loop perforation. In: Proceedings of the 19th ACM SIGSOFT Symposium and the 13th European Conference on Foundations of Software Engineering, ESEC/FSE 2011, pp. 124–134. ACM, New York (2011)

22. Zhang, Q., Tian, Y., Wang, T., Yuan, F., Xu, Q.: Approxeigen: an approximate computing technique for large-scale eigen-decomposition. In: Proceedings of the IEEE/ACM International Conference on Computer-Aided Design, pp. 824–830. IEEE Press (2015)

23. Zhang, Q., Yuan, F., Ye, R., Xu, Q.: Approxit: an approximate computing framework for iterative methods. In: Proceedings of the 51st Annual Design Automation Conference, pp. 1–6. ACM (2014)

A Flexible FPGA-Based Inference Architecture for Pruned Deep Neural Networks

Thorbjörn Posewsky[1] and Daniel Ziener[2(✉)]

[1] Ibeo Automotive Systems GmbH, Hamburg, Germany
[2] Friedrich-Alexander University Erlangen-Nürnberg (FAU), Erlangen, Germany
daniel.ziener@fau.de

Abstract. In this paper, we present an architecture for embedded FPGA-based deep neural network inference which is able to handle pruned weight matrices. Pruning of weights and even entire neurons reduces the amount of data and calculations significantly, thus improving enormously the efficiency and performance of the neural network inference in embedded devices. By using an HLS approach, the architecture is easily extendable and highly configurable with a free choice of parameters like the number of MAC units or the used activation function. For large neural networks, our approach competes with at least comparable performance as state-of-the-art x86-based software implementations while only using 10% of the energy.

1 Introduction and Motivation

For more and more people, *Deep Neural Networks* (DNNs) have become a substantial part of their daily life. Applications like image classification [22] or speech recognition [20] are used by millions on their wearables, smartphones, or tablets. This applies not only to mobile computing, it also holds true for related areas like robotics or autonomous vehicles. Yet, these emerging areas have different power requirements and lack processing power in contrast to high-performance computing which is more often associated with deep learning techniques.

In order to achieve state-of-the-art and beyond classification rates in tasks like object recognition, the number of artificial neurons and layers in DNNs has grown to ever new records in the past years. Despite a significantly increased demand for computational power, the size needed to store such networks has similarly increased. For embedded devices, this is particularly challenging since memory is typically a scarce resource and, more importantly, the access to off-chip memories represents the dominating factor when considering the energy consumption [13]. Hence, to lower both DNN inference time and energy-consumption, this work focuses on techniques that reduce the amount of data to be transferred.

The technique investigated in this work, now known as *pruning*, represents a form of DNN compression [13,17]. Pruning reduces the number of synaptic connections to adjacent neurons such that the overall amount of weights is reduced.

© Springer International Publishing AG, part of Springer Nature 2018
M. Berekovic et al. (Eds.): ARCS 2018, LNCS 10793, pp. 311–323, 2018.
https://doi.org/10.1007/978-3-319-77610-1_23

Most importantly, pruning is often able to eliminate a significant portion of these connections without or with just minor accuracy drops for, i.e., classification tasks. Due to the reduced amount of weights, less data needs to be transferred and less calculations are needed in the hardware. Correspondingly, accelerators are able to compute DNNs much faster. Currently, only a very limited number of previous works exist that consider dedicated hardware support for pruned DNNs [11,12].

As previously mentioned, deep learning can generally be used for many embedded computing applications. The inference efficiency of such embedded solutions plays a pivotal role and is highly dependent on the right hardware architecture for the application-specific neural network architecture. To support a wide area of different networks and, therefore, applications, we use an FPGA-based *high level synthesis* (HLS) [15] approach in order to design a very efficient hardware by rapidly exploring different design parameters, like the number of MAC units or different activation functions. In this paper, we show how a flexible streaming architecture for arbitrarily pruned DNNs can be designed as opposed to designs with partially or completely embedded parameters. We focus particularly on an efficient inference of *fully-connected* DNNs since these layers are the most memory-intensive and build the foundation for all of today's most successful network kinds.

The rest of this paper is organized as follows: Sect. 2 gives an overview of related work. The concept and architecture of our accelerator is explained in Sects. 3 and 4, respectively. Section 5 continues with experimental results. Finally, Sect. 6 concludes the work and highlights future research directions.

2   Related Work

Recently, many accelerator designs for *Convolutional Neural Networks* (CNNs) were introduced. CNNs are often found in image and video recognition systems and typically use a series of kernels or convolution matrices prior to the above mentioned fully-connected network architecture [21]. One example for such an accelerator is given in [10]. Since the number of parameters for convolution matrices is typically only a fraction of the weights of fully-connected network layers, the exploitable compute parallelism is usually greater and thus favors hardware accelerators. However, while such a design and many others (e.g., [8]) are very effective for convolutional layers, their internal buffers and routing elements are not optimized for fully-connected or compressed networks.

An FPGA-based DNN inference architecture that specifically addresses fully-connected layers is presented in [19]. Additionally, the approach enables the reuse of previously transferred weight matrices across multiple input samples, which is referred to as batch processing. Both techniques, the one presented in this work and the one in [19], reduce data transfers for the inference of fully-connected DNNs significantly but are conceptually orthogonal.

A third important type of networks is known as *Recurrent Neural Network* (RNN) [21]. RNNs allow the processing of input sequences through cyclical connections in the network architecture. Like fully-connected layers, these networks are typically memory bound and thus make a parallel execution more difficult. Consequently, corresponding designs are less frequent. However, an early approach for a state-of-the-art RNN, called LSTMs, which uses the same FPGA as this work, is shown in [3] and their results are accordingly compared to ours in Sect. 5.

The theoretical foundation for pruning and, thus, our accelerator was introduced by LeCun et al. in [17]. Originally, it was used to improve generalization and speed of learning in shallow network architectures. However, Han et al. [13] recently revived the technique for DNNs and were able to reduce the number of connections by a factor between 9x and 13x. A corresponding ASIC design with large on-chip memories for the remaining parameters after pruning and quantization (without Huffamn encoding) is given in [12]. As discussed later, our accelerator utilizes a similar format, presented in [24], for the resulting sparse matrices (e.g., after pruning) but does not embed parameters for specific DNNs on-chip. Instead, we propose a streaming architecture for arbitrary DNNs. Very recently their approach was further extended to support LSTMs for speech recognition on high-performance FPGAs [11].

3   Concept

A typical neural network contains several layers $j = 1 \ldots L$. A layer j itself consists of s_j neurons. Fully-connected layers in DNNs are characterized by a bipartite graph of neuron connections between two adjacent layers j and $j + 1$ for $1 \leq j \leq L - 1$. For the rest of this work, we will specify the architecture of these networks through the number of neurons s_j in each layer, e.g., $s_0 \times s_1 \times s_2$ for a $L = 3$ layer network. The synaptic strength of a connection is modeled through a scalar value $w_{i,k}^{(j)}$ called $weight$ that represents the connection to the i-th neuron in layer $j + 1$ from the k-th neuron in layer j. A transition from layer j to the next layer $j + 1$ involves a $weight\ matrix\ W^{(j)}$ where $w_{i,k}^{(j)}$ are the components and the outputs $a_k^{(j)}$ of connecting neurons in the layer j. The result of each neuron $a_i^{(j+1)}$ is computed by the following functions:

$$a_i^{(j+1)} = \varphi(z_i^{(j+1)}), \qquad z_i^{(j+1)} = \sum_{k=0}^{s_j} w_{i,k}^{(j)} \cdot a_k^{(j)}$$

A variety of different types of activation functions φ are known in neural network literature. For example, while before the deep learning era the so called $sigmoid$ function was found most frequently, today's most successful implementations usually deploy $Rectified\ Linear\ Units$ (ReLU) [18] or variations of it [6].

On the hardware side, modern FPGAs typically offer a rich set of DSP and RAM resources within their fabric that can be used to process these networks. However, compared to the depth and layer size of deep neural networks, these resources are no longer sufficient for a full and direct mapping the way it was often done in previous generations of neural network accelerators. For example, given a network with $L = 7$ layers and architecture $784 \times 2500 \times 2000 \times 1500 \times 1000 \times 500 \times 10$ that was proposed in [5]. The network weights need approximately 22 MB if each weight is encoded using 16 bits. Compared to FPGA platforms like the Zynq, where even the largest device is limited to a total BRAM size of less than 3.3 MB [27] (i.e. 26.5 Mb ≈ 3.3 MB for the Z7100 device), a complete mapping with all neurons and weights directly onto the FPGA is no longer possible.

Modern and deep neural networks are usually partitioned into smaller *sections* in order to process them on embedded FPGAs platforms. We refer to a *section* as a certain number m of neurons in a given layer j with $m \leq s_{j+1}$ that can be processed in parallel through our hardware coprocessor with m individual *processing units*. Each processing unit is responsible for the transfer function of exactly one neuron in each section. Each *processing unit* may consists of r different computation resources, e.g., multipliers which are able to consume r weights as inputs in parallel for the calculation of the transfer function.

When comparing the size of the input data (s_j values), the output data (m values), and in particular the weights ($\approx s_j \times m$ values), it can be seen that the transfer of the weight matrix is very costly. In order to reduce the amount of data to transfer from the memory and for calculation, it is possible to remove some connections entirely. After some initial iterations of the training phase, small weights which are below a certain threshold δ can be set to zero:

$$w_{i,k}^{(j)} < \delta \quad \xRightarrow[\text{iterations}]{\text{following}} \quad w_{i,k}^{(j)} := 0$$

Subsequently, these pruned weights are kept at zero and the remaining weights are refined in the following iterations of the training phase. While this can potentially reduce the accuracy if too many weights are pruned, it was shown that over 90% of the weights in fully-connected layers of common CNNs can be pruned without noticeable accuracy drops [13].

Since weights with the value zero neither influence the result of the transfer nor the result of the activation function, these weights don't have to be stored in memory, transferred to the compute units, or used in computations. However, by pruning weights, the weight matrix becomes sparse and the hardware needs to be designed in a way that the involved calculations are computed efficiently.

4   Architecture

We have implemented our design with support for pruned DNNs on Xilinx's *Zynq-7000 All Programmable SoC* platform [27] and using *Xilinx Vivado HLS*. The flexible HLS approach allows us to quickly elaborate the best performing architecture for a given neural network architecture. For example, the number of processing units m and the number of MAC units per unit r can be freely configured during design time. Moreover, the size and format of the weights and the kind of activation function can be easily exchanged. Furthermore, the design time is drastically reduced and our approach is easily extensible to support new kinds of neurons, activation functions, or complete network architectures. An visualization of the overall accelerator structure and all related Zynq peripherals is shown in Fig. 1.

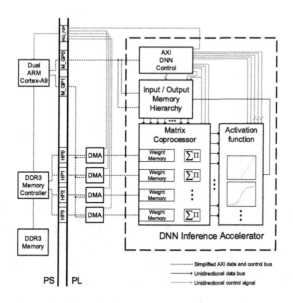

Fig. 1. Overview of our DNN accelerator with the Zynq processing system (PS) on the left and the custom accelerator inside the programmable logic (PL) on the right. The connecting PS-PL interfaces are shown in between. In addition, four DMA master peripherals are used for the weight transfer. All major connections that cross the boundary of our actual DNN accelerator are indicated as dashed lines.

The accelerator has an internal memory hierarchy that is used to store input and output activations for the currently calculated layer (controllable and accessible via software through the GP ports). While the input for the first layer needs to be copied by the ARM cores, the inputs for the following layers are always outputs of previous layers and thus computed and stored inside the memory hierarchy.

The *Matrix Coprocessor* computes the transfer function, i.e., the weighted sum of inputs $z_i^{(j)}$. This involves matrix-vector operations that are mainly implemented with multiply-accumulate units (MACs) by using DSP slices. We use a fixed point data format, known as Q7.8, that consists of one sign bit, seven integer bits and eight fractional bits. Although there exist first results that use fewer bits for both weights and activations (e.g., between 1 and 8 bits) [7], 16 bits are, as of today, the most frequently used bit-width. For the DNN inference, this format is proven to be almost as accurate as single precision floating point weights [4,9,10], whereas weight encodings with very few bits (e.g., 1 or 2 bits) suffer from comparable low accuracy [23]. Note that multiplications use 16 bits, while the subsequent accumulation is done with 32 bits. This ensures that the input of the activation function is provided with full precision (e.g., Q15.16).

Compared to a design without pruning support where it is sufficient to transfer a sequence of weights and the dimension of the matrix operation, pruning requires additional metadata that gives information about the actual position of a weight $w_{i,k}^{(j)}$ within the matrix $W^{(j)}$. We use a format similar to [12] that represents individual rows of the sparse weight matrices using tuples of (w_l, z_{w_l}) entries, with $l = 0 \ldots (1 - q_{\text{prune},k}^{(j)}) \cdot s_j - 1$. Here, w_l encodes a remaining weight after pruning and z_{w_l} denotes the number of preceding zeros that come before w_l in the corresponding row. The number of remaining weights after pruning is $s_j \cdot (1 - q_{\text{prune},k}^{(j)})$, where $q_{\text{prune},k}^{(j)}$ is the pruning factor of row k of the weight matrix $W^{(j)}$. The overall pruning factor $q_{\text{prune}}^{(j)}$ of the weight matrix $W^{(j)}$ can be calculated with

$$q_{\text{prune}}^{(j)} = \frac{1}{s_{j+1}} \cdot \sum_{k=0}^{s_{j+1}-1} q_{\text{prune},k}^{(j)}.$$

Opposed to [12], we do not separate the weights and zeros into two 1-dimensional arrays and store them in on-chip tables, but rather pack a certain number r of consecutive (w_l, z_{w_l}) tuples into one *data word* (cf. [26]). In our architecture we use $r = 3$ tuples, encode w_l with the Q7.8 format, and represent z_{w_l} as an unsigned integer with 5 bits. Using these parameters, a row

$$(0, -1.5, 0, 0, +0.3, -0.17, 0, 0, 0, +1.1, 0, 0, -0.2, 0, +0.1, \ldots)$$

is encoded into the following sequence of 64 bit data words

data word 0						data word 1						
-1.5	1	$+0.3$	2	-0.17	0	$+1.1$	3	-0.2	2	$+0.1$	1	$\cdots$

If z_{wl} would require more than 5 bits, e.g. more than 31 consecutive weights were pruned, we instead use multiple tuples with $(w_l, z_{wl}) = (0, 31)$ until the last tuple of the sequence holds the condition $z_{wl} < 31$. Note that the encoding of a data word uses only 63 bit from the available 64 bit. The advantage is that the data is memory aligned to the 64 bit border which eases the memory access. The corresponding overhead per weight compared to non-pruning implementations is $q_{\text{overhead}} = 64 \text{ bit}/(3 \times 16 \text{ bit}) = 1.33$.

Compared to other sparse matrix encodings that, for example, use separate vectors for the absolute row and column pointers [24], this format works well for streaming architectures since it directly combines both the weight and its relative position in one stream. This means that it does not require synchronization for, e.g., weight and multiple index streams. Since the structure of pruned weight matrices is not as homogeneous as their dense counterparts, the datapath of a corresponding streaming architecture must be design to handle sparse matrices in order to avoid pipeline stalls (see Fig. 2).

Therefore, the coprocessor needs to calculate the address of the input activation $a_k^{(j)}$ for the current weight. This input address is potentially different for

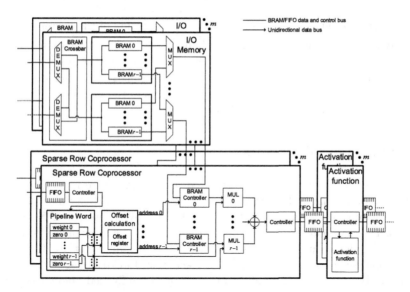

Fig. 2. Datapath for the computation of sparse rows in pruned DNNs. This example presumes a pipeline word with r tuples, each containing a weight and the number of zeros before it. In order to avoid delays when fetching the input activation that corresponds to a given weight, the BRAMs in the I/O memory are also duplicated r times, such that each multiplier has its own memory port. By combining m of these datapath instances, m neurons can be computed in parallel (i.e., m rows of the sparse matrix). In such cases, an IP that merges the activations of different rows must be connected with the I/O memories (indicated through the dashed lines).

every row which makes a parallel distribution of the inputs impractical. Therefore, each of the m parallel sparse row coprocessors has it own I/O memory unit. This means that the I/O memory and the coprocessors are replicated m times. The *offset calculation* IP computes theses addresses for all r weights iteratively using the previously computed and stored offset o_{reg}, the number of non-zero weights before w_l and the zero fields z_{w_l} from the pipeline word:

$$\mathrm{address}_i = o_{\mathrm{reg}} + i + \sum_{k=0}^{i} z_{w_k}, \quad i = 0 \ldots r - 1$$

Having computed the addresses, the coprocessor can multiply the weights and retrieve input activations and subsequently accumulate the partial sums. However, in order to retrieve the weights in parallel and avoid multiple cycles for a sequential fetching of the individual activations, the input memory needs r read ports. Given that RAM resources in current FPGA technologies usually do not provide more than two memory ports, the *I/O memory* stores both input and output activations in r redundant BRAM copies. When m neurons should be computed in parallel, this redundancy is even increased to $m \cdot r$ copies since each of the m coprocessors needs r individual read ports. If the calculated $\mathrm{address}_i$

surpasses the stored number of inputs s_j, the calculation of the current transfer function $z_i^{(j+1)}$ is finalized, the result is handed over to the activation function, and the corresponding processing unit starts calculating the following transfer function $z_{i+m}^{(j+1)}$. After the activation function, a merger IP (not depicted in Fig. 2) distributes the computed output activations of the m neurons to *all* I/O memories (second port of the BRAM crossbar).

5   Experimental Results

To evaluate and verify the so far discussed concept, we have implemented our accelerator on an embedded platform and compared them with different configurations against miscellaneous software platforms. We chose the *Zynq Evaluation and Development Board* [2], short *ZedBoard*, for the implementation of our designs. The design uses two clock domains: the memory interface (e.g., Zynq high performance ports and DMAs) is clocked with 133 MHz and the remaining processing IPs use a 100 MHz clock (f_{pu}). Due to the limited amount of 4 high performance ports on the Zynq, our design utilizes only $m = 4$ coprocessors with $r = 3$ MAC units. This results in a total utilization of only 12 MACs. By using an HLS design flow, the design time was cut down to approximately 8 person weeks. In comparison, an earlier design (see [19]) with a similar complexity needed about 24 person weeks by using a standard RTL-based design flow (using VHDL). Furthermore, a substantial amount of the previously mentioned time for the HLS-based design was spent in creating a suitable testbench that is capable of loading arbitrary networks and transforming the weight matrices in the internal representation for the actual processing.

Throughput Evaluation: For a fair comparison of both hardware and software, we have trained different fully-connected neural network architectures with multiple real-world data set. As many before us, we use the *MNIST database of handwritten digits* [16] as the first benchmark. In addition, we have also performed all tests with a second benchmark that deals with the subject of recognizing human activities (*HAR*) of daily living through smartphone sensors [1]. We have also tested multiple neural network architectures which are taken or inspired from current research in the field. For example, the smaller network for MNIST was proposed in [14] while the larger one is an artificially extended version of that architecture with four additional hidden layers.

In our evaluation, the hardware competes against a software implementation that we have tested on an embedded (i.e., the ZedBoard without FPGA use), a notebook and, a desktop machine. The notebook uses an Intel Core i7-5600U dual core processor with 2.6–3.2 GHz, 4096 KB L3 cache, and 8192 MB single channel DDR3 memory. The desktop CPU is an Intel Core i7-4790 quad core with 3.6–4.0 GHz, 8192 KB L3 cache, and 16384 MB dual channel DDR3 memory. The peak memory throughput is 12.8 GB/s for the laptop and 25.6 GB/s for the desktop system. The ZedBoard has only a memory throughput of 4.2 GB/s.

Furthermore, all presented processors feature some variant of a vector extension to accelerate floating-point intensive calculations through parallelism on instruction level. In order to get the best runtime result on *all* presented platforms, we use the *BLAS* [25] library for the software inference of the DNNs. Xilinx's bare-metal layer is used for the ZedBoard whereas both the notebook and the desktop machine use Linux-based operating systems. By default, bare-metal uses only one core for the software execution. The throughput results for the DNN inference on all software implementations and our hardware platform are depicted in Table 1.

Table 1. Throughput comparison of our hardware design with pruning support and software inference on three different systems. Execution times are averaged over the size of the used test set and given in samples per milliseconds (ms). The best results for both hardware designs and all software runs are highlighted.

Device	Configuration	MNIST [a]		HAR [b]	
		4-layer netw. 1,275,200 Parameters	8-layer netw. 3,835,200 Parameters	4-layer netw. 1,035,000 Parameters	6-layer netw. 5,473,800 Parameters
Hardware-based processing					
	Pruning factor	0.72	0.78	0.88	0.94
HW design	12 MACs	0.439	1.072	0.161	0.420
Software-based processing[c]					
ARM Cortex-A9	#Threads: 1	16.151	48.603	13.120	70.240
Intel Core i7-5600U	#Threads: 1	0.285	1.603	0.223	2.246
	#Threads: 2	0.221	1.555	0.144	2.220
	#Threads: 4	0.247	1.591	0.182	2.417
Intel Core i7-4790	#Threads: 1	0.118	0.917	0.114	1.406
	#Threads: 4	0.057	0.569	0.045	1.205
	#Threads: 8	0.065	0.687	0.055	1.491

[a] Network architectures: $784 \times 800 \times 800 \times 10$ and $784 \times 800 \times 800 \times 800 \times 800 \times 800 \times 800 \times 10$

[b] Network architectures: $561 \times 1200 \times 300 \times 6$ and $561 \times 2000 \times 1500 \times 750 \times 300 \times 6$

[c] Software calculations are performed using the *IEEE 754 floating point single precision* format and using *BLAS*. The i7-4790 utilizes dual channel memory whereas the others only use single channel.

On the software side, we see the fastest inference for the desktop machine with a utilization of 4 threads and dual channel memory. On both the mobile and desktop CPU, the execution times depend mostly on the network size and, more precisely, on the matrix sizes of the individual layers. While the matrices of both 4-layer networks fit completely into the CPU caches and thus enable faster execution times, the tables are turned for matrices of the deep learning era. For example, the 6-layer HAR network with a 2000×1500 matrix represents such a typical fully-connected layer. Here, the hardware, despite its five times slower memory interface, clearly outperforms all software implementations.

Furthermore, we compared our approach with a related FPGA-based neural network accelerator. A fair and direct comparison is only possible with approaches that supply results for fully-connected DNNs or RNNs (RNNs have only slightly more weights due to neuron feedback connections). However, when considering *only* fully-connected layers, our approach clearly outperforms related work like, for example, a recent RNN approach on the ZedBoard [3]. The authors claim an overall throughput of 388.8 MOps/s. With our approach, we reach a throughput of 0.8 GOps/s (only counting MAC operations). However, compared with non-pruned approaches, this is equivalent to 3.83 MOps/1.07 ms = 3.58 GOps/s and 5.47 MOps/0.42 ms = 13.02 GOps/s, respectively (i.e., the non-pruned weight matrix is used as the number of operations, see Table 1).

Energy Efficiency: For determining the energy consumption, we measured the system power for processing the 8-layer neural network and the idle power for all platforms (see Table 2). The overall power consumption on the ZedBoard is evaluated by measuring the average input voltage and the voltage drop on a shunt resistor. Whereas, the average power of the x86-based systems is measured on the primary side of the power supply with an ampere and volt meter. Besides the idle and processing power, the energy consumption with (Overall Energy) and without (Dynamic Energy) idle power consumption is shown in Table 2.

Table 2. Energy consumption comparison of our hardware design and three processors (network: MNIST 8-layer).

Device	Configuration	Power (W)	Overall Energy (mJ)	Dynamic Energy (mJ)
ZedBoard	idle	2.4	—	—
	HW ($m = 4$)	4.1	4.4	1.8
	SW BLAS	3.8	184.7	68.0
Intel Core i7-5600U	idle	8.9	—	—
	#Threads: 1	20.7	33.2	18.9
	#Threads: 2	22.6	35.1	21.3
	#Threads: 4	24.9	39.6	25.5
Intel Core i7-4790	idle	41.4	—	—
	#Threads: 1	65.8	63.9	22.4
	#Threads: 4	82.3	46.8	23.3
	#Threads: 8	81.8	56.2	27.8

Comparing our hardware configuration with pure software approaches, an overall energy efficiency improvement of almost factor 10 can be achieved. Compared to a competing LSTM design [11], our pruning approach is about factor 1.8 more energy efficient using their network with 3248128 weights and their pruning factor of $q_{\mathrm{prune}} = 0.888$ (1.9 mJ for our approach and 3.4 mJ for their approach).

Accuracy Evaluation: The objective for the training with pruning was a maximum accuracy deviation of 1.5% in correctly predicted samples. All networks discussed in the throughput evaluation (i.e., Sect. 5) meet this objective and deliver an accuracy very similar to their non-pruned counterparts (most deviate less than 0.5%).

Table 3. Accuracy evaluation in percentage of correctly predicted test set samples depending on the overall pruning factor q_{prune} of the network

	MNIST[a]		HAR[b]	
Number of parameters	4-layer netw. 1,275,200 parameters	8-layer netw. 3,835,200 parameters	4-layer netw. 1,035,000 parameters	6-layer netw. 5,473,800 parameters
Best non-pruned accuracy	98.3		95.9	
Pruning factor	0.72	0.78	0.88	0.94
Accuracy	98.27	97.62	94.14	95.72

[a] Network architectures: $784 \times 800 \times 800 \times 10$ and $784 \times 800 \times 800 \times 800 \times 800 \times 800 \times 800 \times 10$
[b] Network architectures: $561 \times 1200 \times 300 \times 6$ and $561 \times 2000 \times 1500 \times 750 \times 300 \times 6$

A detailed comparison of accuracy and pruning percentage is shown in Table 3.

6   Conclusions

In this paper, we present a flexible architecture for an FPGA-based embedded SoC that is able to accelerate the inference of previously learned and arbitrary pruned fully-connected deep neural networks. This architecture enables the inference of today's huge networks on energy-constrained embedded devices. By using pruning, the size of external memory as well as the amount of data to be transferred can be significantly reduced which increases the energy efficiency and performance. An application and network-specific design can be easily achieved by using HLS in order to increase the abstraction level of the design entry. The resulting architecture has a comparable performance with state-of-the-art desktop and server processors for large networks. However, only a fraction of energy is needed which enables new applications for embedded systems, even on battery powered devices. Future works on this topic might further increase the throughput and energy efficiency by combining pruning with batch processing [19] into one architecture.

References

1. Anguita, D., Ghio, A., Oneto, L., Parra, X., Reyes-Ortiz, J.L.: A public domain dataset for human activity recognition using smartphones. In: 21th European Symposium on Artificial Neural Networks, Computational Intelligence and Machine Learning, ESANN 2013, April 2013
2. Avnet Inc.: ZedBoard Hardware User's Guide, v2.2 edn, January 2014
3. Chang, A.X.M., Martini, B., Culurciello, E.: Recurrent neural networks hardware implementation on FPGA. arXiv preprint arXiv:1511.05552 (2015)
4. Chen, T., Du, Z., Sun, N., Wang, J., Wu, C., Chen, Y., Temam, O.: Diannao: a small-footprint high-throughput accelerator for ubiquitous machine-learning. In: Proceedings of the 19th International Conference on Architectural Support for Programming Languages and Operating Systems, ASPLOS 2014, pp. 269–284. ACM, New York (2014)

5. Ciresan, D.C., Meier, U., Gambardella, L.M., Schmidhuber, J.: Deep big simple neural nets excel on handwritten digit recognition. CoRR abs/1003.0358 (2010)
6. Clevert, D., Unterthiner, T., Hochreiter, S.: Fast and accurate deep network learning by Exponential Linear Units (ELUs). CoRR abs/1511.07289 (2015)
7. Courbariaux, M., Bengio, Y.: BinaryNet: Training deep neural networks with weights and activations constrained to +1 or −1. CoRR abs/1602.02830 (2016)
8. Farabet, C., LeCun, Y., Kavukcuoglu, K., Culurciello, E., Martini, B., Akselrod, P., Talay, S.: Large-scale FPGA-based convolutional networks. In: Bekkerman, R., Bilenko, M., Langford, J. (eds.) Scaling up Machine Learning: Parallel and Distributed Approaches. Cambridge University Press, Cambridge (2011)
9. Farabet, C., Martini, B., Corda, B., Akselrod, P., Culurciello, E., LeCun, Y.: Neuflow: a runtime-reconfigurable dataflow processor for vision. In: Proceedings of Embedded Computer Vision Workshop (ECVW 2011) (2011, invited paper)
10. Gokhale, V., Jin, J., Dundar, A., Martini, B., Culurciello, E.: A 240 G-ops/s mobile coprocessor for deep neural networks. In: IEEE Conference on Computer Vision and Pattern Recognition Workshops (CVPRW), pp. 696–701, June 2014
11. Han, S., Kang, J., Mao, H., Hu, Y., Li, X., Li, Y., Xie, D., Luo, H., Yao, S., Wang, Y., Yang, H., Dally, W.J.: ESE: efficient speech recognition engine with compressed LSTM on FPGA. CoRR abs/1612.00694 (2016)
12. Han, S., Liu, X., Mao, H., Pu, J., Pedram, A., Horowitz, M.A., Dally, W.J.: EIE: efficient inference engine on compressed deep neural network. CoRR abs/1602.01528 (2016)
13. Han, S., Mao, H., Dally, W.J.: Deep compression: compressing deep neural network with pruning, trained quantization and Huffman coding. CoRR abs/1510.00149 (2015)
14. Hinton, G., Vinyals, O., Dean, J.: Distilling the knowledge in a neural network. ArXiv e-prints, March 2015
15. Koch, D., Hannig, F., Ziener, D. (eds.): FPGAs for Software Programmers. Springer, Cham (2016). https://doi.org/10.1007/978-3-319-26408-0
16. LeCun, Y., Cortes, C., Burges, C.J.: MNIST handwritten digit database (2014). http://yann.lecun.com/exdb/mnist/
17. LeCun, Y., Denker, J.S., Solla, S., Howard, R.E., Jackel, L.D.: Optimal Brain Damage. In: Touretzky, D. (ed.) Advances in Neural Information Processing Systems (NIPS 1989), vol. 2. Morgan Kaufman, Denver (1990)
18. Nair, V., Hinton, G.E.: Rectified linear units improve restricted Boltzmann machines. In: Proceedings of the 27th International Conference on Machine Learning (ICML-2010), pp. 807–814 (2010)
19. Posewsky, T., Ziener, D.: Efficient deep neural network acceleration through FPGA-based batch processing. In: Proceedings of the International Conference on Reconfigurable Computing and FPGAs (ReConFig), Cancun, Mexico, December 2016
20. Sainath, T.N., Kingsbury, B., Ramabhadran, B., Fousek, P., Novak, P., Mohamed, A.: Making deep belief networks effective for large vocabulary continuous speech recognition. In: Proceedings of the ASRU (2011)
21. Schmidhuber, J.: Deep learning in neural networks: an overview. CoRR abs/1404.7828 (2014)
22. Simonyan, K., Zisserman, A.: Very deep convolutional networks for large-scale image recognition. CoRR abs/1409.1556 (2014)
23. Umuroglu, Y., Fraser, N.J., Gambardella, G., Blott, M., Leong, P.H.W., Jahre, M., Vissers, K.A.: FINN: a framework for fast, scalable binarized neural network inference. CoRR abs/1612.07119 (2016)

24. Vuduc, R.W.: Automatic performance tuning of sparse matrix kernels. Ph.D. thesis, University of California, Berkeley (2003)
25. Xianyi, Z., et al.: OpenBLAS, March 2011. http://www.openblas.net. Accessed 02 Mar 2016
26. Xilinx Inc.: Designing Protocol Processing Systems with Vivado High-Level Synthesis, v1.0.1 edn, August 2014
27. Xilinx Inc.: Zynq-7000 All Programmable SoC Overview, v1.9 edn, January 2016

Author Index

Printed in the United States
By Bookmasters